Law and Evil

Law and Evil opens, expands and deepens our understanding of the phenomenon of evil by addressing the theoretical relationship between this phenomenon and law. Hannah Arendt said, 'the problem of evil will be the fundamental question of post-war intellectual life in Europe'. This statement is, unfortunately, more than valid in the contemporary world: not only in the events of war, crimes against humanity, terror, repression, criminality, violence, torture, human trafficking, and so on, but also as evil is used rhetorically to condemn these acts, to categorize their perpetrators, and to justify forcible measures, both in international and domestic politics and in law.

But what is evil? Evil as a concept is too often taken as something that is self-evident, something that is always already defined. Taking Kant's concept of radical evil as a starting point, this volume counters such a tendency. Bringing together philosophical, political and psychoanalytical perspectives, in analysing both the concept and the phenomenon of evil, the contributors to this volume offer a rich and thoroughgoing analysis of the multifaceted phenomenon of evil and its relation to law.

Ari Hirvonen is Adjunct Professor in Philosophy of Law at the University of Helsinki and Senior Researcher at the Centre of Excellence in Foundations of European Law and Polity Research, Academy of Finland. He has published texts on philosophy, psychoanalysis, art, legal and political philosophy, and Greek tragedy.

Janne Porttikivi is a translator and independent researcher, based in Helsinki. He has published articles on psychoanalysis, literature and philosophy. Porttikivi has co-edited and co-translated a collection of Derrida's essays and co-translated a Žižek reader into Finnish.

Law and Evil

Philosophy, politics, psychoanalysis

Edited by Ari Hirvonen and Janne Porttikivi

Routledge
Taylor & Francis Group
a GlassHouse book

First published 2010 by Routledge
2 Park Square, Milton Park, Abingdon, Oxfordshire OX14 4RN

Simultaneously published in the USA and Canada
by Routledge
711 Third Avenue, New York, NY 10017

A GlassHouse book

Routledge is an imprint of the Taylor & Francis Group, an informa business

First issued in paperback 2011

Typeset in Times New Roman by Taylor & Francis Books

British Library Cataloguing in Publication Data
A catalogue record for this book is available from the British Library

Library of Congress Cataloguing in Publication Data
Law and evil : philosophy, politics, psychoanalysis / edited by Ari Hirvonen and Janne Porttikivi.
p. cm.
Includes bibliographical references.
1. Good and evil. 2. Law–Philosophy. I. Hirvonen, Ari, 1960- II. Porttikivi, Janne.
BJ1401.L239 2010
340'.1–dc22

2009013650

ISBN13: 978-0-415-49791-6 (hbk)
ISBN13: 978-0-415-68533-7 (pbk)
ISBN13: 978-0-203-86746-4 (ebk)

Contents

Acknowledgement

We should like to thank the Emil Aaltonen Foundation for its support.

Contributors

Marcia Sá Cavalcante Schuback Associate Professor in Philosophy, School of Culture and Communication, Södertörn University College, Stockholm, Sweden

Simon Critchley Professor of Philosophy, New School of Social Research, New York, USA

Françoise Dastur Professor Emerita, University of Nice, France

Marc de Kesel Senior Researcher, Faculty of Philosophy, Radboud University Nijmegen, Netherlands

Ari Hirvonen Adjunct Professor, Faculty of Law, University of Helsinki; Senior Researcher, Centre of Excellence in Foundations of European Law and Polity Research, Academy of Finland

Jari Kauppinen Researcher, Department of Philosophy, University of Helsinki, Finland

Artemy Magun Associate Professor, European University of St Petersburg, Russia

Angus McDonald Senior Lecturer, School of Law, Staffordshire University, Stoke on Trent, England

Janne Porttikivi Translator, Researcher, Helsinki, Finland

Jacob Rogozinski Professor of Metaphysics, Faculty of Philosophy, University of Strasbourg, France

Sami Santanen Researcher, Department of Aesthetics, University of Helsinki, Finland.

Paul Verhaeghe Professor, Department of Psychoanalysis and Clinical Consulting, University of Ghent, Belgium

Jochem Willemsen Researcher, Department of Psychoanalysis and Clinical Consulting, University of Ghent, Belgium

Véronique Voruz Researcher, Faculty of Law, University of Leicester, England

Chapter 1

Introduction

Ari Hirvonen and Janne Porttikivi

What crime, what sin, had those young hearts conceived
That lie, bleeding and torn, on mother's breast? …
'All's well,' ye say, 'and all is necessary.'
Think ye this universe had been the worse
Without this hellish gulf in Portugal?[1]

So wrote Voltaire in his 'Poem on the Lisbon Disaster' after the first modern catastrophe, the Lisbon earthquake, which took place on 1 November 1755. The earthquake sufficed, says Theodor Adorno, to cure Voltaire from the theodicy of Leibniz,[2] which Leibniz had introduced in his *Essais de théodicée* (1710) to justify the omnipotent, beneficent and infinite Creator in the face of all the evils in the world. For Leibniz, God had in his infinite wisdom necessarily chosen this world we live in, which is the best of all possible worlds.[3] Voltaire continued his criticism of Leibnitz's – and also Alexander Pope's – optimism and dogma of theodicy in his satirical novel *Candide*. It takes quite a belief to take theodicy seriously after having confronted the greatest philosopher in the world, the teacher of 'metaphysico-theologo-cosmolonigology', Dr Pangloss, a parody (unfair) of Leibniz, who goes around Europe repeating again and again after continual moral, physical and natural evils, 'Individual misfortunes result in the general good, with the consequence that the more individual misfortune there is, the more everything is for the best.'[4]

Rousseau, who defended Leibniz, also turned his gaze to human beings. Instead of blaming divinity, one should realize that all their misery, crimes and evil proceed from themselves.[5] Also young Kant heard the news from Lisbon and he published three articles on the subject in 1756 in a local paper, in which he rejected all religious, metaphysical, mystical and astrological interpretations of earthquakes. Earthquakes had nothing to do with divine punishments since we stand with our feet on the cause. 'Man must learn to accommodate himself to nature, but he wishes that he could accommodate it to him.'[6]

Later Kant confronted the problem of moral evil and declared that for its own sake morality does not need religion at all. The cause of moral evil lies neither in the original sin, in turning away from God, in *privatio boni* nor in our desires and needs: 'The history of nature begins thus from good, since it is the creation of God, the history of freedom begins from evil, since it is accomplishment of human being.'[7] For Kant, we are neither angels nor demons. We do have a predisposition (*Anlage*) to good, but it does not mean that we would already actually be good but that we become good or evil by freely choosing good maxims, which incorporate the moral law, or evil maxims, which give primacy to the pathological, non-moral incentives. Then again, we have a propensity (*Hang*) to evil, that is not to follow the moral law. Even if this propensity is innate in our nature, it is based not on our will but our power of choice (*Willkür*). The propensity of evil is brought upon us by ourselves – hence, we are accountable for it. Human being is evil means for Kant that we are conscious of the moral law and yet have incorporated into our maxims the occasional deviation from it. This is what Kant calls radical evil in *Religion within Boundaries of mere Reason*.

Kant does not give formal proof that there is such a propensity but only refers to the multitude of woeful examples that the experience of human acts parades before our eyes, and after Kant this parade has continued. Anyhow, the basic argument for Kant was that we are radically free and hence accountable and responsible for our good and evil maxims and acts. We just can neither exonerate ourselves by blaming the original sin, passions or social expectations, nor turn to a religious fantasy of a perfect world. Evil is a product of humanity and not merely a lack or absence of something that should be there or something that will vanish if we would see things from the perspective of infinity and eternity. All in all, '[t]he human being must make or have made *himself* into whatever he is or should become in a moral sense, good or evil'.[8] As Joan Copjec says, 'Kant sees evil as uniquely the product of a free humanity, and it is this that is new in his thought'.[9]

One more name should be mentioned: Friedrich Schelling, who strictly affirmed the reality of evil. It is something that is present in the world. If Hegel reduced evil to the subordinated moment in the self-meditation of Idea *qua* supreme good, as Slavoj Žižek says, then for Schelling 'evil remains a permanent possibility which can never be fully sublated [*aufgehoben*] in and by the Good'.[10] Thus, there is a universal necessity of evil, since in a dialectical manner good and evil are the same and one who does not have within him either the stuff or the energy of evil, is equally incapable of good. However, evil remains the particular choice of human being – the human freedom means freedom to do good and evil – and in nature there is not evil as such: therefore, evil is spirit, a positive disharmony. The ground and existence, gravity and light, are unified in God but this is reversed in human beings so that the ground becomes the source of evil in human beings.[11] As Richard J. Bernstein confirms, Schelling recognized the unconscious, unruly and dark forces that shape human life and anticipated Nietzsche and Freud.[12]

The first starting point of this book is the inevitable relationship between human freedom and evil. The thinking and speaking of evil have to turn definitely away from theodicy and more generally from all theological explanations of evil. Good and evil are not related to any Supreme Being, transcendent universal principle or infinity. We should not deny the existence of evil by explaining it as something that will in the long run turn out to be part of good. Neither can we see evil as part of the divine plan nor the perfection of the universe, nor, as in a Manichean way, as a transcendent force or principle which is opposing the good. The cosmos is neither ultimately morally good order or a battleground of good and evil forces; these views are not merely philosophically and ethically extremely problematic but politically dangerous, since theological theories of evil are so easily and readily turned into acceptance of suffering and destruction or into demonization of others and justification of war, oppression, and terrorism.

One should not leave evil only for theologians and politicians or reduce it to ultimately dull and boring spectacles of Hollywood movies. One should address evil as 'something' that is in this world, something that is in our being-in-the-world and in our being-together. It is human, an all too human, phenomenon. One does not have to pester the devil to understand evil, Rüdiger Safranski claims, since evil 'belongs to the drama of human freedom. It is the price of freedom.'[13]

Since the aim of the book is to understand evil and how it is conceived in modern thought, the basis for the analysis of evil is the deconstruction of theological concepts of evil already on the way in Voltaire, Rousseau, Kant, and Schelling. Especially Kant's concept of radical evil has in one way or another affected most of the post-Kantian theoretical thinking of evil. For us, it is Kant who truly opens the thinking of modern moral evil. However, some of his contemporaries thought that old Kant had betrayed the principles of the Enlightenment philosophy he had so enthusiastically spoken for, and returned to the firm and safe ground of religious tradition. If we now follow Kant in the opening of this book, do we also, if we take this criticism seriously, turn, after all, back to religion and metaphysico-theological thinking? There is, however, as Joan Copjec has shown, another way to see Kant's turn away from being the new apostle of reason and progress: Kant had 'found in these Enlightenment notions a new source of evil' and had begun to suspect his former optimism.[14] Perhaps Kant saw how the dogma of unlimited progress could become a modern secular theodicy, being not only a new kind of justification of evil but also a source of evil in itself.

The theological and metaphysical stories of good and evil should be interrupted, their truths deconstructed, but so we have also to do with our Kantian heritage if we want to fully grasp the phenomenon of evil in its whole complexity, and this is ultimately also the aim of the essays on law and evil, which are collected here.

In 1945, Hannah Arendt wrote, 'The problem of evil will be the fundamental question of post-war intellectual life in Europe'.[15] One had to articulate and elaborate questions 'What happened? Why did it happen? How could it have happened?'[16] And for Adorno, Hitler imposed a 'new categorical imperative on humankind', which demands to arrange 'thoughts and actions so that Auschwitz will not repeat itself'.[17]

Holocaust was the most extreme form of modern evil and it definitely was not a natural catastrophe, like the Lisbon earthquake, but a human one. The last and this century have continued to be a stage where the human propensity to evil has actualized its possibilities. Neither legal and political institutions nor ethics and philosophy have been able to prevent outbursts of evil. We witness daily evil in different guises and forms: war, terrorism, repression, oppression, racism, xenophobia, imperialism, criminality, violence, torture, human trafficking, exploitation, poverty, pollution, etc. In addition to this moral, political and legal evil, there is evil in the form of diseases and natural catastrophes, which are not completely beyond human responsibility.

Regardless of this, Arendt's demand to think the question of evil has not become true. The conceptual discourse, Richard J. Bernstein writes, 'for dealing with evil has been sparse and inadequate'.[18] Bernstein also cites Andrew Delbanco for whom a gulf has opened up between the visibility of evil and the intellectual resources available for coping with it: 'never have our responses been so weak'.[19] Or as Emmanuel Levinas argues, the Western philosophy has not sufficiently insured itself against the essential possibility of elemental evil.[20] Then again, in recent years there has been discussion on the problem of evil,[21] but still there is a need for theoretical analysis of the concept, idea and phenomena of evil.

The reluctance is related to our starting point. As Ottfried Höffe remarks, for many, evil appears as a metaphysical or theological concept, as the *malum metaphysicum*, as the sum total of the world's imperfections. It is often considered as a subject of philosophy of religion, which cannot easily be accommodated by secular ethics.[22] Peter Dews says that there is an intellectual and cultural dilemma: on the one hand, we feel impelled to resort to the notion of evil in describing horrible events, where the fundamental ethical conditions of human existence are violated; on the other hand, in the predominantly secularized West the majority of people do not share the religious assumptions that gave the notion of its place in our thinking.[23] Therefore, we have to re-think evil in a secular way. We agree with Susan Neiman, for whom 'the problem of evil is the guiding force of modern thought'.[24]

Let us return to Adorno's imperative. Inherent in it there is not merely the categorical necessity, but also impossibility of fulfilling it, as Josh Cohen says, since we can never be assured that nothing similar will happen. That is, 'the judgement of its fulfillment belongs of necessity to an unachieved and unachievable future'.[25] This does not mean that the imperative would be invalid or that thinking should withdraw into melancholy. On the contrary, what gives this imperative philosophical force and ethical urgency is this non-fulfillment, since thinking is prevented to come to rest or 'from seeking a future in which it would be redeemed of its responsibility'.[26] For Cohen, for whom the concentration camps remained 'the site of most radical experiment in exclusion yet known to history', the task of thinking means imagining a political, and so ethical, space liberated from the grasp of identity, from the logic of inclusion and exclusion, belonging and non-belonging.[27]

This is our second starting point: evil is a task of philosophical, ethical, political and psychoanalytic thinking. The book is not just a description of what kind of empirical forms and manifestation evil has in the contemporary world. We don't deny the importance of an empirically oriented account of specific forms of evil, death, destruction, pain and suffering or analysis of different forms of moral, physical and natural evils, but this is not the main subject of the book. For us, the problem of evil is something that needs to be radically addressed, that is one has to go to the roots of evil as a concept and as a phenomenon. Evil as concept is too often taken either as something that is self-evident, something that is always already defined or something that is a concept of bygone days of theology and metaphysics. This kind of unproblematic understanding of evil or turning away from it leads to various ethical and political problems. The purpose of this book is to counter this tendency and give richer and more thoroughgoing analysis of the multifaceted phenomenon of evil in its ethical, political and philosophical ramifications. The aim is to open, expand and deepen our understanding of the phenomenon of evil.

Slavoj Žižek has made a difference between subjective and objective violence. Subjective is the most visible part and it is performed by an identifiable agent. The objective violence has two forms: Symbolic violence is embodied in language and its forms, which is, in Heideggerian terms, our house of being. This violence affects directly our very core of being, because, on the most fundamental level, it pertains to language as such. Systemic violence is the often catastrophic consequence of the smooth functioning of our economic and political systems.[28] Therefore, in analysing law and evil one should not stop at the all too visible level, but try to reach and face the evil operating on other spheres and levels. To do this one has to have valid theoretical 'tools' or 'concepts'.

The main focus of the book is thus how evil has been conceived in modern philosophical, political, juridical and psychoanalytical thinking. Our hypothesis is that only through the analysis of the concept and phenomenon of evil in the modern tradition can one understand more fundamentally what evil truly is, what are the many faces of evil, how evil is used in juridico-political rhetoric, and how the negative effects of evil could be limited. This kind of deeper understanding of evil makes critical thinking possible and also gives theoretical grounds for political action.

Our third starting point is the law. We concentrate on thinking evil in its relation to the law. This may sound self-evident. Even if crimes are seen more and more as unlawful risk-taking, criminals as offenders to be technically controlled and normalized, and punishment as deterrence and cure, not as retribution, many conceive that criminal laws define and criminalize what is considered to be evil in a society or that punishments are an evil for which the offender has to pay. Criminalizations, sanctions and punishments are just one part of the question of how juridical laws and evil are related.

Things are not so simple. Both criminalizations and punishments can be seen as legal violence, evil manifestations of the violence of the sovereign. And even more generally one could speak of legal violence as the anarchist tradition, *à la* Mikhail Bakunin, has done or as Walter Benjamin does in his 'Critique of Violence', where he analyses legal violence, that is law founding and law preserving violence.[29] We also have to recognize as evil the symbolic violence of the language of the law. As Costas Douzinas writes, law carries huge ontological power as it 'prescribes what constitutes a reasonable order by accepting and validating some parts of collective life', as it 'nominates what exists' 'while banning, excluding others, making them invisible.'[30] Therefore, as the law may define evil, it itself is evil as defining what will be recognized and what not. Law may make evil visible and be itself evil in making invisible, or keeping in forgetfulness, some evils.

Anyway, the juridical law may help us to define, locate, condemn and resist evil; and not merely individual crimes but also the crimes committed in the name of a nation, state, ideology or religion. In the preface to the first edition of *The Origins of Totalitarianism*, Arendt defined evil as anti-Semitism, imperialism and totalitarianism. They have 'one after the other, one more brutally than the other demonstrated that human dignity needs a new guarantee which can be found only in a new political principle, in a new law on earth, whose validity this time must comprehend the whole of humanity while its power must remain strictly limited, rooted in and controlled by newly defined territorial entitities'.[31] Of course, there are many problems related to these 'territorial entities', if they are understood as national states. But even if we could speak for a possibility of political constitution of the post-national state, perhaps even speak of Federalism in Europe, Arendt's demand of 'a new law' must be kept open and understood as an urgent not only judico-political but also philosophical and ethical task on the global scale.

At the same time, as has become already clear, the law, the legal system, the state and its constitution themselves may turn into evil. The evil under the rope of the law and legitimate political power did not end with the end to totalitarianism of the twentieth century. Apartheid South Africa, Cambodia, Rwanda, Burma and Yugoslavia, just to mention some place-names, are manifestations of the legal and political evil. Terror can be criminal as well as legal.

For us, the law as legislation, statutory law and legal systems or ideas of justice are just one side of the law. The law also as the moral law is inevitable when we deal with evil. How we understand the difference between the juridical and moral law may also effect how we see evil. And what is the difference between ethically good and evil acts? The universal and eternal substantial moral principles may be questioned in the pluralistic world. Religious systems offer us universal normative orders, but one needs faith to take them as valid norms. One may turn to human rights as the ultimate foundation of law and morality, but then again, they can be also considered 'merely' as positive law, that is legal norms based on conventions, constitutions, and statutory laws. We still have to wonder whether there are any global and generally valid ethical norms? Kant has to offer 'merely' a formal and empty moral law. Or as Jacques Lacan says, "No *de facto* legality can decide if this maxim can assume the rank of a universal rule, since this rank may also possibly oppose it to all *de facto* legalities."[32] Thus, we have to face the question of the moral law itself.

Moreover, the law refers to the law of language and signification, to the law of desire and unconscious, to laws of genre and style. It may as well refer to the Symbolic Order itself. Law itself may be perverse but then again there is no perversion without law: 'It is difficult to comprehend the idea of perversion otherwise than by reference to a norm.'[33] Furthermore, the law opens the question of evil as, or in relation to, transgression, excess, enjoyment and ecstasy. Desire, law and evil are interrelated.

The belief in the infinite scientific, technological and economical progress or the trust on self-sufficiency and limitlessness of an absolute subject, or in a word, the human hubris, has become so self-evident, so natural a state of affairs that we have lost the sense of there being any laws or limits for human being. Perhaps, Greek tragedies could teach us something about the hubris, transgression and law.

Perhaps evil itself is something that exists in relationship to normative phenomena, to various forms of law, something that is not inevitably the other side of the law but also this side of the law, the law itself. Now, we must add, that facing evil in its relation to law does not mean that we would slip back – at least uncritically – into the Augustinian idea that evil does not exist, since it is nothing but a privation of good, a *privatio boni*. There is evil!

To think properly of evil, and also the relationship between law and evil, *Law and Evil* brings together philosophical, political and psychoanalytical approaches on the problem of evil and law. In these articles philosophical, political, juridical, ethical, aesthetical and psychoanalytical questions are often interrelated and cannot be clearly separated from each other. This kind of interdisciplinary approach is needed if we want to face evil as a fundamental problem of our times. The book is divided into three parts.

Freedom

Angus McDonald starts from the first scene of evil, the Fall, in which the evil is unnatural, a loss and a separation. This scene of evil is interrupted by readings of Genesis, Becket, Bataille, Wilde and finally Shangri-la's. If evil is to be defined as interruption, interrupting evil is interrupting the interruption, or restoring a connection, but this re-connection must happen at a different level, at the level of communication and intimacy. Evil is a provocation to the limits of experience and understanding and the response to it may be found in an aesthetics of intimacy.

Françoise Dastur's text is on tragedy and evil. On the basis of the interpretation of tragedy given by Hölderlin, Schelling, Nietzsche, and Heidegger, she shows that the question of evil is tightly linked to human art and culture in general, tragedy being considered as giving the most striking expression of the conflict between art and nature.

Marcia Sá Cavalcante Schuback discusses the concept of interruption and continuity in relation to Schelling and Heidegger. Starting from a reading of Schelling's Essay on Human Freedom she proceeds to Heidegger. In a philosophical dialogue with Schelling and Heidegger she shows that the question of evil touches the problem of the ontological ambiguity of human life.

Sami Santanen analyses the views of Jean-Luc Nancy on evil. For Nancy evil has nothing to do with perversion of good, what is at stake in evil is the question of decision. He examines the possibility of wickedness as correlative to this introduction of freedom. Good and evil (wickedness) are not to be seen any more as something given but as a question of being, as existential possibilities due to freedom that surprises itself in decision.

Jari Kauppinen confronts Jacques Derrida and the concept of arche-evil, which for Derrida is a primordial evil as something which makes possible the system of good and evil, in relation to the Levinasian idea of the Good. It could be also understood as an interruption if it is considered as an introduction of difference, a difference between good and evil as a difference itself.

Terror

According to *Jacob Rogozinski* the experience of the concentration camps invites us to break with the philosophical and theological tradition, which affirms that no one is wicked voluntarily, and to re-think the avatars of not only Good and Evil but also the Law. Thus, Rogozinski reads Hannah Arendt's concept of the banality of evil asking whether the radicality of evil implied by the totalitarian decision can be simply reduced to that of banality. He then describes evil as a decision which projects all the wrong into the Other, which is rejected and annihilated without a trace.

Ari Hirvonen analyses the evolvement of the National Socialist idea of the law and its connection to National Socialist ideology. He asks about the responsibility of those who were representatives of the legal system and of those who were writing the new jurisprudence and legal philosophy. What kind of evil we face in National Socialism is then analysed through lawyers and their action, thinking and writing under National Socialism. The concept of total evil challenges the Kantian moral law and takes us to the limits, even beyond, of radical evil.

According to *Artemy Magun*, the contemporary terrorism as a form of modern evil is actually also the crisis of the Enlightenment subject. This subject is characterized by self-control and self-mastery. But the task of mastering oneself sets the further task of self-affection. Therefore, Enlightenment consists, literally, in the desire to know with empirical certainty, and to add the feeling of self to the feeling of an object. This is why the Enlightenment brings about not just the emancipation of the subject and the victory of reason over prejudice, but equally terror and anxiety. And in today's world of mediatized terrorism this ambivalence of Enlightenment's subject has reached its culmination.

Simon Critchley claims that the problem of politics for Jean-Jacques Rousseau, and for us, is ultimately connected with the paradox of sovereignty at the basis of legal authority, and the question that it inevitably raises of law's relation to religion. According to Critchley, Rousseau gives us the definitive expression of the modern conception of politics: politics is the break with any conception of natural law and has to be based on the concepts of popular sovereignty, rigorous equality and collective autonomy understood as the self-determination of a people. And yet, in order for this modern conception of politics to become effective it has to have a religious dimension, what Rousseau calls a civil religion. Finally he addresses the question of the necessity of fiction at the basis of politics.

Desire

Janne Porttikivi argues that the current political situation with its never-ending war against terrorism is characterized by the excess of ethics over law and politics. In this fight against absolute evil victims and culprits alike fall into the abyss of 'infinite justice'. For this kind of 'bad infinity' he opposes the 'true' (Hegelian) infinite of comedy. Infinite refers here only to the very contradiction in the heart of (the human) being, and which is, he argues, the stuff that comedies are made of. If ethics always refers to the tragic dimension of life, perhaps with comedy we could more easily enter the field of politics. Perhaps the answer to the impasses of international politics is not to refer our constitutive finitude as in tragedy but our paradoxical finitude that is revealed by the fundamental structure of the comedy to be actually infinite.

According to *Marc de Kesel*, the core of Lacanian theory is a new definition of the subject, proper to our modern condition. We are the subject, not of our being, but of our desire for being. We are not what we are, we are desire (for what we wish to be). For him this is the new paradigm according to which we have to rethink 'man and world'. Concerning ethics, this paradigm implies a radical break with all traditional conceptions of morality. The supreme good, on which these are based, turns out to be for Lacan (he is here following Kant) nothing but radical evil. But Lacan's aim is not to bring down or destroy ethics. On the contrary for Lacan non-moralizing ethics is only possible if it acknowledges radical evil as the 'supreme good' which it is aiming at.

According to *Jochem Willemsen* and *Paul Verhaeghe*, before Freud, sexual aberrations were considered to be rare, sinful and criminal, i.e. evil. And actually the contemporary diagnostic includes a strong reference to the illegal character of the perverted act: we have returned to a society in which sexual deviation has become again synonymous with a crime. For Willemsen and Verhaeghe the question is how to understand perversion and psychopathy independently of this contemporary reduction, while at the same time acknowledging the link with the law. Hence, they approach the problem of perversion and psychopathy so that the Oedipal situation, and the relation to the Law and to language are described through Freudian-Lacanian theory.

For *Véronique Voruz*, Kant's invention of a formalist ethics is a construction which responds to his concern with ontological uncertainty. But Freud interprets Kant's categorical imperative as a philosophical rationalization of moral masochism. For Lacan, in spite of a painstaking attempt to separate the subject from all pathological objects, Kantian formalism (categorical imperative) means the return of the Voice (as drive-object) upon the subject. The cause of Kantian ethics inexorably remains the will to jouissance. By contrast, in Lacanian ethics each subject's particular relation to the object has to be included in the subject's ethical position – and this is the key to understanding Lacan's concept of the desire of the analyst, sole 'guarantee' of the ethics of his or her position.

Notes

1 François Marie Arouet de Voltaire, 'Poème sur le désastre de Lisbonne', *Póesis*, Paris: Belles Lettres, 2003, pp. 219–20 ; 'Poem on the Lisbon Disaster', *Selected Works of Voltaire*, London: Watts & Co., 1911. Online. Available at http://en.wikisource.org/wiki/Poem_on_the_Lisbon_Disaster.
2 Theodor Adorno, *Negative Dialectics*, trans. E. B. Ashton, London and New York: Continuum, 1995, p. 361.
3 Gottfried Leibnitz, *Essais de Théodicée sur la bonté de Dieu, la liberté de l'homme et l'origine du mal* I, Amsterdam: François Changuion, 1747.
4 François Marie Arouet de Voltaire, *Candide, or, Optimism*, New York: Modern Library, 2005, p. 15.
5 Jean-Jacques Rousseau, *Les Confessions* II, Paris: Gallimard, 1963, p. 100.
6 Immanuel Kant, 'Geschichte und Naturbeschreibung der merkwürdigsten Vorfälle des Erdbebens, welches an dem Ende des 1755sten Jahres einen

Großen Theil der Erde erschüttert hat' *Werke* I, Berlin: Georg Reimer, 1910, 1968, p. 456.

7 Immanuel Kant, *Mutmaßlicher Anfang der Menschengeschichte. Kleinerë Schriften zur Geschichtsphilosophie, Ethik und Politik*, Hamburg: Meiner, 1973, p. 56.

8 Immanuel Kant, *Religion within Boundaries of mere Reason*, in *The Works of Immanuel Kant, Religion and Rational Theology*, trans. George Di Giovanni, Cambridge: Cambridge University Press, 2005, p. 89.

9 Joan Copjec, *Imagine there's no Woman. Ethics and Sublimation*, Cambridge, MA: MIT Press, 2002, p. 139.

10 Slavoj Žižek, *The Indivisible Remainder. An Essay on Schelling and Related Matters*, London: Verso, 1996, p. 6.

11 F. W. J. Schelling, *Philosophical Inquiries into the Nature of human Freedom and Matters connected therewith*, trans. James Gutmann, Chicago: Open Court, 1936.

12 Richard J. Bernstein, *Radical Evil. A Philosophical Investigation*, Cambridge: Polity Press, 2002, pp. 96–7.

13 Rüdiger Safranski, *Das Böse, oder Das Drama der Freiheit*, Frankfurt am Main: Fischer, 1999, p. 13.

14 Copjec, *Imagine there's no Woman*, p. 136.

15 Hannah Arendt, 'Nightmare and Flight', in *Essays in Understanding, 1930–1945*, New York: Harcourt Brace, 1994, p. 134.

16 Hannah Arendt, *The Origins of Totalitarianism*, New York: Harcourt, 1973, p. 1xxiv.

17 Adorno, *Negative Dialectic*, p. 465.

18 Richard J. Bernstein, *Radical Evil. A Philosophical Investigation*, Cambridge: Polity Press, 2002, p. 1.

19 Andrew Delbanco, *The Death of Satan*, New York: Farrar Straus & Giroux, 1995, p. 3; Bernstein, *Radical Evil*, p. 1.

20 Emmanuel Levinas, 'Reflections on the philosophy of Hitlerism', trans. Sean Hand, *Critical Inquiry*, 17, 1990, pp. 62–71, p. 63.

21 As an example, Joan Copjec (ed.), *Radical Evil*, London: Verso, 1996; Slavoj Žižek, *The Plague of Fantasies*, London: Verso, 1997; Jacob Rogozinski, *Le Don de la loi. Kant et l'énigme de l'éthique*, Paris: Presses Universitaires de France, 1999; Miklos Vetö, *Le Mal*, Paris: L'Harmattan, 2000; Alenka Zupančič, *Ethics of the Real. Kant, Lacan*, London, Verso, 2000; Susan Neiman, *Evil in Modern Thought. An Alternative History of Philosophy*, Princeton, NJ: Princeton University Press, 2002. More books on evil will be found in the bibliography.

22 Ottfried Höffe, *Kant's Cosmopolitian Theory of Law and Peace*, Cambridge: Cambridge University Press, 2006, p. 68.

23 Peter Dews, 'Disenchantment and the persistence of evil. Habermas, Jonas, Badiou', in Alan D. Schrift (ed.), *Modernity and the Problem of Evil*, Bloomington, IN: Indiana University Press, 2005.

24 Neiman, *Evil in Modern Thought*, pp. 2–3.

25 Josh Cohen, *Interrupting Auschwitz: Art, Religion, Philosophy*, London and New York: Continuum, 2003, p. 4.

26 Cohen, *Interrupting Auschwitz*, p. 25.

27 Cohen, *Interrupting Auschwitz*, p. 139.

28 Slavoj Žižek, *Violence. Six Sideways Reflections*, London: Profile Books, 2008, pp. 1–2.

29 Walter Benjamin, 'Critique of Violence', trans. Edmund Jephcott, in *Reflections*, New York: Schocken, 1978.

30 Costas Douzinas, *Human Rights and Empire. The Political Philosophy of Cosmopolitanism*, London: Routledge Cavendish, 2007, p. 298.

31 Arendt, *The Origins of Totalitarianism*, p. ix.
32 Jacques Lacan, 'Kant with Sade', trans. Bruce Fink, in *Écrits*, New York: Norton, 2006, p. 649.
33 Jean Laplance and J. B. Pontalis, *The Language of Psychoanalysis*, trans. Donald Nicholson-Smith, New York: Norton, 1973, p. 306.

Part I

Freedom

Chapter 2

Eden/Shangri-la

Angus McDonald

This argument employs evil obliquely, in order to consider the patterns certain positions fall into when oriented around that idea. Evil is associated with transgression of divine authority, with interruption of natural grace, with unnatural pride, with lust, with justification for the necessity of authority to restrain and punish evil.

Evil interrupts the steady flow of the quotidian. Evil is exceptional, evil is at the extreme other pole to the everyday. Evil is invoked when the behaviour so categorized is inexplicable. Evil is not an explanation; evil is the denomination of the exhaustion of explanation.

However, circulating around the notion of evil, a certain disposition of forces can be described schematically: knowledge of good and evil is the temptation which induces Adam into disobedience of god's taboo, and the prize of this rebellion, which makes Adam a challenger to god's authority. After the fall, there is human authority, god-proxies who take Adam's gain, knowledge of good and evil, as a justification for aping god. And there is punished humanity which has to evade being the object of moral judgement in asserting, first, aesthetic distance, second, human intimacy.

1. (a) Of the many constellations of thought which consider the problem of evil, one is pre-eminent in Western culture, rooted in the early chapters of the first book of the Old Testament of the Bible.[1] The proposition is that knowledge of good and evil is a loss, which separates humanity from nature and from god. The defining image of this notion, two people beside a tree, is found in Genesis 3. So, an atheological reading of this scene.

The first scene of evil, then, is where the loss is a double loss, the loss of intimacy with god, and the loss of unity with nature. In this scene, evil is unnatural. This is evil as the interruption of the otherwise continuous connectedness of everything, because if evil is simply a position in a field, a link in a chain, then it is superfluous, part of normal functioning.

> *Vladimir*: Gogo.
> *Estragon*: *(irritably)* What is it?

Vladimir:. Did you ever read the Bible?
Estragon: The Bible … *(He reflects.)* I must have taken a look at it.[2]

And the Lord God planted a garden eastward in Eden: and there he put the man whom he had formed. And out of the ground made the Lord God to grow every tree that is pleasant to the sight, and good for food; the tree of life also in the midst of the garden, and the tree of knowledge of good and evil. … And the Lord God commanded the man, saying, Of every tree of the garden thou mayest freely eat: But of the tree of the knowledge of good and evil, thou shalt not eat of it: for in the day that thou eatest thereof thou shalt surely die. … And they were both naked, the man and his wife, and were not ashamed. Now the serpent was more subtil than any beast of the field which the Lord God had made. And he said unto the woman, Yea, hath God said, Ye shall not eat of every tree of the garden? And the woman said unto the serpent, We may eat of the fruit of the trees of the garden: But of the fruit of the tree which is in the midst of the garden, God hath said, Ye shall not eat of it, neither shall ye touch it, lest ye die. And the serpent said unto the woman, Ye shall not surely die: For God doth know that in the day ye eat thereof, then your eyes shall be opened, and ye shall be as gods, knowing good and evil. And when the woman saw that the tree was good for food, and that it was pleasant to the eyes, and a tree to be desired to make one wise, she took the fruit thereof, and did eat, and gave also unto her husband with her; and he did eat. And the eyes of them both were opened, and they knew that they were naked; and they sewed fig leaves together, and made themselves aprons. And they heard the voice of the Lord God walking in the garden in the cool of the day: and Adam and his wife hid themselves from the presence of the Lord God amongst the trees of the garden. And the Lord God called unto Adam, and said unto him, Where art thou? And he said, I heard thy voice in the garden, and I was afraid, because I was naked; and I hid myself. And he said, Who told thee that thou wast naked? Hast thou eaten of the tree, whereof I commanded thee that thou shouldest not eat? … And unto Adam he said, Because thou … hast eaten of the tree, of which I commanded thee, saying, Thou shalt not eat of it: cursed is the ground for thy sake … And the Lord God said, Behold, the man is become as one of us, to know good and evil: and now, lest he put forth his hand, and take also of the tree of life, and eat, and live for ever: Therefore the Lord God sent him forth from the garden of Eden.[3]

Is evil the first breach between god and creation? This narrative is so well known that it may escape our notice what exactly it asserts. Consider it afresh. The all-powerful god creates his creatures, but does not endow them with ethical knowledge, a condition of innocence marked by nakedness without shame. That the text makes the linkage ('naked … not ashamed') indicates hindsight, otherwise why would nakedness be linked to shame at all? Nakedness is shameful in the world after the expulsion from Eden, and it is only from this standpoint that the observation makes any sense. Shame is the awareness of having done wrong, as being naked is wrong in the post-lapsarian world. Nakedness in Eden is a natural unselfconscious condition. Awareness of right and wrong is precisely what Adam and Eve lack: they are natural humanity, as integrally harmonious with nature as all the other animals standing naked, shameless – and without ethical knowledge. Into this static situation is added suspense, for god imposes the first taboo, the ban on eating the fruit of one tree. Adam is told, for his own good, supposedly, that eating of that tree will be death. God makes no mention, either to ban access or to allow use, of the tree of life. Is Adam, at this point, immortal? We do not know. Why put that tree there, and then forbid it? Eve is enlightened by the serpent. The serpent lets her know that god has lied. Eating of the tree is not death. In this, the serpent does not lie: when the fruit is eaten, Adam and Eve gain ethical knowledge, and do not die. So, god made the first prohibition on the basis of a lie to his innocent creatures. God does not behave ethically towards his creatures. Indeed, Eve begins to gain ethical knowledge even before she eats, at the moment the serpent causes her to re-evaluate the tree independent of god's taboo ('a tree to be desired to make one wise'). Eve derives two impulses from the serpent: desire, and for wisdom. Two impulses god had not equipped her with. The consequences of ethical knowledge are immediate: self-consciousness, manifested as shame at nakedness, followed by the practical remedy of clothing, and furtiveness when god returns, manifested by hiding. As so often, it is not the breaking of the law, but, quite literally, the cover-up, which undoes them. God knows, by their shame, that they have transgressed. But god must also know, by their transgression, that they know that god lied. Can god be ashamed? Greek gods are shamelessly immoral. This one too? It seems not: his anger could be understood as the shameful anger of a liar caught out. Is this a text of god's fall as well as humanity's? God's shame as well as humanity's?

The theoretical consequence of ethical knowledge is shame; the practical consequence is expulsion. Both, ideally and materially respectively, figure alienation. A separation from nature, a broken relationship with god, a self-awareness which separates humanity from animality and from nature.

Notice, however, that god's motive for the expulsion is not a simple punishment for transgression, but rather a policy of self-defence. God expels Adam and Eve because, having gained ethical knowledge, they might, by eating of the tree of life, also gain eternal life, which would make them 'as one of us'. The tree of life was not forbidden, and had Adam and Eve had the knowledge to eat of it before sampling the fruit of the tree of knowledge … but they could not have done so, lacking the serpent's knowledge. Divinity is revealed as being ethical knowledge plus eternal life. Or, at least, possessing these attributes makes one equal to, and therefore threatening to, divinity.

Before the breach with nature, only the serpent has awareness independent of god's authority. The moral of the story is generally taken to be that humanity must heal its breach with nature and god; an alternative model would be that of the serpent; humanity must become a 'subtil beast'. Certainly god seems to block such an alliance: god says to the serpent, 'I shall put enmity between thee and the woman.'[4] Where the serpent's subtility came from is not revealed. Had it eaten the fruit? If the story is read, as here, without presuming god's goodness or authority – as, with pagan gods, one assumes the latter but not the former – then god's deception and petulant reaction are not justified, putting god in the wrong, and responsible for the breach.

The breach must be considered as twofold. The first breach, when the serpent and the fruit enlighten Adam and Eve, is a breach with nature in the form of self-consciousness which is figured as a first awareness of nakedness, addressed by the adoption of clothing. This leads to the second breach, with god, figured by the hiding from him. God's realization that they have ethical knowledge leads to the expulsion and the setting by god of new terms in the relation between humanity and nature: the terms of hard labour rather than effortless existence. This is not an immediate consequence of self-consciousness, but god's sanction against humanity for disobedience. In Christian teleology the breach with god is healed by Christ's sacrifice, which could be viewed as god's sacrifice for his wrongdoing against humanity in Eden. The breach with nature remains unrepaired. But the figure of the serpent, completely in nature but sufficiently independent to question the veracity of god's claims, suggests a different reconciliation for humanity: with the serpent and against god. However the serpent gained its subtility, humanity can follow, in retaining ethical judgement, a judgement which condemns god, but may allow for reconciliation with nature, a reconciliation which need not be a mere return.

For a more orthodox reading from within the Christian tradition, Hegel's argument that 'as immediately natural human beings, we *ought* to regard ourselves as being what we *ought not* to be. This has been expressed by saying that human beings are *evil by nature*, i.e. they ought not to be the way they immediately are; hence they are as they ought not to be.'[5] To Hegel it is 'only with reference to *cognition* that human beings are posited as evil'.[6] Hegel, in sum, concludes, 'human beings become evil by cognizing'.[7] For Hegel, although this is the story of the fall of humanity, the estrangement from nature and god is a necessary first step towards a later reconciliation at a higher level – with god, through Christ. But this is to accept god's judgement against humanity, of sin, whereas an atheological reading, influenced by Bataille,[8] might ask, why should humanity submit to the liar god?

Which leaves the question of a reconciliation with nature. God's curse stands in the way, his imposition of enmity with the serpent and of labour as how humanity must relate to nature. Can this curse be lifted? Georges Bataille, reading Hegel through Alexandre Kojève, says the way back, the fiction of the nobility of nature imagined even by a writer like Jonathan Swift ('the Houyhnhnms have no word in their language to express anything that is *evil*, except what they borrow from the deformities or ill qualities of the Yahoos')[9] is an illusion. Swift merely inverts terms; nature is noble, Yahoo humanity ugly, whose clothing is the most absurd symbol of estrangement from natural grace in the eyes of the idealized Houyhnhnms. This is not a resolution but a repetition with inverted values which still accepts separation. Bataille might seem to endorse this in phrases such as 'The animal is in the world like water in water'[10] but he goes on to say that 'Man is the being who has lost, and even rejected, that which he obscurely is, a vague intimacy.'[11] In festival, Bataille argues, man seeks a reunion with nature through the operation of sacrifice in the realm of the sacred, but 'to subordinate is not only to alter the subordinated element but to be altered oneself'[12] which is the reality of the world of work, a world opposed to the intimate order, an order of 'intimacy, in the trembling of the individual [which] is holy, sacred, and suffused with anguish'.[13] The contrast is this: to the Christian and the Hegelian, humanity seeks union with god by a distancing from nature, whereas in Bataille humanity seeks an intimacy with nature which necessitates a sacred festivity. The sacred is the route back to intimacy with nature but, for the Christian, intimacy with god lies in a rejection of nature. But Bataille's humanity can no more re-achieve natural intimacy than can the Christian, and the outcome, in the return of a consciousness of separation, is anguish.

If not through sacred festivity, an alternative passage might be aesthetic, the attempt to achieve intimacy through art. One place to think about this would be in the caves of Lascaux. Bataille wrote about the cave paintings of Lascaux as the birth of art. Bataille argued that the birth of representation this art work produces must be understood as a consequence of the painter no longer feeling part of natural animality but being separate: in this separation there may be a nostalgia, a wish to bridge the gap and return, but the way is barred and the reunion may occur only by other paths. The art is an excess, not a utilitarian activity but a celebration of the ability to represent the animal life surrounding the painter with an intimacy thought irrecoverable. When the figure of a man appears, insignificant, Bataille observes that it must surely be the first artist's signature. The birth of art, a fecund birth which also births, in a dimension of transcendence, the essential ideas theorized by Bataille: taboo, transgression, law, the sacred and evil.

In Blanchot's review of Bataille's book[14] he says, of the Lascaux painters, the subterranean paintings of Lascaux 'make us enter into an intimate space of knowledge'.[15] Bataille's hypothesis, according to Blanchot, is that the paintings 'are probably linked to … when man, interrupting the time of effort and work – thus for the first time truly man – returns to the source of natural overabundance … to what he was when he was not yet'.[16]

> He breaks the prohibitions, but because there are now prohibitions and because he breaks them, he is exalted far beyond his original existence.[17]

The 'loss' leads to a greater gain. The art work, Blanchot says, is:

> a return to the first immensity, but a return that is always more than a return, for he who returns … also becomes tumultuously conscious of this impossible return, becomes conscious of the limits and the unique force that allows him to break these limits, does not simply lose himself in the dream of total existence, but instead affirms himself as that which is added to this existence and, more secretly still, as the minute part that, at a distance and through an ambiguous play, can become master of everything, can appropriate it symbolically or communicate with it by making it be.[18]

Where Bataille's festivity was man's attempt to 'lose himself in a dream of total existence', Blanchot's artist achieves a mastery which reconciles humanity with nature through creativity, but does not deny the gap. This is the full achievement of an ethical knowledge, ethical because conscious of the responsibility which a distance from nature imposes on us, but aesthetic knowledge too, as it is through the achievement of art that the higher communication with nature occurs. Blanchot's artist actually creates nature, and thus fulfils god's fear, 'becomes as one of us', in artistic immortality.

(b) And if the art addresses not nature, but the human condition, mockingly, fondly? Once again, two people, a tree, suspense: in *Waiting for Godot* Samuel Beckett returns us to Eden and to two people having trouble with clothing, from first stage direction:

> *Estragon, sitting on a low mound, is trying to take off his boot*[19]

to almost the last dialogue:

> *Vladimir*: Pull on your trousers
> *Estragon*: What?
> *Vladimir*: Pull on your trousers.
> *Estragon*: You want me to pull off my trousers?
> *Vladimir*: Pull ON your trousers.
> *Estragon*: *(realizing his trousers are down)* True.
> *He pulls up his trousers.*[20]

These two people are not, however, troubled by a visitation from the one they wait for. In the episode of Lucky, they see the life of labour to which Adam was condemned for his disobedience, as in a flash forward. Their situation remains static. They are not expelled from their proximity to the tree. The tree is not the key to anything, holds no promise. In fact the ethical apathy of Vladimir and Estragon, and the tedious time filling of their repartee, might suggest a humanity which ate of the tree of eternal life, but not of the tree of ethical knowledge, in a godless Eden. Beckett gives us a humanity that has solved the problem of survival but which, in an inchoate feeling that there must be more than this present existence, spend their time *waiting*. What Godot represents, what understanding they have with Godot which pre-dates curtain-up, is of course the great riddle of the play, and whether Godot, like the edenic god, has contrived to mislead the characters, or even exists outside their minds, is unknowable.

> *Estragon*: What's all this about? Abused who?
> *Vladimir*: The Saviour.
> *Estragon*: Why?
> *Vladimir*: Because he wouldn't save them.
> *Estragon*: From hell?
> *Vladimir*: Imbecile! From death.
> *Estragon*: I thought you said hell.
> *Vladimir*: From death, from death.[21]

Vladimir, who now says, from death, did in fact say hell earlier. To be saved from death is to gain eternal life. To be saved from hell is to be redeemed from sin and reunited with god. Two rather different outcomes. Vladimir and Estragon are saved from death, but not from hell, because the threat of hell does not arise, with them being unfallen humanity. And their dilemma is exactly why Hegel describes the Fall as necessary to humanity's spiritual evolution. Vladimir and Estragon do not evolve. If we view their situation as comic, we may simply conclude, this is the absurd human condition. If tragic, then we are probably buying into a Christian redemptive spiritual history. We might view the absence of a serpent with information about god(ot)'s duplicity as another handicap against the possibility of Vladimir and Estragon making any meaningful choices *and moving away from the tree*. The play never leaves Eden, never enters history – although the glimpse of human society given by Pozzo and Lucky might suggest that staying in Eden is the wiser choice.

This is, however, an Eden where humanity is never embarrassed by the proximity of god. God stays away. In any case, this humanity has an ethical sensibility: a weak one, with no empathy for Lucky's plight, and a constant irritability in the relationship, but one that encompasses a solidarity between Vladimir and Estragon, a commonality, a community in which the extremes of suicide and despair are repeatedly invoked but equally repeatedly evaded. This equivocal Eden, by no means a paradise, still manages to keep the world of work at arm's length, although it is complicated by the world of things. This is an art that knows it cannot return, but establishes human intimacy across the breach, much as the Lascaux paintings commune with nature.

In the next section a strategy for survival without intimacy is examined, by the bifurcation of the sacred and the profane, in a social hierarchy which expels evil.

2. The knowledge of good and evil, propelling humanity into history, may be parlayed by social hierarchy: men who play god, judge and condemn humanity, deny nature. Proxies for god.

Social cohesion has ever been founded on ethical consensus, the achievement of a common view. From Aristotle to Adam Smith, the pressure of sympathy, identity with the community, is the social *sine qua non*. It is the form of consensus rather than the specific content of the values that matters. Ethical values are subsumed to utility, and, if lacking in acceptance, can be imposed.

In Aristotle, knowledge of good and evil, and the consensus around values, makes society possible:

> For the real difference between man and other animals is that humans alone have perception of good and evil, right and wrong, just and unjust. And it is the sharing of a common view in these matters that makes a household or a city.[22]

This is a rather relativistic claim. 'A common view in these matters', which makes a city, is not the same as a claim on the truth, it is just an opinion. Aristotle's perception of good and evil is rather less than Adam and Eve's knowledge of the same.

Augustine asks, 'What is the moral evil in war?' and answers that it is not the deaths which come by war which are the moral evil but 'love of violence, revengeful cruelty, fierce and implacable enmity, wild resistance and the lust of power, and suchlike'.[23] He means not that war stirs such emotions up, but that the suppression of such emotions is the justification for war. Consistently in Augustine authority, by good reason, is justified in acting against evil emotion.

These claims put evil to work. Identifying and punishing evil becomes the great social enterprise. What is the nature of authority's dilemma in controlling crime? Augustine asks, 'What idea can we form of the pitiable predicament of men who sit in judgement on other men without being able to read their consciences?'[24] The problem is the absence in the judges of divine omniscience. Unlike god, the human judge cannot see into the transgressor's evil or innocent soul, and must second-guess as a second best. But ultimately the efficacy of law's judgement does not depend on divine insight: fallible human authority, even in error, remains, precisely, the lesser of two evils – at least, in its own eyes – as it sustains order.

Bataille's theory of sacred festivity has already been mentioned. We can see now that it is subsumed to a social function. Bataille's discussion in *Theory of Religion* aims to analyse what happens when the metaphysics of good and evil are put to work in the name of social order. In what he presents as a speculative anthropology, he contrasts animal immediacy, which lacks any transcendent dimension, with human labouring activity, which posits the object, in the using of tools, and thereby interrupts continuity. This is because tools are developed with an end in view: the tool has no value in itself, but only in relation to an anticipated result. It establishes the clear distinction between the end and the means. Unfortunately, the end is thus given in terms of the means, in terms of utility.

> The absurdity of an endless deferral only justifies the equivalent absurdity of a true end, which would serve no purpose.[25]

For Bataille the problem is the deferral in time of satisfaction, or the impossibility of a true end, which would justify all earlier deferrals. As this true end would serve no further purpose, it would be truly useless, and would make all prior deferrals equally useless.

The world divides into a world of utility, of things, the profane world, and a sacred world, of the useless. To bridge this gap, this alienation, festivity, with sacrifice at its heart, is examined anthropologically. This is another attempt to restore intimacy, figured as a divide between matter, which must be purified by ritual, in sacrifice, emerging as its opposite, spirit.

In matter, in the real, in the profane world, a law ensuring stability in an order of things necessarily develops. Law defines obligatory relations of things with other things, guaranteed by the sanction of public force; but this turns human beings into merely more things in a world of things.

The divine world contained good and evil, equidistant from the profane world, but a shift occurs, with divine purity increasingly becoming identified with good, and profane matter with evil.

Divine sovereignty shifts from evil to good, the divine order sanctions the real order, a good god has operative power over the real, and humanity lives a 'sovereignty of servitude' defined only by glimpses of transcendence. Thereafter intimacy with the divine occurs only through festive sacrifice, and there is no intimacy in the profane world, structured by the externality of divinity. In the next section two strategies for transcending the profane world's utilitarian limits will be considered: the dandy's attempt at personal sovereignty, and the lover's attempt at intimacy.

3. (a)

> … in the lighted room I saw that she was losing what she had had. Her past was coming out on her face like latent handwriting. Her powder and lipstick, alkali and orange in the fluorescent light, were cracking and peeling off. Grime showed in the pores of her nose and at the sides of her neck. Dissolution was working in her rapidly like a fatal disease she had caught.[26]

This is the hard-boiled *noir* version of the Dorian Gray fallacy. The woman's make-up is a mask which has hidden the corruption which now breaks through. Beneath the make-up, beneath the skin, is the skull, the ivory grin. The skeleton in the closet, a rhetorical figure made literal in the novel, the guilty secret, is also the woman's guilty secret: beneath the pretty mask she is ugly, and ugly because evil. The fallacy, the major premise hidden in the fantastical logic of Wilde's novel, is that evil must out.[27] The reader of *Dorian Gray* accepts the minor premise that one might by some kind of magic be able to transfer the physical manifestation of one's spiritual evil from one's own face to the face portrayed in a portrait, and the portrait might become the scapegoat that suffers the ignominy of ugliness, an ugliness, however, that can be concealed. What is accepted in this construction is that evil must show somewhere, and if not in its natural place, on one's own face, then on some simulation of that face elsewhere. However, this is precisely the problem in reality: evil does not show: in an identification parade the mass murderers are not so easily picked out from the ordinary good people. Evil is not a cause whose physical consequence is ugliness.

It is odd indeed that Dorian Gray appears to endorse this logic, to the point of adopting the necessity of an alternative outlet for the ugliness. It is odd, not least because the whole philosophy of the dandy which underlies the novel is most insistent on this point: ethics and aesthetics are separate realms; the good is not the beautiful, the evil is not the ugly this is the founding statement of faith of the aesthete.

The Picture of Dorian Gray stands in English literature as the epitome of the posture of the dandy, but is actually a clearly moral and moralizing fable. The story is well known. A young man finds his wish that he may stay as beautiful as he is at the moment of his portraiture unexpectedly fulfilled. He does not age, decay or become visibly corrupted, whilst the proverbial picture in the attic (actually the schoolroom) bears these marks. But it is on the visibility of corruption that the oddness of the fairy tale revolves. If it were only a matter of arresting the inevitability of the onset of visible signs of ageing, the tale would be merely a narcissistic wish-fulfilment narrative. But this wish is quickly overlaid by the notion that the visible marks of moral corruption also be displaced. Indeed, it is at the crucial moments when Dorian behaves immorally that the portrait becomes uglier, and, logically, he even wonders if, unlike ageing, the process might be reversible – if he commits morally good acts the portrait might be restored to its earlier beauty. The incoherence here – and it cuts to the core of the novel – is that the dandy stance rests entirely on the notion that ethics and aesthetics can be distinguished and kept separate. The founding and defining belief of the dandy is that that which is ethically dubious may nonetheless be aesthetically praiseworthy. Thus the 'beautiful murder', and so on. To the dandy, the evaluative criteria of aesthetics must not be muddied with moral concerns. Art for art's sake is the resistance to morally (read socially, politically) useful art. Only in its uselessness does art meet its purpose, which is purposelessness outside of aesthetic concerns. It is clear: ethics is one thing, aesthetics another. The good is not the beautiful, and the beautiful is not the good. One then has the choice between being a moralist, who can care nothing for the beautiful in the pursuit of the good, and is to the dandy a bore; and being a dandy, who can care nothing for the good in the pursuit of the beautiful, and is to the moralist a decadent.

But the central device of *The Picture of Dorian Gray* confounds this essential distinction, and it is so central, and assumed, in order to make the plot work, that it seems to pass unremarked. The device, which every reader also swallows, is this: ethical or unethical acts have aesthetic consequences. The good is the beautiful, and the evil is the ugly. In the 'natural' course of events Dorian's evils would turn him into an ugly grotesque, and so powerful is this assumption that if the natural process is suppressed by a fairy-tale-like granting of a wish, then the ugliness must come out elsewhere, that is in the portrait. Had the wish not been granted then Dorian's evils would show in his own physical face. But this version of the pathetic fallacy, admittedly a commonplace fictional shorthand, stands in flat contradiction to the founding tenet of the dandy – and reality. The good are not always beautiful, the evil are not always ugly. Evil deeds are not a cause the effect of which is ugly faces.

Dorian is then presented as one subject to a temptation: what if, unlike the universal law, he were allowed to 'get away with' his evils? What if his evils did not carry the natural consequence of ugliness? Would he be tempted by the possibility of evil without personal consequences – evil without punishment – to be more evil than he otherwise would be? Yes, he would. Such is our seduction by this question that we fail to notice that no such universal consequence pertains. It is perhaps the vestige of dandyism that the worst punishment for evil is not god's wrath but to be ugly.

The dandy's attitude is defined in relation to Dorian's seduction by the unnamed decadent text: being 'poisoned by a book', Dorian 'looked on evil simply as a mode through which he could realize his conception of the beautiful'.[28] This is an extra twist. Once the ethical and the aesthetic have been defined as distinct realms with distinct criteria, then not only is it a category error to assess the aesthetic by ethical criteria, but, having discounted the ethical realm – or, in Dorian's case, having become exempt from its rules – the dandy can actually employ the ethical realm to aesthetic ends: the precise inversion of the moralist who would employ the aesthetic realm to ethical ends. (A moralist such as Wilde, for example, whose fairy tale has an unavoidable Big Moral.)

The symptomatic absence in the tale is law. When the tale asks whether corrupting someone is ethically wrong, or perhaps aesthetically pleasing, when it comes to killing people, even, what is clear is that the question never raised is the question of the legal consequences of actions of corrupting and killing.

When an intruder is killed on the estate during a shoot there is no legal consequence. Nor is there any moral qualm. In a book full of consciously amoral attitudinizing, the most amoral attitude, and the only one now shocking, is after the accidental shooting of the intruder, mistaken for a beater:

> 'Good heavens! I have hit a beater!' exclaimed Sir Geoffrey. 'What an ass the man was to get in front of the guns! Stop shooting, there!' he called out at the top of his voice. 'A man is hurt.' … 'Why on earth don't you keep your men back? Spoiled my shooting for the day.'[29]

The beater, a mere servant, is of no consequence: the aristocrat's pleasure has been spoiled, and this is the only cause for anger on Sir Geoffrey's part. An English counterpart to de Sade's libertines. Only the pleasures of the powerful matter, the sufferings of the lower orders to be dismissed. Indeed, in a condensed image, 'two cries heard, the cry of a hare in pain, which is dreadful, the cry of a man in agony, which is worse',[30] the man is more kin to the animal which was killed for pleasure than to the man who killed both of them.

Some sense of social shame intervenes. '"Dorian," said Lord Henry, "I had better tell them that the shooting is stopped for today. It would not look well to go on."'[31] So appearances do matter, even the opinion of the lower orders – but only fleetingly: 'this accident … it's nothing to us. It is rather awkward for Geoffrey, of course. It does not do to pepper beaters. It makes people think that one is a wild shot. And Geoffrey is not.'[32] So the opinion of other aristocrats concerning the hunting prowess of one of their own is the only serious risk to public standing. The matter is closed and dismissed as only a problem in that it may become a bore if 'these fellows keep chattering about this thing at dinner.'[33] They will be told not to. Clearly the young aesthetes are rank amateurs at casual amoralism or simply the typical sons of their callous fathers.

When Dorian kills Basil, and blackmails a friend to help him dispose of the corpse, it is less shocking than the casual killing in the hunting fields. For one thing, Dorian is racked by remorse, and of course there is an aesthetic consequence, the picture becomes uglier. In the contrast between the killing that matters, because Basil is a friend, and the killing that doesn't matter, of the supposed beater (who is actually Dorian's doom, the revenging brother of Sybil, the woman destroyed by him), lies the ethical failing of the novel. Its would-be moral is apparently that evil will out, and that Dorian must suffer after all. The novel has played with the question, how would a person behave if the evil they do has no consequence upon them, specifically upon their appearance? It has presented this as a fabulous exception to the general rule, that the evil we do does have consequences. Maybe it does, but not generally as a direct transformation of our beauty to ugliness. It has proposed that, if one were protected from the consequences, one would act evilly and spread corruption out of one's glamorous inviolability. But Sir Geoffrey kills callously and indifferently and suffers no consequences. And the killing removes Dorian's potential killer neatly from the scene, so Dorian suffers no consequences either. Dorian becomes involved in the killing of Basil only because of the action upon him of what can only be conscience: the need to confess, to tell the secret to someone. He tells Basil, the character most explicitly under the spell of the pathetic fallacy, 'Sin is a thing that writes itself across a man's face. It cannot be concealed. People talk sometimes of secret vices. There are no secret vices. There are no such things. If a wretched man has a vice, it shows itself in the lines of his mouth.'[34] For this fallacy Basil dies, as he is shown the picture which he painted, shown its new ugliness, and draws the conclusion his belief system requires of him, that that ugliness, strangely present on the canvas rather than the skin, reveals nonetheless vice. For this knowledge of vice Dorian kills Basil, as he cannot bear to have his vice witnessed. Dorian is ashamed. No thoroughgoing dandy at all. The notion that the lack of consequences is an anomaly falls. Dorian's corruption has never been without consequences, albeit transposed to the picture. Sir Geoffrey's act of killing is, however, truly without consequence, except a happy twist for Dorian. Dorian is never conscience-free, the picture has become his objectified, externalized conscience, and in his climactic attempt to kill his conscience he succeeds, predictably, only in killing himself. Wilde's confusion concerning consequences renders his novel inconsequential. Evil and ugliness were never split from each other, never mind opposed. A very trite moral fable for a supposed dandy. The glimpse of a coherent philosophy of the dandy, although bungled by a casual unreflective class snobbery, leaves us with a failure, for the dandy in love with himself, or his image, cannot love another. The dandy has attempted a project of personal sovereignty. The element missing in the jousting of the wits is intimacy.

(b)

> 'What colour are his eyes?'
> 'I dunno, he's always wearing shades.'
> 'Is he tall?'
> 'Well, I gotta look up.'
> 'Yeh? Well, I hear he's bad.'
> 'Mmm, he's good-bad, but he's not evil.'[35]

From 'Give Him a Great Big Kiss', by the Shangri-las (1965), we overhear this dialogue between two girls, concerning the boyfriend of the second. The first asks questions of a physical, aesthetic character – eye colour, height – and gets in response slightly evasive answers. She is sceptical, and changes approach, turning to moral criteria. The second answers, once again indirectly, by inventing an ethical distinction: 'good-bad, not evil'. In response to the first girl's moral criticism ('I hear he's bad'), the second responds with a partial concession: yes, he is bad, but bad is not necessarily all bad, he's good-bad, and good-bad is good, or, at least, desirable. The bad to be disavowed is named as evil, and the boyfriend is defended from this allegation ('he's not evil'). In this distinction, between a bad that is good-bad, and an evil which would be beyond acceptability, lies a conundrum. In defusing the allegation, what is the second girl's rhetorical strategy? Perhaps she is refusing the attempt by the first to shift registers from an aesthetic to an ethical evaluation, by folding the ethical shift back into the aesthetic: bad-as-evil would be an ethical criticism, good-bad is an aesthetic compliment. Or perhaps she is embracing the ethical turn, but making a distinction beyond the terms of the first girl – within 'bad' we must distinguish good-bad, evil, and maybe other possibilities:

> 'Yeh? Well, I hear he's bad.'
> 'Mmm, he's good-bad, but he's not evil.'[36]

What does this distinction, in the middle of a pop song, mean? It may help us think through the concept of evil. Because the first clearing of the ground required is this: the pairing 'good–bad' is not the same as the polarity 'good–evil'. And the difference is this. Good and bad are terms of conventional morality: this may be a morality of intentions or a morality of consequences; in any case, it is a question of moral judgement. Good and evil, however, seem to carry a greater air of absolutism. In the dialogue is evil just badness of a greater magnitude, or is it a category occupying a distinctly different vector? A persuasive alternative would be to suggest that the distinction good-bad as distinct from bad-evil is a shift in register from ethical to aesthetic judgement: if he was bad-evil it would be a moral condemnation; as he is good-bad, this is quite attractive, an aesthetic appreciation.

'Evil' is not to signify the extreme end of a moral spectrum running from good to bad. Evil is not merely a moral judgement of 'worse than bad'. Evil is to be defined as interruption, and so interrupting evil is interrupting the interruption, or restoring the connection, but the connection which has been interrupted is not susceptible to reconnection, so reconnection must happen at a different level – this different level might be called communication, but a better word might be intimacy, as this is not the communication envisaged by Habermas, rational and between subjects, but that of Bataille, where communication happens only between abjects.

The girls debating the boy's merits have fallen humanity's knowledge of good and evil, but they do not employ it to condemn; they make judgements, but not as god-proxies: instead, they are assessing whether this boy is worth getting close to, a good companion, a lover. A lover is more seductive if they are a bit 'good-bad'; this is understood by the girls. As Eve was 'good-bad' to Adam, so is the boy here 'good-bad' to the girlfriend. What

Eve had to offer was just more interesting and appealing than god's regime. The knowledge to be sought, a carnal knowledge as much as a spiritual one, lies in intimate communication. The ultimate endorsement of the boy's qualities lies in this clinching observation:

> 'Is he a good dancer?'
> 'What do you mean, "Is he a good dancer?"'
> 'Well, how does he dance?'
> 'Close … very very close.'[37]

The impossibilities of a renewed intimacy with god or nature, the vicissitudes of the aesthetic impulse, finally stand exposed as partial strategies whose ultimate end, the policy of the subtil beast, the serpent, is human intimacy, one with another, in a transgressive complicity.

> 'I don't want to know about evil.
> Only want to know about love.'[38]

In the metaphysical myth the narrative commenced with authority, and prohibition. Then disobedience, the fall from grace, and knowledge of good and evil. In the social scene, hierarchy is replicated, and the god proxies use the fruit of disobedience, the power to judge on the basis of a claim of knowledge of good and evil, to judge and condemn the evil. The attempt at transcendence in sacred festivity is necessarily partial. Finally, at the level of the psyche, the subtil beast attempts to sustain freedom by overcoming the knowledge of good and evil in the embrace of the aesthetic, first, in the role of the dandy, the project of personal sovereignty, which fails, finally in the role of the lover, the project of intimacy which succeeds. The project of intimacy, of course, has been analysed not through intimacy itself, which lacks form, but through an aesthetic strategy, the pop song, embodying a distancing, not mere nearness. Perhaps Shangri-la is back in the caves of Lascaux, after all – almost. Either there, or in Eden, in the intimacy – never closer – shared by Adam and Eve, when caught *in flagrante delicto* by god.

The response to evil is an aesthetics of intimacy; but not intimacy with god, nature, art, which must ultimately be viewed as means to an end, the end being communication with an other person, an other sensibility. Evil, the hardest thing to explain, is a provocation to the limits of explanation and understanding. To be understood, to encounter a different understanding: it is only for this, even, that we read, that we write.

Notes

1 Holy Bible (King James Version), London: Collins, 1958.
2 Samuel Beckett, *Waiting for Godot*, London: Faber, 1956, pp. 11–12.

3 Genesis 2:8–3:23.
4 Ibid. 3:15.
5 G. W. F. Hegel, *Lectures on the Philosophy of Religion* III, trans. R. F. Brown, P. C. Hodgson and J. M. Stewart, Berkeley, CA: University of California Press, 1985, p. 202.
6 Hegel, *Lectures on the Philosophy of Religion*, p. 205.
7 Ibid.
8 Georges Bataille, *Theory of Religion*, trans. Robert Hurley, New York: Zone Books, 1992.
9 Jonathan Swift, *Gulliver's Travels*, London, Pan Books, 1977, p. 265.
10 Bataille, *Theory of Religion*, p. 23.
11 Ibid., p. 56.
12 Ibid., p. 41.
13 Ibid., p. 52.
14 Maurice Blanchot, *Friendship*, trans. Elizabeth Rottenberg, Stanford, CA: Stanford University Press, 1997, pp. 1–11.
15 Ibid., pp. 1–2.
16 Ibid., p. 4.
17 Ibid., p. 4.
18 Ibid., p. 6.
19 Beckett, *Waiting for Godot*, p. 9.
20 Ibid., p. 94.
21 Ibid., p. 13.
22 Aristotle, *Politics*, trans. T. A. Sinclair, Harmondsworth: Penguin, 1981, p. 60.
23 Oliver O'Donovan and Joan Lockwood O'Donovan (eds), *From Irenaeus to Grotius*, Cambridge: Eerdmans, 1999, p. 117.
24 Ibid., p. 149.
25 Bataille, *Theory of Religion*, pp. 28–9.
26 Ross Macdonald, *The Ivory Grin*, London: Fontana Collins, 1952, p. 178.
27 Oscar Wilde, *The Picture of Dorian Gray*, Harmondsworth: Penguin, 1949.
28 Ibid., p. 163.
29 Ibid., pp. 223–4.
30 Ibid., p. 223.
31 Ibid., p. 224.
32 Ibid., p. 224–5.
33 Ibid., p. 225.
34 Ibid., pp. 166–7.
35 Shangri-la, *Give Him a Great Big Kiss*, New York: Red Bird Records, 1965.
36 Ibid.
37 Ibid.
38 John Martyn, *Don't Want to Know*, from *Solid Air*, London: Island Records, 1972.

Chapter 3

Tragedy and evil

From Hölderlin to Heidegger

Françoise Dastur

Tragedy, as we know, was first interpreted by Aristotle in his *Poetics*, but only from the point of view of its effects on the spectators and not from the viewpoint of what was represented in the drama itself. By defining tragedy as the imitation of an action which by giving life to fear and pity operates the *katharsis*, the purgation of these passions,[1] Aristotle was the founder of a tradition which saw in tragedy a moral or a political medication. Nietzsche, in his first and provocative book, *The Birth of Tragedy out of the Spirit of Music* (1872), has shown in a very convincing manner that considering tragedy from the viewpoint of the spectator and not from the viewpoint of the tragic actor or chorus comes in fact from tragedy itself in its development and decline. Nietzsche affirms that tragedy is born from the tragic chorus alone, which simply enacted the celebration of the god Dionysus. Later on, the need emerged to give an explicit representation of the god and to make him part of a drama. The result was the Greek tragedy as we know it, where the balance between the Dionysiac lyric of the chorus and the Apollinian dream world of the scene is maintained, as it is the case in Aeschylus' tragedies and even in Sophocles' ones. But in time dialogue replaced music and the chorus became less and less necessary, so that in Euripides' plays its function is already forgotten.

For Nietzsche, the essence of tragedy was 'destroyed' through the abolition of the chorus and the insertion of dialectic in explanation of action, Socrates being 'closely allied with the Euripidean hero who must justify his action through argument and counter argument'.[2] In Euripides' plays, the spectator himself, that is to say, the ordinary man, climbs on the scene,[3] which means that tragedy is no longer considered as the reflection of life and nature in its full strength,[4] but becomes only the mirror of the present social reality.[5] Because he no longer sees in tragedy a *metaphysical* phenomenon, Euripides is for the young Nietzsche the proclaimer of the death sentence of tragedy itself. Nietzsche therefore left aside the Aristotelian viewpoint of the tragedy as *katharsis* in order to make room for another viewpoint, the Dionysian viewpoint, which allows to see in tragedy the very process of life and becoming in both its creative and destructive aspects.[6] Nietzsche puts the emphasis on Aeschylus more than on Sophocles in order to show how the Greeks understood the relation of the human being to the divine. In his view, Aeschylus' relation with the gods was a feeling of reciprocal dependence, which is what he tried to express in his tragedy *Prometheus Bound*. Prometheus believed that he could defy the gods and nature itself in stealing fire from them and giving it to the human beings. Fire is the most important element in the development of human culture and in Aeschylus' view the fact that its mastery is given to the human beings is a sacrilege that Prometheus has to expiate.

A very important philosophical question is therefore raised here, the question of evil itself: the human being is bound to violate the law of nature and the law of the gods in order to survive, because, in opposition to the other living beings, he is deprived of natural weapons, so that he is in essence a criminal.[7] Each human culture is caught in such a contradiction and this implies that the human being has necessarily to pay for this original crime with which human history begins. But for Nietzsche this Greek conception of evil and crime is different from the Christian conception of Adam's original sin because it gives to the human being a dignity that is lacking in the biblical story of the origin of evil. The Greek hero voluntarily violates the law of the gods, whereas, in the Bible, Adam yields to temptation and disobeys God in a sheer passive way. In the Greek tragedy we find the idea of a crime which has been freely accomplished, as Schelling already explained in the last of his *Letters on Dogmatism and Criticism* (1795).

Oedipus is for Schelling the tragic hero *par excellence*. Being a mortal destined by fatality to become a criminal, Oedipus tries, but in vain, to fight against the fate which was revealed to him by the oracle. He will therefore be punished for a crime which in fact he did not intend to perpetrate but which has nevertheless been accomplished through his hand. How could the Greek reason bear such a contradiction? This is the question raised by Schelling. In his answer, Schelling tries to show that Greek tragedy was a homage paid to human freedom. It was a great idea, he says, to voluntarily accept to be punished for an inevitable crime because it was a way to testify for the reality of human freedom through the very loss of it and to die in proclaiming the freedom of the will. The tragic hero is a being who does not accept to see in some of his actions the effect of destiny alone. He chooses to take the evil upon himself and to be responsible for all he has done, even for what he could not have been consciously doing, because it is the only way for him to have access to the level of an absolute freedom and to identify himself with the *fatum*. But he has to pay for it and the price is his life itself, so that, at the same time he gains an absolute freedom, he loses it.[8]

The same idea can be found in a small essay by Hölderlin, 'The Significance of Tragedies', where it is said that this significance can be understood most easily by way of paradox. The word 'paradox' is also to be found in a letter to his brother dated 4 June 1799 where Hölderlin explains that the artistic and formative drive which constitutes human culture is an authentic service done by human beings to nature. Because, he says, all the streams of human activity have their source in nature and go back to nature and because the human being can only develop the productive forces but not create the force in itself, he should never regard himself as a master and lord of nature.

In a previous letter to his friend Sinclair, dated 24 December 1798, Hölderlin wrote, 'The first condition of all life and all organization is that no force is monarchical in heaven and on earth. Absolute monarchy suppresses itself everywhere because it is without object: in a strict sense there was never something like it.'[9] And he goes on saying that absolute monarchy as well as pure *a priori* thinking is a nonsense because everything that exists is the result of subjective and objective elements, so that it is not possible to completely set apart what is particular and what is whole. The main idea is here that the unique totality – that which Hölderlin, as well as his schoolfellows Schelling and Hegel, named the *hen kai pan* – is always mixed with a particular point of view.

That is the reason why, in 'The Significance of Tragedies', Hölderlin says that 'all original element appears not in original strength but, in fact, in its weakness, so that quite properly the light of life and the appearance belong to the weakness of every whole'.[10] Every whole appears in a living point of view and all that exists is internally divided. Nature cannot appear in its original strength but needs art as something weaker than itself in order to appear. But in art, nature does not appear originally but through the mediation of a sign, i.e. the hero. As such a sign, the hero is insignificant and without effect (*unbedeutend und wirkungslos*), because he cannot do anything against fate and nature and because he will finally be destroyed by them. But when he declines, when, as Hölderlin says, the sign is equal to zero, 'the original element, the hidden foundation of any nature, can also present itself', which means that nature can properly present itself as the winner 'in its most powerful gift'.[11]

For Hölderlin tragedy is a sacrifice through which the human being helps nature to appear as such, to come out of its original dissimulation, of what Heraclitus named its original *krypthestai.*[12] But in order to do such a service to nature, the sign has to become equal to zero, which means that the hero has to die. The conflict of nature and culture is therefore what is represented in all tragedies, but it becomes the subject itself, the theme of the tragedy in *The Death of Empedocles*, the tragedy that Hölderlin wants to write but leaves unfinished in 1799.

In this period, Hölderlin sees in Empedocles the figure *par excellence* of *hybris*, presumption or excess, which is the only form of evil that the Greeks know. Empedocles hates culture, has only contempt for all particular occupations, is an open enemy of all one-sided existence, he suffers from all particular conditions just because they are particular, which means that he suffers from not being a God. He sees in time itself an evil and wants to be delivered from the law of succession in order to gain access to infinite life. The tragedy Hölderlin wants to write is therefore based on the human desire to go beyond the limits of human existence. Kant put the emphasis on the necessity for the human being to assume his own finitude. But he was also quite conscious that evil in a radical form dwells in the human being and he explained in his last book, *Religion in the Limits of Reason Alone*, that this 'radical evil' is nothing else than presumption and egoism, i.e. exactly what the Greeks named *hybris*.

Hölderlin was himself convinced that presumption is deeply rooted in the heart of man and he is conscious that it has become more and more developed in modernity. He explains in 'The Ground of Empedocles' that Empedocles' time, which was a time very similar to modernity, i.e. a time when opposition between art and culture became more acute than ever, required a 'sacrifice', required that the individual perishes in order to restore the integrity of nature. So the need of the time was the sacrifice of the individual, because the danger was positivity, crystallization, freezing of life in dead structures, which is what Empedocles, who dies out of a desire to live like a god, fears above all. In his impatience Empedocles is the incarnation of the premature union with destiny which was only an *apparent* solution, because Empedocles, who, in all his presumption, wanted to be a god, was not able to understand that God is nothing else than time itself, as it will be clearly said in the *Remarks on Sophocles*.

A complete reversal will take place there: what seemed evil for Empedocles, time itself, will reveal itself to be what is good for man. Empedocles' sacrifice was a solution, but only a temporary one, because it is what Hölderlin calls 'a premature union of God and man'. Such a premature union requires the death of the mediator, who is similar to the Christ, because, as Hölderlin says, 'otherwise the universal would be lost in the individual and, which is even worse than all great movements of destiny and by itself impossible, the life of a world would expire in some particular instance'.[13] If the reconciliator does not die, then the divine dimension will be lost, the totality will become particularity, the intensity of life will crystallize in a particular being and thus there will be no world, no sphere at the same time human and divine, but a total flatness of a 'human, all too human' life, which is the danger that menaces, the real danger being not the death of the individual, of the mediator, but the death of light itself, of the divine horizon of human existence. Such a danger, the impossibility for the human being to be human, the regression to a mere animal life, reveals itself as the extreme form of evil.

Hölderlin sees here with the greatest clarity the objective law of life, the formal condition which allows the life of the totality, its staying alive – it is the death of the individual. But, as will become clear in the *Remarks on Sophocles*, there are two different kinds of death, the Greek one and the

Hesperian or modern one, a death which is a farewell to the world and a death which is a living death, the endurance of separation. The possibility of this other kind of death begins to appear in the third version of his tragedy *The Death of Empedocles*, with the figure of a new protagonist, the adversary, who is also mentioned in the last part of the essay 'The Ground of Empedocles'. The adversary also gives a solution to the problems of the time, not like Empedocles, by achieving a 'premature' union or reconciliation with nature, but by maintaining the tension between art and nature and keeping both of them inside their respective limits. Whereas Empedocles incarnates impatience and *hybris*, the adversary is the incarnation of patience, of perseverance, of steadiness, he is not inclined to unite the extremes, but he tries to 'tame them and tie their reciprocity to something permanent and stable',[14] which can only be a political structure or a work of art. Compared to Empedocles, the adversary is 'a daring open soul', a more passive kind of person who is able to endure the opposition between nature and culture.

This becomes clear in the third version of the tragedy, when the figure of the adversary seems to take two different forms: the royal brother on one side, who maintains the opposition, and on the other side the priest sent by God, Manes, 'the one who remains'[15] and who questions Empedocles' right to reconcile the extremes. On both sides, on the side of the human *polis*, as well as on the side of the heavenly domain, Empedocles' drive to reconciliation is contested and both the king and the priest utter a warning and try to show him that the human being is committed to find his dwelling in the *Zwischen*, the in-between of earth and heaven.

From there, we can perhaps understand why Hölderlin gave up his project of writing a modern tragedy. If the theme of *The Death of Empedocles* is the justification of 'speculative suicide or sacrifice', and if in working out the drama the necessity of enduring separation, which was already Hyperion's final discovery, was once more revealed to him, it becomes clear that the kind of death Empedocles wanted could not be compatible with what requires modernity. Empedocles' desire to escape all determinations, to leave behind the law of succession, is the desire to escape finitude into death, whereas in the *Remarks on Sophocles*, Hölderlin stresses on the contrary that 'the striving from this world to the other' has to be reversed into 'a striving from another world to this one'.[16] Hölderlin could not confer on Empedocles' death an authentically modern meaning, because, as he says in the first letter to his friend Böhlendorff, 'this is the tragic for us: that, packed up in any container, we very quietly move away from the realm of the living and not that, consumed into flames, we expiate the flames that we could not tame'.[17] The modern *Schicksal*, the modern destiny, is not as impressive as the Greek one, but, as Hölderlin stresses, it is 'more profound', because it requires that the limits between humanity and divinity should be maintained and acknowledged.

On the basis of what the *Remarks on Sophocles* are saying about the necessity of a 'categorical reversal' of the human being towards the earth, what is therefore evil? It remains the same: *hybris*, the transgression of the limits of human finitude, leading to the madness of the modern man, which is nothing else than the desire for absolute knowledge and domination upon earth.[18] The same idea can also be found in Heidegger, especially in the second part of his work.

It is first necessary to try defining Heidegger's conception of evil, which, as we will see, he developed on the basis of his interpretation of Greek tragic experience and in a certain proximity to Kant's idea of radical evil. Hannah Arendt, who, in spite of her great knowledge of Aristotle's philosophy and of the Greek world in general, was not really interested in tragedy, seeing in it only a social phenomenon, explained her own view of the *banality* of evil in *Eichmann in Jerusalem*, a book published in 1963. She defines this conception in a passage of a letter she wrote to Gershom Scholem in the same year, 1963, during the controversy following the publication of her book:

> It is indeed my opinion now that evil is never 'radical', that it is only extreme, and that it possesses neither depth nor any demonic dimension. It can overgrow and lay waste the whole world precisely because it spreads like a fungus on the surface. It is 'thought-defying', as I said, because thought tries to reach some depth, to go to the roots, and the moment it concerns itself with evil, it is frustrated because there is nothing. That is its 'banality'. Only the good has depth and can be radical.[19]

For Hannah Arendt, as it seems, evil can be understood only from an ethical viewpoint, and not from a philosophical one.

Heidegger himself seems to think on the contrary that there is indeed, as Kant and Schelling declared, a *radicality* of evil. He is even more radical than either of them because for him evil is not external to spirit and has its centre not in the material or in the sensible but, on the contrary, *in* spirit itself, as he says in his 1936 lecture course on Schelling.[20] Already in *Being and Time*, in section 82, when opposing his own conception of time to the Hegelian one, Heidegger takes up the word *spirit* as his own, but with quotation marks.[21] Spirit is there not opposed as the intemporal to the temporal (as is the case with Hegel, who speaks of the 'fall' of spirit into time), but understood as originary temporalization, as time itself. From the very beginning, Heidegger identifies spirit and time and thinks that time is affected by an internal duplicity which makes it both proper and not proper, *eigentlich* and *uneigentlich.*

Much later, in his essay on Trakl (1959),[22] Heidegger insists on the radicality of evil with formulas sometimes literally Schellingian. The metaphysics of evil, which Heidegger seems then to support, is a metaphysics which separates in a radical manner animality from humanity. According to this metaphysics, evil is reserved to mankind alone because only man as a free being can disjoin his ontological fit, whereas the animal cannot get out of its natural unity. In the 1936 lecture course on Schelling, Heidegger tried to withdraw the Schellingian thinking of evil not only out of a purely Christian space but also out of the ethical horizon, which, as he underlines, 'is not sufficient to conceive evil'.[23] This led Heidegger to inscribe evil in the profundity of the history of spirit as its internal duality or dissension (*Zwietracht*). Dissension constantly menaces spirit insofar as spirit *is* time, that is, it is always outside itself (*ausser sich*), deported from itself (*entsetzt*), thrown out of itself (*aufgebracht*).[24] Spirit is the *element* which, by auto-affective spontaneity passes ecstatically outside itself, while remaining, however, one in its most internal discord.

But it is in 'The Sayings of Anaximander' (1946) that Heidegger confronted the problem of evil in a direct manner.[25] According to the literal translation, the first sentence of the saying speaks of the genesis and of the perishing of beings, of the necessity of this process of universal emergence and disappearance, of justice, injustice and punishment in regard to the beings, and it is usually considered as normal for a primitive way of thinking to use moral and juridical concepts to approach the realm of nature. But, as Heidegger stresses, this way of understanding Anaximander's saying presupposes that the spheres of ethics and law have already been differentiated from the sphere of mere nature, which is not yet the case for the so-called Presocratics.[26] The second part of the saying, which is in fact, according to Heidegger, the real saying that can be attributed to Anaximander,[27] is again divided into two sentences: the first one speaks of 'necessity', the second one speaks, according to the received translation, of justice and of the penance that the things pay one another for their injustice. The word *adikia*, injustice, names the main feature of the beings. This word is a negative term and for Heidegger it names the privation of *dike*, which, seen in the light of Being, understood as presence, has the meaning of juncture and accord.[28] That which is coming into presence (*das Anwesende*) has therefore to be understood as being in the disjunction (*aus der Fuge*).[29] But the coming into presence is a process that takes place in the interval between two absences – the absence of past and the absence of future – so that which comes into presence is *das je Weilige*, what whiles at a time. This interval is that which allows us to understand the dynamic 'arrangement' of the coming into presence, the *dike* of beings, but not their *adikia*. However, the saying is speaking of *adikia* as being the main feature of beings. In which sense is there *adikia*? It seems that it can be the main feature of the beings only if there is in them a tendency to rigidity, to persist in the dynamic process of emergence and disappearance, as if each of them were inclined to persist into presence, to instigate an insurrection against the passing of time, to spread out in the self-will of persevering and to no longer turn towards the other beings.[30]

Such a view of becoming which sees in it a fundamental 'injustice' can only be pessimistic or even nihilistic. This is in fact the way of understanding the Greek experience of Being that we find in Schopenhauer and also in the young Nietzsche. But is it really what the saying means? Are injustice and punishment really in question? In fact the saying does not speak of *paying* penance, as it says in Nietzsche's translation, but, in Heidegger's translation, of *giving* juncture. The moral appreciation of becoming stays under the domination of the spirit of revenge which requires payment for the past and does not see the gift of presence, a gift which is not a giving away, but consists more originally in granting to the other what properly belongs to it. Such a gift is the gift of Being, an *ontological* and not moral accomplishment.

Therefore a letting the beings belong to Being, a *Gehörenlassen*,[31] is a more originary gift. For what belongs properly to each being is precisely not its 'self-will' of persistence, but on the contrary its 'obedience'[32] to the transitory character of its whiling: that which comes to presence is only present in so far as it lets itself belong to the non-present and 'assumes' (*verwindet*) disjunction in the sense that it continuously gives way to non-presence. There is assumption (*Verwindung*) and not overcoming (*Überwindung*) of disjunction and discord precisely because disjunction is not merely left behind but assimilated as constituting the *reciprocal* 'structure' of each whiling. Heidegger names tragic and not pessimistic or nihilistic such an experience of Being, noting that the word 'tragic' remains here overbearing (*überheblich*), but that it is possible to begin to conceive the essence of the tragic merely in a non-aesthetic or psychological sense, but in its essential ontological dimension. We may assume from what Heidegger suggests here that tragedy comes from *hybris*, the process of insubordination of beings, which opposes itself to the necessary accord of the whole.

For the process of coming to presence involves a plurality of beings which have to come to presence as a *whole*, as an ensemble. Each being must not only 'assume' his own tendency to remain into presence, but must also retain its own place in the general accord and maintain the relationship which binds it to the other beings and to the whole. It means the taking account of the whiling of the others, the consideration (*Rücksicht*) for them, which defines the manner according to which the beings 'while' in presence, so that the dynamic process of coming into presence involves a general 'compatibility' of all beings within the domain of non-concealment. It means, to underline it once more very clearly, that the beings have to 'assume' – that is to say, get over[33] – their tendency to deny their own 'momentaneity' which is in fact the very condition of their coming into presence. Giving care to each other is the *manner* into which the beings can in general while and be present. The assumption of disjunction is therefore nothing else than letting be the reciprocity of care. But we must ourselves be careful in our understanding of what is care here: not simply the ethical respect for the otherness of the other, but the ontological regard of the Being of the other, which involves in itself a relation to Being as such.

Disjunction is therefore inscribed in the very core of Being itself, which cannot be thought of as accord without being *at the same time* seen in the light of discord or *adikia*. But Heidegger refuses to speaks here of justice and injustice, because, as he declares, in staying in great proximity to the Nietzschean identification of morality and metaphysics, that too often in the ethical viewpoint, *das Gerächte*, the revenged, constitutes *das Gerechte*, the just.[34] Can we consider the domain of what is called 'right' or 'justice' without any reference to the idea of revenge, payment and penance? The question should be asked. But what is in fact revenge, if it can be at the very origin of the ethical as such? Nietzsche gave us the answer in his *Zarathustra:* the *ressentiment* against time which depreciates all that is transitory,[35] that is, in the Heideggerian view of the non-difference between Becoming and Being, a lack of care for Being itself, for the *finitude* of Being which there is only as long as *Dasein* is. There can be a separate ethical domain and separate moral and juridical representations only on the ground of such a spirit of revenge against Being and Time, a 'spirit' which does not want to *let* Being be *at the same time* accord and discord, to *let* Being be *finite.* For such a finitude means at the same time the belonging of man to Being and the possibility of his turning against it.

What has to be respected in man can therefore not only be his irreducible singularity or otherness, his 'share' of time, but the *freedom* which makes him able or not able to *affirm* Being and to say yes to time. That is the reason why, in opposition to those who want to give to ethics, and not to ontology, the first place in philosophy, Heidegger declared in the *Letter on Humanism* that the thinking of the truth of Being, as fundamental ontology, i.e. as ontology of *Dasein*, is already in itself the originary ethics.[36]

Notes

1 Aristotle, *Poetics* (*Peri Poietikes*), 1449b, 25 ff.
2 Friedrich Nietzsche, *Die Geburt der Tragödie. Kritische Studien Ausgabe*, ed. G. Colli and M. Montinari, Munich: DTV/De Gruyter, 1988, §14; my translation.
3 Ibid., §11.
4 Ibid., §8.
5 Ibid., §11.
6 Friedrich Nietzsche, *Ecce homo. Kritische Studien Ausgabe* VI, ed. Giorgio Colli und Mazzino Montinari, Munich: DTV/De Gruyter, 1988, § 3.
7 Nietzsche, *Die Geburt der Tragödie*, § 9.
8 Friedrich W. J. Schelling, *Sämmtliche Werke* I, Stuttgart: Cotta, 1856–61, pp. 336 ff.
9 Friedrich Beissner and Jochen Schmidt (eds), *Hölderlin Werke und Briefe* II, Frankfurt am Main: Insel, 1969, p. 886.
10 Friedrich Hölderlin, *Essays and Letters on Theory*, trans. and ed. Thomas Pfau, New York: State University of New York Press, 1988, p. 89; translation modified.
11 Ibid.
12 Hölderlin does not quote the Heraclitus fragment, saying that 'nature likes to dissimulate itself' (*physis krypthestai philei*) – no edition of the *Fragments* was

then available – but his understanding of nature is as near as can be in modern times to the Presocratics' approach to *physis.*

13 Hölderlin, *Essays and Letters on Theory*, p. 56.

14 Ibid., p. 61.

15 The name *Manes* can be put in connection with the Latin verb *manere*, to stay, but it can also be referred to the Greek word *mantis*, diviner (cf. Wolfgang Binder, 'Hölderlins Namenssymbolik', *Hölderlin-Jahrbuch* XII, 1961–62, pp. 95–204, pp. 201 ff.).

16 Hölderlin, *Essays and Letters on Theory*, p. 112.

17 Ibid., p. 150.

18 See Françoise Dastur, 'Tragédie et modernité', *Hölderlin. Le retournement natal*, La Versanne: Encre Marine, 1997.

19 See Hannah Arendt, *The Jew as Pariah: Jewish Identity and Politics in the Modern Age*, ed. R. H. Feldman, New York: Grove Press, 1978, pp. 250–1. Hannah Arendt's letter to Gershom Scholem dated 14 July 1963.

20 Martin Heidegger, *Schelling Abhandlung 'Über das Wesen der menschlichen Freiheit' (1809)*, Tübingen: Niemayer, 1971, p. 177.

21 On the meaning of these quotation marks see Jacques Derrida, *Of Spirit, Heidegger and the Question*, trans. Geoffrey Bennington and Rachel Bowlby, Chicago: University of Chicago Press, 1989. (*De l'esprit* was originally a lecture given 14 March 1987 at the end of a conference entitled 'Heidegger: Open Questions', organized by the Collège International de Paris.)

22 See Françoise Dastur, 'Heidegger et Trakl: le site occidental et le voyage poétique', *À la naissance des choses. Art, poésie et philosophie*, La Versanne: Encre Marine, 2005, pp. 173–95.

23 Heidegger, *Schelling Abhandlung 'Über das Wesen der menschlichen Freiheit' (1809)*, p. 176.

24 Martin Heidegger, 'Die Sprache im Gedicht', *Unterwegs zur Sprache*, Pfullingen: Neske, 1959, p. 60.

25 See Françoise Dastur, 'Heidegger on Anaximander: being and justice', in Charles E. Scott and John Sallis (eds), *Interrogating the Tradition. Hermeneutics and the History of Philosophy*, Albany, NY: State University of New York Press, 2000, pp. 179–90.

26 Martin Heidegger, 'Der Spruch des Anaximander', in *Holzwege*, Frankfurt am Main: Klostermann, 1963, p. 305.

27 Ibid., p. 314.

28 Ibid., p. 329. Heidegger here uses the words *Fug* (joint) and *Fuge* (accord), which do not have the same origin. (*Fuge* comes in fact from the italian *fuga*, whereas the German verb *fügen* means to join, fit together.) In fact the Greek *dikè* comes from the Indo-European root *deik*, which means 'to show' and 'to say'. (See Emile Benveniste, *Le Vocabulaire des institutions indo-européennes*, Paris: Minuit, 1969, II, p. 108.)

29 Ibid., p. 327.

30 Ibid., p. 328.

31 Ibid., p. 329.

32 Ibid. It should be stressed here that, in the reflexive form *sich fügen*, the verb *fügen* means to adapt oneself or to obey, so that the discourse of juncture and accord in itself involves the dimension of adaption and obedience.

33 The German verb *verwinden*, translated here by 'to assume' means to get over, to recover from something, for example from a disease.

34 Ibid., p. 328.

35 See Martin Heidegger, 'Wer ist Nietzsches Zarathustra?' *Vorträge und Aufsätze*, Pfullingen: Neske, 1954, pp. 115 ff.

36 See Martin Heidegger, 'Brief über den "Humanismus"', in *Wegmarken*, Frankfurt am Main: Klostermann, 1967, p. 187.

Chapter 4

Interrupting evil and the evil of interruption

Revisiting the question of freedom

Marcia Sá Cavalcante Schuback

'Interrupting evil' – in these words we hear urgencies and assumptions. We hear the urgency of interruption and an assumption on continuity. Not only does evil continue to befall and overcome us but the question of conceiving evil also continues to challenge contemporary philosophy. We face natural and political catastrophes almost everywhere. We recall Hannah Arendt's statement that the question of evil should be the central philosophical issue after the Second World War. Evil has become a huge subject for studies focusing on its aesthetic, political, social, psychological, theological, philosophical, cultural, natural, and other aspects. We have probably never spoken and philosophized so much about both natural and moral evil than today. However, we have probably never been so passive and conformist towards evil. We testify today, even more than natural and moral evil, to the *evil of indifference and ambiguity*. But in post-Enlightenment analytical discourse on ethics and morality, which more and more governs our institutions and our souls, evil is disguised. We could so often utter Phaedra's words in Euripides' *Hippolytus*:

> Women of Trozen, dwellers in his extreme forecourt to the land of Pelops, I have pondered before now in other circumstances during the night's long watches how it is that the lives of mortals are now in ruins. I think it is due to lack of understanding that they fare worse than they might, since many people possess good sense. Rather one must look at it this way: we know and understand what is noble to do but do not bring it to completion.[1]

The fact that we may know what should be done, deducing it from rational argument, does not imply that we are able to do it. Despite all clever arguments, the gap between theory and practice is still the biggest riddle of our ethical-philosophical issues. In rare moments of sincerity we may perhaps admit that best arguments are still not enough to face the multiple faces of evil. The face of one's suffering; the face of one who provokes the suffering of others; the evil face of egoism and indifference, of despair and madness, of hunger and death continues to surpass reason. Here we face an 'I don't know what to say or to think'. Nevertheless, we remain convinced that reason – in its widest philosophical spectrum of meanings – is the only way of interrupting evil. It seems that we have first to *know* what evil is in order to act for the sake of interrupting evil.

Western philosophical tradition has developed some knowledge of evil, which centres evil in the heart of the metaphysical question about negativity. As a negative concept, evil is what negates the Good and what can be thought only in relation to the Good. Negation of the Good has traditionally been conceived in two major senses: as *privation* and as *perversion*. Defined as *privatio boni*, recalling the Augustinian definition, evil is not only what is negatively related to the Good but privation as such is evil. Privation, absence, lacking, losing – all these words name the worst of all sins, that is the sin of not having, which constitutes the negative economy of evil. As privation, evil expresses what is lacking and wanting, something that is unaccomplished and incomplete. Metaphysically, evil as privation is located in finitude. Evil, placed in finitude and defined as deprivation or absence of the Good, appears as 'condition for the Good', and as 'almost nothing', recalling Leibniz's expression: a little thing if compared with the incommensurable plenitude of the Good. Evil is thus non-Good. But even if evil is to be conceived from the perspective of the incommensurable plenitude of the Good as 'almost nothing', this still does not answer why evil exists. We do not have to be a Castilian king to wonder that God could have created a better world than ours – a world without evil. Does not evil hide at the end a nature which is independent from the Good? However, to affirm that evil has an independent nature outside the totality of the Good both threatens the absolute plenitude of the Good and denies the negativity of evil. It seems that ontologically, as well as theologically and logically, there is no other way left than to admit that evil is located within the Good as much as lacking finitude is located within infinite plenitude. At this point there appears a dangerous insight, namely that the Good *is* somehow evil and evil *is* somehow the Good. The danger of pantheism is the danger of the identity of good and evil. Kant's concept of *radical evil* is an attempt to clear up the danger of possible identity of the Good and evil defining evil as *perversion* of the Good.[2] Assuming evil as perversion, Kant had also to admit the possibility of perverting this perversion, the possibility of evil becoming good. Admitting that the perversion of evil can be perverted, Kant reaffirmed the sovereignty of the Good. Kant's position seems to be a position of hope: radical evil implies the possibility of perverting the perversion of evil. From this point of view, the Good would be non-evil. But we still have to ask what kind of Good is the one that emerges from the perversion of evil? Is non-Evil good enough? As perversion of evil perversion, the Good could be considered a normalized Good, but is normalized Good enough or even able to interrupt evil? All these questions need to be asked. However, in order to answer them it is necessary to ask a very principal question, the one about how to conceive interruption as such? In order to reflect upon this question, I will follow Schelling's and Heidegger's thinking, concentrating on Schelling's essay on human freedom[3] and Heidegger's dialogue between a younger and an older prisoner-of-war in Russia.[4]

Schelling on evil and freedom

Schelling's *Freedom* essay can be read as a 'deconstruction' – even if the essay is very idealistic – of the metaphysical meaning of interruption. I use the term deconstruction here in the sense Miklos Vetö gave to it: 'the works of the spirit that, through a genetic method ... decompose and break down rigid forms in order to reveal the living articulation of its productivity', that is of its coming to a form.[5] In its basic metaphysical meaning, interruption has been conceived as the fundamental character of finite existence, of individuality and singularity. Finite individual existence can be considered as an interruption of the continuity of a lineage, in so far as it is a unique life and thereby *ineffable,* incomparable. Continuity of species is though only possible through the 'interruption' as discontinuity of individual life, a central thought developed by Georges Bataille in his *L'Érotisme.*[6] A child is at the same time interruption and continuity of a lineage. *Antigone* is undeniably the most accomplished tragic expression of this basic paradox of life. That which unites divides at the same time. Interruption means the life of continuity itself. In this tragic sense of interruption, which outlines Greek understanding of life as a whole, interruption or mortality is integrated in continuity, in the being-forever of life. It is fundamentally understood as discontinuity. Life and death, continuity and discontinuity, being-forever and interruption are integrated in the rhythmic and circular being-forever of bio-cosmological life. That is why Greek words that could be used to translate the word 'interruption' express the idea of a pause or break, in the sense that sleep is a break in our waking life or rest is a break in movement.

For the Greeks, however, the individual existence of animals and plants shall be distinguished from the individual existence of human beings. From a rigorous point of view, only finite human existence can be considered mortal, can be seen as interruption because it represents a 'cut' in the circular movement of bio-cosmological life. By the distinction between bio-cosmological life and human-biographical life, between the concepts of *zoe* and *bios,* between immortality of life and mortality of human life, between *athanatoi* and *thanatoi*, an idea of interruption as *cut* within continuity is also present in the ancient Greek cosmology and ontology.[7] That is why human death is rather 'evil' than natural, as Sappho meant in one of her fragments when she said, 'Death is evil. Otherwise Gods would have chosen to die.'[8] However, this human cut is to be understood as a cut *within* continuity and not as a cut or interruption of continuity of life as a whole. There is not enough hubris in the human hubris to cut itself away from the continuity of bio-cosmological life. Human life, finitude, as a cut or break *within* continuity is therefore not evil. Instead, evil takes place when human mortal life and human interruption strive to become as immortal and continuous as divine continuity. Evil appears as not accepting the discontinuous and interruptive nature of human life. But human freedom is self-limitation and acceptance of its discontinuous, mortal and interruptive nature. The Greeks conceived it as the virtuous self-delimitation of Theseus. This ancient experience of discontinuity and interruption is still present in Schelling's *Freedom* essay. Indeed, Schelling will deepen this view by casting upon it what I would like to call the *light of paradox*. Under the light of paradox, interruption is brought back to possible and future meanings.

Christianity represents an interruption in this ancient experience of *interruption within continuity*. For it, human finite life is neither a break in continuity nor a cut within continuity. It is a *fall*. The scenario of fall, which Vetö described well in relation to Schelling's position, is the scenario of a hard separation, which is the event of *selfness*.[9] Interruption means fall, and fall means the constitution of finitude as selfness. However, selfness means not only separation but the possibility of unredeemable separation. With Jewish-Christian metaphysics of creation, interruption becomes the place of evil, the place of unredeemable separation from God, of a life outside God. But this place of evil, this place of unredeemable separation, this outside God, must still be within God, otherwise God would not be *deus pantocrator et creator*, God would not be creation. As fall, interruption makes even more explicit the challenge of conceiving human freedom within absolute freedom, finitude within infinitude, conditional within the unconditional, evil within the Good. This is the basic question of the pantheistic struggle, which is in its turn a central point in the idealistic attempt to go beyond Kant through Spinozism. Schelling's *Freedom* essay presents a solution to this struggle by means of deconstructing the question itself and its presuppositions. The presupposition of the pantheism struggle is the idea of interruption as fall, which assumes 'fall' as an expulsion, a throwing outside what was inside. One of the most obscure fundaments of this long history of trying to conceive evil within creation is the distinction between interiority and exteriority, between an inside and outside creation, between immanence and transcendence. Schelling's solution is to bring this discussion to a more radical, mystical experience of creation, liberating it from dogmatic theological views. Creation is not exteriorization and expression but *self-revelation*, *Selbstoffenbarung*.[10] As Schelling claims, 'God is not a God of the dead, but a God of the living.'[11] God is a living God, and life is fundamentally self-revelation. Finitude, fall, interruption and human freedom are to be understood as God's life, that is as self-revelation. However, self-revelation is not a transition from inside to outside, which implies that something was first one and then other. *Self-revelation is a self which only is itself becoming other*. Self-revelation is the paradox of one being other, the paradox implied in self-formation, that is in being a becoming. God is becoming, God is living God. Hence, Schelling says, the big problem with Spinozism is not really the idea of immanence. It is the idea of thinghood, of being as substance or as thing.[12] Understood as becoming, the concepts of immanence and transcendence also have to be dimensioned anew. Becoming is a paradoxical proposition: fulfilment is unfulfilment, continuity is interruption, Good is evil. Becoming means a transformation of the meaning of copula itself by which the copula leaves behind its logical-gnoseological sense and discovers its *creative* sense. Copula, the *Ist*, is creation, as Vetö says, closely following Heidegger.[13] Becoming as creation means that the principle of identity discovers itself as the *light of paradox*. Schelling's position can be summarized as follows: self-revelation is the ontological constitution of becoming as the paradox of one being other.

Let us now approach how Schelling describes self-revelation as the ontological constitution of becoming. Self-revelation is a speculative concept in a literal meaning. It is understood from out of the miracle of a reflected or mirrored (*speculum*) image, the miracle of an *Ein-bildung* and *Lichtblick*, which are both important concepts in Schelling's philosophical vocabulary. At the same time, the image *is* and *is not* what it reflects. Both what is imaged and an image are distinct and paradoxically identical. Janus' face is nothing but the image of what an image is. An image is at once difference and identity and as such it reflects on its own reflection what an image is. It images its 'model' but also its imaging action. This imaging action is, according to Schelling, language. It is Word. To say a 'tree' is to bring a tree to presence but also to say that we are saying.

Man is the image of God. Man reveals in his structure the creational becoming that God himself is. But in order to really understand human finite life as image of God's becoming, and not of God's being, the life of God must become visible as life. Nature is life becoming visible as life. God's life becomes visible in the life of nature. Or, in more speculative terms, *the nature of life becomes visible in the life of nature.* The life of nature is productive reproduction; it reproduces continuously the species by producing infinite numbers of finite forms of life. Nature is the life of forms. However, there is no form of life that would be able to exhaust the life of forms. Nature makes 'becoming' visible as productive reproduction. It reproduces itself by means of producing new forms of life which both interrupt and give continuity to former lives. Or with Schelling's own formulation in the lectures held at Erlangen in 1821, the nature of life is 'to go through all things and to be nothing, namely, to be nothing such that it could always be otherwise – this is the demand'.[14] On the one hand, this means that the abundance of life forms can never exhaust the life of abundance; that life's nature is infinitude in so far as it can never accomplish itself in one absolute form. On the other hand, it says that the life of life, *vita vitae,* is *nothing*; it is no thing. This nothingness of the life of life makes it possible not only to recognize the paradoxical structure of continuity through discontinuity and interruption, which characterizes the ancient Greek understanding of nature and life, but also to discover the optic of this paradox, the constitution of its own light.

Schelling shows that self-revelation means, for the first, that one can only show itself in its contrary – love in hate, good in evil, God in man. That is the tragical constitution of self-revelation as the ontological constitution of a becoming. Schelling moreover underlines the sliding away or withdrawing structure of this paradox. Becoming other in finite forms of life, means a withdrawing of life's own ground. In order to expand itself, life's nature has to expand itself both outwards, becoming a new life, and inwards, letting its own unaccomplishment alive. The ground of existence designates this never fulfilled remainder that expands as remainder when a new life expands life beyond itself. The infinitude of life wants to remain infinite. However, in order to remain infinite, life has to become the infinity of finite forms of life. Only losing itself in finite forms, life can win itself as infinitude. This insight in the sliding away or withdrawing ground of life in the coming out of a new finite existence is very central in Schelling's philosophy of nature. He says explicitly that the properness of his philosophy of nature lies in having assumed the distinction between ground of existence and existence.[15] This distinction is not a difference between stages in a development or process. It is the co-incidence of two eternal beginnings, the co-incidence of two movements, the movement towards the ground and the movement towards existence, a movement towards the depth of gravity and a movement towards the lightness of light. Paul Klee's paintings and writings are perhaps the closest to Schelling's description when we recall his images of stairs ascending and descending at the same time, or of trees' leafy branches ascending toward the open and lightened sky, which is simultaneously the movement of roots descending toward obscure earthly depths. This withdrawing of the ground in the coming out of existence shows the properness of the nature of life. It shows the proper nature of God. God's nature is nature in God. God's self-revelation is the revelation of the withdrawal of nature in the coming out of creatures. Created existence has its fundament in what in God slides away when something comes to existence. This withdrawing nature in God is the 'indivisible remainder', the *nie aufgehende Rest,*[16] the alchemic *Basis*,[17] which intensifies itself as ground when something comes to existence and thereby separates from the ground. The tendency to remain as ground is the tendency to remain in itself and thereby to not come out to existence and become another. One aspect of the will to ground is universal will, because it is the obscure realm of possibilities in becoming. However, as it wants to remain as ground, it becomes the abyss of selfness and its selfishness, the abyss of particular will. Other aspect of the will to existence is particular because it is the enlightened realm of determinations. However, wanting to remain as existence, it has to will the ground of existence and thereby to become universal. The difficult dialectic of universal and particular will, which differs notably from Kierkegaard's discussion about the demonic in *The Concept of Anxiety*, is an attempt to show that evil does not come from finitude but from *finitude elevated to selfness*.[18] In God, each centre or movement, the will to ground and the will to existence, universal and particular will, in their own contrary directions, contractive and expansive forces, live in harmonic coincidence, that is in *continuous tension*. Only in man, who is the image of this divine coincidence of opposites, each centre can become irreconcilable contraposition. This is because continuous tension can reveal itself only in its contrary, that is in an irreconcilable contraposition.[19] Being the image of God's becoming, man is the place where the pulsing tension between the power of the obscure principle of ground and the force of the light of existence becomes visible. Man is himself the 'anxiety of life', the *Angst des Lebens*,[20] the anxiety of the whole creation, being the force of intensification of this in-between. Consciousness is anxiety, *Angst*, of nature itself. This means, however, that in man, and only in man, the intensification of the tension of contrary wills, the will to ground and the will to existence, can become so strong that the balance of forces breaks down. The breaking down of the harmonic and continuous tension of forces is the *irruption* of evil. The spirit of evil, as Schelling affirms, is of 'meteoric nature'.[21] *Evil is irruption, rather than interruption*. Evil can take place only when selfness wants to leave its own centre and expand itself to the whole periphery. Evil takes place when selfness wants to universalize its egoism, when selfness begins to burn as 'tantalic anger',[22] an expression used by Franz Baader under the influence of Jacob Böhme's mystical visions. It aims to show the *irruptive* character of evil from within the divine balance of forces. In analogy with the irruption of a disease, evil is neither perversion nor interruption but irruption from within the pulsing life of divine coincidence of opposites. The irruption of the destructive force of selfishness is the risk of every existence. It is the risk of willing so much to remain existence that all becoming must be destroyed. Because becoming implies necessarily abandoning of being and existence is struggle for possessing being, existence struggles against becoming and hence against itself. This risk of every existence, the risk of determination, is the risk of inflaming selfness into universal selfishness.

Human finite life is an image of the whole creational process of God. What in God is continuous tension, balance of forces, reveals itself, in human finite life, in its opposite. Schelling considers the concept of *indifference* as the most adequate concept for this divine continuous tension or balance of inseparable forces.[23] Indifference, as Kuno Fischer insisted, is not the contrary of difference. It is not the lack of difference but the life of differentiation.[24] It means to live *within* differentiation. This continuous tension, balance, coincidence of opposites, this divine indifference, can reveal itself only in its opposite by sliding away and withdrawing itself when revealed. The opposite to divine continuous tension, divine balance of forces and divine indifference is indecision, *Unentschiedenheit*. Indecision is the finite image of divine continuous tension or indifference, constituting its most extreme opposite.

According to Schelling, divine indifference, divine balance of forces defines absolute freedom. The *image* of absolute freedom, of divine indifference, is indecision. Human freedom is to be understood from this condition of man, which is indecision, and this as an 'image' of absolute freedom as non-indecision. That is why Schelling says that 'the real and vital conception of freedom is that it is a possibility of good and evil'.[25] Man is the *Scheidepunkt* of creation;[26] man is the point of rupture, cision (*Scheidung*), being, but, at the same time, the point of jointure, love. It is always the same door that opens and closes. Being the opposite of divine indifference or creative balance of forces, human indecision is the place where divine indifference, continuous tension, reveals itself in a tragic mode. But this also means that human finite existence exists in such a way that it has to continuously decide for itself assuming the divine tension of forces from which human life is possible. With other words: as continuous tension of wills, of forces, life still has to become alive. For humans, it is not enough to live. Life has still to become 'sharp', using another expression of Schelling. Life demands decision for life. Decision means to rejoin the conjunctive tension of contraries, to rejoin divine indifference. This is the meaning of religiosity, defined by Schelling in the *Freedom* essay in terms of *Gewissenhaftigkeit*, of consciousness, a concept that has affinity with Heidegger's *Gewissen* in *Being in Time*. A very important aspect in both Schelling's and Heidegger's discussions of those closely related concepts is the fact that decision is understood ontologically and not ontically. As an ontological concept decision means, not an ontic choice between this or that, but an action of rejoining the pulsing jointure of contrary wills. This rejoining divine in-difference is the force or spirit of love. Rather than in enthusiastic words, the rigorous laws of this *Gewissenhaftigkeit* find their expressions in a serious insight 'that this has to be done because it cannot not be done'. Love is the vigour of such rigour. Decision is decision for rejoining the perspective of the balance of forces, of indifference breaking down, interrupting indecision, and interrupting ambiguity.

Heidegger and the ambiguity of malignity

At this point in our discussion we see a central thought in Schelling's *Freedom* essay that shows its actuality when articulated with Heidegger's thoughts concerning evil. One could say a lot about Heidegger's reading of Schelling and of his essay.[27] Instead I will relate Schelling and Heidegger from another perspective, that is through reading Heidegger's 'Abendgespräch' dialogue dated May 1945. It was probably written the day Germany capitulated and it involves questions regarding Heidegger's relation to the Second World War and Nazi Germany. I will focus on allusions to Schelling's *Freedom* essay that pervade this dialogue regarding the problem of interrupting evil and that even appear in Heidegger's *Letter on Humanism* from 1946.

In the dialogue, Heidegger leaves behind the concept of evil (*Böse*) and assumes, already at the beginning of the dialogue, the concept of *malignity* (*Bösartigkeit*). The concept of malignity is conceived here by analogy with the irruption of a disease. Hence he follows a metaphorical realm as Schelling did in his *Freedom* essay. Heidegger defines malignity, *das Bösartige*, as 'anger of irruption', *Ingrimm des Aufrurhrs*, which comes very close to Schelling and Baader.[28] Heidegger uses the same expression and reasoning in his *Letter on Humanism*.[29] In the dialogue, Heidegger refutes the concept of Good, insisting upon the necessity of not moralizing the question of evil. For Heidegger, Nietzsche's claim of a beyond good and evil is still a moral demoralization. For him, the concept of the *Heilsame*, the *salutary*, becomes central. Although conceiving 'malignity' and 'salutary' in analogy with the irruptive character of a disease, Heidegger directs those concepts towards another dimension when relating the salutary feeling of freedom to *openness*. While the salutary is related to openness, malignity is connected with prison, with the act of enclosing. Prison is described in this dialogue as a 'camp', and more specifically as a labour camp, which as reality of malignity frames for Heidegger the hermeneutic situation from within the question of evil and interruption is being asked. The hermeneutic situation is not the devastation of the Second World War but the devastation of a technical era, of the workers' era. Technique is, according to its essence as *Gestell*, as 'enframing', the enclosure of Being. An enclosure means commonly the *space* where sheep are allowed to graze unattended. The dialogue takes place at the open space within a labour camp. It takes place in the ambiguous space of being imprisoned within openness and walking in the openness of a labour camp. Already, in this real and historical landscape of the dialogue, we are able to follow what may be considered the main experience of the dialogue, namely ambiguity. Every concept, image and description depicts the experience of ambiguity, of what is but what could as well be its contrary. This ambiguity is one of the most central concepts in the dialogue. And, especially in relation to the experience of ambiguity, the dialogue with Schelling's *Freedom* essay becomes very inspiring for our problematic.

Ambiguity is a central concept in Heidegger's analysis of decadence in *Being and Time*. It is related to Dasein's projection into its existential possibilities.[30] Ambiguity inhibits patient dedication to the coming to be, confusing the coming to be with vestiges of probabilities and anticipated results. The concept of ambiguity becomes more and more central in Heidegger's texts after the war. In the dialogue, we can observe that the question of technique, which for Heidegger, and in consonance with Ernst Jünger's meditations on this topic, is a question profoundly connected with one of the deserts of nihilism. It is essentially related to the phenomenon of ambiguity.[31] Focusing on Heidegger's dialogue, we can see how ambiguity exposes indecision as the *place* (and time) of man's finitude. In the dialogue, the main key to this central concept is to be found in the definition of malignity. Malignity is, as well as evil in Schelling, the tantalizing anger of irruption. Heidegger observes, however, that the anger of irruption, which is the anger of the selfishness of selfhood, never breaks through completely. 'When it breaks through, it conceals itself. In its hidden threat, this anger of irruption frequently exists as if it did not exist.'[32] This central definition of malignity that we can read in the beginning of the dialogue explains Schelling's reflections. Not only is evil what irrupts from indecision and ambiguity, but irruptive anger, malignity, is the structure of ambiguity itself. Ambiguity, or in Schelling's terms indecision, is the negation of differentiation. It is not indifference as life of differentiation in its idealistic ontological meaning, but indifference in the common sense of lack of difference, of incapacity to make distinctions and above all decisions. In the enclosed world of the worker, of technique, in the world of 'our today', we experience incapacity not only to distinguish good and evil, but above all to distinguish the wide-openness of life from desertification of life. What pervades technical ambiguity is inability to decide for life. This dialogue is one of Heidegger's few texts in which he explicitly says that Being means life: 'We understand the word "life" in the way that since quite long in western tradition is already the case, that is, quite wide, relating the signification realm of life to "Being".'[33] The dialogue can be read as a description of how in the world of ambiguity, the technical world of the worker, the most opposite experiences glide into the other, so that ontological difference becomes almost imperceptive. The experience of wideness, *die Weite*, quickly glides into the experience of the desert, *die Wüste*. Desertification of life takes place through the mobilization of all efforts to assure the control of life. To assure life, to control life for the sake of saving life from destruction – living for living's sake – is to desert from life. In the global mobilization of all efforts to control everything for the sake of avoiding the destruction of life, life is systematically deserted. In the dialogue, Heidegger describes the ambiguity of 'our today', of *Heute*, as he repeats in several texts, we can read between the lines how the question of malignity is related to the imminence of total destruction of life and above all to the destruction of the life of totality.

The malignity of ambiguity is, however, the most revealing, since it is paradoxically as such an image of truth's essence. In his *The Question of Technique* Heidegger says, 'The essence of technique is ambiguous in an elevated meaning. This ambiguity points toward the mystery of every unconcealment, i.e. of truth'. Following Heidegger, we could say that ambiguity is the most dangerous 'image' of the mystery of truth as *aletheia* because it shows it hiding it in different ways. Our today is the today of an 'on line', of an *Über die Linie*, recalling the adjustment made by Heidegger to Ernst Jünger's expression, when pointing out that the question at stake in the technique's planetary era is the one of assuming the hard position of a being 'on the line', *de linea*, and not striving beyond the line, *trans lineam*.[34] The most dangerous in this being 'on the line', *de linea*, lies not simply in the possibility that the human may *fall* but because we do not see the danger any longer. The hidden threat exists as if it did not exist.[35] This is the decisive mark of ambiguity. Ambiguity is self-hiddenness, self-concealment. Self-concealment is self-revelation but from the point of view of the veil. That is why ambiguity becomes the language of nihilism. Nihilism is a central issue not only in the dialogue but also in Heidegger's thought as a whole. As nihilism talks the language of ambiguity it describes the strange life of desert as the desertification and desertion of life. The desert of nihilism does not mean merely that life does not grow. The desert grows, as Nietzsche said. Heidegger understands this strange life of the desert, of nihilism, as the 'abandoned wideness proper to the abandon of all life'.[36] At stake here is an abandonment that abandons everything even abandoning. The abandonment can no longer be seen as abandonment. This abandonment, in second potency, of all life means that desert does not reveal itself in lack, as the absence of life, but in its contrary, in abundance, in the abundant production and exploitation of every level of life.[37] In the dialogue Heidegger develops the question about ambiguity and nihilism, describing different levels of paradoxes that sustain the technical age of ambiguity. Reading together the dialogue and Heidegger's texts on the essence of technique, from the four lectures held at Bremen in 1949 to lectures during the 1960s dealing with the topics of Cybernetics, it is possible to seize some paradoxes that Heidegger indicates.

Let me formulate some of these paradoxes that constitute the technical age of ambiguity as follows. Ambiguity is so wide that wideness becomes ambiguity. Ontological distinctions such as nature and culture, nature and technique, body and soul, transcendence and immanence become more and more confused and mixed in everyday life: to be here means to be connected with a thousand things abroad. Nature is so cultivated that artificial things seem quite natural; culture has become so naturalized that nature seems artificial. To search for such distinctions sounds in the age of planetary and global technology an anachronism; our bodies are already mixed with our machines and our machines are becoming more and more human, interactive, sensible; to control our lives, our bodies, our environment according to our willing machines is presented by us and to us as the highest signs of human free sensitivity. Equality is confused with uniformity and uni-dimensionalization of all differences to the one and only way of existing, the way of ambiguity. Political, ethical and religious issues and arguments can be used by the torturer and the sufferer, the persecutor and the persecuted, as devices of the Right and Left. Words say nothing even if they are more than abundant. Man is compelled to compel beings to his control, and thus he becomes a slave of his will to control, a slave of his own rights. Individuals become so individualistic that they become nothing more than a 'lonely crowd'.[38]

In Heidegger's dialogue the question is no longer how to interrupt evil or malignity but rather how to interrupt ambiguity when ambiguity is, as said, an indication towards the mystery of the truth of Being.[39]

How to interrupt ambiguity? Heidegger's answer or way towards an answer in the dialogue, as also in his later philosophy, is related to the question concerning waiting, *Warten* and serenity, *Gelassenheit*. These ways towards an answer – to wait in serenity (*Warten in Gelassenheit*) and serenity in waiting (*gelassen zum Warten*) – have a strong philosophical affinity with Schelling's claim for rejoining the tensional force of the contraries through love. At the end of the *Freedom* essay Schelling claims for a loving decision, which is the rigorous vigour of a 'not being able not to do'. Instead of a moral ought, the claim is for loving – I cannot not do it. Giorgio Agamben defined Heidegger's understanding of love as the experience of 'being able to not be able'.[40] Even if Agamben's interpretation can and should be criticized in so far as he understands Heidegger's 'love' from Aristotle's metaphysics of force, it has the importance of having thematized the question of powerlessness in relation to Heidegger. Schelling's moral claim of a decisional love that says, 'I cannot not do it,' and Agamben's interpretation of Heidegger's notion of love as a 'being able to not be able' are symmetrically opposed. However, they may show a common path that is related to a certain experience of powerlessness and impotence. This is decisive in the realm of ambiguity because it points towards the force of the negative. The force of the negative is not the violence of a cut, of an interruption, but the strength of a learning to dis-learn. Powerlessness does not mean the weakness of resignation or the passivity of an 'anything goes'. Powerlessness does not mean inability, not having the capacity. Powerlessness means rather leaving power behind, something as disempowering. Heidegger discussed this in terms of *Warten* and *Gelassenheit*, a word issued from the vocabulary of German mysticism which Schelling also used as a decisive philosophical term. Affirming immemorial Being as Will, Schelling comes to the concept of *Unwille*, of non-willing. Heidegger reads Schelling's philosophy of freedom with admiration, keeping his concepts such as *Angst des Lebens, Lichtblick des Seins, Ingrimm des Aufruhrs*, as we have seen, but not without critique. For Heidegger, Schelling's philosophy remains a completion of German Idealism, understood as the Metaphysics of Subjectivity and of the Will. Powerlessness, in Heidegger's sense, is will-lessness, and not simply non-willing, because the latter would still mean willing the will, as he also argues in relation to Nietzsche. However, in his readings of Hölderlin, and more precisely Hölderlin's poem 'Andenken', Heidegger recalls a fragment in which Hölderlin relates the will to a coming. This will, says Heidegger, is quite different from the will of subjectivity because it is a willing the coming.[41] Even if for Heidegger fundamental differences between Schelling and Hölderlin must be observed, this willing the coming may help to understand in what sense *Gelassenheit*, serenity, interrupts ambiguity when admitting powerlessness and will-lessness. As discussed in *Being and Time*, ambiguity is intimately connected to *Dasein*'s possibility of projecting itself to its own being-possibility. What Heidegger's late discussion points to is the fact that ambiguity reveals the coming precisely in hiding it. In ambiguity, the coming appears as indecision in regard to the possible, as indecision of an either–or which is even the indecision of a not-yet-real. At the same time, ambiguity shows the coming or the not-yet-real as an *in-between* reality and unreality. The coming appears as what can be neglected because it can show itself as coming only in its absence, in its unreality. Ambiguity reveals the in-between as human finitude. It reveals *Dasein* as an in-between, showing it under the rigorous light of paradox.[42] This light is the light of what can appear only when withdrawing and sliding away. Moreover, ambiguity reveals the *in-between* as its nearest but nevertheless most opposite and interruptive instance. *Zweideutigkeit* reveals life's *Zwischendeutigkeit*, that is ambiguity reveals the in-between-voqueness of life but precisely in hiding it. The question is therefore not of overcoming ambiguity (*Zweideutigkeit*) or wanting non-ambiguous univoqueness (*Eindeutigkeit*). The experience is rather of facing ambiguity in such a way that within ambiguity the *Zwischendeutigkeit*, the light and the voice of the in-between of existence, can become transparent, can be seen with 'clairvoyance'. This light is the light of paradox, under which it becomes possible to learn another meaning of difference, beyond the dualism of oppositions and negations, of positive and negative. Schelling intuited this light in his late positive philosophy and in *Clara*, in which he presented the experience of clairvoyance.[43] Heidegger enlarged this light in his concept of *Lichtung*. Under this light, ambiguity is the light under which the desert, in which we exist, can appear as a 'silk ground', recalling another verse of Hölderlin. This silk ground is the mark of oscillation (*Schweben*), of the continuous tension of contraries, where a 'concealed undefined already is intimately decided', a concealed indeterminate already is inner decision.[44] What appears to us as what is to be interrupted is, rather than evil or even ambiguity, oppositional thought, positive and negative dualisms, which are indifferent to the silk ground of differentiation. This is what Hölderlin showed in a fragment, 'Root of all Evil': 'To be united is divine and good; from where then is the addiction/Among humans that there are only just units and single things.'[45]

This dialogue between Schelling and Heidegger on the question about interrupting evil and the evil of interruption points toward the necessity of learning to dis-learn dialectics of difference for the sake of approaching a thinking in living differentiation. The path of this dis-learning is a hard one because it obliges thinking to abandon common sensory ideas about difference and thereby to confront the arduous realm of ambiguity that pervades the challenge of philosophizing in the age of global technique. This dis-learning has to do with a difficult learning to cultivate a desert as if it were a reversed garden and thereby to follow, as Heidegger pointed out in a quite

Schellingian way, the indications of the truth of Being in the age of ambiguity. Perhaps only then will we be able to revisit the question of freedom from within the heart of freedom and the freedom of the heart.

Notes

1 See Euripides, *Hyppolitos*, Swedish trans. Hjalmar Gullberg, Stockholm: Geber, 1930, v. 375.
2 Immanuel Kant, *Die Religion innerhalb der Grenzen der bloßen Vernunft*, GS 6, Kant Akademie Ausgabe, Berlin: Reimer, 1914.
3 F. W. J. Schelling, *Philosophical Inquiries into the Nature of Human Freedom and Matters connected therewith*, trans. James Gutmann, Chicago: Open Court, 1936; *Philosophische Untersuchungen über das Wesen der menschlichen Freiheit und die damit zusammenhängenden Gegenstände*, Hamburg: Meiner, 1997.
4 Martin Heidegger, *Feldweg-Gespräch*, GA 77, Frankfurt am Main: Klostermann, 1995.
5 Miklos Vetö, *Le Fondement selon Schelling*, Paris: BAP Publications de l'Université de Paris X Nanterre, 1977, p. 141. 'Cette deconstruction correspond à l'oeuvre de l'esprit qui decompose les choses par la méthode génétique et brise l'enveloppe de la facticité pour retrouver derriére elle l'activité, qui decompose le produit figé pour faire apparaître en lui l'articulation vivante de la productivité.'
6 Georges Bataille, *L'Érotisme*, Paris: Minuit, 2001 (*Eroticism*, London: Marion Boyard, 1987).
7 See here Hannah Arendt's remarks on this Greek experience in Hannah Arendt, 'The concept of history, ancient and modern', in *The Portable Hannah Arendt*, ed. Peter Baehr, New York: Penguin Books, 2000, p. 279.
8 Alcée et Sappho, *Fragments*, Paris: Belles Lettres, fragment 170. ('[T]o apothneskein kakón. oi theoi gar houto kekríkasin. apethnéskon gar an.')
9 Vetö, *Le Fondement selon Schelling*, pp. 417–69.
10 Schelling, *Philosophical Inquiries*, p. 19; 'Die Folge der Dinge aus Gott ist eine Selbstoffenbarung Gottes' (p. 19).
11 Ibid. 'Gott ist nicht ein Gott der Toten, sondern der Lebendingen' (ibid.).
12 Ibid., p. 22. '[E]r Fehler seines Systems liegt keineswegs darin, dass er die Dinge in Gott setzt, sondern darin dass es Dinge sind-in dem abstrakten Begriff der Weltwesen, ja der unendlichen Substanz selber, die ihm eben auch ein Ding ist' (p. 22).
13 Vetö, *Le Fondement selon Schelling*, pp. 470 f.
14 F. W. J. Schelling, *Initia Philosophiae Universae*, Erlanger Vorlesung WS (1820/21), Bonn: Bouvier, 1969, p. 16. 'Durch alles durchgehen und nichts seyn, nämlich nichts so seyn, dass es nicht auch anderes seyn könnte.'
15 Schelling, *Philosophical Inquiries*, p. 31. 'Die Naturphilosophie unser Zeit hat zuerst in der Wissenschaft die Unterscheidung aufgestellt zwischen dem Wesen, sofern es existiert, und dem Wesen, sofern es bloss Grund von Existenz ist' (pp. 29–30).
16 Ibid., p. 32.
17 Ibid., p. 48.
18 Ibid., p. 46 n. 2. 'Das Böse kommt nicht aus der Endlichkeit an sich, sondern aus der zum Selbstsein erhobenen Endlichkeit' (p. 42).
19 Ibid., 39. 'Diejenige Einheit, die in Gott unzertrennlich ist, muss also im Menschen zertrennlich sein – und dies ist die Möglichkeit des Guten und des Bösen' (p. 36).

20 Ibid., p. 59, p. 53.
21 Ibid., p. 57.
22 Ibid., p. 43 n. 1. 'So ist nun allgemein die Ichheit, Individualität freilich die Basis, das Fundamentoder natürliches Centrum jedes Kreaturlebens; sowie selbes aber aufhört dienendes Centrum zu sein und herrschend in Peripherie tritt, brennt es als tantalischer Grimm der Selbstsucht un des Egoismus (der entzündeten Ichheit) in ihr' (p. 39).
23 Ibid., 93. 'So haben wir den bestimmten Punkt des Systems aufgezeigt, wo der Begriff der Indifferenz allerdings der einzige vom Absoluten mögliche ist' (p. 83).
24 Kuno Fischer, *Schellings Leben. Werke und Lehre*, Heidelberg: Winter, 1899, pp. 563 ff.
25 Schelling, *Philosophical Inquiries*, p. 26. 'Der reale und lebendige Begriff aber ist, dass sie ein Vermögen des Guten und des Bösen sei' (p. 26).
26 Ibid., pp. 33 ff.
27 Martin Heidegger, *Schellings Abhandlung über das Wesen der menschlichen Freiheit*, Tübingen: Niemeyer, 1971.
28 Heidegger, *Feldweg-Gespräch*, p. 208.
29 Martin Heidegger, *Brief über den Humanismus*, in *Wegmarken*, Frankfurt am Main: Klostermann, 1978, 355. 'Mit dem heilen zumal erscheint in der Lichtung des Seins das Böse. Dessen Wesen besteht nicht in der blo ssen Schlechtigkeit des menschlichen Handelns, sondern es beruht im Bösartigen des Grimmes. Beide, das Heile und das Grimmige, können jedoch im Sein nur wesen, insofern das Sein selber das Strittige ist. Im ihm verbirgt sich die Wesensherkunft des Nichtens.'
30 Martin Heidegger, *Sein und Zeit*, Tübingen: Niemeyer, 1986, § 38, pp. 173, 175. 'Die Zweideutigkeit ... hat sich schon im Verstehen als Seinkönnen, in der Art des Entwurfs und der Vorgabe von Möglichkeit des Daseins festgesetzt; and further: Sie liegt schon im Miteinandersein als dem geworfenen Miteinandersein in einer Welt. Aber öffentlich ist sie gerade verborgen.'
31 We can see here a connection between Heidegger's views on ambiguity and Hannah Arendt's view on the *Sprachregelung* as the organ of evil's banality. Even Simone de Beauvoir's moral of ambiguity is not to be neglected here.
32 Heidegger, *Feldweg-Gespräch*, p. 208. 'Das Wesen des Bösen ist der Ingrimm des Aufruhrs, der nie ganz ausbricht, und der, wenn er ausbricht, sich noch verstellt und in seinem versteckten drohen oft ist, als sei er nicht.'
33 Ibid., 212. 'Das Wort "Leben" denken wir dabei, wie es auch von altherher im abendländischen Denken oft geschieht, so weit, dass sein Bedeutungsumkreis sich mit dem des Wortes "Sein" deckt.'
34 Martin Heidegger, *Zur Seinsfrage*, in *Wegmarken*, Frankfurt am Main: Klostermann, 1978, p. 370.
35 Heidegger, *Feldweg-Gespräch*, p. 208.
36 Ibid., p. 212. '[V]erlassene Weite der Verlassenheit von allem Leben.'
37 For Heidegger's discussion of this abundance of voidness see both Heidegger, *Zur Seinsfrage*, p. 406, and Heidegger, *Die Zeit des Weltbildes*, in *Holzwege*, Frankfurt am Main: Klostermann, 1980, p. 93.
38 See David Riesman. *The Lonely Crowd*, New Haven CT: Yale University Press, 1961, 2001, a book that Heidegger read and discussed in connection with the topic of Cybernetics. See Martin Heidegger, *Überlieferte Sprache und technische Sprache*, St Gallen: Erker-Verlag, 1989.
39 Heidegger, *Feldweg-Gespräch*, p. 213. 'Wenn wir diesem Gedanken Raum geben, müssen wir nämlich dies denken, dass das Sein von Allem, was ist, im innersten zweideutig bleibt. – Ohne zunächst erfahren zu können, worin diese Zweideutigkeit

gründet und ob mit dieser Kennzeichnung des Seins das Geringste von ihm selbst gesagt ist. Vermutlich sprechen wir da nur von einer Verlegenheit des menschlichen Deutens in Bezug auf das Sein, aber nicht von ihm selbst. Es ist rätselhaft.'

40 Giorgio Agamben and Valeria Piazza, *L'Ombre de l'amour. Le concept d'amour chez Heidegger*, Paris: Rivages Poche/Petite Bibliothèque, 2003. (Agamben's original text in Italian was published 1988.)

41 Martin Heidegger, *Erläuterungen zu Hölderlins Dichtung*, GA 4, Frankfurt am Main: Klostermann, 1981.

42 Heidegger, *Sein und Zeit*, § 72, p. 374. 'Als Sorge ist das Dasein das "Zwischen".'

43 See Schelling's discussions of clairvoyance in Friedrich Wilhelm Schelling, *Clara oder über den Zusammenhang der Natur mit der Geisterwelt*, Stuttgart: Frommannn, 1948.

44 Martin Heidegger, *Erläuterung zu Hölderlins Dichtung*, GA 4, Frankfurt am Main: Klostermann, p. 109. ('[V]erhüllendes Unbestimmtes (ist) doch schon innig Entschiedenes'.)

45 Friedrich Hölderlin, 'Wurzel alles Übel', SW, vol 1.1., 1946, p. 305. 'Einig zu seyn ist göttlich und gut; Woher ist die Sucht denn Unter den menschen dass nur Einer und Eines nur sei?'

Chapter 5

Wickedness inscribed in freedom

Jean-Luc Nancy on evil

Sami Santanen

Does wickedness have something to do with the world becoming more and more crowded with bodies? Let this general question remind us that when in what follows I discuss the views of Jean-Luc Nancy on evil, his subtle analyses have in any case what he calls 'the world of bodies' as their context. This notion crystallizes Nancy's conceptualization of our current world.[1]

In addition to context, Nancy's views have a background. It consists of some particular key ideas, such as the inscription of evil in freedom as well as the so-called positivity of evil. The former implies a certain conception of freedom as freedom to good and evil; the latter makes it clear that evil is not to be understood as privation of good but as something that has its own peculiar reality. Nancy draws from this Kantian and Schellingian legacy, but his orientation differs from it in one important respect. In his opinion evil has nothing to do with perversion of good. For him, what is at stake in evil, or, to be precise, in wickedness, is the question of decision.

In addition to these key ideas there are some relevant matters worth mentioning, that are often associated with the phenomenon of evil, e.g. the abyss and fascination with it. I bring these issues up in this presentation, and I think that they can be discerned quite clearly in Nancy's thought.

My curiosity arose some years ago when I stumbled upon a perplexing question in one of Nancy's texts: how can we distinguish one nothingness from another? This question is extremely interesting, particularly with respect to evil, the context of its appearance.[2] Could the abyss and the network provide us with an answer? Be that as it may, they are the fixed points in my presentation, because they bring us closer to the problem of decision. And it is the problem of decision, in its concreteness, which summarizes the examination of evil for Nancy.

The emphasis on decision is something that Nancy shares with (for example) Kant. But there are also differences between the two. Nancy examines decision on the existential level, that is to say, ontologically, whereas for Kant it is an issue of morals. It should also be noted that Nancy's focus is on malice, or rather on wickedness, meaning an existent's possibility to refuse and destroy existence. According to Kant, this kind of evil, evil for the sake of evil, is something quite impossible and incomprehensible as far as human beings are concerned. Kant excludes wickedness, the diabolical evil, from the field of radical evil. But does radical evil then become slightly too human?

Considering the thematic of evil, another important figure for Nancy is Heidegger.[3] This may sound strange, if we consider e.g. the objection made by the Italian philosopher Luigi Pareyson. According to him, the Heideggerian notion of *Nichts*, the nothing, entirely lacks the destructiveness proper to evil, and has nothing to do with the kind of negation that is destructive.[4] One is tempted to think that this objection is caused by a well-known formulation by Heidegger. He says that the nothing is – as other than the being, *Seiende* – only the veil of being, *Sein*, that arouses anxiety. This setting changes, however, if we focus on the implications that Nancy draws from the Heideggerian notion of *Nichten*, nihilation. Below I will try to illuminate how he unveils the possibility of devastation from this concept in the context of *Letter on Humanism*. The nothing proves to be double-edged.

On the whole Nancy takes the destructiveness, the positivity of evil or of wickedness seriously, because at its worst it has caused the extreme negation of existence. Faced with a fact like this, our culture of freedom has proved powerless and even worthless. Evil is something that is unjustifiable.[5] Nevertheless, we cannot avoid its inscription in freedom. Wickedness *is* freedom, in a sense.

Before I go deeper into these reflections I must sketch a background for Nancy's constitutive ontological viewpoint mentioned above. I will do this with two facts. The facts in question are the fact of being and the fact of freedom, and – as one may guess – we are not talking about facts in the everyday meaning of the word. The first fact, the fact of being, originates from Heidegger's thinking of being, in other words from the notion of withdrawal or concealment of being understood as the condition for the unconcealment of the being. Nancy reads Heidegger's existential analytic from this angle. For him the notion means the existentiality of existence, that is the withdrawal of being in *Dasein* and as *Dasein*.[6] Thinking of being, then, is thinking of existence. The second fact refers to the Kantian notion of the fact of freedom, as defined in the last pages of *Critique of Judgement*.[7] However, Nancy revises this notion with the result that the fact in question comes quite close to the fact or factuality[8] of *Dasein* in Heidegger.

It goes without saying that the question of freedom has an important role also in Heidegger's thinking. The concept of freedom as such, however, is replaced by him with the thought of the history of being, but this conception is followed by themes like the 'free', *das Freie*, or the 'free space'.[9] In this context it is nevertheless interesting that also Heidegger, in his Schelling Lectures, speaks about the fact of freedom.[10] In these lectures he traces real human freedom as a capacity for good *and* for evil and accordingly opposes the conception of moral decidedness, *Entschiedenheit*, for good *or* evil.[11]

This is worth keeping in mind in view of what follows, because Nancy, who studies wickedness ontologically, here ends up with 'for good *and/or* evil' – and finally with a solution to the benefit of the latter: freedom decides for good *or* evil.[12]

In what follows I will try to clarify the facts of being and freedom, albeit rather schematically. Even if I examine these facts separately, it should be noted that they overlap, because freedom turns out to be an element of being, as Nancy claims.[13] It is well grounded to examine them as facts that are not to be taken in the usual way, that is as given or empirical. They introduce a paradoxical, non-empirical reality marked by a tensional differentiality in its concreteness. Nancy calls this paradoxical reality *aréalité*, areality. It means finite transcendence, and that is what the facts of being and freedom are all about.

At this point I should sound a note of warning. In the following descriptions of these facts very few – if any – traces of evil or wickedness can be found. This could give rise to an impression that wickedness is of secondary importance in comparison with the reality that is being described. However, I have just claimed that wickedness, for Nancy, is not a perversion of anything preceding or 'originary'. Following this partial point of view I will try to introduce a level on which wickedness can be discussed as inscribed in freedom. It is my aim to complement the point of view further on.

First, the fact of being. As stated above, Nancy thinks of existence – *Dasein's* way of being – from the Heideggerian viewpoint of the withdrawal of being. Besides the categorical determinations, it is essence as the preceding and grounding instance in particular from which being withdraws. At the same time it draws the being to the nothingness of its freedom. Being, then, offers existence, which in itself, as groundless, constitutes essence – instead of preceding or following (from) essence. At that point the concepts of existence and essence lose their traditional, metaphysical meaning and opposition and, according to Nancy, end up in a chiasmatic relation with one another, to which being in its withdrawal is abandoned. In *Being and Time* this is formulated as follows: 'The "essence" of *Dasein* lies in its existence.'[14] Nancy holds this assertion as central to the whole existential analytic. Simultaneously he claims that the chiasm between existence and essence implies freedom.[15] 'Existence as its own essence is nothing other than the freedom of being.'[16]

Existence is thus offered as factual, as the factuality of *Dasein*. Nancy emphasizes that the essence of *Dasein* lies in its (having)-to-be, *Zu-Sein*, or in its possibilities, which are each time possible for it to be.[17] These possibilities are existential and factual, in other words, they have to be existed; they don't float free, nor are they anything appropriable. Deciding for them, or 'to choose oneself', means to decide 'to be one's own as the existent that one is, which means always, as this being whose existence *surprises* it, as existence and as its own'.[18] The surprise clearly brings out the difference of existence to itself, which is what the fact of being is about. In the following it is precisely the relation to these possibilities that will be of crucial significance, but things get complicated by the fact when freedom is introduced, it will bring along with it the possibility of evil.

Second, the fact of freedom. Nancy's point of departure is the Kantian, that is the practical, non-empirical version of this fact. However, he emphasizes the point that if freedom is real, it has to be viewed ontologically, as an element of being; not causally as Kant does, but as liberated from the causality (of freedom). Understood in this way, freedom deals with 'the reality of man'. Heidegger, who uses this expression in his Kant interpretation, also gives a hint about the existential dimension of the reality of this freedom.[19] He speaks about the categorical imperative and emphasizes the inner function of this law for *Dasein*.[20] Nancy follows Heidegger's thought, with a quite unconventional interpretation as a result.[21]

According to Nancy, in the light of Heidegger's idea the fact in question proves to be the reality of the ought-to, the duty of being-there, *Sollen des Daseins*. The abandonment of existence to obligation is due to existence not having an essence as given, but having to receive it as alterity, as the law of existing. Freedom is given as a law of singularity, as Nancy says, that is to say, as the categorical imperative: *Act only on that maxim through which you can at the same time will that it should become a universal law.*[22]

The reality of the ought-to, then, means a situation of being exposed to the imperative as well as being responsible to it. This does not imply, however, that the existent could not disobey it or act against it. Freedom allows for radical evil (Kant) or the maxim of wickedness (Nancy).[23] In any case, being subject to duty means a situation in which a decision in favour of the 'ought to', *Sollen* – having to will one's existence – is called for as a ceaselessly recurrent task: one ought to legislate in a universal manner. Freedom means a destination to this universal legislation.[24] Praxis, enjoined by the imperative – *Act!* – is reduced to this kind of decision of existence. However, the universal, here, is not given, which means that it is set as a task.[25] The universal has to be found in the decision itself, in an unpredictable way – that is to say, without preceding instances (e.g. general law), as Kant has shown in his analysis of reflective judgement. Nancy is ready to see in the not-given universal a determination of *the other existent*. But this other existent is to be understood as plural.[26] The determination, then, means existents sharing their singular alterity.[27] Each time, however, it is dependent on decision, whether we permit our alterity to coexist.[28] Such viewpoints lend themselves well to emphasizing responsibility, especially if we take into account the aforementioned possibility of evil.

To summarize, we can conclude from these facts that Nancy's idea is to think of the withdrawal of being as freedom. The fact *that there is existence* is not due to any necessity but is freely given or offered.

How does Nancy understand freedom, then? His point of departure is that the factuality of existence is a matter of factual freedom. This means that freedom *precedes* the existential possibilities. It is what makes these possibilities possible. However, freedom is now comprehended in a radical way, as liberation, as e.g. Heidegger has emphasized.[29] Freedom as factual is not to be taken as quality or property, as the power of spontaneity, etc., because it is by itself only its own liberation. Nancy finds in later Heidegger the idea of leap, *Sprung*, and thinks that factual freedom is precisely that kind of leap.[30] Another term that according to him characterizes freedom is surprise, which we already touched upon, and this surprise concerns freedom itself: factual freedom surprises itself. Surprising itself is a mark proper to freedom.[31]

But this surprising relates to existence, as we have seen. We get more clarity to the surprising nature of factuality if we take into account that liberation surprises the course of time. It is not difficult to think that the moment of surprise overtakes at the cost of the past as well as of the future. Besides ignoring both the bygone and the coming present, as Nancy remarks, liberation does not keep itself within its own present or event, either. Surprise is untimely. It spaces time in a manner that brings to mind the Heideggerian notion of the 'free space of time'. The consequence is a syncope of time and presence, '*wherein that which does not present itself as present presents itself*, namely, the withdrawal of essence in which existence *exists*'.[32] We see here how being, in its withdrawal, can show a surprising generosity.[33]

Even though Nancy is aiming at the experience and finitude of freedom, he does not limit his investigation to the commonly accepted democratic liberties.[34] Today these liberties seem to be so far beyond reasonable doubt that they can be said to be the current representation of freedom in general. Their seeming self-evidence is revealed by the reaction of intolerance which occurs when they are suppressed or even momentarily suspended. This kind of reaction is not caused only by moral values but, as Nancy says, it is due to the fact that those liberties 'delimit necessary conditions of contemporary human life'.[35] The consequence is that evil has started to incarnate itself in everything that threatens or destroys those liberties. The horizon is thus narrowed worryingly, because the potential menace extends also to concerns that are beyond these more or less clearly defined liberties. One such example is the idea of freedom, which is implicated as their common but transcendent concept. Because this kind of idea is unexplainable, the efforts to put it into practice will probably only lead to chaos or terror and jeopardize these liberties. Consequently it is better not to touch upon it by any means.

Nancy doesn't examine freedom from the point of view of liberties or the idea of freedom. Instead, he aspires to set the stakes of freedom differently, that is ontologically. If my understanding is correct, the background for this is a judgement about the coming to the fore of wickedness in the current world. Evil is neither graspable in terms of privation, as a lack of the good, nor can it be articulated or approached as a perversion of the good, as Kant's radical evil still was, but as wickedness taken as positive, that is as a peculiar reality.[36] But how is the possibility of wickedness effectively present in freedom's factuality? Following this train of thought is obviously impossible from the Kantian point of view.

If we draw together what Nancy says about factual freedom, we notice that it is characterized by liberation, that is to say, being outside of itself or detached from itself. He thinks that freedom has to be comprehended according to this logic of liberation or detachment, as the 'self' of the being-outside-of-itself.[37] It is finite, then, if we bear in mind that it is essential to finitude not to contain its own essence in itself. Consequently, finite freedom does not return or belong to itself, but instead it can turn against itself unexpectedly: freedom is precisely what is free for and against itself.[38] Nancy claims that the possibility of wickedness lies in this turn of freedom against itself. Hence we can conclude that, for him, freedom is freedom to good and to evil, even as freedom of being.

Thus Nancy considers good and evil as existential possibilities, that is as possibilities of existence. The approach is based on the idea that being offers these existential possibilities in its withdrawal, or, in other words, in its no-thingness. Finitude, which is at issue in this offering, is to be understood so radically that it puts also the opening of the possibility of wickedness at stake.[39] This conception differs from the view that takes finitude as privation of good and consequentially as evil. The crucial point is that the possibilities of wickedness and good are equally original and evil is not regarded any more as a perversion of the primordial good.[40] But at this point it becomes difficult to discern between them. This is perceptible e.g. in the difficulty of distinguishing between senseless insanity and the moment of lack of sense, which according to Nancy is constitutive of the opening of the dimension of the sense (of being) exceeding all the disposable significations as well as expectations or demands.

The discernment in such a situation depends on the freedom that surprises itself in the decision which takes its pick, makes the choice. But as will be shown more accurately later on, good and evil exist only because of decision. If freedom now allows itself evil *as* evil, as Kant defines wickedness in his essay *Radical Evil*, it appears that even if evil is not the privation of good, it is 'absolutely relative' to good, as Nancy emphasizes.[41] Deciding for evil is to decide to break down the possibility of good in the very act of decision. Wickedness consists in surprising, crushing and ruining the good where it has not even occurred. It is, as Nancy says, a stillborn good.

Thus freedom becomes concrete in the f(act) of decision, a bit in the same way as in Kant above. However, the matter does not acquire weight before good takes its turn. First we have to follow how wickedness struggles to 'steal the show', so to speak, and to manifest freedom. Nancy offers very exciting ideas about how wickedness in its very negativity makes an appearance as the positivity of freedom, as the peculiar positive possibility. He also sees here a motive for the modern fascination with evil in its different forms.[42]

The possibility of wickedness is, as said, in the freedom's turning against itself. But even then the bottom line is liberation, or, to put it ontologically, existing, in other words detachment of freedom from itself. According to Nancy this detachment can turn into unleashing, with the result that freedom unleashes itself – against itself. 'Freedom knows this as a "good" and it is this good that freedom devastates as it exercises itself as freedom. Freedom destroys itself in every freedom as if with an initial self-hatred.'[43] Wickedness, in its progressive work of ruining, follows this logic. Nancy emphasizes that wickedness, its tenacity, means nothing but being freely bound to this unleashing and not e.g. the waiting for the victory of freedom.[44] What is essential is that this unleashing represents the detachment (of freedom) that is characteristic to wickedness, it does not include all detachment or liberation. But as Nancy remarks, freedom attains there its first discernible positivity.[45] In its negativity wickedness is probably even *the* positivity of freedom, positivity now understood as the manifestation of freedom.[46]

In my opinion the originality of Nancy's approach is beginning to show itself here. The positivity of evil includes its attestation as if by essence: 'Evil must attest to its operation, it must show its devastation.'[47] Good does not have this kind of positivity. It does not belong to the front page but to a different order, because it is unnoticeable and covers its traces. While evil leaves its mark, good remains in the dead zone: '[T]he attestation of evil is equal to the attestation of the good that is not there, to the extent that it is not there and has no positivity.'[48]

Is there anything to be discerned in the shade of evil, then? Further on it will become evident that for Nancy wickedness represents only one version of freedom, of its liberation. But before we get there we need to prepare ourselves by concentrating briefly on Nancy's interpretation of one of the enigmatic formulations in Heidegger's *Letter on Humanism*. The terms that appear in it – fury, *Grimm*, and grace, *Huld* – refer to wickedness and good; this inference is justified by virtue of Heidegger's comment on evil: '[t]he essence of evil is in the malice of fury, not in the mere baseness of human action'.[49] The enigmatic formulation in question is as follows: 'To healing Being first grants ascent into grace; to fury its compulsion to ruin.'[50] According to Nancy, these words and some related developments in the text refer to his basic idea, to wickedness inscribed as a possibility in the withdrawal of being.

Fury ruins, as Nancy emphasizes. This is interesting from the viewpoint of our subject matter, because it echoes his earlier formulation of wickedness as a stillborn good. Thus if 'fury' seems to be equal to 'grace' in Heidegger's formulation, 'this equality is immediately shattered in the very principle [because fury] ruins "healing", but healing does not repair ruin'.[51] If we take into account the logic of wickedness described above – unleashing the detachment proper to freedom, marked here with the tenacity of fury – it is not difficult to conclude that a furious freedom will annihilate itself. Nancy, however, points out that this annihilation is not to be taken as self-suppression of fury or freedom. If anything, what is at issue is total devastation, in other words 'an empirico-transcendental unleashing' of furious freedom that progresses by ruining singularities in a potentially infinite way. Fury is the free devastation that leaves freedom devastated.[52]

The issue can also be expressed in terms of Heidegger's *Letter*. As a matter of fact, fury has its possibility in being, because, as Heidegger says, being 'conceals' in it 'the essential source of nihilation'.[53] In Nancy's view being then conceals the origin (of nihilation) in freedom, that is to say, in freedom of its withdrawal.[54] What this means is that in the withdrawal of being, freedom itself can be essentially withdrawn, that is 'devastated by the fury of nihilation that it *is*'. Above we have discussed the freedom of being or withdrawal in terms of nothingness. Now the focus is more specifically on nihilation, *Nichten*, which seems to follow from the unleashing of that nothingness.[55] This sharpens the earlier characterization of the unleashing as self-hatred of freedom. Hatred does not so much concern freedom itself as it concerns singular existence as such, with the result that it will be withdrawn by the existent into the abyss of being, as Nancy says. '[E]vil is in the existent as its innermost possibility of refusing existence.'[56]

Talking about the abyss of being may sound strange in this particular context. However, it is to be noted that being is also the nothingness where fury precipitates it.[57] Nancy indicates here the motif of pure immanence (or pure transcendence), which is constitutive of wickedness. The important point that he makes is that the withdrawal of being can unleash itself to *essential* devastation and again, by way of that, to the hold of essence in the form of nihilation. Is this perceptible in the tenacity of fury? In any case the withdrawal of being from *essence*, what liberation is all about, turns into an *essential* devastation, where the groundlessness of being gets discernible abyssal features. The result is reappropriation, 'existence taken up again in essence': 'concentration in itself'.[58]

But what does the discernment of those abyssal features mean regarding the groundlessness of being? Nancy gives attention to the fascination of evil and to the manner in which it is connected to being tempted, due to freedom, to bear the unbearable. Fascination becomes abyssal: evil engulfs and repulses. What is at issue in the horror and attraction of the abyss is the question of groundlessness and the nothingness of liberation, but in a form that is marked by thickness as well as peculiar presence. Nothingness figures as a sort of a shadowy substance, with 'too much figure', as Nancy says, because of the contours of the abyss.[59] He asks with good cause whether evil arises from the abyss of will to presence.

Now one figure of groundlessness has become clear: the abyss, representing the withdrawal of being. Yet Nancy points out that liberation, its 'syncope', which we have already touched on, is so groundless that the discernment of this kind of figure is possible in it. According to him there is no reason, however, to equate groundlessness with abyss.[60] But are there other ways to think about it? At this point Nancy turns to decision in order to find an answer.

Freedom is discussed above as freedom to good and evil. But it is approached as a question of being, not as a choice between given alternative norms or values. This comes close to Heidegger's view mentioned above: moral choice between separated alternatives – good *or* evil – does not give an account of 'real freedom', which according to him demands attention to the common ontological ground of the alternatives. So far we have followed liberation in the form of wickedness. Nancy, however, very sharply points out the dangers of this path. He asks, if Heidegger in his Schelling Lectures maybe remains caught in the logic of idealism of freedom, 'according to which freedom "for good and for evil" is first established and can only be established through evil', which implies a justification of evil in one way or another.[61] In our examination liberation has ultimately proved to be unleashing of the unleashing itself, that is nihilation in its own terms, indifferently, 'concentrated in itself'.[62] Still, this unleashing of nihilation is just one form of the withdrawal of being.

In order to reach another form we shall concretize our examination to the f(act) of decision, which is to be taken as existential, because existence without essence depends entirely on decision. The question still concerns good and evil, but as we will see, these can be distinguished as two different kinds of decisions.

Nancy approaches the problematic of decision by examining Heidegger's existential analysis of conscience, *Gewissen*, in *Being and Time.* Following him we can draw from it the essential points relevant to our discussion.[63] Of those points Heidegger's idea of the originary indebtedness, *Schuldigsein*, of *Dasein* is especially worth mentioning, because it orients Nancy's view on decision.

According to Heidegger, in conscience is attested *Dasein*'s 'ownmost potentiality-for-being', in so far as *Dasein*, as *Dasein*, 'is *never* in possession of its ownmost being' due to its existing as thrown-into-the-world.[64] Here the negation, 'never', indicates that thrownness is marked with nullity – this recalls the nothingness characteristic of groundlessness of being. For *Dasein* this existential nullity, that is to say, existing as thrown, implies indebtedness or guilt, as the ambiguous word *schuldig* reveals. In Nancy's interpretation, then, 'the existent, as existent is indebted to and guilty for the being-itself which it is not and which it does not have'.[65] With regard to our subject matter it is nevertheless illuminating that he introduces his crucial notion of the withdrawal of being also here, in the context of indebtedness. According to him the existent, as existent, is indebted to the withdrawal of being. Does this lead to the conclusion that thrownness or existence – as well as the disclosedness of *Dasein*, further below – is to be taken as an offer of being in its withdrawal? And that the existent, then, has to answer *to* and *for* this offer or generosity of being?[66] At this point it is, however, too early to answer these questions.

Let us turn back to the analysis of conscience. According to Heidegger's ontological interpretation, the debt is originary.[67] It is revealed to the existent by the call of conscience, which calls *Dasein* back to its thrownness marked with nullity. The call gives the fact of being-evil, *schuldig*, to be heard. The connotations of guilt, which the term *schuldig* produces, are naturally connected with bad conscience. As Heidegger remarks, bad conscience has primacy in the experience of conscience.[68] Nancy seizes this kind of primacy of bad conscience, but also the attestation in it of being-wicked, *Bösesein*, of *Dasein*, like Heidegger says. He is ready to acknowledge that this kind of being-wicked, conveyed by bad conscience, corresponds to being-indebted.[69] Of course bad conscience comprehends only half of the debt when it apprehends that conscience reprimands for a wrong already committed as a lived experience. This kind of ordinary comprehension prevents us from seeing that the debt as originary, as well as the attestation of being-wicked, is more ancient than every act committed and submitted to judgement.[70] This, however, should not stop us from thinking that what is ordinarily considered as 'bad' in bad conscience turns out to be 'being-guilty of not properly being one's being'. Nancy talks about the ontological archi-decision of the existent, which, judging from the call of conscience, is wrong.[71]

What Nancy is after here is that the existent is not innocent, if my understanding is correct.[72] Above, the experience of conscience has shown that the existent does not float free; as thrown-into-the-world or abandoned it is in debt and has to decide. In this fact of abandonment freedom comes into play in its factual mode, with which we have already been acquainted. The existent meets with having to decide on (answering to) the call that calls the existent back to thrownness by calling it forth to the possibility of assuming its indebtedness by way of existing. The existent has to decide on its existing. Let us remark that this 'ought to', subject to which the deciding in its fact is, is expressed in German with the word *Sollen*, which also has the meaning of 'being in debt'.

The existential relevance of the decision in question becomes clear when we notice that it cuts, *ent-scheidet*, as Nancy says, between an undecided state and a state of decision.[73] This brings to mind the detachment proper to freedom, as discussed before. The cutting does not mean neutral choice between alternatives but a decision which already by itself decides for decision – as well as for decidability, as Nancy adds. The addition is crucial with regard to our subject. Preliminarily we can state that decidability concerns the existential possibilities of the existent, which have been considered above in terms of good and evil. Decidability means freedom to decide on good and evil; consequentially it both demands decision and makes it possible. Thanks to the decision, the existent exposes itself to these possibilities, here barely distinguishable from each other. In terms of Heidegger's analytics of *Dasein* we can say that decision, then, makes the existent exist as 'resolute' or 'decided', *entschlossen*.

Decidability extends the problematic of decision. The new issues emerging can be specified into a question: where does decision take place? The question is appropriate, because decision, being existential, is similar to the leap mentioned before. I have already touched on this groundlessness when I spoke about the surprising nature of freedom and decision. Nancy points out the passive moment in decision: the act of decision is the action of being-thrown-into-the-world.[74] But with respect to our question, we can examine it in the light of Heidegger's notion of decisiveness or resoluteness,[75] *Entschlossenheit*, just mentioned. The importance of this notion for our subject matter becomes obvious if we remember that the existent's indebtedness concerns the being-itself; according to Heidegger decisiveness means this being-itself as proper, *eigentliches Selbstsein*.[76] In this connection it is essential, however, that *Entschlossenheit* in Heidegger also signifies openedness. A question arises: toward what does *Dasein* disclose itself in decisiveness? According to Heidegger the answer can be given only by decision itself, because 'resoluteness [or decisiveness – *S.S.*] 'exists' only as a decision, which understandingly projects itself'.[77] The answer Heidegger gives here allows for a couple of remarks, but before getting into that I will give a hint in view of continuation: in connection with his answer, Heidegger talks about decisiveness of *Dasein* in terms of being determined (or destined) to indetermination.

What is noteworthy in Heidegger's answer is the 'answer', especially because it can take only the form of decision. How should it be understood, then? Recall that our purpose is to find out where the decision takes place. Ordinarily an answer is taken to be an answer to a question. I think that in this connection we have to take into account also the fact that the openedness of decisiveness, as well as that toward which *Dasein* discloses itself in decisiveness, depend on the decision. This means that decision *answers for* these matters. Decisiveness 'exists' only as a decision, as we just have read from Heidegger. On the other hand, the decision is simultaneously an *answer to*[78] the offer of being (in its withdrawal), from which these matters in part stem.

The gist of decisiveness lies in the affirmation, in the 'for the there, *für das Da*', due to freedom.[79] This shows how what is at stake in decisiveness is the factuality or situation of *Dasein*, instead of the latter being detached from its world, floating free. As Heidegger says, 'decisiveness, by its ontological essence, is always the decisiveness of some factual *Dasein* at a particular time'.[80] The *Da*, 'there', brings forth the spacious aspect of *Dasein*, being-there, that is to say, its disclosedness, *Erschlossenheit*, that being offers in its withdrawal. In decisiveness, *Entschlossenheit*, the question concerns the assuming of this spaciosity of being-there by way of spacing it. 'The making-the-difference of disclosedness in its very self', as Nancy calls this spacing, takes place by decision.[81] The result is that decisiveness, in its openedness, turns out to be disclosedness proper, *eigentliche Erschlossenheit*.[82] In other words, disclosedness receives itself as such when it reaches its decision.[83] The prerequisite for this is that decision itself is disclosive.[84]

The disclosedness is concretized in this way, which is crucial to our questioning. Its spacing in its very self brings it to what is proper to it: to exist. This means that it cannot be appropriated[85] – unless in a paradoxical way, by maintaining its inappropriable difference. I mentioned above the indetermination (of being) to which *Dasein* is determined or destined in decisiveness. In my view, the question in it concerns this maintaining of difference, that is to say, maintaining itself in the openness of difference. If this indeed is the case, it can be thought that the indetermination is an offer of disclosedness in its inappropriable spacing. In the stead of indetermination we could also be discussing ontological undecidability. The undecidability – in which *Dasein* holds itself in suspension, as Nancy points out[86] – concerns good *and* evil as the existential possibilities for the existent. These possibilities, to which the existent – thanks to decision – exposes itself, appear indistinguishable, as previously has come up, but here in terms of the (un)decidable that calls to decide. At the same time it is interesting to note that, according to Nancy, the undecidability can be thought to imply the consistency of existence, which is noteworthy because existence as groundless is entirely in its decision.[87] I will return to this briefly.

The undecidability makes it possible to discern between decisions. As I mentioned previously good and evil mean two different kinds of decision. In both it is a question of freedom but understood as freedom for and against itself. Wickedness has already acquainted us with the manner of liberation of the latter. However, the spaciosity of being discussed in the here and now also implies another possibility, because it means freedom can be opened rather than engulfed.[88] Next to freedom (as free for *and* against itself) we have now been able to outline the undecidability (of good *and* evil). It offers a way to distinguish between the two decisions – good *or* evil – because good and evil, here, are not in a symmetrical relation to it.

We have already gotten to know the decision that liberates freedom by unleashing it in fury against itself. It is not difficult to conclude that this decision is a decision to suppress decision (of existence), and consequently, as Nancy adds, 'to suppress the undecidable that renders decision possible and necessary'.[89] Such decision – decision for wickedness – is a decision for what leaves nothing more to be decided. It is the suppression of the existentiality of existence.

The difference with the other decision could hardly be clearer, because in it *the relation to existential possibilities* rises to a central role. The question, as I see it, concerns the maintaining of the difference of disclosedness, or, in other words, the maintaining of the possibilities (for good and evil) offered as undecidable by the disclosedness. The spacing of the disclosedness – existence as groundless – is at every moment the responsibility of the disclosive decision, as has been shown. But at the same time the disclosedness, in its inappropriable difference, offers for its part the possibility of this decision of existence in the undecidability.

Now it will be possible to give an answer to where the decision takes place. From what is said above it becomes clear that the decision cannot be separated from the undecidable. In fact, it is a question of the exposition of these two terms to each other. Nancy claims that the decision takes place in the undecidable, by definition.[90] But what does this mean regarding decision? As I see it, the decision, then, does not belong to itself any more. This is so because the relation to existential possibilities means for it a limit, at which it is forced to open up to a difference from itself. The relation is thus built as (in)decision. The decision gives access to the letting-be singular existence, as Nancy says, which is its maintaining as indecision – this indecision, in its turn, is *passable* for decision.[91] This means a decision that reopens at every moment in itself the difference of indecision, the possibility of each time deciding anew. Such a decision is a decision for existence, for maintaining decision as such. The aforementioned consistency of existence relates to it.

What is interesting is that this kind of decision does not become recognised because it differs from itself. It is made in the indecision and comes as surprise. Good passes without being noticed – it cannot present itself as good – whereas evil is always after a spectacle, as we have seen.

Such a decision for existence means that the withdrawal of being can get another form. The spacing, which has proved to be a characteristic of it, gives being a possibility to withdraw from being 'concentrated in itself', which was shown above to be a characteristic of the furious devastation. What it comes down to is that existence offers a spacious shelter for being to withdraw to finitude.[92]

In this case, also, what is at issue is the groundlessness of being. This groundlessness, however, is not *Abgrund*, an abyss, but rather an 'unground' *Ungrund*, that can be thought of as a network.[93] Previously I discussed the existents sharing their singular alterity. Now, we can say that the surprise that the freedom of existing is signifies that the withdrawal of being, its groundlessness, is constitutively shared with others, in otherness – perhaps in an ontological network.

Notes

1 Jean-Luc Nancy, *Corpus*, Paris: Métailié, 1992.
2 Jean-Luc Nancy, *La Pensée dérobée*, Paris: Galilée, 2001, p. 108.
3 Also Schelling and Hegel can be mentioned.
4 Luigi Pareyson, *Ontologia della libertà*, Turin: Einaudi, 2000, p. 460.
5 Jean-Luc Nancy, *L'Expérience de la liberté*, Paris: Galilée, 1988, p. 159; Jean-Luc Nancy, *The Experience of Freedom*, trans. Bridget McDonald, Stanford, CA: Stanford University Press, 1993, p. 123. Page references will be given first to the French text and second to the English translation.

6 Ibid., p. 169; p. 130.
7 Immanuel Kant, *Kritik der Urteilskraft*, *Werkausgabe* X, ed. W. Weischedel, Frankfurt am Main: Suhrkamp, 1977, § 91.
8 Nancy prefers 'factual' for Heidegger's *faktisch*. According to him, this translation allows one to preserve 'the value of the mundane, material, carnal, existential *fact*, which is what matters' – without forgetting the singularity of the 'fact' distinguished by Heidegger from *Tatsächlichkeit*, the immediate state of things (Jean-Luc Nancy, *Une pensée finie*, Paris: Galilée, 1990, p. 138 n. 2; English translation of the chapter 'La décision d'existence' in Jean-Luc Nancy, *The Birth to Presence*, 'The decision of existence', trans. Brian Holmes, Stanford, CA: Stanford University Press, 1993, p. 406 n. 48). I will follow Nancy's suggestion.
9 Nancy, *L'Expérience de la liberté*, pp. 51–63; pp. 33–43.
10 Heidegger, in his Schelling Lectures (Martin Heidegger, *Schelling: Vom Wesen der menschlichen Freiheit* (1809), GA 42, Frankfurt am Main: Klostermann, 1988). Benjamin S. Pryor has discussed Nancy's and Schelling's views in a very interesting way, with special reference to Heidegger's Schelling Lectures: Benjamin S. Pryor, '"Giving way to … Freedom": A Note after Nancy and Schelling', in Jason M. Wirth (ed.), *Schelling Now*, Bloomington, IN: Indiana University Press, 2005.
11 Heidegger, *Schelling*, p. 270.
12 See Nancy, *L'Expérience de la liberté,* pp. 157–90; pp. 121–47.
13 Ibid., *see*, p. 14; p. 10.
14 Martin Heidegger, *Sein und Zeit*, 15th edn, Tübingen: Niemeyer, 1979, p. 42.
15 Nancy, *Une pensée finie*, pp. 138–9; p. 104; Nancy, *L'Expérience de la liberté,* p. 13; p. 9.
16 Nancy, *L'Expérience de la liberté*, p. 29; p. 23.
17 See Heidegger, *Sein und Zeit*, p. 42.
18 Nancy, *L'Expérience de la liberté*, p. 152 n. 1; p. 199 n. 8.
19 Martin Heidegger, *Vom Wesen der menschlichen Freiheit*, GA 31, Frankfurt am Main: Klostermann, 1982, p. 293.
20 Martin Heidegger, *Kant und das Problem der Metaphysik*, 4th (enl.) edn, Frankfurt am Main: Klostermann, 1973, p. 251.
21 Jean-Luc Nancy, *L'Impératif catégorique*, Paris: Flammarion, 1983, pp. 133–7; in greater detail see Nancy, L'Expérience de la liberte, pp. 27–39; pp. 21–32, and Jean-Luc Nancy, 'Dies irae', in Jacques Derrida et al., *La Faculté de juger*, Paris: Minuit, 1985.
22 Immanuel Kant, *Grundlegung zur Metaphysik de Sitten*, Werkausgabe, ed. W. Weischedel, VII, Frankfurt am Main: Suhrkamp, 1977, p. 52. I refer to the page numbering of the first edition (1785).
23 Nancy, *L'Expérience de la liberté,* pp. 37, 162; pp. 30, 125.
24 Nancy, 'Dies irae', p. 44.
25 *See* Jean-Luc Nancy, *La Création du monde – ou la mondialisation*, Paris: Galilée, 2002, p. 69.
26 See Nancy, *La Pensée dérobée*, p. 136.
27 Nancy suggests that Heidegger's notion of 'being-there-with', *Mitdasein*, is interpreted in this light (see Nancy, *La Pensée dérobée*, p. 136).
28 Jean-Luc Nancy, *La Communauté dés Oeuvrée*, rev. enl. edn, Paris: Bourgois, 1990, p. 278.
29 Heidegger, *Kant und das Problem der Metaphysik*, p. 257.
30 Nancy, *L'Expérience de la liberté*, p. 81; p. 58.
31 Ibid., p. 20; p. 15.
32 Ibid., p. 151; p. 116.
33 Ibid., p. 155; p. 120.

34 The finitude of freedom does not mean 'a limited freedom having no space of play except between certain borders or frontiers' (ibid., p. 111; p. 83).
35 Ibid., p. 42; p. 2.
36 Ibid., p. 159; p. 123.
37 Ibid., p. 96; p. 70.
38 Ibid., pp. 80, 205; pp. 57, 161.
39 Nancy, *Une pensée finie*, p. 33.
40 Nancy, *L'Expérience de la liberté*, pp. 159, 163; pp. 123, 125.
41 Ibid., p. 163; p. 126.
42 Ibid., p. 160; p. 123.
43 Ibid., p. 164; p. 126.
44 It is worth noting that we cannot talk about 'the wicked being' in terms of pure empirical figure any more, because experience itself, here, is transcendental. Instead, according to Nancy, 'there are apparatuses, mechanisms, institutions and calculations that can present wickedness as such' (ibid., p. 164 n. 1; p. 201 n. 10).
45 Ibid.
46 Ibid., p. 172; p. 133.
47 Ibid., p. 164 n. 1; p. 201 n. 10.
48 Ibid.
49 Martin Heidegger, *Wegmarken*, 2nd (enl.) edn, Frankfurt am Main: Klostermann, 1978, p. 355.
50 Ibid., p. 357. In the original: 'Sein erst gewährt dem Heilen Aufgang in Huld und Andrang zu Unheil dem Grimm.'
51 Ibid., p. 165; p. 127.
52 Ibid., p. 166; p. 128.
53 Heidegger, *Wegmarken*, p. 355.
54 Nancy, *L'Expérience de la liberté*, p. 166; p. 128.
55 See ibid., p. 184; p. 143.
56 See ibid., pp. 166–7; pp. 128–9.
57 Nancy, *La Pensée dérobée*, p. 108.
58 Nancy, *L'Expérience de la liberté*, pp. 167, 180; pp. 129, 140.
59 Ibid., p. 171; pp. 132–3, see also p. 112; pp. 83–4.
60 Nancy, *Corpus*, p. 89; see also Nancy, *Une pensée finie*, p. 103.
61 Nancy, *L'Expérience de la liberté*, p. 170; p. 131.
62 Ibid., p. 175; p. 136.
63 See ibid., pp. 176–7; pp. 136–7.
64 In greater detail see Heidegger, *Sein und Zeit*, pp. 279, 284.
65 Nancy, *L'Expérience de la liberté*, p. 176; p. 137.
66 See Nancy, *Une pensée finie*, p. 140; p. 105.
67 Heidegger, *Sein und Zeit*, pp. 286–7.
68 See ibid., pp. 290–1.
69 Nancy, *L'Expérience de la liberté*, p. 177; p. 137.
70 Ibid.
71 Ibid.
72 Ibid., p. 178; p. 138.
73 Ibid.
74 Nancy *Une pensée finie*, p. 117; p. 88.
75 *Entschlossenheit* is ordinarily translated 'resoluteness'. However, I use 'decisiveness', suggested by Nancy.
76 Heidegger, *Sein und Zeit*, p. 298.
77 Ibid. Note that *Entschlossenheit* is derived from the verb *entschliessen* that also includes the (old) meaning 'to open' (cf. *ent-schliessen*).

78 Let us mention here Nancy's suggestion for translation. In his opinion the term *schuldig* should be understood (and translated) as 'responsible'. 'Responsible' covers both the too moral 'guilt' and the too economic 'debt' (Nancy, *Une pensée finie*, p, 140 n. 1; pp. 406–7 n. 51).
79 Heidegger, *Sein und Zeit*, p. 300.
80 Ibid., p. 298.
81 Nancy *Une pensée finie*, p. 122; p. 92.
82 See Heidegger, *Sein und Zeit,* pp. 296–7.
83 Nancy, *Une pensée finie*, p. 140; p. 105.
84 Nancy, *L'Expérience de la liberté*, p. 185; p. 144. According to Nancy, the word *Entscheidung* can also be read literally as 'cutting separation' and therefore as 'disclosive' (see Nancy, *Une pensée finie*, p. 116; p. 87). As to the word *Entschluss*, which Nancy also translates as 'decision', it is derived from the verb *entschliessen* discussed above, note 77.
85 See Nancy, *Une pensée finie*, p. 128; p. 97.
86 Ibid., 127; p. 95. Here Nancy refers to *Being and Time:* '[*Dasein*] holds itself in suspension, *hält sich in einer Schwebe*' (Heidegger, *Sein und Zeit*, p. 170). Let it be noted that here suspension, *Schwebe*, does not mean floating free, but rather concerns being-thrown-into-the-world.
87 Nancy, *L'Expérience de la liberté*, p. 206; p. 163; see also Nancy, *Une pensée finie*, pp. 135–6; pp. 102–3.
88 Nancy, *L'Expérience de la liberté*, p. 188; p. 146.
89 Ibid., p. 205; p. 162.
90 Ibid., pp. 183, 204; pp. 142, 161.
91 Ibid., pp. 184, 205; pp. 143, 162, see also Nancy, *Une pensée finie*, p. 114; p. 86.
92 Nancy, *L'Expérience de la liberté*, pp. 180, 188; pp. 140, 146.
93 Nancy, *La Communauté dés Oeuvrée*, p. 70.

Chapter 6

Arche-evil

Derrida's philosophy explained through the concept of evil

Jari Kauppinen

> The world is going badly [*Le monde va mal*], the picture is bleak, one could say almost black.[1]

Introduction

The aim of this text is to gather together the systematic interpretations of Jacques Derrida's philosophy in relation to evil, which are not usually considered to be key terms in 'understanding Derrida'.[2]

Derrida's notion 'arche-evil' already opens this path: it can be understood as an atopology,[3] as a limit of the system or as something outside it that at the same time makes this system possible. Hence it is something that makes possible the system of good and evil, something that is actually beyond this system or the primordial unity of good and evil. The concept of evil that Derrida uses refers also to the Kantian radical evil, and to the notion of *la pire violence*, the worst violence, as he calls it in his argumentation about the violence of the discourse and about original violence. The concept of evil also relates to the sacred and to God, to the relation to the other, to what comes from the other and to the notion of to-come.[4] Then again, Derrida is not a negative theologian, like Emmanuel Levinas or Jean-Luc Marion, because he does not want to determine the other or the other of the other who is coming; there is no *Deus absconditus* or Wittgensteinian ineffability as a transcendental signifier. Moreover, what makes Derrida's discussion about evil different from the theological perspectives is the recognition of psycho-analysis. Freud speaks about evil in terms of radical evil, which Derrida makes clear: 'We do not like to be reminded, Freud notes, of the undeniable existence of an evil which seems to contradict the sovereign goodness of God.'[5]

The concept of violence: Derrida and Levinas

I shall show first how Derrida uses the concept of evil (and violence) in his early work, first in 'Violence and Metaphysics' and then in *Of*

Grammatology. Derrida starts to ask questions of evil, ontology and violence in relation to the philosophy of Levinas. We confront the notion of worst violence in Derrida's argumentation against Levinas's notion of original peace in *Totality and Infinity*.

> Discourse, therefore, if it is originally violent, can only *do itself violence* (*se faire violence*), can only negate itself, in order to affirm itself, make war upon the war which institutes it without ever *being able* to reappropriate this negativity, to the extent that it is discourse. *Necessarily* without reappropriating it, for if it did so, the horizon of peace would disappear into the night (worst violence (*pire violence*) as previolence). This secondary war, as the avowal of violence, is least possible violence, the only way to repress the worst violence (*la pire violence*), the violence of the primitive and pre-logical silence, of an unimaginable night which would not even be the opposite of day, an absolute violence which would not even be the opposite of nonviolence: nothingness (*le rien*) or pure non-sense.[6]

Let me say immediately that Derrida should not be read in the context of structural linguistics but in the context of phenomenology and the philosophy of Being. This concerns the structure of the original violence, or the first violence of Being, that is discussed in Derrida's critique of Levinas in 'Violence and Metaphysics'. In early Derrida[7] the focus is on the violence of language. Even if Derrida based his criticism of Lévi-Strauss and his reading of Rousseau's *The Essay on the Origin of Languages* on the argument of transcendental violence, he himself, as he analyses the origin of violence, makes a Rousseauistic move. The structure of Derrida's argument goes from transcendental violence to ontological violence. First there is the opening of the ethical relationship to the other and the determination of violence in the case of Levinasian pre-theoretical ethics of ethics. For Levinas the religious is the ethical and we need it because of evil; and of course philosophy for Levinas derives from religion. Thus the problem of evil is placed in a Levinasian context, and Derrida explains how the relation to the other is the transcendental origin of irreducible violence, namely pre-ethical violence.[8] This is the famous passage against Levinas that leads to the earlier quoted passage on the worst violence; it also introduces the notion of an economy: 'For this transcendental origin, as the irreducible violence of the relation to the other, is at the same time nonviolence, since it opens the relation to the other. It is an *economy*. And it is this economy, by this opening, that will permit access to the other to be determined, in ethical freedom, as moral violence or nonviolence.'[9]

This is what the non-ethical opening of the ethics means which means also the necessary violence. In this arche-evil, or primary war in the case of Levinas, is needed so that that ethics can be founded as first philosophy.

Derrida argues that the possibility of peace can be founded only on the basis of secondary war, because this represses the worst violence – the radical evil – of primitive violence. As already mentioned, Derrida speaks about arche-evil as absolute violence and the worst violence as pre-violence. Here violence also means history.[10]

> Further, without the thought of Being, which opens the face, there would be only pure violence and non-violence. Therefore, the thought of Being, in its unveiling, is never foreign to a certain violence. That this thought always appears in difference, and that the same – thought (and) (of) Being – is never the identical, means first that Being is history, that Being dissimulates itself in its occurrence, and originally does violence to itself in order to be stated and in order to appear. A Being without violence would be a Being which would occur outside the existent: nothing; nonhistory; non-occurrence; nonphenomenality.[11]

Thus we need Being with history, with politics, and with ethics: violence is in the final analysis finity as the ethical is opened as a relation to infinity. Or as it is known, from Levinas, that being is evil. Finally, Derrida states that it is in articulation that violence begins, 'Violence appears with *articulation.*'[12]

Although evil is always in the background of Levinas's philosophy he makes only rare comments on it. For example, Levinas says that evil is something unintegratable, evil is excess: 'The ontological difference is preceded by the difference between good and evil,' which makes ethics primordial.[13] His comments on evil can also be found from his writings on the Jewish tradition. As an example of evil I take 'Damages due to Fire', a Halakhic commentary which deals with the responsibility to violence or terror of fire:

> It affirms responsibility for damages caused by a disaster, due, to be sure, to human freedom, but which, as fire, immediately escapes the powers of the guilty party. Fire, an elementary force to which other elementary forces will add themselves, multiplying damages beyond any rational conjecture![14]

When we read this in relation to the problem of fire, cinders and remains in Derrida it can be seen that in Derrida's reading impossibility and nothing are more radical than the Levinasian theodicy of a heavenly firewall against the enemy. This leads to Derrida's later theory of hauntology. It is enough to point out the argument of *Of Spirit*, in which the spirit leads to the ashes and to the hauntology, where the spirit is also the ghost which always doubles itself when it returns, as is explained in *Specters of Marx*. It implies the general structure of becoming and the peculiar temporality of the future without present and the shift from the messiah to messianicity. This is also implied in the coming of the worst because the old evil always doubles itself and in the becoming of evil is always the possibility of impossibility, absolute evil, where the dead should bury the dead – as is already implied in history.

Rousseau and the violence of the letter

But to return to our argument. In *Of Grammatology* Derrida harshly criticizes Claude Lévi-Strauss's 'modern Rousseauism', for which violence means writing.[15] The question is what links writing (in the normal sense) with violence. Derrida considers that the complex structure of violence, as arche-violence, arche-writing or arche-ethics, is analogical to the structure of metaphysics and as complex as the system of writing. First there is primary violence, the naming and being named. Out of this comes the violence of law, that is reparatory and protective violence that institutes morality. The third, and the most complex, violence is related to these two inferior kinds of violence. This is empirical violence, violence of reflection, a classificatory and identificatory violence.[16] It is 'what is commonly called evil, war, indiscretion, rape'.[17] This is the structure of violence. Thus we get to the origin, or to nature, because in Derrida's interpretation of Rousseau we have the structure of the supplement, and evil comes through the supplementarity. There is always something more, something that is lacking from the origin and now it is culture which appears as evil through the chain of supplements and substitutions. There is something proper, without a name, and this impropriety appears in the form of culture or of language. This is the Derridian argument about voice and speech in relation to Rousseau's notion of the original cry. In a section called 'Writing, political evil and linguistic evil' there is discussion of the determination of absence as the origin in relation to presence and supplement. Derrida comments: 'Among all its representations (exteriority of nature and its others, of good and evil, innocence and perversity, of consciousness and non-consciousness, of life and death, etc.) one in particular requires our special notice.'[18]

Derrida's philosophical examination of linguistic and political evil shows the way in which Derrida deals with the first passion in Rousseau, be it pity (as in the Second *Discourse*) or fear (as in *The Essay*). It is passion that starts both culture and society, or language and culture, because it is possible to 'reread all the texts describing culture as the corruption of nature: in the sciences, the arts, spectacle, masques, literature, writing'.[19] These things mean history – and of course this movement is classical, because speech makes the difference between animality and humanity. It is not merely that war means animality, it is the imagination as a supplement that is a passion above animality. Nature is another name for impossibility or a limit, in relation to addition and imagination. But where Rousseau is different from Hobbesian fear and aggressivity – and not only in the sense of fear and pity – is that according to Derrida Rousseau reduces or neutralizes, *Epokhè*.

> What Rousseau thus reveals is the neutral origin of all ethico-political conceptuality, its field of objectivity, and its axiological system. All the oppositions that follow in the wake of the classical philosophy of history, culture and society must therefore be neutralized. Before this neutralization, or this reduction, political philosophy proceeds within the naiveté of acquired and accidental evidence.[20]

Indeed, in the *Second Discourse* and *The Essay* Rousseau says nearly the same: that in his theory of sovereignty Hobbes concludes too hastily that the first men were enemies. It is like Rousseau says, one cannot conclude wickedness from a lack of goodness.[21] Nevertheless, the argument here is that nature signifies radical nonpresence. Derrida's argument as a whole, if one looks again at the last pages of *Of Grammatology* is that exteriority – death, violence, evil and supplement – makes violent movement a force, a Heideggerian *dynamis*, a structure of reversal.[22]

Another point is to see how pity, in relation to the suffering of suffering, leads to auto-affection as a suffering. Auto-affection, the other name for living in general, also means suffering, just as an animal bears the double value of innocence and radical evil. But in the case of Rousseaustic reversal and the system of corruption as evil, one can also see how writing, or speech, or language has the double value of good and evil. Derrida's most notorious text is of course 'Plato's Pharmacy', where is the function of mimesis in relation to good and bad imitation and writing presenting speech and speech thought. I shall merely quote Derrida's litany of Platonic oppositions that govern Western metaphysics:

> One cannot, in fact, speak – and we don't really know what the word could mean here anyway – of a borrowing, that is, of an addition contingent and external to the text. Plato had to make his tale conform to structural laws. The most general of these, those that govern and articulate the oppositions speech/writing, life/death, father/son, master/servant, first/second, legitimate son/orphan/bastard, soul/body, inside/outside, good/evil, seriousness/play, day/night, sun/moon, etc., also govern, and according to the same configurations Egyptian, Babylonian and Assyrian mythology.[23]

This means that violence begins with articulation, and the articulation of Greek philosophy, or *logos*, in relation to Asiatic *mythos*. These oppositions are what classical Derridian deconstruction constitutes and then displaces, Derrida continuing the argument between the relation of evil, speech and language. Some twenty years later, in 'The Eyes of the Language', Derrida sees a multiple structure of evil. Here he deals with Gershom Scholem's 'ghostly letter' to Franz Rosenzweig about the language of Palestine and the problem of the profane language of the not-yet-born nation. According to Derrida, Scholem makes a confession to Rosenzweig:

> It is a confession before Rosenzweig the anti-Zionist, because Scholem is a Zionist – that is what he wants to be, that what he remains and confirms being. Yet, he cannot recognize in Zionism an *evil*, an inner evil, an evil that is anything but accidental [*un mal qui n'a rien d'accidental*]. More precisely, one cannot but recognize that the accidental that befalls Zionism or that lies in wait for it threatens it essentially, in its closest proximity: *in its language* [*au plus proche de lui-même* dans sa langue], and as soon as a Zionist opens his mouth. This evil has the triple form of threat or danger, first, then of failure, and finally as the root of the danger and the failure, the form of profanation, of corruption and sin … This linguistic evil does not let itself be localized or circumscribed.[24]

This is the traditional argument about Babel and Hebrew concerning the question of the language as opposed to the secularization and materialization of language. The evil of the secularization of Zionism is a distinct possibility: 'The linguistic evil is total: it has no limit because first of all it is political.'[25] In Scholem's letter it is the Zionist who does not understand the essence of language according to Derrida's interpretation; it is the accidental against the essential. For Scholem Palestine is like a volcano in which language boils.

The problem of linguistic evil is well known in Derrida since *Of Grammatology* and 'Plato's Pharmacy'. The debate goes back further to the first *Discourse* of Rousseau, where he claims that *le grand mal* was the invention of the sciences, and this is the fault of the Egyptian god Theuth, who brought letters to the human world.

Radical evil in 'Faith and Knowledge'

In Derrida's later philosophy there are three main texts where Derrida speaks about the radical evil, in relation to Kant's *Religion within the Boundaries of mere Reason*. 'Chaire vacante' is about the university and the status of philosophy in relation to other faculties.[26] In 'Psychoanalysis searches for its States of the Soul' Derrida refers to Freud and the problem of cruelty, *Grausamkeit*, which could not be extirpated from the human being. From Derrida's perspective, radical evil is central to Freudian thought.[27] Then there is Derrida's most famous text on religion in 'Foi et savoir' ('Faith and Knowledge'), to which I turn now. As he analyses religion Derrida wonders why we need the concept of evil and what the different forms of evil are, whether salvation is necessarily redemption before or after evil, fault or sin. Moreover, where is evil (*le mal*) today, and he asks, could there at present be an exemplary and unprecedented figure of evil, even radical evil, which would mark our time as no other?[28]

Derrida links radical evil to questions concerning the return of religion and he asks if radical evil institutes or destroys the possibility of religion and then he even states that at least radical evil destroys and institutes the religious.[29] When there are different interpretations of religion that are distinct from the religious (be it the basis of faith or not) the religious seems to be the same as the religion, as far as it is instituted (and destroyed) by evil. Radical evil is described as the phallic machine that rapes but it functions in the same way as ontotheology. Evil is as necessary as ontotheology – we cannot avoid violence and evil, as faith is tied to the future, the to-come that is machinal. This also reminds us that the Lacano-Freudian structure of the world is necessarily phallic. It means also the coming of the worst or even the menace of radical evil.[30] Monotheistic religions involve the violence of the sacrifice in the name of non-violence; and the sacrality and the sacredness of life involves the interruption of the opposites of the machinal and the holding back (*Gelassenheit*, for example) in relation to the good to come.[31] Opposites are in suspension, '*suspending* themselves and, in truth, interrupting themselves'.[32] When radical evil takes the form of the mechanical it is domesticated; it shifts from the general economy of evil to the restricted economy of evil.[33]

The second theme in 'Faith and Knowledge' is the historicality of evil that Derrida wishes to update.[34] From Kant's *Religion within the Boundaries of mere Reason* Derrida takes the perversion of the human heart that is not given at once, is not one, and can express itself only as figures. Derrida underlines Kant's dictum that evil is inconceivable to reason and as a consequence we have the historical mode of representation of the Scriptures that speak in figures about human frailty. This implies a distinction between religion as a cult and moral religion, as well as the epiphany as history rather than myth. Derrida goes on to emphasize that it is the reflective faith that opens a space of discussion, because it is on the same lines as practical reason in contradistinction to dogmatic faith that ignores the distinction between faith and knowledge. This is the place of conflict for Derrida, because this means in a sense globalatinization, meaning the globalization of Christianity as the religion of morality and as a religion where we must act morally without depending on the favours of God as in a cult.[35] At the same time Christianity means the religion of the death of God, because only in Christianity is the sacrifice of a corporeal God central, unlike other Abrahamic religions, namely Judaism and Islam.[36] Derrida sees Heidegger's *Being and Time* opening up to other philosophical resources. When Heidegger emphasizes, following Nietzschean genealogy, moral concepts like *Gewissen* or *Schuldigsein*, these concepts open themselves to pre-moralistic, pre-ethical and pre-religious modes of being.

The third theme in 'Faith and Knowledge' is the coming of the worst. It is formulated against the Hegelian temporality of theodicy; the Spirit that could 'heal the wounds'. The future is not to be anticipated as the history of the future. The theme is more Heideggerian, and it implies the distinction between the time of farewell and the time of 'to God'. (This Derrida develops in *Adieu à Emmanuel Levinas*. Of course, this means an *a dieu/à dieu* distinction between the privation of God, *pas de dieu* as no God and a step to God, and the vocation of God, or to God.)[37] In 'Faith and Knowledge' this temporality is put in the form of messianicity. It is what is meant by chora, or arche-originary or messianicity without the messiah. This is something that comes from the other and comes in the form of interruption; it also means the advent of justice, undecidability, revolution, and the interruption of tearing history apart:

> The coming of the other can only emerge as a singular event when no anticipation sees *it coming*, when the other and the death – and radical evil – can come as surprise at any moment. Possibilities that both open and can always interrupt history, or at least the *ordinary* course of history. But this ordinary course is that of which philosophers, historians and often also the classical theoreticians of the revolution speak.[38]

This is what is called in Derrida's words the general structure of experience and in *Of Grammatology* is called auto-affection or life that starts from symbolizing or language, by which he meant the possibility of going over the performative level. This in turn is related to the performative level of promises and lying; Derrida simply will not admit that lying is a radical evil as Hannah Arendt claims.[39]

Gift, death and the economy of sacrifice

One cannot sufficiently understand the later Derrida on religion and faith unless one considers Derrida's critique of the sacrifice that started in relation to general and restricted economies as in the case of the economy of violence in relation to ontology.

Johannes Hoff has noted that the central point for Derrida's critique of Christian theology is that it is the doctrine of sacrifice and hence too bloody.[40] According to Derrida Christianity is the only one of the three Abrahamic monotheisms in which God could be dead. This means that God has taken human form and is mortal. This implies a sacrificial structure in which God as a human being sacrifices itself. This is central to Derrida's critique of the Eucharist, a common feature in the Christian Ecumenical tradition, embracing Orthodox, Catholic and Lutheran traditions.[41] Of course, Abrahamic religions are based on the sacrifice, as Derrida's *The Gift of Death* shows in his reading of the offering at Mount Moriah, where a ram is substituted for Abraham's son, Isaac, animal to human. It must also be read as a critique of self-sacrifice and in relation to Levinas's 'Mourir pour', which was also a primary reference in Derrida's *Aporias*.[42] In his essays Levinas gathers together all his arguments against Heidegger since the 1930s. These include his arguments against *Dasein*'s *Jemeinigkeit* and *Eigentlichkeit*, against the event of Being, and about the question of the ontologization and temporalization of being in relation to the others (*être-avec, miteinandersein*) and about the care for others (*souci pour, Fürsorge*); and finally he refers to section 47 of *Being and Time*, from which the title of the text (*Sterben für*) is taken. Of course, Levinas takes issue against Heidegger in speaking about 'dying with others' and about love, and he takes sacrifice or death and the problem of authenticity to a level beyond ontology. One must underline here that Derrida's deconstruction of the structure of *Dasein* in *Aporias* and the relation between both human and animal, and the capability of dying and just ending must be re-read against Levinas' 'humanism of the other human'.

Hoff's contribution is that he shows how Derrida sees the Eucharist as one example of the general economy of sacrifice. This is based on a reading of the theme of blood, which is important for Derrida, from the 'Force of Law', the general economy from *Economimesis, The Gift of Death, Given Time* and 'Il faut bien manger'. Hoff places sacrifice and the offering of animals at the centre of Western metaphysics. For me, the formation of the logic of sacrifice is most important in *The Gift of Death*, especially where it concerns the communicative sacrifice of Abraham and the Derridian theory of decision.[43] Derrida summarizes the Kierkegaardian reading of the sacrifice of Abraham in relation to Abraham's decision and the Heideggerian 'blink of the moment'. This is an economy.

> The sacrifice of economy, that without which there is no free responsibility or decision (a decision takes always place beyond calculation), is indeed in this case the sacrifice of the *oikonomia*, namely the name of the home (*oikos*), of the heart, of that which is one's own or proper, the private, of the love or affection of one's own kin. This is the moment when Abraham gives the sign of absolute sacrifice, namely, by putting to death or giving death to his own, putting to death his absolute love for what is dearest, the only son; this is the instant in which the sacrifice is as it were consummated, for only an instant, a *no-time-lapse* separates this from the raised arm of the murderer himself; this is the impossible to grasp instant of absolute imminence in which Abraham can no longer go back on his decision, nor even suspend it.[44]

The relation between God and Abraham is 'to speak of the secret between God and Abraham' and this leads to communication as non-communication: 'in order that there be this gift as sacrifice, all communication between them must be suspended, whether that be communication as an exchange of words, signs, or promises, or communication of as exchange of goods, of things, riches or property'.[45]The absolute gift, the gift of death, is outside the economy of change, as it puts (as an arche-evil) the system on exchange to work as an articulation.

In relation to radical and satanic evils, Hoff's intention is to show how satanic evil cannot be historized, as the banality of evil can, because it also involves the *unheimlich* and undecidability. What is important is not human evil but the relation to 'other temporality'. There is the problem of the doubleness of evil – evil always doubles itself in relation to religion or technical – as satanic and radical evil. The radical evil is always human, Hoff notes.

In Hoff's interpretation, satanic evils are connected with heterogeneity, against the Levinasian face of the other as a human face. This links us with Derrida's tirelessly asked question: if animals are others do they have a face? The status of the other(s) began with Derrida's debate with Levinas in 'Violence and Metaphysics' concerning the question of the other and the same as unreduced alterity. In *The Gift of Death* Derrida again refers to the famous appresentation of Husserl's fifth *Cartesian Meditation.* In the chapter called 'Tout autre est tout autre' he discusses Levinas:

> If every human is wholly other, if everyone else, or every other, is every bit other, then one can no longer distinguish between a claimed generality of ethics that would need to be sacrificed in sacrifice, and the faith that turns towards God alone, as wholly other, turning away from human duty. But since Levinas also wants to distinguish between the infinite alterity of God and the 'same' infinite alterity of every human, or the other in general, then he simply cannot be said to be saying something different from Kierkegaard.[46]

In *The Gift of Death* Derrida reads religion in relation to the cult and morality as he did later in 'Faith and Knowledge' in relation to Kant's *Religion*. This is related to Jan Patočka's Nietzschean genealogy that Christianity originated in a Platonic cult as orgiastic mystery and Christian mystery that was opposed to a European heritage.[47] It is difficult to say whether there is in the phenomenological language any advance from the darkness of mystery into the metaphysics of light because of the supplementary structure of genealogy, even when this is presented as inverse Platonism, because there is orgiastic origin in Platonism.[48] This leads to the secret, secrecy and death. The problem of gift and death leads to temporality, namely finitude, as my death is not to be given away as *Jemeinigkeit*; and it is impossible to give death to oneself.

Derrida points out how 'our society' is based on sacrifice of the other in relation to the giving of death or giving death. He could not be clearer when he refers to the dictum of giving food to the one who is hungry and water to the thirsty which constitutes the basis of Levinasian meta-ethics and does not simply give moral orders for everyday duties.

> On the other hand, the smooth functioning of such a society, the monotonous complacency of its discourses on morality, politics, and the law, and the exercise of its rights (whether public, private, national or international), are in no way impaired by the fact that, because of the

> market that society has instituted and controls, because of the mechanisms of external debt and other similar inequities, that same 'society' *puts to* death or (but failing to help someone in distress accounts for only a minor difference) *allows* to die of hunger and disease tens of millions of children (those neighbors or fellow humans that ethics or the discourse of the rights of man refer to) without any moral or legal tribunal ever being considered competent to judge such a sacrifice, the sacrifice of others to avoid being sacrificed oneself.[49]

This is what commonly happens every day, and we all are aware of it, as we know how responsibility or unconditional hospitality has its rupture and can be impossibility in practice. This is also shown in de Vries's excellent reading where he interprets Abraham's sacrifice as everyday, and relating it to the impossibility of absolute responsibility. He interprets it as a sacrificial structure which both constitutes intentionality as subjectivity and ruptures it as the sacrifice of the other, and as hostility to the intentional object.[50] The question of Abraham's sacrifice is not just the offering but also concerns its relation to ethics or principles and the notion of responsibility as impossibility. What is at stake when there is a question of what to sacrifice is the aporia of responsibility and the distinction between absolute responsibility and general responsibility, when the latter is the secret and singular translated to the level of discourse?

In Derridian parlance, it is the sacrifice that is never sacrificed. This structure of the sacrifice is implied in certain discourses of the gift, as at the end of *Given Time.*[51] In general, sacrifice in Derrida is positioned between two levels of economy: the restricted economy and the general economy. There is first the limited and reciprocical exchange of goods or marks and then there is the non-limited level of the gift, or, as the saying goes, giving what oneself does not have. But one point here is to read the sacrificial discourse in relation to Heidegger, and not just to Bataille, Blanchot and Nancy. In 'Philopolemology' (which originally bore the name 'Le Sacrifice de Heidegger', in both meanings) there are few remarks on this subject. In it Derrida speaks about the logic, or better, the economy of sacrifice where the sacrifice in itself is never sacrificed. For example, the poet (Hölderlin) sacrifices himself, as well as the Rousseauistic *legislateur*, as being the one outside that constitutes the system (the State). Sacrifice is also the future, or the destiny of the people. Thus in *The Origin of the Work of Art* the truth is sacrificed as the truth of sacrifice. And in the end it is the *polemos*, *Feindseligkeit*, that brings out the best and the worst when we hear the silent call of the friend's voice.[52]

Of flames, psychoanalysis, sovereignty and arche-evil

There is a temporal and an ontological note on the development of Derrida's philosophy. First, the temporal one.

Often it is thought that Derrida does not offer any 'positive' theory after the famous 'deconstruction of time' in 'Ousia et Grammè'. It is in general the notion of to-come, the future without, the futurality of the future, the temporality of may-be and perhaps that Derrida put forward and in particular 'the coming of the worst'. This means that the to-come is not so strong a temporality as the second future, the Hegelian time of Theodicy, as Derrida states in *Les Temps des adieux*. The to-come is weaker, contingent, singular, a possibility of a coming, or as Derrida puts it, it is weak messianicity instead of the coming of the particular messiah or *parousia*.

Derrida refers to the temporality of time being out of joint. There is a disjointure, *adikia*, in a different temporality, as in the globalatinization in which the world is going badly, 'it wears as it grows'.[53] The temporality of *à venir* refers to a yet unknown evil, the worst, that occurs in disjointure, namely the impossibility of absolute evil. There is another temporality, in which the arche-evil emerges, i.e. the coming of the worst: 'To be "out of joint," whether it be present Being or present time, can do harm or evil, it is no doubt the very possibility of evil. But without the opening of this possibility, there remains, perhaps, beyond the good and evil, only the necessity of the worst.'[54]

The ontological one is that it is often thought that Derrida's *Of Spirit* leaves just cinders as nothing and no-thing, and there is no positive 'content' in the deconstruction of Spirit, be it Heidegger's or Hegel's. But as *Specters of Marx* shows there is hauntology instead of phenomenological ontology as the coming of the ghost as *re-venant* – the spirit and ghost always doubles itself, and it is at the phantasmatic level of *phainesthai* that the relation to the other, or the big Other, becomes meaningful as something non-being. The structure of coming and to-come (as anticipation and *malum futurum*) in relation to the *pathè* of Aristotle's *Rhetoric* was already described in Heidegger.[55] For him, this is one of *Dasein's* modes of disclosedness in being in the world. Heidegger worked the structure of fear and anguish in the 1920s as a reversal of Augustinian *Timor Domini*: the difference between fear and anguish is that unlike the former the latter does not have an object.

Finally, I will make three concluding remarks.

1. The 'Spirit in ashes' can be found already in the remarks that Derrida makes in *Of Spirit* about evil and the worst. Derrida talks about the determination of spirit 'In the affirmative determination of Spirit – *spirit in-flames* – the internal possibility of the worst (*du pire*) is already lodged. Evil has its provenance in spirit itself.'[56] From there Derrida continues to explain the double logic of evil and the spirit in relation to Heidegger's determination of spirituality and his explication of Trakl's last poem, 'Grodek': 'It is not born of spirit but, precisely, of a spirit which is not metaphysico-platonic *Geistigkeit*. Evil is not on the side of matter or the sensible matter opposed to spirit. Evil is spiritual, it is also *Gei*st, whence this other internal duplicity which makes spirit into the evil ghost of the other.'[57] Moreover, 'this

duplicity affects all thinking up to and including that of ash, that whiteness of ash which belongs to destiny consumed and consuming, to the conflagration of the flame which burns itself up,' and finally 'Is ash the Good or Evil of the flame?' when Heidegger speaks about the *heissen Flamme des Geistes.* This is noteworthy, because Derrida alludes to ash 'The white of ash, one could say, here figures the destruction according to radical evil. Evil and wickedness are spiritual [*geistlich*] and not simply sensible of material, by simply opposition to that which is *geistig*.'[58] Derrida also offers here a topological reading where spirit is read in relation to several traits as a trait, also in the direction of the displacement. This is related to the question of *ruah raa*, where the spirit has the possibility of being an evil spirit, and also to Heidegger's interpretation of Schelling's *Freedom Treatise.* Derrida simply says that Heidegger employs Schellingian language to avoid the metaphysical and Christian opposition between spirit and nature or spirit and sensibility of the spirit of nature. Unfortunately, Derrida here provides a rather conventional reading of Schelling in terms of metaphysical oppositions. However, his final position in reading evil as a trait, 'the trait of the re-trait of what *has trait* [*a trait*] inscribes evil',[59] could be interpreted as a Schellingian position, in relation to the difference of ground and existence and in relation to the *abgrund*, as the positivity of evil. Of course, the Derridian structure of the worst and the best is confusingly close to the Heideggerian structure of the *Gefahr*, the saving danger.

Let us then summarize two current interpretations of Derrida's notion of evil or the worst to come. Hent de Vries contrasts the doubling of the best and the worst, or the risk of the worst of the worst as an analogy of the best and the worst in relation to absolute hospitality and absolute hostility within the risk of incalculability.[60] Björn Thorsteinsson notes how the worst in relation to justice (*la justice*) is the constructing principle for constituting the possibility of justice as undeconstructable (*indéconstructible*).[61] This is discussed in de Vries as an 'arche-something' that constitutes the good and the evil, or pre-hospitality as a condition to both welcoming hospitality and unwelcoming hostility. In short, the relation of the good and the bad was made possible by hauntology, and therefore justice is possible by hauntology; justice does not come about through the best and the worst – whatever comes from the big Other – but it is opened through the possibility of evil. Obviously, there is the problem of justice in relation to sacrifice and suffering. One would hesitate to say that if there is some kind of justice then the Most High ought to be postulated unless this Heideggerian *Dike/Adikia* from the Anaximander Fragment and *La Différance* does not already incorporate deconstruction as justice and some kind of undeconstructable.

There is always violence at the origin, archival violence, as Derrida calls it; there is never peace. To found any primordial ethics of the Good, there ought to be an atopical, an arche-evil, or a Platonic *chora*, that is weaker than God. This leads Derrida to affirm unconditional hospitality that does not mean simply tolerance, limited or conditional hospitality, towards the other in the sense of Christianity or brotherhood.

2. There is no transcendental law, the right of God, in Benjamin's sense, that could measure the Human: 'Divine violence will always have preceded but will also have *given* all the first names. God is the name of this pure violence.'[62] We only have this law, even if it is called a positive law. There is no Sovereignty in the strong sense, only the weak sovereign: 'Sovereign is the violent power of this originary appellation.'[63] *In concreto*, the last phase of Derrida's philosophy was to argue that there is no metaphysical base for Sovereign law to decide about the right of living and death; there is the struggle against the death penalty. The death penalty is against the sovereign subject, or the Sovereign State, statism, be it sovereign, subject, state, law, etc. Indeed, Derrida in *La bête et le souverain* refers via his critique of Rousseau's state of nature to Hobbes's artificial concept of the Sovereign.[64] Leviathan is a sea monster that could swallow the sun, but it also relates to the Creator's ontological question to the poor creature at the end of the *Book of Job* concerning the origin and causes of evil: where were you when I created?

In Derrida's thought of the new justice and the new international law-to-come the most important thing is its relation to unconditional hospitality as an ideality (be it phenomenological or within the realms of phenomenology) or, as it would be put in deconstructive terminology, whether it is unfilled or under 'indeterminacy'.[65] In the eyes of an international lawyer Derrida's references to international law are too traditional, too general and too European, and they presuppose the untenable difference between political and international law, that is to say, they refer to the Kantian realm, or to pureness of law.[66] From this perspective Derrida idealizes international law and justice because he does not take into consideration the pragmatist reality (instability) of international law.[67] The critique of Derrida overlooks, however, the most important point of the ideality of hospitality or the new justice – it is always impossible and thus to be interrupted, as the theme of interrupting and of interruption of evil reminds us. In this sense one can better understand the idea that *différance* has the same function as 'deconstruction is justice': there is always a contamination of finity and infinity, there is no pure right. The new international law is not just to be reduced to the old law in a new form; the new law (*droit*) is something we do not know yet. It is not utopia but atopia, as I have already suggested.[68]

Derrida says, 'There is thus as yet no true international law.'[69] This means that nations are not yet ready to renounce their sovereignty. Derrida notes the interdependence of modern mass murder or death in relation to technique, and the establishment of modern international law.

> An enormous, bottomless memory where the worst cruelty, the cruelty of a paregicide that still remains to be thought, the cruelty of the Terror,

> the cruelty of the death penalty on a massive scale, the cruelty of all tortures and executions in the aftermath of 1917 revolutions, the still open list of the most relentless cruelties, *Shoah*, genocides, mass deportations, and so forth, go side by side indissociably, as well as the two processes were inseparable, with the invention of human rights, the foundation of the grounds of modern international law undergoing transformation.[70]

Usually it is said that Derrida deals with cruelty and evil too abstractly but how could one be clearer when dealing with violence and law?

3. When we re-read *Psychoanalysis Searches for the States of its Soul* through Derrida's last seminar 'Le Souverain bien' we get a strong impression of the importance of psychoanalysis in understanding the problem of evil and suffering. Derrida says in his conference presentation that perhaps the Supreme or absolute Good needs radical evil[71] – a thesis that had already been worked out by Jacques Lacan in *The Ethics of Psychoanalysis.*[72]

Sovereignty and evil are repeated themes in 'Psychoanalysis Searches for the States of its Soul', where Derrida elaborates on cruelty, or evil for evil's sake (*le mal pour le mal*), the destructivity of humankind (war) and the Freudian 'myth' of *Todestried.* Indeed, Derrida sees psychoanalysis as the only force in working against cruelty. In this respect psychoanalysis has a special signification:

> Whenever a question of suffering *just to* suffer, of doing or letting to do evil *for* evil, wherever, in short, the question of radical evil, or an evil worse than radical evil would not be abandoned to religion and to metaphysics, no other discourse of knowledge stands ready to take an interest in something like cruelty – except what is called psychoanalysis, whose name is now associated with evil.[73]

There is also the resistance of psychoanalysis to the subjectivity, to *l'état*, to the sovereignty of onto-theology (academic institutionalism, spiritualism or religiousness), to globalization, to positive and cognitive sciences. (Physicalism cannot deal with cruelty and evil.) Derrida also notes that psychoanalysis must be deconstructed, since psychoanalysis is dead. He asks psychoanalysis to do its work of mourning and through this suffering its relation to the reality of cruelty is opened up. It is the relation of psychoanalysis to the notions of cruelty (*cruor, crudelitas, Grausamkeit*) or the economy of evil that is to be deconstructed. This new psychoanalysis that is to-come would be like justice and the new forms of international law and it must build upon several possibilities such as the three discourses. Psychoanalysis must be neutral in deciding what would be cruelty or evil, because that also involves undecidability in relation to responsibility, and the effect is more indirect:

> The task, which is immense and remains entirely to be done, both for psychoanalysts and for whomever, citizen, citizen of the world, or mega-citizen, concerned with responsibility (in ethics, law, politics), is to organize this taking account of psychoanalytic reason without reducing the heterogeneity, the leap into undecidability, the beyond of the possible, which is the object of the psychoanalytic knowledge and economy, in particular, of its mythological discourse on the death drive and beyond the principles.[74]

Undecidability and the beyond of the possible are related to the discourses of the other and the question of evil, to evil in relation to suffering and making evil without wanting evil or suffering. It means also the interruption of evil, that comes from the (big) Other as evil for evil. This refers to the question of what Derrida means by the life worth living: 'It is attached to life, certainly, but to a life other than that of the economy of the possible, an im-possible of life no doubt, a sur-vival, not symbolizable, but the only one that *is worthy* of being lived, without alibi, once and for all, the only one from which to depart (notice I say which *to depart*) for a possible thinking of life.'[75] This reminds us of the economy of life and violence, or life in general (as a question of finity), but now, with the concrete nuance of the impossible, to survival; and of course, the problem of the impossible work of mourning.

Derrida tries to formalize three levels, orders or instances. In fact, he applies here the deconstructive methodology that implies the production of a pair or a binary opposition, and then turns it round, proceeding to the level of *différance*, or to the impossible. First there is the level of the *constative*, or the (phenomenological) description of evil and suffering, in relation to technics and juridical processes. This is also one of clearest expositions of what Derrida does with the troubling pair of the performative–constative. In the order of the constative, that is theoretical or descriptive knowledge, which is habitually opposed to the performative, psychoanalysis could be in the future, as Freud himself prescribed, take seriously into account the totality of knowledge, in order to keep a rigorous account of it, and in particular to all scientific knowledge that stands on the border of the supposedly pure physical realm (the organic, the biological, the genetic with their theoretical and therapeutic powers – for let us not forget that our theme will have been evil, suffering, torment, torture).[76] This 'how of suffering and evil' also implies a relation to technology.

Then there is secondly the performative level that concerns economic, juridical and political changes in relation to reducing the sovereignty. The performative level was already found in phenomenology as the work of the proto-geometrician, who establishes a new kind of knowledge which has its force through the medium of writing (or in a form of law), as it is now, through tele-techonological-scientific system. Psychoanalysis must take its responsibilities, invent or reinvent its law, its institutions, statutes, norms, in the order of the performative, where it is not a matter knowing, describing, prescription.[77] This aim of psychoanalysis is, of course, for Derrida, indirect, but it implies a relation to the problem of the death penalty and to crimes against humanity. Therefore, this order poses the question of human freedom that is always implied in the question of evil. Derrida has reservations about the classical metaphysical terminology of humanism and sovereignty; and this means one more turn.

Thirdly there is for Derrida the level of impossibility, between the constative and the performative, namely the level of interruption, the coming of the other, the irruption of knowledge and the symbolic. This is the step that will have been made possible through deconstruction. 'Here, beyond the most difficult, the im-possible itself ... [A]n event, the coming of an event worthy of this name, its unpredictable alterity, the arrivance of the arrivant, all of this is what exceeds any power, any performative.'[78]

There is perhaps something 'beyond beyond', *au delà et en deça*, the impossibility that has been called here arche-evil. This is also the level of the coming of the other: 'The unconditional coming of the other, its event without possible anticipation and without horizon, its death or death itself are interruptions that can and must put to rout the two orders of the constative or the performative, of knowledge and the symbolic. Perhaps beyond any cruelty.'[79]

Notes

1 Jacques Derrida, *Specters of Marx. The State of the Debt, the Work of Mourning, and the New International*, trans. Peggy Kamuf, London and New York: Routledge, 1994, p. 78.

2 Cf. Jack Reynolds and Jonathan Roffe (eds), *Understanding Derrida*, London and New York: Continuum, 2004. Even the dictionaries of Charles Ramond (*Le Vocabulaire de Derrida*, Paris: Ellipses, 2001), Niall Lucy (*A Derrida Dictionary*, London: Blackwell, 2004) and Manola Antonioli (*Abécédaire de Jacques Derrida*, Brussels: Sils Maria, 2006) do not recognize these terms. Pier Paolo Portinaro's (*Il concetti di male*, Turin: Einaudi, 2002) excellent general vocabulary mentions Derrida only in relation to violence and alienation. Peter Fenves ('Out of the blue. secrecy, radical evil, and the crypt of faith', in Richard Rand (ed.), *Futures. Of Jacques Derrida*. Stanford, CA: Stanford University Press, 2001, p. 123) claims that Derrida does not give 'a direct response to Kant's thesis of radical evil'; his response is 'oblique' but, interpreted in the context of Levinas, everything proves to the contrary. The reference to the worst violence was noted by Hent de Vries (*Philosophy and the Turn to Religion*, Baltimore, MD: Johns Hopkins University Press, 1999) and Serge Margel ('Les dénominations orphiques de la survivance. Derrida et la question du pire', in Marie-Louise Mallet (ed.), *L'Animal autobiographique. Autour de Jacques Derrida*, Paris: Galilée, 1999).

3 On the interpretation of Derrida's philosophy as a series of atopologies, such as law, literature, death and undecidability, see Jari Kauppinen, 'Atopologies of Derrida', dissertation, Helsinki: University of Helsinki, 2000.

4 The relativistic argument claims that that deconstruction is nihilist. This is simply wrong. The concept of evil is something that makes the later Derrida more

understandable. Derrida's later work does not merely move from phenomenology to something else, be it the so-called turn to the political, or the turn to the ethical or to religion. The themes of political, ethical and religious have been already in his work. In fact, charting the constellation of evil in the work of Derrida has important consequences for the way he is read not only in literary studies but also in philosophy.

There has been a wide discussion of Derrida's relation to negative theology. The most comprehensive study is in Jayne Svenungsson, *Guds återkomst. En studie av Gudsbegreppet inom postmodern filosofi*, Munkdal: Glänta, 2004; see also Peter Zeillinger and Matthias Flatscher, *Kreuzungen Derridas. Geistergespräche zwischen Philosophie und Theologie*, Vienna: Turia & Kant, 2004, de Vries, *Philosophy and the Turn to Religion*, and Jari Kauppinen, 'Derrida and Blanchot. From the nothingness of literature to writing as arch-ethics', in Päivi Mehtonen (ed.), *Illuminating Darkness*, Helsinki: Finnish Academy of Sciences, 2007. I argue against the tendency of literary scholars to reduce Derrida and Blanchot simply to negative theology. Usually Derrida's own comments are taken from *Denegations* and *Passions*, where Derrida is distancing himself from negative theology or apophatics.

5 Jacques Derrida, *Archive Fever. A Freudian Impression*, trans. Eric Prenowitz, Chicago: University of Chicago Press, 1995, pp. 12–13.

6 Jacques Derrida, 'Violence and Metaphysics', trans. Alan Bass, in *Writing and Difference*, London: Routledge & Kegan Paul, 1978, p. 130.

7 I use the notion of early Derrida to imply that the positive force of language, or performatives, has not yet been worked out by Derrida.

8 For the limitation and the concept of violence see Hent de Vries, *Religion and Violence: Philosophical Perspectives from Kant to Derrida*, Baltimore, MD: Johns Hopkins University Pres, 2002, pp. 123 ff. The genealogy of violence is from Levinas to Eric Weil, and then back to Kierkegaard's *Fear and Trembling* and finally to Hegel.

9 Derrida, 'Violence and Metaphysics', pp. 128–9.

10 Ibid., p. 130. According to Johannes Hoff, history should be understood in a Foucauldian sense, because Derrida was writing '*Cogito* and the History of Madness' at the same time as 'Violence and Metaphysics'; Johannes Hoff, *Spiritualität und Sprachverlust. Theologie nach Foucault und Derrida*, Paderborn: Schöningh, 1999.

11 Derrida, 'Violence and Metaphysics', p. 147.

12 Ibid., pp. 147–8.

13 Emmanuel Levinas, 'Transcendence and Evil', trans. Alphonse Lingis, in A. T. Tymieniecka (ed.), *Analecta Husserliana* XIV, Dordrecht: Reidel, 1983, p. 160.

14 Emmanuel Levinas, 'Damages due to Fire', trans. Annette Aronowitz, in *From the Sacred to the Holy* in *Nine Talmudic lectures*, Bloomington, IN: Indiana University Press, p. 185.

15 Jacques Derrida, *Of Grammatology*, trans. Gayatri Spivak, Baltimore, MD: Johns Hopkins University Press, 1983, p. 106.

16 For a commentary see Arthur Bradley, *Derrida's* Of Grammatology, Edinburgh: Edinburgh University Press, 2008, pp. 87–9.

17 Ibid., p. 112.

18 Ibid., pp. 167–8.

19 Ibid., p. 180.

20 Ibid., pp. 188–9.

21 Ibid., p. 189.

22 Ibid., pp. 315–16.

23 Jacques Derrida, *Dissemination*, trans. Barbara Johnson, Chicago: University of Chicago Press, 1981, p. 85.
24 Jacques Derrida, 'The eyes of language: the abyss and the volcano', trans. Gil Anidjar, in *Acts of Religion*, London: Routledge, pp. 194–5.
25 Derrida, 'The eyes of language', p. 195.
26 See de Vries, *Religion and Violence*, pp. 20–122. The reading would combine Kant's *The Conflict of Faculties* and *Religion within Boundaries of Mere Reason* and Derrida's 'Theology of Translation'.
27 Jacques Derrida, 'Faith and Knowledge', trans. Samuel Weber, in *Acts of Religion*, London: Routledge, 2002. In 'Psychoanalysis Searches for the States of its Soul' Derrida even speaks about evil that is worse than the radical evil which only psychoanalysis can deal with: neither metaphysics nor theology is able to do it.
28 However, Derrida discusses the problematic of religion and God already in 'Violence and Metaphysics'. Because of the different editions of *Faith and Knowledge*, I refer to Derrida's numbering and in the quotes also to the pagination of *Acts of Religion*. Jacques Derrida, 'Faith and Knowledge', No. 2.
29 Ibid., No. 36, No. 51.
30 Ibid., Nos 37–8.
31 Ibid., No. 41.
32 Ibid., No. 40, p. 85.
33 Ibid., No. 45a.
34 Ibid., Nos 14–15.
35 Ibid., No. 15a.
36 Ibid., No. 15b.
37 The analysis of de Vries (*Religion and Violence*, pp. 178 ff.) is indispensably here in relation to *adieu*. See also de Vries, *Philosophy and the Turn to Religion*.
38 Derrida, 'Faith and Knowledge', No. 21, p. 56.
39 Jacques Derrida, 'History of the lie: Prolegomena', trans. Peggy Kamuf, *Without Alibi*, Stanford, CA: Stanford University Press, 2002.
40 Hoff, *Spiritualität und Sprachverlust*.
41 Slavoj Žižek argues of the Christian sacrifice and the Hegelian triad instead of the Judaic doubleness of the other but he prefers earlier Derrida compared with the latter. Žižek could not be clearer when he says that radical evil means totalitariansm; clearly he avoids any 'empty messianism' only as a Kantian form. Slavoj Žižek, *The Puppet and the Dwarf. The Perverse Core of Christianity*. Cambridge, MA: MIT Press, 2003, pp. 138–41.
42 Emmanuel Levinas, 'Mourir pour', in *Entre nous. Essais sur le penser-à-l'autre*, Paris: Grasset, 1991; Jacques Derrida, *Aporias*, trans. Thomas Dutoit, Stanford, CA: Stanford University Press, 1993.
43 See Hoff, *Spiritualität und Sprachverlust*, p. 174–93.
44 Jacques Derrida, *The Gift of Death*, trans. David Wills, Chicago: University of Chicago Press, 1995, 2008, p. 95.
45 Ibid., p. 96.
46 Ibid., p. 84.
47 More on Derrida's reading see Rodolphe Gasché, 'European memories: Jan Patočka and Jacques Derrida on responsibility', in W. J. T Mitchell and Arnold J. Davison (eds), *The Late Derrida*, Chicago: Chicago University Press, 2007.
48 Derrida, *The Gift of Death*, p. 29 ff.
49 Ibid., pp. 85–6.
50 De Vries, *Religion and Violence*, see the chapter 'Violence and testimony', esp. pp. 159, 194, 201–202, 210.

51 A footnote on Kant's radical evil in *Given Time* brings the Baudelairian theme of circulating and counterfeit money in relation to the radical and the diabolic evil (the bestiality of man is between the diabolic and the bestiality). There is also the notion of satanic cruelty that goes beyond Kant and a rare reference to de Sade (not to mention 'Kant avec Sade') and Kantian problem of freedom and human nature. Jacques Derrida, *Given Time*, trans. Peggy Kamuf, Chicago: University of Chicago Press, 1994, p. 165 n. 31.

52 Jacques Derrida, 'Heidegger's Ear. Philopolemology (*Geschlecht* IV)', trans. John P. Leavey, in John Sallis (ed.), *Reading Heidegger. Commemorations*, Bloomington, IN: Indiana University Press, 1993. In 'Le sacrifice' Derrida explained the economy of sacrifice in relation to the theatre and philosophy. He explained how in the sacrificial economy one just cannot put an end to sacrifice in sacrificing the sacrifice, because there is the supplementary structure of the foreclosed. Jacques Derrida, 'Le sacrifice', in Daniel Mesguih, *L'Éternel éphémère*, Paris: Verdier, 2006; *Le Sacrifice*, p. 148.

53 Derrida, *Specters of Marx*, p. 53.

54 Ibid., p. 29.

55 Heidegger, *Being and Time*, §§ 29–30; about the temporality of the worst cf. Margel 1999.

56 Jacques Derrida, *Of Spirit. Heidegger and the Question*, trans. Geoffrey Bennington and Rachel Bowlby, Chicago: University of Chicago Press, 1989, p. 97.

57 Ibid., p. 97.

58 Ibid., p. 102.

59 Ibid., p. 106.

60 Hent de Vries, *Religion and Violence.* Dooley and Kavanagh (*The Philosophy Derrida*) do not understand this kind of argumentation when they claim that Derrida's attitude in *Philosophy and the Time of the Terror* has serious shortcomings and he fails to pass his own criteria of singularity, ethnicity and justification. They label Derrida as European Marxist who sees conspiracies and fails to see the singularity of 9/11; they do not accept that Derrida reminds us that one man's terrorist could be another man's freedom fighter and that in *The Rogues* all states are rogues. They say that things are simpler. Derrida should have drawn qualitative distinctions like: The United States is not a terrorist state but Iraq is.

61 Björn Thorsteinsson, *La Question de la justice chez Jacques Derrida*, Paris: Harmattan, 2006.

62 Jacques Derrida, 'Force of Law', trans. Mary Quaintance, in *Acts of Religion*, London: Routledge, 2002, p. 293.

63 Derrida, 'Force of Law', p. 293.

64 Jacques Derrida, 'La bête et le souverain', in *La Democratie à venir. Autour de Jacques Derrida*, ed. Marie-Louise Mallet, Paris: Galilée, 2004.

65 For a recent study of the constitution of ideality and law see Tomi Kaarto, *Jacques Derrida and the Question of Interpretation. The Phenomenological Reduction, the Intention of the Author, and Kafka's Law*, Frankfurt am Main: Lang, 2008.

66 See for example Martti Koskenniemi's review of Borradori's Derrida/Habermas interview in *German Law Journal*, No. 10, 2003.

67 There is a huge discussion going on about Derrida's Kantianism, or its legacy. Although it is commonly admitted that Derrida distances himself from the regulative ideas, it is also supposed that he falls back to them in the undeconstructable concepts like justice. This confusion is based on teleological understanding of to-come, and not to the to-come that is opposed to the eschatological future, or the second future. Justice may happen at once and every

possible moment, every day, and not in some distancing future, that means the sacrifice.

68 See Jari Kauppinen, 'Law without Place', *Law and Critique*, 9, 1998, pp. 225–48.

69 Jacques Derrida, 'Psychoanalysis Searches for the States of its Soul. The Impossible Beyond of a Sovereign Cruelty', trans. Peggy Kamuf, in *Without Alibi*, Stanford, CA: Stanford University Press, 2002, p. 271.

70 Ibid., p. 266.

71 Jacques Derrida, 'Le souverain bien – ou l'Europe en mal de souveraineté. La conférence de Strasbourg du 8 juin 2004', *Cités*, No. 30, 2007, pp. 103–42; p. 125.

72 Jacques Lacan, *Le Séminaire VII. L'éthique de la psychanalyse*, Paris: Seuil, 1986. The basic version is Jacques Lacan, 'Kant avec Sade', in *Écrits*, Paris: Seuil, 1966.

73 Derrida, 'Psychoanalysis Searches', p. 240.

74 Ibid., p. 273.

75 Ibid., p. 276.

76 Ibid., p. 277.

77 Ibid., p. 277.

78 Ibid., p. 278.

79 Ibid., p. 278.

Part II

Terror

Chapter 7

Hell on earth

Hannah Arendt in the face of Hitler[1]

Jacob Rogozinski

In 1933 Karl Kraus, an Austrian writer and journalist, decided that his review *Die Fackel* would no longer appear. He announced, 'Mir fällt zu Hitler nichts ein' ('I can't think of anything to say about Hitler').[2] It is quite possible that there is nothing to be said on the question of Hitler and of everything that the name implies. It is quite possible that any discourse, with all the inevitable pathos and narcissistic posturing which it would involve, would be out of place, and that any effort of thought would be incommensurable with what happened. And yet silence too does injustice to memory. It is this fact which requires us, as Hannah Arendt writes, to try to say and 'to understand and to come to terms with' what happened.[3] To understand, she continues, 'examining and bearing consciously the burden which our century has placed on us – neither denying its existence nor submitting meekly to its weight', and without trying to deny what is repugnant.[4] But here thought runs up against its limit, against the limit of an experience, which cannot be communicated, the memory of which cannot provide us with any more illumination 'than can the uncommunicative eye-witness report'.[5]

This limit is the limit of language itself. There is no name which could capture this reality. For this event, which breaks the bounds of common sense, implies 'the appearance of some radical evil, previously unknown to us'.[6] It is unnamable, because it is radically new and without precedent in the long tradition of human misery. As is well known, this is one of Arendt's central theses: 'totalitarianism differs essentially from other forms of political oppression known to us such as despotism, tyranny and dictatorship'.[7] It is the essence of total domination which is revealed in the camps. 'There are no parallels to the life in the concentration camps', not penal colonies, nor religious persecutions, nor ancient slavery – these are superficial analogies which lead our judgement astray.[8] Nevertheless, when Arendt struggles to think the unspeakable, one word recurs in her text. The word is 'hell'.

> Concentration camps can very aptly be divided into three types corresponding to three basic Western conceptions of a life after death: Hades, Purgatory, and Hell. ... Purgatory is represented by the Soviet Union's

> labor camps, where neglect is combined with chaotic forced labor. Hell in the most literal sense was embodied by those types of camp perfected by Nazis, in which the whole of life was thoroughly and systematically organized with a view to the greatest possible torment.[9]

To understand what happened, we must try to grasp what she means by hell. But this is precisely what has become impossible. As belief in God has diminished in the modern West, belief in the immortality of the soul, in hell and in heaven, in the devil and the angels, has lost all meaning. And here we have a paradox: at the very moment when human beings cease to believe in a hell located in the beyond, the reality of this world becomes infernal. Confronted with this paradox, Arendt's thought branches out in two very different directions. In 'The Crisis of Culture', the doctrine of hell is presented as a political myth, consciously elaborated by Plato to allow the philosopher king to subjugate the multitude by using the threat of eternal punishment.[10] St Augustine is said to have deliberately introduced this 'noble lie' into Christian dogma in order to reinforce the political authority of the Church. It certainly looks as though Arendt shares this 'Platonic' confidence in the political efficacy of religious myths. She does not hesitate to reduce the religious dimension to a mere political myth, an instrumental fiction consciously forged for purposes of domination. This type of analysis betrays one of the limits of her thought: her failure to acknowledge the importance of the symbolic.[11] This leads her, for example, to abandon any interpretation of Nazi anti-Semitism based on religious schemas, in favour of vague socio-economic considerations which in no way make it possible to understand why the Jews should have been the primary target of Nazi terror.[12] This failure derives from a fundamental tendency of her thought, which leads her to limit politics to the immanent scene of action in the domain of the visible, to reduce it to the phenomenon of the political, as this is revealed in the clear light of action, without taking any account of the invisible horizon which surrounds it.

However, her remarks on the camps and on hell pointed on to another direction. She suggested that what is at stake here is not simply an external analogy, but that the emergence of total domination is closely and strangely related to the religious belief in hell, that it materializes this belief by incarnating it in immanence. In a strict sense the camp realizes hell on earth. And this monstrous incarnation is undoubtedly integral to the delirium which claims to realize the Millenium or the New Jerusalem as a classless, communist society or as a thousand-year Reich, as if the beyond were collapsing entirely into the here and now, and heaven and hell were being joined together on a devastated earth.

> Suddenly it becomes evident that things which for thousands of years the human imagination had banished to a realm beyond human competence can be manufactured right here on earth, that Hell and

> Purgatory, and even a shadow of their perpetual duration, can be established by the most modern methods of destruction and therapy. … Nothing perhaps distinguishes modern masses as radically from those of previous centuries as the loss of faith in a Last Judgement: the worst have lost their fear and the best have lost their hope. Unable as yet to live without fear and hope, these masses are attracted by every effort which seems to promise a man-made fabrication of the Paradise they had longed for and of the Hell they had feared. … The one thing that cannot be reproduced is what made the traditional conceptions of Hell tolerable to man: the Last Judgement, the idea of an absolute standard of justice combined with the infinite possibility of grace.[13]

We are here brought back to the heart of the paradox. Arendt tries to reach the core of truth in the myth of religion. She attempts to grasp what it is, in the belief in hell, which arouses the anxiety of men and orients their desire. It thus appears that representations of hell and of paradise – far from being an illusory dogma – perform a major symbolic function. They allow us to project into the beyond, outside the power of the human being, the focuses of fear and hope. When the belief in immortality disappears, the representations which supported it do not vanish, but continue to orient desire. The way is then open for the fabricators of heaven and hell, who promise to give substance to the blissful communion of the saints and the torments of the damned in this world. '[T]he totalitarian hell proves only that the power of man is greater than they ever dared to think, and that man can realize hellish fantasies without making the sky fall or the earth open.'[14] And yet, in this gesture of mad excess, which claims to make hell incarnate here below, the truth of the Christian hell has already been lost. What 'realizes' total domination is a mutilated hell, devoid of its ultimate core of meaning, devoid of 'the idea of an absolute standard of justice combined with the infinite possibility of grace';[15] in other words, devoid of – although Arendt avoids naming him – the idea of God. God is he whose sovereign justice and love justify the existence of hell for the believer. Are we even capable of understanding the strange figure of a God of goodness, whose infinite love is unleashed in the form of anger and hatred? How can we account for this enigmatic movement, for this historical turn – this 'rescendence', to use Heidegger's term – in which God and his Law, heaven and hell, are reappropriated by the human Subject?

In this metaphysical transposition of the religious horizon, it is not only the avatars of the idea of God, and Good and Evil, but also those of the Law which must be analysed. In fact it is impossible to understand totalitarianism, and its radical newness, without taking account of its relation to the Law. What distinguishes it from the tyrannies of the past, 'lawless' regimes submitted to an arbitrary will, is the fact that 'it operates neither without guidance of law nor is it arbitrary, for it claims to obey strictly and unequivocally those laws of Nature or of History from which all positive laws always have been supposed to spring'.[16] Thus totalitarian politics promises 'to establish the rule of justice on earth because it claims to make mankind itself the embodiment of the law'.[17] Arendt underlines this fact repeatedly: this immanent law of movement, which legitimates extermination, has nothing in common with the eternal Law of Justice which the tradition identified with the divine will. And yet is it not after all the same law which the totalitarian project seizes hold of, even though monstrously disfigured? What are we to make of this law of Hitler, whose imperative Eichmann claimed to respect to the very end? It is not only in an ironic sense that Arendt describes Eichmann as 'a law-abiding citizen' who only did his duty in organizing the extermination.[18] She recounts that, during his police examination, Eichmann 'suddenly declared with great emphasis that he had lived his whole life according to Kant's moral precepts, and especially according to a Kantian definition of duty'.[19] Taking in consideration Kant's moral philosophy, 'this was outrageous, on the face of it', Arendt comments.[20] Eichmann himself admitted that 'from the moment he was charged with carrying out the Final Solution he had ceased to live according to Kantian principles'.[21] He seemed to recognize that there was nothing in common between the Kantian law of duty and the law of Nazi terror except the nominal identity of the word 'law'. But such is not Arendt's view. According to her, Eichmann 'had not simply dismissed the Kantian formula as no longer applicable, he had distorted it'.[22] He had assimilated it to the Hitlerian 'categorical imperative' formulated by Hans Frank: 'Act in such a way that the Führer, if he knew your action, would approve it.'[23] This amounts to reducing the universal law of practical reason, which exceeds all finite subjectivity, to the judgement of a particular subject: to considering Hitler as the author of the Law, its sovereign Subject. For Arendt, such a 'deformation' would maintain intact the essential structure of the Law. She concludes that 'there is not the slightest doubt that in one respect Eichmann did indeed follow Kant's precepts'.[24] Thus the meaning of this distortion must be elucidated. However, Arendt is scarcely interested in this. The Eichmann case attracts her attention for other reasons. For her, it is an exemplary image of the banality of evil.

The reference to hell appeared at first as the metaphor of an unspeakable horror. It was the only name appropriate to the appearance of a radical evil which was unknown to us before. But this metaphor is without doubt the indication of a limit of thought.

> It is inherent in our entire philosophical tradition that we cannot conceive of a 'radical evil', and this is true both for Christian theology, which conceded even to the Devil himself a celestial origin, as well as for Kant, the only philosopher who, in the word he coined for it, at least must have suspected the existence of this evil even though he immediately

> rationalized it ... Therefore, we actually have nothing to fall back on in order to understand a phenomenon that nevertheless confronts us with its overpowering reality and breaks down all standards we know.[25]

The Western tradition has continually affirmed that no one is wicked voluntarily, that Being and the Good are the same, and that evil comes from nothingness, that it is nothing but impotence and privation of being. It is for this reason that judgement found itself disarmed when confronted with the outbreak of radical evil. The experience of the camps invites us to break with this tradition, to try to approach the mystery of a bad will, which could decide freely for evil 'as evil' – something which, according to Kant, cannot be found in man, since the consequence would be that 'the subject would be made a *diabolical* being'.[26]

In the final chapters of *The Origins of Totalitarianism* it is evident that Arendt's thought should have followed this path. In fact, when she tackles the question again, in connection with the Eichmann trial, it is no longer the radicality of evil which she emphasizes, but its banality. She claims that there was no 'diabolical or demonic profundity' in Eichmann, not even perverse or pathological profundity.[27] 'He "personally" never had anything whatever against Jews.'[28] There was no desire to do evil as a matter of principle, since Eichmann was precisely incapable of knowing or feeling that he had done evil: '[h]e *merely ... never realized what he was doing*'.[29] The true moral challenge which is posed by the Eichmann case consists in its frightful normality. Does this mean that every 'normal' human being is threatened by the same 'banality': that in certain circumstances any of us could have been Eichmann? This is an almost unbearable question, whose challenge a radical ethics could not avoid taking up. Arendt, however, refuses to take it into account: Eichmann's banality is said to be too banal to be universal. In fact, she defines it in a purely negative manner, by incriminating Eichmann's 'lack of imagination', 'sheer thoughtlessness', his 'inability to *think*, namely, to think from the standpoint of someone else'.[30] Evil becomes, in the most classical manner, a mere lack, a failure of judgement, an involuntary fault. The 1951 text already supported such an interpretation. Arendt wrote that 'radical evil has emerged in connection with a system in which all men have become equally superfluous'.[31] It is the desolation of the individual lost in the mass – in the 'economically superfluous and socially rootless human masses' of the modern society – which brings about the lack of common humanity characteristic of Eichmann.[32] In this sense, the radicality of evil is not opposed to its banality: it is here that it finds its source. It originates in this feeling of desolation and of abandonment (a word which has the same root as 'banality'), in this banalization of life which deprives the individual of all belonging to the world; which annihilates the capacity for judgement and action. It is then that this banal individual emerges, the totalitarian murderer, who is all the more dangerous in that he mocks himself for never having lived, for never having been born, who is equally capable of taking on either the role of victim or that of torturer. Radical evil is not the work of a bad will, but of an absence of will, of a freedom which has renounced itself, to the point of identifying with blind necessity. No one is wicked voluntarily. The judges of Nuremberg and Jerusalem condemned only puppets.

The flaw in this analysis is that it examines only the attitude of the agent, who carries out his sinister task without remorse and without hatred. Eichmann, it seems, was painfully surprised when his boss informed him of the decision to put the Final Solution into effect. But where did this order itself come from, if not from an initial decision? By concentrating on the case of Eichmann, Arendt avoids the essential issue. If one wishes to understand the hell of totalitarianism, it is the decision of Hitler himself which must be elucidated. But Arendt cannot bring herself to do this, and for good reason. It would destroy the keystone of her thought, that is, her conception of freedom, which she identifies with transcendental freedom, with the power of absolutely beginning a series of events, dissociating it from ethical freedom, from the capacity to commit oneself to good or evil. This prohibits her from evaluating the advent of the new from an ethical standpoint. For her, every beginning, as a beginning, is already a miracle of Being and should be celebrated as such. Undoubtedly, this is the price which she has to pay for her continuing fidelity to Heidegger's thought. That the totalitarian movement, the most implacable enemy of human freedom, could itself originate in a free decision, which makes a breach in time and brings something new into the world, that it therefore belongs to the sphere of action – this is what Arendt cannot tolerate.[33] In denying that it could be the result of an act of freedom she tends, paradoxically, to accept the representation of itself which the totalitarian movement puts forward. For we know that it considered itself as the agent of an objective necessity, of inexorable laws of nature and history. However, some of Arendt's analyses allow us to glimpse another dimension of the totalitarian project. In the course of her examination of the organization of the Nazi party she points out that it was constituted on the model of a conspiracy, like 'secret societies established in broad daylight'.[34] This is not a matter of a tactical choice intended to facilitate the conquest of power. 'The totalitarian movements which, during their rise to power, imitate certain organizational features of secret societies and establish themselves in broad daylight create true secret society only after their ascendancy to rule'.[35] The clandestine organization is in fact in charge of a secret: 'the strictly esoteric knowledge' concerning the camps and extermination programme, which makes every SS man a *Geheimnisträger*, the bearer of a secret.[36] Thus the movement tends to develop into a vast conspiracy, organized around the opaque core of a secret, into a global conspiracy directed towards world conquest. Arendt even goes as far as to suggest that the Nazi party used 'the "Protocols of the Elders of Zion" as a model for the future organization of the German masses for "world empire"'.[37] This 'model', rather than the 'pompous scientism' of official discourse, is said to represent the true ideology of the regime. 'Thus the Protocols presented world conquest as a practical possibility' which 'did not depend upon objective and unalterable conditions, but only on the power of organization'.[38] Moreover, they 'implied that the affair was only a question of inspired or shrewd know-how'.[39] The choice of such a model tells us that at the heart of the totalitarian project we find desire and hate, vengeance, trickery and envy. We find that for Hitler the law of the world is the law of the Subject, of a conscious will which aspires to domination. Or, more precisely, that he imagines history to be a closed arena in which two hostile wills confront each other and struggle to the death for the mastery of the world. Hitler imagines that, in this implacable struggle, the sovereign place, that of master and model, is at present occupied by the Jew, whom Hitler must therefore imitate. He must take him as a model, identify with him – the better to annihilate him.

I believe it is possible to analyse this motif of world conspiracy in the light of the Arendtian categories of work and of action, and of her interpretation of revolution. When she evokes the Protocols, which Hitler is said to have learned by heart, Arendt points out that the notion of 'the uninterrupted existence of an international sect that has pursued the same revolutionary aims since antiquity is very old and has played a role in political backstairs literature ever since the French Revolution, even though it did not occur to anyone writing at the end of the eighteenth century that the "revolutionary sect" ... could be the Jews'.[40] So we must ask why the myth of the conspiracy acquires such an importance, from the French revolution onwards, and why the figure of the 'Jew' finally displaced those of the Jesuit and the Freemason. On closer inspection, the ideology of a 'world conspiracy' seems to be determined by two incompatible logics. To declare that the apparent agents of political life are merely puppets whose strings are pulled by an invisible power is to affirm that the true cause of events is hidden from view, that the will and intelligence of human beings are unable to grasp the hidden driving forces of history. But this is in order to restore immediately, in the background, the reign of an all-powerful will endowed with boundless knowledge. Thus the mythology of the conspiracy lays an ideology of necessity over metaphysics of the will. Through its faith in the limitless power of will and action it participates in the modern experience of politics. And it is remarkable that it should have developed in connection with the French revolution, at the moment when men became aware that an event could result from action, and even from the conscious intention of man.[41] With the collapse of the traditional hierarchies and points of reference, in the euphoria of a free beginning of history, there is a great temptation to consider every obstacle, every objective limit, as a result of action, as the effect of an opposing will. To perceive in the least resistance the sign of a hostile intention which must be exposed so that it can be confronted in broad daylight. However, the experience of the French revolution immediately takes on a different meaning, which further intensifies the suspicions of the revolutionaries and their will to unmask the hidden enemy. This is the notion of an irresistible movement which escapes the grasp of action, as though 'a force greater than men had interfered when men began to assert their grandeur and to vindicate their honour',[42] as though freedom could appear only behind the petrified features of necessity. This is a paradox which the myth of the conspiracy magically makes it possible to resolve by projecting the fiction of a sovereign will behind the anonymous necessity of history. In their very delirium the fanatical ideologues of the conspiracy pay homage to the power of action, to the lost treasure of human freedom.

But only at the cost of a transposition which disfigures, and finally annihilates, the meaning of freedom. They believe that they can find this power of action, which they despair of finding in the political domain on an imaginary scene. What they are seeking, however, on the scene of phantasm is no longer the free agent of action, but an invisible Author, who weaves his intrigues and manoeuvres men according to a secret plan. This allows them to exorcise, by means of the representation of total knowledge and an infallible plan, the indeterminacy of history and of action: 'In this French Revolution, the Abbé Barruel wrote, everything was foreseen, premeditated, constituted, resolved upon, instituted: everything was the effect of the most profound wickedness, since everything was prepared and brought about by men who held alone the threads of the conspiracies which had long been woven in secret societies.'[43] In fact it is an essential characteristic of action that, even if it reveals an agent, a 'hero', a history, it nevertheless remains authorless, without a pre-established model, irreducible to the calculus of means and ends. For Arendt '[t]he real story in which we are engaged as long as we live has no visible or invisible maker because it is not made'.[44] This makes it different from the work, which is conceived and produced by its creator. But this essential demarcation was very quickly erased, at the very beginning of political philosophy, and the reduction of acting to making, of *praxis* to *poiesis*, becomes even more acute in the modern age, with the victory of *homo faber*. Is it certain, however, that the 'Jew' of the Protocols is the distant successor of the Platonic demiurge or of the divine Providence? The Western tradition has continually asserted that God is not the cause of evil, that, if evil is allowed to appear in this world, it is necessarily to further the good, in accordance with the wise calculations of a providential plan. The ambiguity and the mystery of God's will, of his anger and his vengeance, are pushed into the background, concealed by the reassuring image of a supreme Maker who uses evil in the service of the good. The ambivalence of the divine will is therefore split between a focus of love and a focus of hate. Thus faith in the infinite goodness of God brings forth as its opposite the limitless malice of the Prince of Darkness. This opposition turns out to be precarious, since the devil is God's creature, the instrument of his Providence; and above all because the demarcation is strangely lacking in consistency: it threatens to become undecidable, at the extreme point of desolation, evoked by Luther, when 'God wears the mask of the devil, and the devil wears the mask of God'.[45] It is this split, and the phantasm to which it gives rise to belief in the malignant will of a hidden enemy, which we rediscover in the myth of the conspiracy. This distinguishes it from other, worldly versions of providence, in their liberal, Hegelian or Marxist variants. It leaves open the chasm of the Thing, the abyss of hate and abjection which they tend to conceal or to annul. Arendt is mistaken when she affirms that in the modern age the masses have ceased to believe in the devil. In the fable of the conspiracy this belief re-emerges at the point of intersection of delirium and the real. This is enough to set Europe aflame with a new witch hunt.

It is possible, however, that this mythology of the conspiracy, with the sharp demarcations which it establishes, with its rigid splitting of good and evil, of the same and the other, is not adequate to explain the Final Solution. An additional feature may be necessary: the instability of a limit. Arendt may be said to be sensitive to it when she tries to identify the specific characteristic which distinguishes Nazism from the various tendencies of 'everyday racism'. Indeed, she points out that:

> The use of the Protocols was not restricted to the Nazis; hundreds of thousands of copies were sold in postwar Germany, and even their open adoption as a handbook of politics was not new. Nevertheless, this forgery was mainly used for the purpose of denouncing the Jews and arousing the mob to the dangers of Jewish domination. In terms of mere propaganda, the discovery of the Nazis was that the masses were not so frightened by Jewish world rule as they were interested in how it could be done, that the popularity of the Protocols was based on admiration and eagerness to learn rather than on hatred, … It was the motif of a global conspiracy in the Protocols which appealed most to the masses, … The delusion of an already existing Jewish world domination formed the basis for the illusion of future German domination.[46]

This is what Himmler had in mind when he declared that 'we owe the art of government to the Jews, namely, to the Protocols'.[47]

In contrast to traditional anti-Semitism, Nazism is not satisfied with denouncing a fictional Jewish conspiracy. It tries to imitate it, to reconstruct the exact replica of its phantasm in reality. This is why it is organized as a secret society, as an inverted reflection of an imaginary plot. 'Seduction', 'eagerness to learn' and 'admiration' are the terms which Arendt uses to describe this paradoxical logic.[48] But she is mistaken when she affirms that such feelings can temper or eliminate hatred and fear. What the Nazi finds fascinating, in the image of the Jew as 'master of the epoch,' serves only to excite his rage and envy. One need only glance through *Mein Kampf* in order to be convinced of this. It is with one and the same gesture that Hitler vomits his hatred against the 'Jewish plague,' against the parasite, the vampire, the 'slimy and stinking bloodsucker', and at the same time salutes the infinite power of the Jewish people, their 'intellectual faculties developed over thousands of years', its 'limitless tenacity' which has allowed it to 'preserve its race' and the purity of its blood. The Aryan race is for Hitler 'already internally contaminated', 'only one race struggled for long years with an unshakable consistency, and this was the Jewish. The Star of David continued to mount ever higher in the firmament as the will to preserve our own race weakened.'[49] Thus Hitler's delirium raises the Jew to the status of a master and model. He wishes to identify himself with precisely that which he execrates. Only a diabolical intention, according to Kant, could wish evil as evil, and establish it as a universal law.[50] It is indeed possible that this absolute evil will cannot be found in the human being, but the structure of the delirium which we have described comes as close as possible to it, since this delirium assigns the Other to the place of the Devil and identifies itself with this fiction of a demonic will. It is Gnostic, but as an inverted Gnosticism which preaches the imitation of the evil demiurge.

Does this mean that Hitler aspires to 'be Jewish'? This is a fatal misunderstanding which must be avoided. Hitler's 'Jew' is merely a delirious construction which bears no relation to real Jews, until the moment when the delirium bursts in on reality with the acting out of the Final Solution. All the same, is there absolutely no relation between Jewish reality and the 'Jew' of phantasm with whom the Nazi identifies? In order for such an identification to be possible, must it not be supported by a distinctive feature, an effective determination which could be said to constitute the kernel of truth of the delirium? In the representation of the Jew as 'the master of the world', of a people apart, enjoying an exorbitant privilege, one ought perhaps to recognize a deformed echo of the manner in which the Jews have thought of themselves since biblical times – as the Elect People of God. This is how Freud claimed to explain anti-Semitism. Hatred of the Jews could be said to arise from the founding myth of the Jewish people and the 'jealousy' which it arouses in other peoples, to the extent that they believe this myth: 'I venture to assert that jealousy of the people which declared itself first-born, favourite child of God the Father, has not yet been surmounted among other peoples even today: it is as though they had thought there was truth in the claim.'[51] '[I]t was the religion of their primal father to which were attached their hope of reward, of distinction and finally world domination. This last wishful phantasy, long abandoned by the Jewish people, still survives among that people's enemies in the belief in a conspiracy by the "Elders of Zion".'[52] According to Freud, anti-Semitism is a Jewish affair: the imaginary reversal, the recoil of the originary phantasm which cements the unity of the Jewish people. It is this murderous game of mirrors which Freud strives to shatter: by showing precisely that being chosen by God is merely a phantasm, which is based on a denegation, the denial of a founding murder; that the jealousy of the nations is directed at an illusory privilege, a primitive belief which has been 'long abandoned'.[53]

What, we asked, is the 'law' of Hitler? And why does he designate the Jew as his worst enemy? If Freud's hypothesis is correct these two questions require a single answer. Nazi hatred is based on envy. It is focused on the Jew, because it imagines him to be God's favourite, the master and possessor of the Law. In the logic of his delirium the Nazi reveals himself to be a strict monotheist. The Nazi believes in the chosen people of a unique God, in a sovereign place, one and indivisible, access to which ensures undivided enjoyment of the Law. The banality of evil, we have suggested, is not sufficient to account for its radicality. And we wished to elucidate Hitler's decision. It seems that Arendt's thought is no longer of any help here, since it cuts modern anti-Semitism off from its religious roots. Yet Hitler declared the principle of his decision very clearly, and of the mad 'reason' which justified it: 'There cannot be two Chosen People. We are God's people. Does not that fully answer the question?'[54] What dooms the Jewish people to extermination is thus the promise to Abraham, the Election on Sinai which made him the hostage of the Law. It is the mastery of the Law, or rather, of what a Nazi can comprehend of the Law, a Law which reappears in Hitler's discourse as the 'law of race and blood' which 'takes vengeance without mercy when its commandments are broken'.[55] In what sense is this 'law' of Hilter still the Law? Can we say, to use Arendt's terms, that Hitler did not 'simply dismiss' the Law, but that he 'distorted' it:[56] that he nevertheless preserved it and took it over, respected it, through the very process of its deformation? Or is there 'nothing in common' between the Law which forbids murder and the Nazi invocation of the 'law,' in which the term, now reappropriated in blood and soil, legitimates extermination, in which the blustering claim to an authentic law merely covers a hatred of the Law?

The Nazi borrows an objectified law from the discourse of science, which is converted into a law of nature and whose docile servant he wishes to be. He wishes to be the historical agent of its fulfilment. But we know that this biological determinism is merely a surface ideology. In fact, the movement is organized around the fiction of an all-powerful will, capable of controlling the course of history and the laws of life, or, more precisely, of fusing with the superhuman sources from which these laws derive. So that each of the Führer's orders has the value of an unconditioned imperative, his will made the law. By contrast, what characterizes the position of the law in Judaism, and its reworking in Kant's ethics, is the fact that the subject is placed in the position of addressee, that the subject is determined as obliged or held hostage by a prescription whose source remains for ever indeterminate. A law without author or master, which is uttered in an empty place, is inaccessible to a finite subject. The pure practical imperative, which 'gives us nothing to see', assures us of no theoretical knowledge, no power, no enjoyment; which demands nothing but our respectful listening, the obedience of the being who is obliged; his abandonment of self.[57] This empty place of the Other is that of the dead father, whose withdrawal is marked by the Law. Freud taught us to recognize, in the murder of the father, the primordial event which inaugurates the symbolic debt binding each subject to the Law. According to him, the myth of Election which constitutes Jewish identity is organized around a blind spot, the denial of this primitive murder, repeated in the murder of Moses by his people. It is in this way that the deepest motive of Western anti-Semitism can be explained, the accusation of having killed God. The following would be the full text of this accusation: 'You [the Jews] will not *admit* that you murdered God (the primal picture of God, the primal father, and his later incarnations). There should be an addition declaring, "We did the same thing, but we *admitted* it, and since then we have been absolved."'[58] In refusing to admit to the founding murder, the Jewish position escapes the phantasm of its expiation. In this respect it avoids giving way to the illusion of a sacrificial redemption which would claim to cancel the debt and abrogate the Law.[59] Such would be the ultimate meaning of the Election of Israel: it would entrust to Israel the safekeeping of the debt, the memory of what has been forgotten. The Election signifies that there is no chosen people, if by that is understood a kind of 'superior race' enjoying a supernatural privilege. We should reject any confusion of the Election with its imaginary inversion, the narcissistic self-consciousness of the Jewish people, which is perhaps merely a way of bearing the burden of Election.

We are now in a better position to grasp the 'distortion' which is at work in Hitler's delirium. Taking the 'Jew' for a model, it projects on to him its own representation of the Law. It is in fact the totality of symbolic determinations of the Law and the Other, of Election, of murder and of debt, which is discarded: rejected, but also reinstated through a displacement. It is retranscribed into another register, into a new language, which retains nothing of its initial meaning. It is exiled within a strange horizon where its truth is lost. The place of the Other, which is always empty, becomes a place which could be occupied, delivered up to the conquering will of a Subject. Its withdrawal will thus be interpreted as the sign that this place is already occupied by a usurping rival. The vacancy of the Other, the indeterminacy of a Law which gives nothing to be seen, become so many indicators of the fact that this all-powerful rival is enjoying his mastery behind the protective screen of secret societies: in a place which is both withdrawn and accessible, the source of a total knowledge and a limitless power. From now on, this delirious desire to possess the Law will find the trace of the invisible enemy everywhere as its target. Time and again it will run up against this obscene and ferocious figure that is never anything other than an imaginary projection, than the truth of its own phantasm, foreclosed and rejected into the Other. The mediation of the Law, with the sharing-out or pact which it sanctions, is missing from this duel to the death: With the Jew, Hitler proclaimed, one cannot make agreements, but only decide: all or nothing, and there will be only one winner. What is lacking here is the possibility of accepting the murder of the father, as it appears, always denied or displaced, in the Sacrifice of Abraham or the Passion of Christ; of facing the ordeal which, beyond the image of the threatening rival, would give access to the Law and the debt. This is the gaping chasm of an impossible representation, which allows murder to be unleashed in the real. In the economy of his delirium the Nazi admits to no debt. By contrast with its Judaic denial, or its Christian *Aufhebung*, the founding murder here 'always remains to be accomplished'.[60] It is tirelessly repeated, since it remains without effect for him, as if it had never taken place. The exterminating machine goes out of control, since it is running wildly, disconnectedly, relentlessly repeating the same unrepresentable crime. It is not on jealousy that this hatred feeds, as Freud thought: for this presupposes a ternary structure – the jealousy of the brothers towards the favourite son of the father, or the jealousy of the Eternal One, who forbids his people to adore other gods. In this deadly confrontation it is a question of envy, of envious hatred, projected on to an evil double, as on to a mirror.[61] It is no longer a matter of representing oneself as the Lord's Elect, given a special task by the Other and submitted to his law, but of setting oneself up as a god in the place of God. For 'the good Lord is Jewish': in this cry of Louis-Ferdinand Céline's the ultimate meaning of Nazism is perhaps revealed, as metaphysical revolt, as hatred of God and the Law.

This revolt is metaphysical in the strict sense that it is grounded in a sovereign subject, which establishes itself as the supreme measure at the heart of beings. Nazism is a sinister offshoot of the metaphysics of the Subject, which annihilates every trace of humanity. It is without doubt an inheritor of our modernity. In its will to eliminate all modernity's achievements – democracy, Enlightenment, human rights – and to return to the myths of the primitive horde, the savagery of the 'blond beast', the Nazi reaction against modernity is deployed on the basis of modernity and on the revolution which inaugurates it. 'After democracy and against it,' this is how Claude Lefort's work has taught us to think of totalitarianism: as the negation and as the 'extension' of modern democracy, as an 'adverse power which it bears within itself' and which actualizes representations which it already contained potentially.[62] In order for the ideology of the conspiracy to emerge, it was necessary for the image of the Evil One to accompany the images of the divine in their rescendence and in their decline. It was necessary for it to encounter the representation of an unstable power, which is divided and limited, always in search of its own legitimation, and whose precariousness gives rise to the illusion that true Power is elsewhere, almighty but hidden. The Law, now delivered from its anchoring in the body of the king or the will of God, had to be exposed to the risk of its emptiness, its inconsistency, to this indeterminacy which totalitarianism claims to exorcise by reincarnating the law in the inflexible will of a Subject. It is the extent of these displacements, of these ruptures, which are constitutive of modernity, which Freud overlooks. Written as his testament, in the face of the menacing pressure of the 'new enemy', his *Moses* is undoubtedly aimed at the foundations of Nazi anti-Semitism. But Freud perceives in it, apparently, nothing more than a resurgence of traditional Western anti-Semitism. The strategy which he outlines consists, as we know, in a deconstruction of what it is in the founding myth of the Jewish people which gives rise to the jealousy of nations. He does not grasp – could he have done so in 1938? – that the classical schemas are no longer any use, that, in Nazism, one is no longer dealing with Oedipal jealousy, but with a primary envy, provoked by a peculiar delirium, structured like a psychosis. It seems that Freud has difficulty grasping what separates modern anti-Semitism from its primitive religious roots. For him, it is always the ancient phantasy of world domination, which he attributes to the Jews, which 'survives among that people's enemies' when the latter continue to believe 'in the conspiracy of the "Elders of Zion"' as if one and the same illusion had persisted, unchanged, for thousands of years.[63] Thus he has no hesitation in identifying the Election of Israel with its delirious reinterpretation in the anti-Semitic mythology of the conspiracy. The latter thus appears as a mere reaction to Jewish narcissism, its symmetrical and complicit reflection. Thus Freud makes a double mistake: concerning the symbolic significance of Election – which, in the Bible, does not imply any promise of 'world domination' – and concerning the historical significance of Nazi anti-Semitism, the kernel of which is a modern myth, which has developed only since the French revolution. The lack of a sense of history, which characterizes Freud's work, as it does that of the majority of his successors, leads him to erase the discontinuity of epochs, the difference of times. We have identified the opposite tendency in Arendt. In her effort to define the specificity of modern anti-Semitism, she ended up separating it entirely from its theological foundations. In both cases, it is the double movement of rescendence which is hidden: both what it deforms and what, at the same time, it preserves of an old configuration, by translating it in another level.

Arendt's approach at least preserves her from any position of timeless survey. This permits her, at times, to come nearer to the enigma of rescendence. In *The Origins of Totalitarianism* she wondered how the imaginary international conspiracy which was first attributed to the Jesuits or the Freemasons came to be attributed, at a later date, to the Jews. In considering narcissistic racism as a consequence of the old religious concept of election Arendt seems to converge with Freud's position. However, rather than making it a timeless feature of the Jewish condition, she understands it as the denaturing of religious beliefs, which were formerly authentic, into superstitions. It is the 'laicization of the Jews' which deformed the idea of election and gave rise to this incredible illusion, shared both by non-believing Jews and by non-Jews, according to which the Jewish people were naturally more intelligent, better, more healthy, and better equipped to survive: the motor of history and the salt of the earth.[64] This is degradation similar to that undergone by the belief in hell: the trace of a mutilated election, deprived of its messianic dimension, reduced to the sordid claim of 'believing on self chosen, without believing in him who chooses'.[65] Thus the attention which she pays to the emergence of the new in history enables Arendt to avoid overlooking the symbolic dimension of the Promise, collapsing it into its narcissistic inversion. It also helps her to unlock the paradox of contemporary anti-Semitism, to understand why 'it became most extreme at the very moment when the Jews had lost their public functions and influence'.[66] The work of Tocqueville provides us with the key. He perceives in the demand for equality the most powerful driving force of our modern societies; he discovered the peril which overshadows the Democratic Age:

> The great challenge to the modern period, and its peculiar danger, has been that in it man for the first time confronted man without the protection of differing circumstances and conditions. And it has been precisely this new concept of equality that has made modern race relations so difficult, ... It is because equality demands that I recognize each and every individual as my equal, that the conflicts between different groups, which for reasons of their own are reluctant to grant each other this basic equality, take on such terrible cruel forms. Hence the more equal the Jewish condition, the more surprising were Jewish differences.[67]

Arendt is suggesting here that, in a world where long-standing differences of condition and status are being effaced, it is the last difference which survives: the discrimination of 'races', which has to bear the whole weight of a lost alterity and to carry the burden of hatred which is attached to it. It seems possible to push this analysis one stage further. One could say that hatred increases even more as the wavering of this limit, the imminent disappearance of the final index of alterity, is sensed. Just as, according to Tocqueville, the aristocrats were never so unanimously detested as on the eve of the loss of their privileges, so anti-Semitism becomes more intense when directed against Jewish communities which are in the process of being assimilated entirely.

This is doubtless because such a situation intensifies anxiety in the face of the indeterminacy, because it reinforces the belief in an omnipresent enemy who is all the more disturbing in that he can no longer be distinguished. The rescendence of the divine goes together with this delimitation, this movement of reduction of alterity which erases or de-marks distinctions and points of references, thus condemning them to delimit themselves again, to re-mark themselves violently in the real. Since the Great Confinement of the insane, the history of our modernity is punctuated by these mad attempts to circumscribe difference in the other, to hollow out once more the gap which is closing, to expel a menace which re-emerges within. This logic of delimitation was surely at work in the French revolution, when the decree of Prairial, extending without limit the notion of 'suspect', tended to dissolve any criterion of political judgement, thereby constituting the Terror as the sole authority capable of designating the enemy, of producing in a social domain without landmarks the mark of an absolute distinction.[68] Can we not perceive in the Nazi terror the last offshoot of this history, which pushes its logic to the limit and completes it?

I do not think so. What such logic can explain is the ghetto, not Auschwitz: enclosure and expulsion, not extermination; at most, 'limited' massacres, auto-da-fés or pogroms, but not the Final Solution. The anxiety provoked by the elision of differences, the aggression aroused by the absorption of otherness, are not enough. The problematic of Tocqueville, adopted by Arendt, reaches its limit here. For the emergence of the implacable determination to annihilate a whole people without remainder, to the last of its members, a far more profound hatred, a more radical panic is required. The alterity being absorbed must already be the focus of all hatred and all envy. A delirious projection must already have set it up as a pole of abjection, as the grimace of the Thing which it struggles to keep at a distance. It is this defence which collapses, the last bulwark against horror, when such a projection fails. It is this doubling that is delimited, that returns to the Same. Only at this point anxiety turns into panic as the subject discovers itself, in Hitler's words, 'already inwardly contaminated' by the Thing – as close as possible to its double, almost identical with it, dispossessed of itself by this evil other which it is. This forces it to traverse a point of extreme desolation where the limits of the subject and of the object tremble, where God and the Devil exchange masks, undecidably. If it were here simply a matter of the evening out of differences, it would doubtless be enough to re-mark the old landmarks: to forbid all cross-breeding, to enforce the wearing of a distinctive sign, to exile or enclose. This cannot be enough when this other who is delimited is already the infamous, the malignant double which infects everything and proliferates everywhere, and whose very existence represents the threat of a chaos into which all identity dissolves. At this point its least trace is unbearable and must be annihilated.

The historical dynamic of rescendence and delimitation is not adequate on its own to render the Final Solution comprehensible. Other analyses are required, which would take into account the structure of unconscious phantasm, the logic of foreclosure, of abjection implied by the Nazi delirium. Perhaps even this is insufficient. If this delirium is underpinned by panic and hatred, it immediately reinscribes them into another register, into the density of a carnal dimension. It is no accident that *Mein Kampf* draws upon the most archaic images of the parasite, of the vampire, of cancer, of gangrene, if it attributes 'a frightful poisoning of the body of our people by syphilis' to the 'Judaization of life'.[69] When the frontiers of the proper and the improper, of the Same and the Other, are erased, these collapsing divisions can maintain themselves only by being embodied, by cutting the very flesh into an inside and an outside, into one's own body and the alien body. In so far as totalitarianism represents the social in accordance with the image of a body, in so far as it aims to 'remake a body' in a society condemned to an irreversible disincorporation, this can be only – as Lefort's work has shown – a monstrous body, in which 'the attraction of the whole is no longer distinct from that of fragmentation'.[70] The only thing which holds this threatened, unstable body together, which is always on the point of disintegration, the only thing which holds it back on the brink of chaos and death, is hatred. The hatred, which is older than love, according to Freud, as old perhaps as flesh itself, as this panic of origins from which emerges the precarious unity of a body. The same terms which Céline projected on to 'the Jew' describe the Nazi image of the body, the flesh of the Nazi phantasm: 'It has only one authentic thing in the depths of its excremental substance, and this is its hatred for us, its contempt, its furious desire to make us sink deeper and deeper into the sewer.'[71]

The failure of Arendt's thought, of her phenomenology of action, is to have missed the dimension of unconscious phantasm and, what is more, not to have been able to approach the invisible horizons of the flesh: this flesh which, for each subject, bears the promise of his birth to the world and to others, but also retains the traces of a primordial panic, of the hatred which is always ready to unleash itself again on the world. In a certain sense, nothing could be more banal. Nothing could be more common than these birthmarks, than these bruised traces, deposited in the flesh of each one of us by dead-ends and dramas of our genesis. Is this banality, which is the sign of our finitude, at the basis of what Arendt terms 'the fearsome, word-and-thought-defying *banality of evil*'?[72] Can the radicality of evil implied by the totalitarian decision be simply reduced to that banality?

We have tried to describe this evil decision: as a counter-blow which, at the blackest moment of desolation, demarcates itself and cuts into the indecidable – which decides for evil and hatred, which decides to project all the wrong, all the abjection of its flesh, into the Other. To reject this Other, which it also is, to annihilate it without a trace. The instant of decision is always madness. In this instant something was lacking; a mark, an appeal must have been lacking, thereby abandoning the decision to itself, to its own infernal essence. 'Banality', as we have indicated, comes from the same root as 'abandon.' A mill was said to be 'banal' when its use was conceded to the community, abandoned to all by the sovereign. *Banality* is the condition of man who has been forsaken, *banished.* Man is he who asks, 'Why hast thou forsaken me?' The affliction of our century is that we are not even able to ask this question, that we no longer even know from what land we have been banished, that we can no longer even name what has abandoned us. This delivers us without appeal to banality, to 'the fearsome, word-and-thought-defying *banality of evil*',[73] to the desolation which Hannah Arendt has taught us to think.

Notes

1 This is a newly edited version of 'L'enfer sur la terre. Hannah Arendt devant Hitler', *Revue des sciences humaines*, 213, 1989, pp. 183–206, trans. Peter Dews as 'Hell on Earth. Hannah Arendt in the Face of Hitler', *Philosophy Today*, 37, 1993, pp. 257–74.
2 Karl Kraus, *Die Dritte Walpurgisnacht*, Frankfurt am Main: Suhrkamp, 1989, s. 12.
3 Hannah Arendt, *The Origins of Totalitarianism*, New York: Harcourt, 1973, p. xl.
4 Ibid., p. viii.
5 Ibid., p. 441.
6 Ibid., p. 443.
7 Ibid., p. 460.
8 Ibid., p. 444.
9 Ibid., p. 445.
10 Hannah Arendt, 'The crisis in culture: its social and its political significance', in *Between Past and Future*, New York: Penguin, 1993.
11 It seems that the majority of the criticisms which Lefort addresses to Arendt – rigid opposition between the political and the social, misunderstanding of human rights and of democracy – indicate, more or less directly, the overlooking of the symbolic dimension. Claude Lefort, 'Hannah Arendt et la question du politique', in *Essais sur le politique XIXe–XXe siècles*, Paris: Seuil, 2001.
12 Cf. Arendt, *The Origins of Totalitarianism*, pp. 3–120.
13 Ibid., pp. 446–7.
14 Ibid., p. 446.
15 Ibid., pp. 446–7.
16 Ibid., p. 461.
17 Ibid., p. 462.
18 Hannah Arendt, *Eichmann in Jerusalem. A Report on the Banality of Evil*, New York: Penguin, 1994, p. 135.
19 Ibid., p. 135–6.
20 Ibid., p. 136.
21 Ibid., p. 136.
22 Ibid., p. 136.
23 Ibid., p. 136.
24 Ibid., p. 137.
25 Arendt, *The Origins of Totalitarianism*, p. 459.
26 Immanuel Kant, *Religion within Boundaries of pure Reason*, in *The Works of Immanuel Kant, Religion and Rational Theology*, trans. George di Giovanni, Cambridge: Cambridge University Press, 2005, p. 82.
27 Arendt, *Eichmann in Jerusalem*, p. 288.
28 Ibid., p. 26.
29 Ibid., 287.
30 Ibid., p. 287, p. 49.
31 Arendt, *The Origins of Totalitarianism*, p. 459.
32 Ibid., p. 459.
33 Although she was, at one point at least, very close to, recognizing it: in the crucial – and highly aporetic – passage on pardon and promise which concludes her analysis of action in *The Human Condition:* 'This is the true hallmark of those offences which, since Kant, we call "radical evil" … All we know is that we can neither punish nor forgive such offences … Here, where the deed itself dispossesses us of all power, we can indeed only repeat with Jesus: "It is better for him that a millstone were hanged about his neck, and he cast into the sea."'

Hannah Arendt, *The Human Condition*, Chicago: University of Chicago Press, 1958, p. 241.

34 In relation to this definition Arendt refers to Alexandre Koyré's 'The Political Function of the Modern Lie', published in 1945 in *Contemporary Jewish Record*; Arendt, *Eichmann in Jerusalem*, p. 376.

35 Arendt, *The Origins of Totalitarianism*, p. 435.

36 Ibid., p. 435.

37 Ibid., p. 358. This is why Goebbels could proclaim that 'the nations that have been the first to see through the Jew and have been first to fight him are going to take his place in the domination of the world'. Ibid., p. 360.

38 Ibid., p. 360.

39 Ibid., p. 360.

40 Ibid., p. 359. See also the notes, where Arendt refers to pamphlets against the Jesuits (the *Monita secreta* of 1612) and the Freemasons. Ibid., p. 359. Cf. also the documents assembled by L. Poliakov in *La Causalité diabolique*, Paris: Calmann-Lévy, 1980.

41 Cf. Hannah Arendt, *On Revolution*, New York: Viking Press, 1963.

42 Ibid., p. 49. In this book Arendt attempts to show that this triumph of necessity is not a tendency inherent in revolution as such, as the example of the American revolution shows.

43 Cited by S. Hutin, *Les Francs-maçons*, Paris: Seuil, 1961, pp. 10–11. As is well known, Barruel's *Memoires pour servir à l'étude du jacobinisme* (1798–99) are the first attempt to 'explain' the revolution as a 'Masonic plot'.

44 Arendt, *The Human Condition*, p. 186.

45 Martin Luther, 'Commentary of St Paul's Epistle to the Galatians', in *Works* XLVII, trans. T. C. Graebner, Philadelphia, PA: Fortress Press, 1955, p. 43.

46 Arendt, *The Origins of Totalitarianism*, pp. 358–60.

47 Ibid., p. 360.

48 Ibid., p. 358.

49 Adolf Hitler, *Mein Kampf*, Band 1 & 2, Franz Eher Nachf. 1925/26. In his interviews with Rauchning, Hitler frequently emphasizes this 'fraternal' rivalry with the Jew: 'Has it not struck you how the Jew is the exact opposite of the German in every single respect, and yet is as closely akin to him as a blood brother?' Hermann Rauchning, *The Voice of Destruction. Conversations with Hitler*, New York: Putnam, 1940, p. 238.

50 Kant, *Religion within Boundaries of pure Reason*, p. 82.

51 Sigmund Freud, *Moses and Monotheism. Three Essays. The Standard Edition of the Complete Psychological Works of Sigmund Freud*, XXIII, trans. James Strachey, London: Hogarth Press, 1964, p. 91.

52 Freud, *Moses and Monotheism*, p. 85.

53 Ibid.

54 Rauchning, *The Voice of Destruction*, p. 241.

55 Hitler, *Mein Kampf.*

56 Arendt, *Eichmann in Jerusalem*, p. 136.

57 Cf. Jean-François Lyotard, *Le Différend*, Paris: Minuit, 1983, pp. 159–86.

58 Freud, *Moses and Monotheism*, p. 90. We have based our argument here on the interpretation proposed by Jean-François Lyotard in his *Heidegger et les 'Juifs'*, Paris: Galilée, 1988.

59 It is possible that the Christian position in relation to the Law cannot be reduced to this 'phantasm of expiation'. But that would require further analysis.

60 Guy Rosolato, *Essais sur le symbolique*, Paris: Gallimard, 1964, pp. 92–3, 360–1 (which refers to Lacan's theory of psychosis).

61 The distinction between envy and jealousy, see Melanie Klein, *Envie et gratitude*, Paris: Gallimard, 1968, p. 18.
62 Cf. Claude Lefort, *L'Invention démocratique*, Paris: Fayard, 1981, pp. 41, 144, 170–5.
63 Freud, *Moses and Monotheism*, p. 85.
64 Ibid., p. 166.
65 Ibid., p. 164.
66 Arendt, *The Origins of Totalitarianism*, p. 4. This interpretation has been challenged by Claude Lefort in his 'Hannah Arendt et le totalitarisme', in *L'Allemagne nazie et le génocide*, Paris: Gallimard/Seuil, 1985, pp. 517–35.
67 Arendt, *The Origins of Totalitarianism*, pp. 54–55.
68 Cf. Claude Lefort, 'La Terreur révolutionaire', in *Essais sur le politique XIXe–XXe siècles*, Paris: Seuil, 2001, pp. 75–109.
69 Cf. the proclamations of Hitler cited and analysed by Wilhelm Reich, *Psychologie de masse du fascisme*, trans. Pierre Kamnitzer, Paris: Payot, 1977, pp. 90–2.
70 Lefort, *L'Invention démocratique*, p. 175.
71 Louis-Ferdinand Céline, *Les Beaux Draps*, cited by Julia Kristeva, *Pouvoirs de l'horreur*, Paris: Seuil, 1980, p. 218.
72 Arendt, *Eichmann in Jerusalem*, p. 252.
73 Ibid., 252.

Chapter 8

Total evil

The law under totalitarianism

Ari Hirvonen

Jurists at Nuremberg

'The dagger of the assassin was concealed beneath the rope of the jurist,' the Nuremberg Military Tribunal stated in its opinion in the so-called Justice Case (United States of America v. Altstoetter et al.), which took place during 1947. The defendants, who had served as officials of the Reich Ministry of Justice, judges and prosecutors of the Special Courts and People's Courts in National Socialist Germany, were charged with participation in a conspiracy to commit war crimes and crimes against humanity, of committing these crimes and of membership in a criminal organization, like the SS, SD and the Leadership Corps of the NSDAP.[1] The prosecutor Telford Taylor argued that the case was unusual in that the defendants, who were the embodiment of what passed for justice in the Third Reich, 'engaged in an unholy masquerade of brutish tyranny disguised as justice … distorted, perverted, and finally accomplished the complete overthrow of justice and law in Germany'.[2]

In the opening statement for all the defendants, the defence counsel Egon Kubuschok's main point was that no new legal system was created during National Socialism. German law was codified law, which in itself demanded observance of legal standards. According to legal positivism, which occupied a very important position in German legal thinking, only 'the written law (statutory law) and not general ideas on morals and rights constituted the directive for administration of law and justice'.[3] Moreover, Ministry of Justice and judiciary sought to defend the concept of constitutional state and independence of the judiciary from interventions by Himmler's powerful police forces.

All the defendants pleaded not guilty. The highest official on trial, Franz Schlegelberger, Acting Reich Minister of Justice, pleaded, 'I was never fooled or influenced by Hitler's demoniacal qualities, and I saved my own conscience,' and 'I was out to fight for justice and against arbitrariness.'[4] He was 'a man whose life was devoted to the law', but who understood 'how certain sacrifices had to be made to this storm of power in order to prevent it from triumphing completely'.[5] He remained at his post to prevent something worse, but when he realized on 20 August 1942 that he had to build up a National Socialist administration of justice, he resigned.

The same excuses were repeated again and again: 'I was a German judge. I followed the laws of my country and my knowledge and my conscience in passing judgment' (Nebelung).[6] 'I served my country … in faithfulness, with a pure heart, and without malice. … Nobody in our position at that time could be of the opinion that the State which we served could be accused of being altogether illegal … I applied the laws of my country in the manner in which they were intended, to the best of my conscience and belief' (Rothaug).[7] 'I always acted in the belief and in the conviction that I was doing right, by obeying the law to which I was subjected and applying it in the manner in which my conscience told me to' (Oeschey).[8] '[T]he obedience to the law and the norm created by the State has been the only task of the jurist. … What legal and factual opportunities were open to me I used in favour of justice … To revoke laws and norms which have existed for years was not in my competence' (Klemm).[9] 'These proceedings … prove that I always only served law and justice' (Altstoetter).[10] 'I decided with all my energy to influence the development of National Socialism in the sphere of justice' (Rothenberger).[11] 'Only a judge who is a saint is free of errors' (Cuhorst).[12]

According to the Tribunal, the acts of defendants involved 'an element of evil to the State which is not found in frank atrocities which do not sully judicial robes'. Most of them were convicted.[13]

Law is law – a diabolical principle?

One of the most important German legal philosophers, Gustav Radbruch, who had been Social Democrat Minister of Justice during the Weimar Republic and who was stripped of his professorship in 1933, wrote immediately after the war that for a lawyer the principle in the Third Reich was: a law is a law (*Gesetz ist Gesetz*). A positive law (*Gesetz*) was valid since it was a law, and it was a law since it was enacted in correct procedure and secured by state power. This reflected the doctrine of legal positivism which had held sway over German jurists. Therefore, he concluded, legal positivism had rendered lawyers defenceless in the face of the criminal content of laws in the National Socialist legal order.[14] (I translate *Gesetz* as 'a law' or 'laws' referring to particular laws and degrees, and *Recht* as 'the law', referring to the law as the general phenomenon or idea of law or as a legal system.)

Radbruch's observations were followed by a stream of texts that demonized legal positivism. Because of this positivistic orientation jurists were considered to have been unconditionally loyal and devoted to statutory laws. They adhered to the will of the lawgiver, considered that the only criterion for legal validity was that legal norms were enacted in a formally correct way, and then interpreted these norms objectively. Moral and political considerations were excluded from legal thinking and legal practice as extra-legal elements. Hence judges were not allowed to use any moral criteria with which they could evaluate the legitimacy of formally valid laws.[15]

But was there any legal system in the Third Reich?[16] Franz Neumann denied this in his famous *Behemoth*.[17] However, National Socialists did not deny that the state must be based on a certain respect for the law.[18] Germans had prided themselves, and continued to do so in the National Socialist period, that their state was a state based on the rule of law. Hitler's dictatorship 'imposed its rule to a large degree through properly issued laws and administrative degrees'.[19]

We can distinguish three legal phases that lead to the Holocaust. First, the Enabling Act (Law for Removing the Distress of the *Volk* and the Reich) was passed in the Reichstag on 23 March 1933. This 'temporary Constitutional law [*Verfassungsgesetz*] of the new Germany',[20] as Carl Schmitt called it, made the legislative powers of the Reichstag obsolete by giving legislative powers, even the right to make constitutional changes, to the Reich Cabinet, practically to the Reich Chancellor.[21] This law, together with the Emergency Decree for the Protection of *Volk* and State that the Reich President Hindenburg gave on 28 February 1933, which suspended personal basic rights, and a law passed on 1 August 1934, which united the offices of the Reich President and the Reich Chancellor in Hitler's person upon the death of Hindenburg that followed the next day, formed the constitution of the Third Reich. Hitler had become the supreme legislator, administrator and judge. Second, this legal revolution was followed by discriminatory legislation and directives against Jews and also against political opponents and racial minorities – the aim of which was to persecute, humiliate, disenfranchise and finally exclude from the *Volksgemeinschaft*, the German national community, Jews and other targeted groups.[22] Jews were legally deprived of their position as citizens and legal subjects. They were positioned between two deaths: the civil death (legal incompetence and lack of rights) and the physical death. Third, when it comes to the mass-murder operations and genocide there are no promulgated and published laws. However, the euthanasia programme, the establishment of *Einsatzgruppen*, first in Poland and then in Soviet Union, to murder 'the Jewish-Bolshevik intelligentsia', and finally the launching of the Final Solution, were all based, beyond any reasonable doubt, on the will and order of Hitler, which had the force of law in the Third Reich. The law was therefore a necessary instrument of the Holocaust, which was a legal, bureaucratico-governmental economico-technological event: 'It occurred within the German legal system' and evil was 'perpetrated through the rule of law'.[23]

The National Socialist idea of law

Even if the German jurist respected law and order, was loyal to authority and cherished legality, legal positivism and formalism were seen as 'a manifestation of the spiritual foreign infiltration' of liberalism.[24] The more materialist-technical liberalism increased, the more legal positivism dominated.[25] According to Schmitt, 'this positivism of the legal rule has until now been known to pass itself off as *the* juristic method'.[26] Schmitt said that legal positivism 'identifies statutory governing with *Recht*; it recognizes … instead of *Recht*, only normative fixed legality'.[27] It rejects everything '"extra-legal", all *Recht* not created through human statutes', which leads to '*Recht* thinking becoming legality thinking'.[28] In Schmitt's words, 'the age of juristic positivism has ended'. Because of general clauses, indeterminate concepts, the leadership principle and references to extra-legal criteria, there is 'a renunciation of the foundation of positivism, namely the detached lawgiving decision embodied in the norming'.[29]

One can trace two directions in the development of the law and legal thinking under National Socialism: on the one hand, the destruction of both the democratic-liberal idea of the law and the doctrine of value-neutral positivism, and, on the other hand, the construction of a radically new idea of the law, a *völkisch* renewal of the law based on the National Socialist world view.[30] Ernst Forsthoff announced that 'with the National Socialist revolution the German *Volk* entered the twentieth century'.[31] In the legal revolution of National Socialism, Helmut Nicolai declared, 'the spirit of the state and the law was totally changed'.[32] 'National Socialism has made in Germany a new, specifically German idea of the law [*Rechtsidee*] valid' and this began 'a new historical epoch', Karl Larenz emphasized.[33] Karl Michaelis added that German legal science (*Rechtswissenschaft*), which had to free itself from old abstract legal concepts and foreign methods, was 'not at the end, but in the front line of a new beginning'.[34] For Erik Wolf 'the essential of the renewal of the law cannot take place through the reform of laws but through the formation of a new type of German jurist as a true man of the law'.[35] Schmitt spoke of a new concept, not only of the law, but also of the German jurist.[36] 'The victory of the National Socialist movement had also awoken the German jurist to self-knowledge.'[37] For Schmitt, Hans Frank, the head of the National Socialist Jurists Association (BNSDJ), was 'the Führer of our German legal front line, the protagonist for our good German law, the model of the National Socialist German jurist. Heil!'[38]

To understand how these new types of jurists understood the idea of law and their role as jurists, I will map legal thinking under National Socialism. I will concentrate on legal thinking during the first years of National Socialism, the time legal scholars were enthusiastically participating in the revolutionary renewal of the idea of the law (*Rechtserneuerung*).[39] Even if the dogma and method of National Socialist jurisprudence, or legal philosophy and theory, did not exist, even if there were constant conflicts concerning the revolutionary renewal of the law and the state, there were shared juridical, constitutional, philosophical and political ideas and concerns.[40] I will bring forth these in relation to discourses on the topics of the state, the Führer, the *Volk* and the judiciary.

The state

Nicolai argued that after the revolution the new state leadership had the task of giving, instead of the democratic parliamentary form of the state of the Weimar, 'a new, National Socialist form of the state' to the German *Reich*.[41]

In a speech on 13 November 1934 Hermann Göring spoke about legal security being the ground of the new *Volksgemeinschaft*.[42] Otto Koellreutter was sure that 'the eternal value of *Rechtsstaat*', which would reconcile the tension between political and legal values, was guaranteed under National Socialism.[43] The German national revolution, which had 'a real revolutionary character', had changed 'the bourgeois liberal *Rechtsstaat* into a national *Rechtsstaat*', into 'a Führer and authority state'.[44] It is a 'wilful political form of living order of the people' and it recognizes 'the sanctity of the law', but 'the determining value of the law is in the legal form and safeguarding of the national living order'.[45] Referring to Ernst Jünger, Koellreutter defined it as 'the state of workers', whose figure plays a crucial role in the National Socialist idea of state.[46]

For Schmitt, Koellreutter's concept of a national *Rechtsstaat* was still connected with liberalism and a neutral and plural state. *Rechtsstaat* represented un-German liberal ideas of the law and the state, liberal constitutional dualism, the separation of powers, and individual freedom, which had turned the law and justice into the net of positivistic norms as it withdrew from both religion and ethics.[47] Schmitt emphasized that 'the National Socialist state is a just state [*gerechter Staat*]'.[48] Even if he was not in favour of the concept of *Rechtsstaat*, he accepted its use, since what was decisive was what specific content one gave to this ambiguous word.[49] Therefore, he turned to a definition provided by Frank, namely 'the German *Rechtsstaat* of Adolf Hitler'.[50] Moreover, the state under National Socialism was for Schmitt a tool of *völkisch* strength and unity.[51]

Hans Helfritz reminded that the concept *Rechsstaat* was not a problem as long as one kept in mind that '*Rechtsstaat*' and 'liberal state' are not the same.[52] Also Gustav Adolf Walz said that 'the "legal" National Socialist revolution' led to an anti-liberal state, to 'a *völkischer Führerstaat*'.[53]

For Forsthoff, the all-encompassing 'total state is … an answer against the liberal state', but it was not merely against former models of the state, since it 'has its own form, which has no immediate historical models'.[54] The National Socialist will for reform aimed at 'the establishment and affirmation of the authoritative order [*Herrschaftsordnung*] and the rehabilitation of the people's order [*Volksordnung*]', both of which had been 'victims of bourgeois society'.[55] The order of domination had a dual structure. It included, on the one hand, the dynamic leadership and personal rule ('the leadership order of the National Socialist state is the leadership order of the National Socialist Movement') and, on the other hand, the bureaucratic administration, which operated predictably and according to statutes and rules.[56] The *Volksordnung* was a racially and spiritually homogeneous community, which was basically a pre-political order. On the other hand, it is not a non-political fact, and therefore it needs the authoritative order, which must be based on the living conditions of the *Volksordnung*.

Georg Dahm remarked that the total state did not mean, using Jünger's phrase, 'total mobilization' through the omnipotence and totality of the state but through the community and the unity of conviction and world view.[57] For Nicolai, the concept of totality meant the negation of the dualism of the people and the state, making the private and public person the same, and the abrogation of parliament, parties and basic rights. The state had no limits in regulating human lives by laws or acts. Instead of basic rights, the state had the duty to preserve the law of the people. That was 'the only basic right of the citizen'.[58] If the 1789 revolution was about freedom of the person, the 'national revolution' was about combining individual freedom and social duty and 'subordinating the individual to the whole'. Its task was to create 'the national law of the future'.[59]

For Wolf, the claim of the National Socialist state captured the temporal existence (*Dasein*) of man in an extensive way. Neither historical tradition nor basic and human rights demarcated its limits.[60] Forsthoff also saw that in the total state duties were emphasized rather than abstract and formal liberal freedoms: 'The total state must be the state of total responsibility': both in private and in public life everyone was responsible for the fate of the nation.[61] Therefore, Heinrich Lange wrote, 'duty came to the fore instead of rights. The *Volk* is above the individual.'[62]

The Führer

'An authoritarian state leadership means: at the apex of the state is the Führer, whose spirit and will command the being of the state.'[63] 'The new state is a *Führerstaat*, in as much as government and legislation are combined in one hand', that is, the Reich Chancellor, who is the Führer of the Reich, the *Volk*, and the political followers of the NSDAP.[64] The foundations of the order of the *Volk* were 'the German *Volk* with its Führer as the head of the state and supreme judge of the nation; the order of the National Socialist movement as the protector of the constitution, the German *Wehrmacht*, with the Führer as the supreme commander'.[65]

'One could say, "Hegel died"' on 30 January 1933 as Hitler became the Reich Chancellor, Schmitt declared, as on that day the nineteenth-century Hegelian administrative state came to an end, even though, he quickly added, it did not mean that the work of that German political philosopher had lost its significance or that the idea of political leadership transcending the egoism of social interests had been abandoned: 'What in Hegel's powerful spiritual construction is perennially great and German continues to be influential in a new form.'[66] From the Hegelian state Schmitt turned toward the Führer and the *Volk*. 'Today the political cannot be defined from the perspective of the state; instead the state must be defined from the perspective of the political.'[67] The political unity of the new state was a triadic structure of state, movement and *Volk*, which might be used both to express this political unity and specific sides of it: 'the state in the narrower sense as the political-static part, the movement as the political-dynamic element and the *Volk* as the unpolitical side, thriving under the protection and shade of political decisions'.[68] This unity, which overcomes the liberal democratic order's dualist system of state and *Volk*, government and *Volk*, citizen and civil servant, and state and party, is established through the fact that the movement pierces and leads the state and the *Volk*. Thus Schmitt legitimized the leading role of the National Socialist movement, whose leader is the the Führer. The concept of political *Führung*, or leadership, emanated from the 'concrete, substantial thinking of the National Socialist Movement'; it was a concept of 'immediate present and real presence'.[69] Moreover, it demanded 'unconditional racial similarity or commonality [*Artgleichheit*] between the Führer and followers'.[70] Only it could prevent the power of the Führer turning into tyranny and despotism. Racial similarity was thus not 'a theoretical postulate': 'Without the principle of racial similarity the National Socialist state could not exist and its legal life would be unthinkable.'[71] For Koellreutter too, every society needs leadership and it means ordering together a racially similar group of people and warding off or demolishing hostile forces.[72]

In the area of the law, Frank said, 'the state is merely the means of the Führer for realizing National Socialism', and 'the law, as the state does, serves only the *Volk*'.[73] It is the Führer who is 'the portrayer of the law and portrays the law of the concrete order', and the Führer's 'figure stands before and over a law', Helmut Seydel wrote, as he drew a distinction between the Führer and *Leiter*, an ordinary leader without followers.[74]

'The Führer protects the law,' Schmitt said as he attempted to legitimize the execution of Ernst Röhm and his SA men, as 'he at the moment of danger, by the power of his leadership as the supreme judge, immediately creates the law'.[75] The Führer's judgeship arises from the same legal source as all the law of all the people: 'All the law emerges from the right to life of the *Volk*.'[76] Later Schmitt confirmed that 'Today the will and plan of the Führer are a law.'[77] According to Larenz, only the Führer can make the final decision whether a specific rule is valid. As the protector of the constitution by the force of his leadership, he does not need any guarantee for the preserving of justice (*Gerechtigkeit*). Hence a law based on his will is not subject to judicial review.[78]

The Volk

'The Weimar state was a state without the *Volk*,' Fortshoff declared.[79] Walz spoke for the *völkischer Führerstaat* instead of the *nationaler Rechtsstaat* or authoritative state, since national was still too 'Western' a term and authoritarian referred too much to the presidential powers of the Weimar constitution, but *völkisch* caught the sense of unity and identity of the *Volk* in the new state. The *Volk* must here be understood in a *völkisch* sense, that is, referring to 'the racially similar [*artgleichen*] German *Volk*'.[80] It 'is more than the incidental sum of individuals in a territory'; it exists as 'an intrinsically allied unity of racial togetherness'.[81] If the liberal *Rechtsstaat* and its assimilation theory accepted foreign groups in the being of the people (*völkische Sein*), 'the national *Rechtsstaat* as the living order of the people is based on the *Volk*', Koellreutter wrote.[82] The new state must through legislation ensure and protect the racial population of the *Volk*.[83] Michaelis made a difference between 'the new, *völkisch* determined concept of the law' and 'a juridical state and normative thinking'.[84]

The law, as Wolf said, 'is something that lives in the blood' and 'the correct law [*Richtiges Recht*] in the National Socialist sense is also the law that is in accordance with the essence of the *Volk*'. The idea of justice (*Gerechtigkeit*) does not get its particular substance from philosophy or ethics but immediately from the *Volk*, which lives as a natural-spiritual unity.[85] Theodor Maunz confirmed that the principle of legality was not based on laws but on the law in general, which was rooted in the *Volk*.[86]

Roland Freisler criticized the universal law as being a system that is something one thinks but does not experience and live – and the German jurist was 'a German man', who stands in the middle of 'the river of the life of the people'.[87] Hence, Lange declared, the principle in 'the fight over the renewal of German law' was 'for German law against Roman law', which was related to the individualist and materialist law of liberalism, from which one should turn back to Hegel, the Romantic and the Historical school.[88] 'The law is the order of the life of the community. … The norm is just a form of the law … The law is thus merely a sub-species of the ethical living order.'[89] A decision in a particular case was 'an ethical decision that must be rooted in the life of community so long as the law shall coincide with it'; and finally, '[t]he judicature belongs thus only in the hands of the *Volksgenossen* [comrades of the people] who are rooted in the German *Volkstum* [ethnicity]'.[90] Frank put it thus: 'The function of the legal life is not the securing of the application of paragraphs, but the securing of the life of the people.'[91]

Schmitt considered that from the Nuremberg racial laws onwards 'blood and German honour are the main concepts of our law [*Recht*]', the state being 'the means of force and unity of the people'.[92] Schmitt hence attacked 'foreign-blooded and groundless legal theory', which had a general template.[93] He saw 'a concrete order thinking', which had been displaced by the reception of both Roman law since the fifteenth century and the liberal constitutional normativism since the nineteenth century, which had still been alive in Fichte's, Schelling's, Hegel's and Savigny's thinking, as an alternative to normativistic-constitutional legal thought. Concrete orders – families, social groups, armies, institutions, associations, corporations in which people live and work – were the ground from which this legal thinking must start. 'The norm or rule does not create order; on the contrary, only on the basis and in the framework of a given order does it have a certain regulating function.'[94] Schmitt affirms Pindar's *nomos basileus*, law as king, *Lex* as *Rex*, if it is not understood normativistically, but 'if *Nomos* means precisely the concept of *Recht* encompassing a concrete order and *Gemeinschaft*'.[95] Laws evolve from these concrete orders, norms being merely the medium of their values and needs. Therefore, the task of the German jurist rooted in German legal life should be 'a *Sachgestaltung* [thinking shaped by the needs of a concrete situation] that conforms to the German spirit'.[96] He has 'a big new task', namely 'to shelter the law of the German people'.[97] The jurist belongs intrinsically 'to the living reality of developing law and to the contemporary common order of our German people' and he was bound to 'the order of the *Volk* that is grounded on racial similarity and in which the jurist and his spiritual work also belong'.[98]

Reinhard Höhn spoke strongly for the dynamic community and substituted the legal community, *Rechtsgemeinschaft*, and the juridical concept of a state personality, the foundation of the previous constitution, by the *Volksgemeinschaft*, which is the starting point and also the foundation and cornerstone of the new constitution. This concrete community of the people follows the Führer and is bound together through loyalty. The state as a legal person and the concept of community are mutually exclusive, Höhn thought. *Völkisch* principles are the main principles and race is the insurance of community.[99]

For Larenz, the 'substance of one's spiritual life is the *Volksgeist*'.[100] The *Volksgeist* is the source and creator of the law as the law carries in itself the *völkisch* idea of the law. But, as Fichte and Hegel argued, 'the general spirit, which lives in us and determines our own spiritual existence, is not abstract-general but the spirit of a designated community, the spirit of our own *Volk*.'[101] This concrete substance is – Larenz referred here to Hegel – 'the sacred, which bounds human beings and spirits together'.[102] *Volksgeist* is a singular form, which is given through blood relationship and creative life. 'Blood must become spirit and spirit blood. That is possible only when blood is spirit. … Spirit is bound to blood as long as it is creative.'[103] The law is rooted in the *Volk* and its tradition and hence it is sought 'not so much from abstract norms or arbitrary enactments as from the form of life of the *völkischen Gemeinschaft*', from 'a concrete order of community', 'a living order', which is actual in the activities of its members.[104] The binding force of the law is based not on the system of legal norms but on one's 'existence in the community' and thus it is 'an existential, not a normative type'.[105] Existence means the unity of an individual and the substance. 'Ought' (*Sollen*) comes from the being of substance (because of the blood relationship the law of community's life is not merely *Sollen* but *Müssen*, 'must'). If the law is experienced as a demand and a limit and not as a constituent of one's own *Dasein*, the existential bond turns into a normative one, which means – Larenz refers to Heidegger's *Being and Time* – fall into the way of life of *das Man*.[106] Moreover, only a will that expresses the common spirit and will of the *Volk* is able to enact valid laws. The lawgiver is also existentially bound to the *Volksgeist*; that is, 'the idea of the law of his *Volk'* is 'the substance of his own thought and will'.[107]

Based on these ideas, Larenz applied Hegel's idea of concept in the field of jurisprudence and turned from abstract and formal general legal concepts – which Schmitt saw as 'the ghost world of general concepts'[108] – to concrete-general concepts, which are immanent in things themselves and in which the living spirit of reality is present. The abstract concepts of person or legal subject and legal capacity, which reflected the Kantian idea about equal ethical freedom and thus equal legal capacity, were to be abandoned.[109] The concrete concept of legal capacity means the capacity to be a partner in the legal life of society and be in a determinate position in the *Volksgemeinschaft*. Thus, 'for the legal status of an individual his being-person altogether is not decisive any more but his concrete being-member'.[110] Decisive is one's belonging to one's people, family, religion, profession, etc., which makes one 'a concrete personality'.[111] It is not the capacity to have subjective rights but the capacity to partake in the legal life of the community and to belong to the *Volksgemeinschaft* that is crucial for the concrete concept of legal capacity. Therefore, 'not every human being as a person has a legal capacity, but only the *Volksgenosse* [the comrade of the people] as the '*Rechtsgenosse*' [the comrade of the law]'.[112] Who was outside this comradeship of the people was also outside the law, that is was not a *Rechtgenosse.* Even if this concrete-general concept of the person was Larenz's proposition for a new first paragraph in the German Civil Code, this norm would merely be a confirmation of the valid law, which was already immanently in the racially similar community of the people as a concrete concept and order.[113]

Also Nicolai emphasized that the *Volksgeist*, not the lawgiver, is the basis of the law.[114] Contrary to positivism, 'the state merely formulates and administers the law'; hence 'the legal order is constructed from the bottom up'.[115] 'The original act of National Socialism is the production of a united *Volksgeist.*'[116] The National Socialist state lacked a formal constitution, but it had 'a spiritual constitution'; as it lacked the formal constitution it had one *Volk*, which the Weimar constitution lacked.[117] Nicolai defined 'the nation or the *Volk*' as 'a group of people who belong together through a blood relationship' and hence 'blood (race) is decisive'.[118] For him, the legal philosophy based on the National Socialist world view was a racial jurisprudence.[119] Since the law is a precondition for living together, innate in human beings and born with them, the race of the people determines the law. The German law is 'the national law', 'a unity of the law, ethics, religion and morality', 'the law of the racially pure *Volk*', which is 'an absolute criterion'.[120] Thus the state is subject to the law, which is only what serves the racially determined *Volksgemeinschaft*, that is the blood community (*Blutsgemeinschaft*), whose *Volksgeist*, the spirit of the people, Nicolai equates with *Rassenseele*, a racial soul. Therefore, even if they lived in Germany, 'Jews, national minorities, gypsies' did not belong to the German *Volk*.[121]

Thus *Artgleichheit*, racial similarity, to which we have already referred, was a basic concept of constitutional and administrative law, as Schmitt said in October 1933.[122] As Schmitt praised the Nuremberg laws as the constitution of freedom and the heart of the German law, he declared freedom from foreign spiritual domination. The legal and constitutional thinking must purify itself and become German.[123]

If the *Volk* did not keep its blood pure, Wilhelm Frick argued, 'the inevitable result is that its unity and unanimity are fractured and its originality is lost'; and because 'for Germany the racial problem means the Jewish problem', 'all the influence of those who belong to the Jewish people on the German people's own life will be dismantled'.[124] Frick said, 'The leading idea of National Socialist revolution was the German *Volk's* longing to once again became master in its own house in all areas of its *völkischen Lebens* [life].'[125] Hence all kinds of interior and exterior foreign domination are to be 'abolished through legal means'.[126]

The Jews became an enemy since, as Forsthoff professed, they had infringed the territorial and spiritual living space (*Lebensraum*) of the German *Volk*, which was a community based on a homogeneity of being and species, homogeneity arising from the sameness of race and the destiny of the people.[127] As enemies they must 'be rendered harmless'. Then again, if they withdrew into their Jewishness and stopped attempting to 'participate in the spiritual, intellectual and political existence of the German people', they ceased to be enemies and became merely *Artfremden*, different types, that is, racially dissimilar.[128]

The judiciary

According to Roland Freisler, the function of the judge was to draw the law from the source of norms which the *Volk* had enacted through the Führer, since the *Volk* and its conscience were the ultimate source of the law.[129] In interpreting the law, according to Heinrich Henkel, the judge did not merely have to take into consideration the living world view of *Volk* as an empirical fact but also had to recognize it as a normative element: 'Thus we don't see the National Socialist judge as an unbound judge of the Free Law School, nor as the bound judge, bound by a law'; only when the judge is bound to the state leadership and its leading principles is 'the true independence of the judge thinkable'.[130] However, the jurisdiction was seen as independent and impartial.[131] Schmitt, who emphasized the importance of the question of 'the judge's relation to a law',[132] explained that the principle of the independence of the judiciary was recognized under National Socialism. One should not, however, associate this principle with the concepts of the liberal state, but embed it in the structure of the National Socialist state itself.[133] For Schmitt, pre-National Socialist laws continued to be valid but only as functional norms. The spirit and basic principles upon which those laws were founded were no longer valid. If concepts like 'good faith' and 'common decency' are linked not to the individualistic society, but to the interest of the entire nation, 'the entire *Recht* changes in reality without it being necessary to change a single "positive" law'.[134] Therefore, in legal interpretation, one must overcome the false opposition of letter and spirit, the word and meaning of a law, and instead oppose the former valid spirit to the new one, which is now valid. The meaning of not merely general clauses and concepts but also determinate words might change because 'the basis of the legal system has been completely renewed'.[135] Jurisdiction must grow from the National Socialist spirit.[136] For Schmitt, the first principle of interpretation was that the whole of German law must be 'governed exclusively and solely by the spirit of National Socialism' and every interpretation must be 'an interpretation in the spirit of National Socialism'.[137] 'Today's legislator sees in the German judge' – who belongs to the *Volksgemeinschaft*, a follower of the Führer – 'a co-operator with the Führer's will and plan'.[138] A judge in the Führer state is 'a co-operator in law'.[139] Since judges and officials are not mechanically and automatically bound to legal norms, since they are not 'law-application automats', who concretize abstract norms as they do in the normativist legality, 'everything depends on the brand and type of our judges and officials'.[140] They have to abandon 'the legal blindness of liberal legal thinking'.[141] Therefore, the judge is a moral and ethical, a creative 'personality', not a personality in the sense of liberal individualism, but as someone who belongs to 'the concrete German *Volk*'.[142]

Total law and community

The aforementioned discourses in the field of jurisprudence, and also in the fields of constitutional theory and legal dogmatics, were forming the juridical context (it was not fixed once and for all during the first years of National Socialism but was fluid and changing) in which the actions of the defendants in the Justice Case took place. In National Socialism the principle of *law is law* – and the principles of legality, the rule of law, legal obedience, etc. – was still valid, if one understands the concept of law in accordance with the National Socialist idea of the law, though it has become quite clear that in the National Socialist legal order, legal thinking was not formalistic-positivistic, abstract and value-neutral.[143]

The law was fraught with substance. These texts of legal scholars we have gone through show how the new idea of the law was formulated, new legal concepts and principles were constituted and the substance of the old terminology was changed. The basic, and relatively constant, concrete concepts were: *Rasse*, *Blut*, *Seele*, *Boden*, *Volk*, *Volksgenosse*, *Volksgemeinschaft*, *Artgleichheit*, and Führer.

The legal thinking under National Socialism repeated, as the texts of legal scholars reveal, the main concepts of National Socialism and followed a certain kind of logic, that is the National Socialist ideology. For Hannah Arendt, even more important than any particular idea of an ideology is the logical process developed from it, 'the logic with which this "idea" is carried out'.[144] The National Socialist racist ideology was the totally self-fulfilling logic of the idea (race, the conflict of races, care for racially similar Germanic *Volk*) that the unfolding of history can be explained as one consistent process: whatever happens, happens according to the logic of this idea. The National Socialist ideology is hence a political explanation of the world, that is of history, on the basis of the concept of race and all the aforementioned concepts based on it. It showed contempt for reality and factuality as it aimed at making the world completely consistent, as it aimed 'to remake humanity and the world such that "the facts" reflect the truth of the ideological supersense' (the superiority of the Aryan race in the Darwinian struggle).[145] This explanation and conception of the world – *Weltanschauung*, vision, intuition, and comprehension of the world – attempted to be a total explanation and conception, that is indisputable, leaving no gaps or surplus.[146] It was the total domination of the law of the motion of nature. According to Philippe Lacoue-Labarthe and Jean-Luc Nancy, there is 'a logic of fascism', that is 'a certain logic is fascist', and this logic is not entirely foreign to the general logic of rationality in the metaphysics of the Subject. Therefore, it was 'the ideology of the subject'.[147] The texts of legal scholars include, follow and also disclose five ideological steps:

1) There was the lack of a German identity, and the National Socialist movement, which was the becoming-of-the-*Volk*, promised an end to the alienation and homelessness of the German *Volk*. It appealed for a new beginning, where the German *Volk* would return to its home, come back to itself and be developed into the reality of its existence by appropriating the unique and exclusive origin of Germans, by identifying itself as a German nation, by creating its own subject and itself as the subject. The precondition for all this was awakening the capability of the race, which was the principle and locus of mythical power. Or, as Lacoue-Labarthe and Nancy say in

their analysis of the National Socialist myth (and Alfred Rosenberg): first, the power of myth had to be reawakened in opposition to the inconsistency of the abstract universalities of science, philosophy and democracy; second, the power of the race and the *völkisch* power had to be reawakened, and this power is characterized as the productive and formative power of the myth and as its fulfilment, which requires the active adherence of the *Volk* to its myth, that is its total participation and act of faith. And the Aryan is seen as the founder of civilization. It forms itself and types itself as an absolute and free creator and self-creator, whose position is formed from an immediate and absolute natural essence, that of blood and race. The Aryan race is *the* Subject.[148] The immanence of the Aryan spiritual body was the Absolute as the ultimate foundation and guarantor of the final meaning.[149]

2) National Socialism was a struggle for the effective realization of the concept of *Volksgemeinschaft*, which was exactly the concept of the myth.[150] It was formed in accordance with the National Socialist *Weltanschauung* as the unified subject of history, in which the *Volk*, the state, the law and the identity came in their presence. This common being, a community of internal unity, was based on one blood and *Volk*, on one truth and destiny. Because individual rights, interests and desires were subordinated to common communal duties and values, there prevailed an undividedness and harmony in the *Volksgemeinschaft*, which made the natural *Volk* the political *Volk*, which was present in itself as an absolute subject, as a carrier, source and aim of will, determinedness and representation. Moreover, contradictions of nature and spirit, body and soul, history and future, value and reality, factual and normative were annulled.[151] All in all, *Volksgemeinschaft* was supposed to be a complete and completely immanent community, that is a self-sufficient common being with a common substance, a community, which was closed upon itself, which had an undivided common identity and in which there was the full presence of the *Volk* to itself without flaw and without any outside.[152]
3) The German lack of identity also was the lack of the true German law. The *Volk* had to find its law to become itself and to be totally enclosed within itself without any lack in the complete communal fusion. National Socialism promised to re-find the law and 'to establish the rule of justice on earth because it claims to make mankind itself the embodiment of the law'.[153] The law was innate in the thick presence of the blood and soil of the *Volk*, in the German type, in the *Volksgemeinschaft* and concrete orders of German people. The race was thus the carrier of the law and the *Volk* the ultimate source of the law and the ground of its legitimacy. The law was the absolute and immanent natural law, and thus its binding force was absolute and existential.
4) The Führer was the highest embodiment and expression of the being of the *Volk*, the one who knew the demands and necessities of the *Volksgemeinschaft*. Through the Führer the *Volk* gave itself its laws from itself and thus

constituted itself as a juridico-political community, which the state apparatuses preserved. As Hitler told his followers, 'All that you are, you are through me; all that I am, I am through you alone.'[154] The *Volksgemeinschaft* and its law had therefore 'the autarky of absolute immanence'.[155]

5) Only those who shared the common blood and spirit were considered members of this community. 'These racial dominants demand the creation of a type' ('the time-bound plastic form of an eternal racial spiritual content') only within which is 'truly organic freedom' possible, as Alfred Rosenberg declared.[156] Thus the task of National Socialism was 'to create a new human type out of a new view of life'.[157] The founding of this German type with its ownmost characteristics was possible only through a negative movement. National Socialism needed in its figuration others, not-same, to become itself and secure its identity and borders. In this paradoxical inclusive exclusion, the German defined itself through that which it cast out.[158] Others were not others with whom to share the world or to be together, but the absolute Other, the evil enemy, who threatened with their existence the homogeneous, total and absolutely immanent community. The Other had to be annihilated from the German type and life, from blood and soil, from the law and community. The Jew was defined as the Other. The Jew was considered to be an abstract universal being as opposed to the concrete and particular German identity. For Rosenberg, the Jew was not even the opposite type but the absence of type.[159] The Aryan world would not be merely a world exploited by Aryans but a world that would have become Aryan, which demanded the elimination of the antitype and all non-Aryan types.[160] And here the law again comes in play: it was the natural law of the *Volk* that demanded this, and laws that immediately expressed the natural law were protecting the unity of the community by drawing lines between friend and enemy and excluding all alterity and difference. The totalitarian laws were constructing and affirming the Aryan figure, which was part of the combat over the *Weltanschauung*, construction, and conformation of the world according to the vision and image of the creator of forms, the Aryan, according to its total *Anschauung*, total view.[161]

This National Socialist idea of 'idyllic community', as Sarah Kofman writes, 'erases all trace of discord, difference, death, which pretends to rest on a perfect harmony, a fusion conferring immediate unity, is necessarily a fiction of community, a beautiful story (psychotic?)'.[162] It destroyed the plurality, or, more properly, the plurality of singularities, which is the essential part of any political community. In reality this National Socialist unitary community and incarnated communion of racially similar people was the annihilation of community, of the open space of co-appearing, spacing, distinctness and difference, of the activity of sharing and being-with, of the singularity of finite beings: 'the fulfilment of community is its suppression'.[163] And the result of this logic of racist ideology was the Holocaust: 'the desire to fix the origin, or to give the origin to itself, once and for all' is, as Nancy puts it, 'a desire for murder', a desire 'for an increase of cruelty and horror', which ends in 'the massacre, the mass grave, massive and technological execution, the bookkeeping of the camps'.[164] Justice on earth, that the National Socialist ideology had promised, turned out to be – and had been from the beginning – hell on earth.[165]

Ethical blindness

After all, why? There was a terrible silence. Jurists were reluctant to look into that which had taken place. Schmitt, once again, represents this willingness to forget when, in 1949, he wrote an essay for the amnesty, which meant forgetting, the power of forgetting, which would end 'the civil cold war', namely denazification – the other way, the communist way, to end it would be, according to Schmitt, 'the annihilation of the other' (*Vernichtung des anderen*).[166] When these jurists spoke, as in the Justice Case, only hollow words were uttered. For these jurists forgetting was made easy by the fact that the legal profession remained essentially untouched – and anyway the blame could be put on legal positivism.[167]

Before returning to the Justice Case let us remember Arendt's report on the case of Adolf Eichmann, who stood trial in a Jerusalem court. Eichmann saw himself as a law-abiding citizen who 'not only obeyed *orders*, he also obeyed the *law*.'[168] He also argued that he had lived his life according to Kant's moral precepts, and especially according to a Kantian definition of duty.[169] Arendt says that even if Eichmann perverted Kant's definition of duty, he did follow Kant in one respect, that is a law is a law and there can be no exception. This justified him in his own eyes. Since there were no exceptions to laws, he did his duty against his sentimental inclinations or self-interest. Even though his deeds were monstrous, Arendt found neither any diabolical profundity nor firm ideological conviction in Eichmann. Instead, his speech was empty talk. His inability to speak was closely connected to his inability to think, that is, to think from the standpoint of others. He was surrounded by 'safeguards against the words and the presence of others, and hence against reality'.[170] He relied on various bannisters, ready-to-hand principles and value judgements that enabled him to navigate life without having to stop and think. The lack of imagination and sense of responsibility, the failure of any faculty of judgement and sheer thoughtlessness predisposed him to become one of the greatest criminals of that period, whose crimes 'took place within a "legal" order', which 'was their outstanding character'.[171] Arendt said that in Eichmann we confront 'word-and-thought-defying *banality of evil*'.[172] It is the banality of excessive and depthless normality. 'Eichmann was indeed normal in so far as he was "no exception within the Nazi regime". However, under the conditions of the Third Reich only "exceptions" could be expected to react "normally".'[173] Eichmann was an example of the new figure of evil and crime to have appeared with totalitarianism.[174]

The evil of the defendants may be defined as banal evil. However, they were not merely Eichmanns, who 'did not have to fall back upon his "conscience", since he 'acted in accordance with the rule, examined the order issued to him for its "manifest" legality, namely regularity'.[175] The judges and officials did not merely obey laws but actively applied and interpreted them in accordance with the National Socialist ideology and its idea of the law.

In the National Socialist legal order, the law bound both legally and morally. The distinction between legal and moral duty was lost. Moreover, the law bound not merely normatively but also existentially. Those who shared the German biological and spiritual being were seen as the embodiments of the law. The *Volksgemeinschaft* and its laws, which were based on absolute sameness, absolute intolerance, annihilation of otherness, immediate biologico-spiritual connectedness, being-with merging into being-in-common-with, left no possibility for critical distance or antagonism. This led to the decline in the capacity to think and judge legal, ethical and political matters. It was not legal positivism that made it impossible to criticize valid laws from a moral perspective using moral criteria but the National Socialist idea of the law, which declared the collapse of difference between law and morality, legal and moral validity and obligation. One could not even argue that, even though racist positive laws had formal legal validity, they were unjust laws and could and should be resisted on moral grounds. Moreover, the merging of *Sollen*, Ought, and *Sein*, Is, that is normativity (legal norms) and factuality (Aryan race and blood, the nature of the *Volk*) diminished the possibility of criticism. The antidote would have been Radbruch's words from 1914: 'Nothing is ever to be regarded as right simply because it is, or because it was, or because it will foreseeably be.'[176] Since the law was immediately present and legally-morally-existentially binding, there was no critical and ethical locus from which to condemn the legal order.

This does not mean that jurists would avoid responsibility by putting the blame on the evil of the National Socialist law. Jurists accepted it and became not merely more or less willing servants, but also creators and embodiments of this idea of the law. They did realize what they were doing as juridical instruments of the legal machinery of mass murder. The constant noise of blood made them deaf to the possibility of there being others. They were excessively normal in the National Socialist order, in which the relationship between normality and exception was overturned so that everything happened as if the proliferation of evil rendered all almost numb to its advent, as Fabio Ciaramelli says.[177]

Next, the legal scholars who did not apply laws or give degrees but thought the essence of the law. For Schmitt, 'legal science (*Rechtswissenschaft*) cannot lead an encapsulated existence in the life of peoples and times'.[178] For that reason, legal thinking was figuring and erecting the order of absolute law in accordance with the National Socialist racist ideology, which penetrated all their ideas, concepts and principles. Even if some of the legal scholars withdrew from their enthusiastic support of National Socialism, even though they would not have predicted that National Socialism was going to turn into the Holocaust, they put their thought at the service of this ideology, and its logic.

As Arendt says, the danger in an ideology is that one exchanges 'the freedom inherent in man's capacity to think for the straitjacket of logic with which man can force himself almost as violently as he is forced by some outside power'.[179] 'As soon as logic as a movement of thought – not as a necessary control of thinking – is applied to an idea, this idea is transformed into a premise', deduced from which everything and every occurrence is explained.[180] This movement of thought carries the individual along with the premise. 'You can't say A without saying B and C, and so on, down to the end of the murderous alphabet.'[181] Hence, we can say that legal scholars had changed the 'necessary insecurity of philosophical thought for the total explanation of an ideology and its *Weltanschauung*'.[182]

On the one hand, the legal thinking of the legal scholars imitated the National Socialist ideology. On the other hand, legal thinking itself was part of the construction of the National Socialist ideology as an ideological knowledge of the law. All the analysis and descriptions of the law aimed at total – that is undisputable and continuous – explanation. The texts promised to provide a truer reality of the law, which had been concealed behind normative-empirical positive laws, in which the German *Volk* had lost its true sense of justice. This juridico-ideology that proceeded 'from the premise of nature' (the natural law of the *Volk*) promised 'to explain all historical happenings, the total explanation of the past, the total knowledge of the present, and the reliable prediction of the future' of the law.[183] Their juridical and philosophical thinking partook in the formation of the fundamental norm of legal genocide: *You must die*.[184] The juridical, philosophical and political texts of legal scholars may be seen as, in Paul Celan's words, a 'thousand darknesses of deathbringing speech'.[185]

Legal scholars did not merely submit juridical, ethical and philosophical thinking to ideological truths and logic, but they also produced actively the absolute, immediate and immanent natural law. Their thinking and judgement were dissolved into blood and soil and their freedom was submitted to the internal tyranny of the fulfilment of the idea of the law. They created the ideology of the law and then submitted themselves to this law.

This is an ethical blindness, which is the result of the lack of thinking, which does not mean that their writings would be irrational non-thought or that they would not have known the European tradition of philosophy and jurisprudence, which they actually used, even if this tradition was submitted to the ideological truths and world view, and continued in their construction of total theories of the law, which became absolute rules and criteria for further legal thinking. This blindness meant the renunciation of the activity of thinking, that is the activity of reason (*Vernunft* in Kant's distinction to

Verstand, intellect and knowing); a dialogue with oneself, the constant questioning and making sense of the world we share with others and one's action or thoughts in this shared world of pluralities; thinking from the standpoint of others, an anticipated communication with others, the representation of absent others in one's mind, an imagination that goes visiting.[186] Following Arendt, for whom thinking and judging are independent but interrelated activities, one could say that since thinking, which deals with invisibles and representations of things that are absent, 'the two-in-one of the soundless dialogue' that 'actualizes the difference within our identity as given in consciousness and thereby results in conscience as its by-product' is lacking, also judging, which is 'the by-product of the liberating effect of thinking', which realizes thinking in the world of appearances as the ability to tell right from wrong, is also lacking.[187] The judgement that was lacking in National Socialism was not so much determinant judgement, which subsumes particulars under universal norms or positive laws and decrees, but reflective judgement, which Kant deals with in his analysis of aesthetic judgement, that is the judgement of the particular for which no norms exist and which, as free of personal interests, takes place on the basis of what one shares with others, or, as Kant put it, such judgement is achieved through enlarged thought. According to the maxim of Kant's enlarged thought one has to put oneself in thought in the place of everyone else, to test one's judgement against the imagined judgements of others, to reflect upon judgement from a universal standpoint. Judging is activity in which the sharing the world with others takes place and the absence of this sharing is exactly what the thoughtlessness, both of legal scholars and judges, prosecutors and officials, ultimately meant. They failed in thinking and henceforth in judging. They failed in existing outside of themselves and the immanent totality of their communal community and its laws, in exposing themselves to others, in exposing itself. Or, in other words they failed in affirming transcendence within immanence – transcendence here referring to no sacred meaning, either to gods or to eternal principles of justice, but signifying resistance to immanence, resistance to communion, fusion, sameness and the murderous exclusion of the Jews.[188]

Destruction of the moral law

To finish, in addition to this thoughtlessness and blindness there may be evil as a phenomenon that is deeper than the banal evil. One more time: Kant. His notion of radical evil refers not to extreme acts of evil, such as the Holocaust, but to a natural propensity (*Hang*) to disregard the moral law and to subordinate moral incentives to non-moral, 'pathological', incentives (self-regard, pleasure, empathy, will to power, etc.), which are brought upon human beings by themselves. It is not our passions and pleasures that are evil but the fact that we have chosen to give them priority – therefore, we are fully responsible as free subjects.[189] Particular human beings have the power of choice (*Willkür*) to adopt good maxims, which incorporate the moral law, or evil maxims, which give primacy to non-moral incentives. Hence we may consider as an ethical act an act that can be universalized in accordance with the categorical imperative and that is performed in accordance with a good maxim based only on respect for the moral law.

But does Kant's radical evil fall short when we face the evil of, and in, National Socialism? Arendt notes that the greatest evils have 'nothing to do any more with such humanely understandable, sinful motives'.[190] What about those whose maxims and actions were motivated purely by the duty to National Socialism and respect for its law? This is exactly what the texts of legal scholars advocated: the National Socialist law was legally, morally and existentially valid and binding law, and one should, as a member of *Volksgemeinschaft*, act out of respect for it.

Don't we actually confront here a diabolical evil, in which opposition to the moral law is made the universal principle? Kant denied the possibility of devilish being. For him, human beings are conscious of their transgression of the law, considering themselves as culpable and guilty. I agree with Kant as far as he denies the possibility that the human species, or even some individuals, would be innately and naturally devilish.[191] Then again, if human beings have the power of choice, there is no reason why anyone should not be able to freely adopt 'a disposition [*Gesinnung*] in which he consistently refuses to do what the moral law requires' and consistently adopts evil maxims.[192] Considering the jurists under National Socialism this seems to be what took place.

Then again, I have a couple of reservations. First, as Karl Jaspers reminded us, all talk of demonic and diabolic would give these acts 'satanic greatness'.[193] Second, what does one really oppose when opposing the moral law? If the moral law would include some substantial norms (as an example, the Ten Commandments or their secularized version, human rights) one could say without a doubt that the horrible crimes done in the name and for the sake of National Socialism were diabolically evil acts, since they systematically and intentionally opposed, and thus destroyed, the law. But Kant's moral law is formal and empty of content. It does not include norms, which would order what to do and what not. It 'merely' demands one to do one's duty. So if opposition to the moral law is elevated to the level of a maxim and a principle, it would no longer be opposition to the moral law but would become the law itself, as Alenka Zupančič remarks.[194] Thus National Socialist diabolical evil would have the same form as the ethical act. Here we come to an impasse: it seems impossible to argue that all these juridical and academic acts and texts we have dealt with should be considered ethical because they were motivated purely by the (National Socialist) law. An even more perverse conclusion would be that jurists who sent Jews to concentration camps for the sake of duty would be considered as morally good since their acts were based on the National

Socialist idea of the law; those who opposed the legal terror and terrorist laws because of empathy or some other non-moral incentive were morally evil.

However, I still insist that there is something beyond the radical evil, which is related exactly to the emptiness of the moral law. The Kantian moral law and its excess, which transcends all pre-given positive legal and moral norms, demands the autonomous subject to transform the abstract demand of the empty moral law and categorical imperative in particular maxims and actions, to always take a risk, since one does not know in advance whether an act is truly an ethical act. The moral law does demand neither something nor nothing; it has the structure of '*enunciation without a statement*'.[195] Thus the law is a law of the unknown: the moral law is not present as something that waits for the subject to submit itself to the law; it is constituted only in the act.[196] We know the existence of the moral law merely as the always singular voice of conscience. We know the law without substance only because we are conscious of our transgression of the law, that is, as Joan Copjec puts it, 'the law makes itself known only in the negative experience of guilt, of not being up to the task of our freedom'.[197]

During National Socialism the natural law based on National Socialist ideology of the law took the place of this purely formal moral law, which was phenomenalized and substantialized – the moral law became a positive law filled with the content of norms, normative ideas, principles and concepts based on the National Socialist ideology. All action could be justified as acts, not only in conformity with this absolute immanent natural law, but also motivated purely by respect for this law. This is what Arendt also refers to as she says that Eichmann – even if she insisted that one cannot trace any ideological convention in Eichmann – distorted the Kantian categorical imperative to read: 'Act as if the principle of your actions were the same as that of the legislator of the law of the land'.[198] This new law, which had substance and object, became the ultimate ground and principle. The moment thought concerns itself with National Socialist evil, it is not frustrated merely because there is nothing, as Arendt sometimes seems to suggest (however, the banal evil was not for her the only form of evil) but terrified that there is the totalitarian ideology and its law.[199]

Human beings as human beings were made superfluous in this process, in which firstly the legal subject as carrier of rights, then the moral person and finally human individualism, spontaneity, freedom and solidarity were destroyed.[200] The possibility of ethical freedom, the ethical being itself, was thus annihilated. In other words, one chose to relinquish one's thinking and judgement, chose to submit oneself to the absolute substantial law and became the instrument of the supreme 'good' of the ideology represented in the law. By letting oneself become the instrument of National Socialist law one became numb to the pressure of the moral law. The new law 'freed' the subject from its always singular voice of conscience and, since that was the only way the subject knew the moral law, from the moral law itself. The subject under National Socialism did thus choose, using its power of choice, *Willkür*, to obey unconditionally the new law, to let it become the motive of its action and to incorporate it in its maxims. Perhaps we could take one more step and consider the possibility that one even chose to submit the moral law to the new law which took the place of the legislative capacity or the normative aspect of the will, the law of freedom, the practical reason, *Wille*, which exerts the pressure of its own normative nature upon the *Willkür*.[201] As a result, *Wille* itself became evil. We come closer and closer to a consistent principal rejection of the moral law. Instead of the pseudo-theological concept of diabolic evil, let us call this total evil, or total ideologico-legal evil.

This is what judges, prosecutors and bureaucrats of the Justice Case and legal scholars we have dealt with chose to do. (Sometimes the submission was motivated by pathological reasons, sometimes not.) Moreover, the texts of legal scholars under discussion were producing National Socialist law, which took over the positive juridical law and the empty moral law. I have traced the argumentation of these texts, since they present empirically how the total evil works, namely, how the substantial ideological law is presented as the normative essence, nature and destiny of being, how this law is destined to take the place of the moral law, and how the moral law is thus destroyed. Moreover, these texts confirm that there is evil beyond the radical evil, that the total evil is connected both to the subject and the symbolic order (the National Socialist language, law and ideology). The texts and acts of the jurists were manifestations of the total evil of 'deathbringing speech'.

Notes

1 The Tribunal declared that the overt acts with which defendants are charged occurred after September 1939. Acts prior to this were referred to, since they illuminated the defendant's knowledge, intent and motivation in transforming the entire judicial system into a tool for the propagation of the National Socialist ideology, the extermination of opposition and the advancement of plans for aggressive war and world conquest. Count 1 of conspiracy embraced the period between January 1933 and April 1945, but it was declared as being outside the jurisdiction of the Tribunal and in so far as it charged the commission of the alleged crime of conspiracy as a separate substantive offence, distinct from any war crime or crime against humanity, the Tribunal disregarded that charge. All but one of the defendants were professional jurists. *Trial of War Criminals before the Nuernberg Military Tribunals* III, (NMT III), Washington, DC: US Government Printing Office, 1951, p. 956.

2 Ibid., p. 31.

3 Ibid., pp. 108–9.

4 Ibid., p. 291.

5 Ibid., p. 303.

6 Günther Nebelung, Chief Justice of the Fourth Senate of the People's Court. Ibid., p. 950.

7 Oswald Rothaug, Senior Prosecutor of the Public Court. Ibid., p. 947.

8 Rudolf Oeschey, Judge and Chief Justice of the Special Court in Nuremberg. Ibid., p. 952.

9 Herbert Klemm, State Secretary in the Reich Ministry of Justice. Ibid., p. 943.

10 Josef Altstoetter, Chief of the Civil Law and Procedure Division of the Reich Ministry of Justice. Ibid., pp. 952–3.

11 Curt Rothenberger, State Secretary of the Reich Ministry of Justice. Ibid., p. 943.

12 Hermann Cuhorst, Chief Justice of the Special Court in Stuttgart. Ibid., p. 951.

13 Ibid., p. 1086; Altstoetter, von Ammon, Joel, Klemm, Lautz, Mettgenberg, Oeschey, Rothaug, Rothenberger and Schlegelberger were sentenced to imprisonment. Barnickel, Cuhorst, Nebelung and Petersen were acquitted. Engert's case was declared a mistrial and Westphal committed suicide. By 1951 all the convicted had been released, except Rothaug, who was released in 1956.

14 Gustav Radbruch, 'Fünf Minuten Rechtsphilosophie' (1945), p. 78, 'Gesetzliches Unrecht und übergesetzliches Recht' (1946), p. 83, 'Die Erneuerung des Rechts' (1946), p. 80, 'Die Erneuerung des Rechts' (1947), p. 108, all in *Gesamtausgabe 3. Rechtsphilosophie* III. Heidelberg: Müller, 1990.

15 See Hubert Schorn, *Der Richter im Dritten Reich*, Frankfurt am Main: Klostermann, 1959; Hermann Weinkauff, *Die deutsche Justiz und der Nationalsozialismus. Ein Überblick*, Stuttgart: Deutsche Verlags-Anstalt, 1968.

16 On legislation in the Third Reich, Martin Hirsch, Diemut Majer and Jürgen Meinck (eds), *Recht, Verwaltung und Justiz im Nationalsozialismus*, Cologne: Bund-Verlag, 1984.

17 Franz Neumann, *Behemoth. The Structure and Practice of National Socialism, 1933–1944*, New York: Harper & Row, 1944.

18 According to Walter Jones, the National Socialists drew a distinction between the law in general (*Recht*) and statute law (*Gesetz*). J. Walter Jones, *The Nazi Conception of Law*, Oxford: Clarendon Press, 1939, pp. 11–12.

19 Henry Friedlander, 'German law and German crimes in the Nazi era', in F. C. DeCoste and Bernard Schwartz (eds), *The Holocaust's Ghost. Writings on Art, Politics, Law and Education*, Edmonton: University of Alberta Press, 2000, pp. 283–9; see also David Fraser, *Law after Auschwitz. Towards a Jurisprudence of the Holocaust*, Durham, NC: Carolina Academic Press, 2005, p. 15.

20 Carl Schmitt, *Staat, Bewegung, Volk. Die Dreigliederung der politischen Einheit*, Hamburg: Hanseatische Verlagsanstalt, 1933, p. 7. According to Schmitt, along with the Enabling Act the parliamentary legislative state was subverted, since the new legislator created not merely decrees but in a formal sense Reich laws. For Schmitt, the Enabling Act was both constitutional and an expression of the victory of the national revolution. Carl Schmitt, 'Das Gesetz zur Behebung der Not von Volk und Reich', *Deutsche Juristen-Zeitung*, 38, 1933, pp. 455–8.

21 The Act was limited initially to four years. It was renewed in the Reichstag in 1937 and 1941, two of the few laws the Reichstag passed after this Act. Its validity could be questioned. It was passed through formally correct procedure and got the required two-thirds of votes, but the Communist deputies were excluded from the Reichstag. The voting was also manipulated by threats and procedural changes. In the Justice Case the defence witness, Hermann Jahrreiss, had referred to a leading expert in constitutional law in Weimar, Gerhard Anschütz (who gave up his Chair in Heidelberg in 1933 for political reasons), according to whom the assurance of the Reich President, who examined whether a law has been passed in a constitutional manner, excluded all scrutiny afterwards as to whether a law had been passed in an orderly manner. Thus this Act was formally valid law. *NMT III*, pp. 255–6. The acts of state between 1933 and 1945 'were, at least in part, voluntarily recognized as legal acts at

home and abroad'. Michael Stolleis, *The Law under the Swastika. Studies on Legal History in Nazi Germany*, trans. Thomas Dunlap, Chicago: University of Chicago Press, 1998, p. 6. Then again, the validity of the Act was limited to the time of the Cabinet in power and there had been changes in the Cabinet. But according to Georg Kaisenberg the change of individual Ministers did not count, only the resignation of the Reich Chancellor would have meant a change of Cabinet. Georg Kaisenberg, 'Das Ermächtigungsgesetz', *Deutsche Juristen-Zeitung*, 39, pp. 458–61, p. 461. Schmitt agreed, saying that the Cabinet got its identity from the Führer. Carl Schmitt, 'Das Gesetz zur Behebung der Not von Volk und Reich', p. 457.

22 Ernst Fraenkel had argued in 1940 that the Third Reich was a dual state: a normative and prerogative state, where normality and terror existed side by side. Ernst Fraenkel, *The Dual State. A Contribution to the Theory of Dictatorship*, trans. E. A. Shills, New York: Octagon Books, 1969. Also Michael Stolleis says that law and despotism coexisted. A legal black hole was formed and extended continuously. Michael Stolleis, 'Law and lawyers preparing the Holocaust', *Annual Review of Law and Social Science*, 3, pp. 214–31, p. 214.

23 Deborah E. Lipstadt, 'Witness statement', *Irving v. Lipstadt: Denial on Trial*, Available online: www.hdot.org, p. 68. See Raul Hilberg, *The Destruction of the European Jews*, Chicago: Quadrangle Books, 1961; Saul Friedländer, *The Years of Extermination. Nazi Germany and the Jews, 1939–1945*, London: Weidenfeld & Nicolson, 2007.

24 Karl Larenz, *Deutsche Rechtserneuerung und Rechtsphilosophie*, Tübingen: Mohr, 1934, p. 11.

25 Heinrich Lange, *Liberalismus, Nationalsozialismus und bürgerliches Recht*, Tübingen: Mohr, 1933, p. 5.

26 Carl Schmitt, *On the Three Types of Juristic Thought*, trans. Joseph W. Bendersky, Westport, CT: Praeger, 2004, p. 64. According to Schmitt, legal positivism (nineteenth century) was a combination of Hobbesian decisionism (seventeenth century) and rational-law normativism (eighteenth century): there is a decision of the legislator, which has to have firm and inviolable value as norm, then the legislator is subjected to valid norms and the legal system rises above the power decision of the state.

27 Ibid., p. 64.

28 Ibid., pp. 64–5.

29 Ibid., p. 90.

30 Oliver Lepsius, 'The problem of perceptions of National Socialist law, or, Was there a constitutional theory of National Socialism?' trans. Iain L. Fraser, in Christian Joerges and Navraj Singh Ghaleigh (eds), *Darker Legacies of Law in Europe. The Shadow of National Socialism and Fascism over Europe and its Legal Tradition*, Oxford: Hart, 2003, p. 21; Bernd Rüthers, *Entartetes Recht. Rechtslehren und Kronjuristen im Dritten Reich*. Munich: Beck,1989, p. 18.

31 Ernst Forsthoff, *Der totale Staat*, Hamburg: Hanseatische Verlagsanstalt, 1933, p. 51.

32 Helmut Nicolai, *Der Staat im nationalsozialistischen Weltbild*, Leipzig: Schaeffer, 1933, p. 19.

33 Larenz, *Deutsche Rechtserneuerung und Rechtsphilosophie*, p. 38.

34 Karl Michaelis, 'Wandlung des deutschen Rechtsdenkens seit dem Eindringen des fremden Rechts', in Georg Dahm et al., *Grundfragen der neuen Rechtswissenschaft*, Berlin: Junker & Dünnhaupt, 1933, p. 61.

35 Erik Wolf, *Richtiges Recht im nationalsozialistischen Staate*, Freiburg: Wagnersche Universitätsbuchhandlung, 1933, p. 27; see also Erik Wolf, 'Das Rechtsideal des nationalsozialistischen Staates', *ARSP*, 28, 1934–35, pp. 348–63.

36 Schmitt, *On the Three Types of Juristic Thought*, p. 97.
37 Carl Schmitt, 'Der Weg des deutschen Juristen', *Deutsche Juristen-Zeitung*, 39, 1934, pp. 691–8, p. 691.
38 Carl Schmitt, 'Der Neubau des Staats- und Verwaltungsrechts', in Rudolf Schraut (ed.), *Deutscher Juristentag 1933*, Berlin: Deutsche Rechts- und Wirtschafts-Wissenschaft, p. 251; cf. Raphael Gross, *Carl Schmitt und die Juden. Eine deutsche Rechtslehre*, Frankfurt am Main: Suhrkamp, 2005, p. 70.
39 I use the term 'legal scholars' when I speak of those jurists whose texts we are discussing. The most famous was Carl Schmitt, who was professor in Berlin and from June 1934 the chief editor of *Deutsche Juristen-Zeitung*, one of the most important legal journals. His student Ernst Forsthoff was a professor at Frankfurt am Main, later in Hamburg. Karl Larenz, Georg Dahm and Karl Michaelis belonged to the Kiel school, i.e. the Department of Law at the University of Kiel, which was playing a leading role in building National Socialist legal thinking, especially through the application of a Hegelian legal philosophy. In Breslau, another 'shock troop university', there were Rector Gustav Adolf Walz, Heinrich Lange and Hans Helfritz. Otto Koellreutter was a professor at Jena and Munich, Heinrich Gerland at Jena, Heinrich Henkel at Marburg. Theodor Maunz was associate professor at Freiburg, where Erik Wolf, a friend of Heidegger, was a dean of the Law Faculty. Georg Kaisenberg was Ministerial Secretary. Helmut Seydel was an attorney-at-law. Then there were devoted party jurists: Hans Frank, Minister of Justice for Bavaria, the Reich Minister, the head of the National Socialist Jurists Association and president of the Academy of German Law, Roland Freisler, State Secretary at the Ministry of Justice, Reinhard Höhn, professor at Heidelberg and Berlin, Helmut Nicolai, Ministerial Director and later tax consultant, and Wilhelm Frick, Interior Minister.
40 Rüthers, *Entartetes Recht*, p. 19; Hubert Rottleuthner, 'Substantieller Dezisionismus. Zur Funktion der Rechstphilosophie im Nationalsozialismus', in Hubert Rottleuthner (ed.), *Rechts, Rechtsphilosophie und Nationalsozialismus*, Wiesbaden: Steiner, 1983. According to Stolleis, there was no 'real "legal doctrine" (legal philosophy, legal theory) of National Socialism (Stolleis, *The Law under the Swastika*, p. 20); see also Diemut Majer, *Grundlagen des nationalsozialistischen Rechtssystems. Führerprinzip, Sonderrecht, Einheitspartei*, Stuttgart: Kohlhammer, 1987, p. 23.
41 Nicolai, *Der Staat im nationalsozialistischen Weltbild*, p. 20.
42 Hermann Göring, *Die Rechtsicherheit als Grundlage der Volksgemeinschaft*, Hamburg: Hanseatische Verlagsanstalt, p. 935.
43 Otto Koellreutter, 'Der nationale Rechtsstaat', *Deutsche Juristen-Zeitung*, 38, 1933, pp. 517–24, p. 517.
44 Ibid., p. 517.
45 Otto Koellreutter, *Grundriss der Allgemeinen Staatslehre*, Tübingen: Mohr, 1933, pp. 108–9.
46 Koellreutter, 'Der nationale Rechtsstaat', p. 523.
47 Cf. Carl Schmitt, 'Nationalsozialismus und Rechtsstaat', *Juristische Wochenschrift*, 63, 1934, pp. 713–18; Carl Schmitt, 'Was bedeutet der Streit um den "Rechtsstaat"', *Zeitschrift für die gesamte Staatswissenschaft*, 95, 1935, pp. 189–201; Carl Schmitt, 'Der Rechtsstaat', in Hans Frank (ed.), *Nationalsozialistisches Handbuch für Recht und Gesetzgebung*, Munich: Zentralverlag der NSDAP, Franz Eher Nachf., 1935. On the dispute about the *Rechtsstaat* see Stolleis, *A History of Public Law in Germany*, pp. 349–58; Peter Caldwell, 'National Socialist and constitutional law: Carl Schmitt, Otto Koellreutter, and the debate over the nature of the Nazi state, 1933–1937', *Cardozo Law Review*, 16, 1994, pp. 399–427.

On Schmitt and jurisprudence under National Socialism see Gross, *Carl Schmitt und die Juden*.

48 Carl Schmitt, 'Neue Leitsätze für die Rechtspraxis', *Juristische Wochenschrift*, 62, 1933, pp. 2793–4, p. 2793.

49 Ibid., p. 2793; Schmitt, 'Nationalsozialismus und Rechtsstaat', p. 717.

50 Schmitt, 'Was bedeutet der Streit um den Rechtsstaat', p. 199; Hans Frank, 'Der deutsche Rechtsstaat Adolf Hitlers', *Deutsches Recht*, 4, 1934.

51 Schmitt, 'Die Verfassung der Freiheit', *Deutsche Juristen-Zeitung*, 40, 1935, pp. 1133–5, p. 1135.

52 Hans Helfritz, 'Rechtsstaat und nationalsozialistischer Staat', *Deutsche Juristen-Zeitung*, 39, 1934, pp. 426–33, p. 433.

53 Gustav Adolf Walz, 'Autoritärer Staat, nationaler Rechtsstaat oder völkischer Führerstaat?' *Deutsche Juristen-Zeitung*, 38, pp. 1334–40, pp. 1336, 1339.

54 Forsthoff, *Der totale Staat*, pp. 9–10. Koellreutter criticized the term 'total state', which Schmitt had also used, even though he had turned away from it after April 1933. For Koellreutter the theory of the total state is the theory of the power state, whose aim is to maintain its own power. This continued the dualism of liberalism, where power and the individual are opposed and politics is not about integration into a national community. Alfred Rosenberg and Roland Freisler also criticized the term 'total state'.

55 Ibid., pp. 33–4.

56 Ibid., p. 38.

57 Georg Dahm saw a difference here from the Italian fascist total state. Georg Dahm, *Nationalsozialistisches und faschistisches Strafrecht*, Berlin: Junker & Dünnhaupt, 1935, pp. 9–10.

58 Nicolai, *Der Staat im nationalsozialistischen Weltbild*, p. 23.

59 Heinrich Gerland, 'Rechtserneuerung und Revolution', *Deutsche Juristen-Zeitung*, 38, 1933, pp. 1065–9, pp. 1066, 1069.

60 Wolf, *Richtiges Recht*, p. 23.

61 Forsthoff, *Der totale Staat*, p. 46.

62 Lange, *Liberalismus*, p. 3.

63 Nicolai, *Der Staat im nationalsozialistischen Weltbild*, p. 27.

64 Walz, 'Autoritärer Staat', p. 1339.

65 Schmitt, 'Die Verfassung der Freiheit', p. 1135.

66 Schmitt, *Staat*, p. 32. In another connection Schmitt said that 'Hegel's state … is neither mere sovereign decision nor a "norm of norms" … It is the concrete order of orders, the institution of institutions.' Schmitt, *On the Three Types of Juristic Thought*, pp. 78–9. Hegel's state as the realization of reason and ethics did not go well together with the idea of a racially determined unity of the community of the *Volk* and the leadership of Hitler, which Schmitt and his neo-Hegelian supporters did not recognize, Koellreutter argued. Rüthers sees this as one reason for Schmitt distancing himself from Hegel. Otto Koellreutter, *Volk und Staat in der Weltanschauung des Nationalsozialismus*, Berlin: Pan, 1935; Rüthers, *Entartetes Recht*, pp. 78–80.

67 Schmitt, *Staat*, p. 15.

68 Ibid., p. 12.

69 Ibid., p. 42.

70 Ibid.

71 Ibid.

72 Koellreutter, *Grundriss der Allgemeinen Staatslehre*, p. 54.

73 Hans Frank, 'Die Einwirkung des nationalsozialistischen Ideengutes auf das deutsche Rechtsleben', *Deutsche Juristen-Zeitung*, 39, 1934, pp. 1169–74, p. 1171.

74 Helmut Seydel, 'Führer und Leiter', *Deutsche Juristen-Zeitung*, 40, 1935, pp. 1213–18, p. 1213.
75 Carl Schmitt, 'Der Führer schütz das Recht. Zur Reichstagsrede Adolf Hitlers vom 13 Juli 1934', *Deutsche Juristen-Zeitung*, 39, 1934, pp. 945–50, p. 946.
76 Ibid., p. 947.
77 Carl Schmitt, 'Kodifikation oder Novelle? Über die Aufgabe und Methode der heutigen Gesetzgebung', *Deutsche Juristen-Zeitung*, 40, 1935, pp. 919–25, p. 924.
78 Larenz, 'Deutsche Rechtserneuerung und Rechtsphilosophie', p. 34.
79 Forsthoff, *Der totale Staat*, p. 42.
80 Walz, 'Autoritäter Staat', p. 1339.
81 Lange, *Liberalismus*, pp. 3–4.
82 Koellreutter, *Grundriss der Allgemeinen Staatslehre*, p. 200.
83 Ibid., p. 50.
84 Michaelis, 'Wandlung des deutschen Rechtsdenkens', p. 9.
85 Wolf, *Richtiges Recht*, pp. 3, 12.
86 Theodor Maunz, *Neue Grundlagen des Verwaltungsrecht*, Hamburg: Hanseatische Verlagsanstalt, 1934, pp. 32–3.
87 Roland Freisler, *Das Werden des Juristen im Dritten Reich* I, Berlin: Junker & Dünnhaupt, 1933, p. 20.
88 Lange, *Liberalismus*, pp. 1, 6.
89 Ibid., p. 7.
90 Ibid.
91 Frank, 'Die Einwirkung des nationalsozialistischen Ideengutes', p. 1171.
92 Schmitt, 'Die Verfassung der Freiheit', p. 1135. Schmitt commented of Italian Fascism: 'The problem of race is ignored in Italy'. Carl Schmitt, 'Faschistische und nationalsozialistische Rechtswissenschaft', *Deutsche Juristen-Zeitung*, 41, 1936, pp. 619–20, p. 620. Dahm also drew a distinction between National Socialism and Fascism, which emphasized the concept of the nation, the spiritual and historical unity created through will and historical act, and not of the *Volk*, the unity of race and blood. Dahm, *Nationalsozialistisches und faschistisches Strafrecht*, p. 7.
93 Carl Schmitt, 'Der Weg des deutschen Juristen', *Deutsche Juristen-Zeitung*, 39, 1934, pp. 691–8, p. 691.
94 Schmitt, *On the Three Types of Juristic Thought*, pp. 48–9.
95 Schmitt referred to Hölderlin's note to his translation of Pindar's fragment (which Schmitt misread) in order to show how *nomos* and king are related to each other, in order to affirm the connection between the will of the Führer and the *nomos* of the German *Volk*. Schmitt, *On the Three Types of Juristic Thought*, pp. 50–1; Gross, *Carl Schmitt und die Juden*, pp. 111–12.
96 Schmitt cites here the Reich Minister of Justice, Hans Frank. Schmitt, *On the Three Types of Juristic Thought*, p. 97; see also p. 114 n. 73.
97 Schmitt, 'Die Verfassung der Freiheit', p. 1135.
98 Schmitt, 'Der Weg des deutschen Juristen', p. 698.
99 Reinhard Höhn, *Rechtsgemeinschaft und Volksgemeinschaft*, Hamburg: Hanseatische Verlagsanstalt, 1935, pp. 72–81; see also Reinhard Höhn, *Vom Wesen der Gemeinschaft*, Berlin: Heymann, 1934; Reinhard Höhn, *Der individualistische Staatsbegriff und die juristische Staatsperson*, Berlin: Heymann, 1935.
100 Karl Larenz, 'Volksgeist und Recht. Zur Revision der Rechtsanschauung der historischen Schule', *Zeitschrift für Deutsche Kulturphilosophie*, 1, 1935, pp. 40–60, p. 42.
101 Ibid., p. 43.
102 Ibid., p. 43.
103 Ibid., p. 42.

104 Ibid., pp. 40, 45.
105 Ibid., p. 47.
106 Ibid., p. 48.
107 Ibid., p. 57.
108 Schmitt, 'Nationalsozialistisches Rechtsdenken', *Deutsches Recht*, 4, 1934, pp. 225–9, p. 225.
109 Karl Larenz, 'Rechtsperson und subjectives Recht. Zur Wandlung der Rechtsgrundbegriffe', in Georg Dahm et al. (eds), *Grundfragen der neuen Rechtswissenschaft*, Berlin: Junker & Dünnhaupt, 1933, p. 228.
110 Larenz, *Deutsche Rechtserneuerung und Rechtsphilosophie*, p. 40.
111 Larenz, 'Rechtsperson und subjectives Recht', p. 229.
112 Ibid., p. 259.
113 Cf. Rüthers, *Entartetes Recht*, p. 92.
114 Helmut Nicolai, 'Zum Gesetz über den Neuaufbau des Reiches', *Deutsche Juristen-Zeitung*, 39, 1934, pp. 233–8, p. 238.
115 Nicolai, *Der Staat im nationalsozialistischen Weltbild*, pp. 16, 19.
116 Nicolai, 'Zum Gesetz über den Neuaufbau des Reiches', p. 238.
117 Ibid.
118 Nicolai, *Der Staat im nationalsozialistischen Weltbild*, p. 36.
119 Ibid., p. 14.
120 Ibid., pp. 17–18.
121 Ibid., p. 39; cf. Nicolai, *Die rassengesetzliche Rechtslehre. Grundzüge einer nationalsozialistischen Rechtsphilosophie*, Munich: Eher, 1934.
122 Schmitt, 'Der Neubau des Staats- und Verwaltungsrecht', p. 251. According to Raphael Gross, Schmitt saw a connection between *Art*, type, race, species, and *Denken*, thinking, and hence racially dissimilar, could not think in a German way. Gross, *Carl Schmitt und die Juden*, p. 70; see also Schmitt, *Staat*, pp. 32–46.
123 Schmitt, 'Die Verfassung der Freiheit', p. 1134–5.
124 Wilhelm Frick, 'Das Reichsbürgergesetz und das Gesetz zum schutz des deutschen Blutes und der deutschen Ehre vom 15 September 1935', *Deutsche Juristen-Zeitung*, 40, 1935, pp. 1389–94, p. 1389.
125 Wilhelm Frick, *Die Rassengesetzgebung des Dritten Reiches*, Munich: Zentralverlag der NSDP, F. Eber Nachf, 1934, p. 3.
126 Ibid., p. 5.
127 Forsthoff, *Der totale Staat*, p. 42.
128 Ibid., p. 43.
129 Roland Freisler, 'Recht, Richter und Gesetz', *Deutsche Justiz*, 49, 1933, pp. 694–6, p. 695; Roland Freisler, *Nationalsozialistisches Recht und Rechtsdenken*, Berlin: Spaeth & Linde, 1938, p. 54. The will of the Führer, *Volksgemeinschaft* and the party programme were legal norms, which were superior to old statutory laws. However, there was a tension between a subjective-teleological interpretation that was orientated to the will of the legislator and an objective one, orientated to the dynamic development of the will of the law of the *Volksgemeinschaft*. Rüthers, *Entartetes Recht*, pp. 29, 35–6; see also Majer, *Grundlagen des nationalsozialistischen Rechtssystems*.
130 Heinrich Henkel, *Die Unabhängigkeit des Richters in ihrem neuen Sinngehalt*, Hamburg: Hanseatische Verlagsanstalt, 1934, pp. 33–4.
131 Helfritz, 'Rechtsstaat und nationalsozialistischer Staat', p. 432.
132 Schmitt, 'Der Weg des deutschen Juristen', p. 692.
133 Schmitt, 'Nationalsozialismus und Rechtsstaat', p. 716.
134 Schmitt, *On the Three Types of Juristic Thought*, p. 91; cf. Schmitt, 'Nationalsozialismus und Rechtsstaat', p. 717. According to Arthur Kauffman, in actual legal practice there existed a two-track strategy: if one was dealing with pre-1933

laws the rigours of positivism did not prevail, but if one was dealing with National Socialist laws, then one had to obey and follow the laws literally, even if they were flagrantly unjust. Arthur Kaufmann, 'National Socialism and German jurisprudence from 1933 to 1945', *Cardozo Law Review*, 9, 1988, pp. 1629–49.

135 Schmitt, 'Der Weg des deutschen Juristen', p. 694.

136 Ibid., p. 695.

137 Schmitt, 'Nationalsozialismus und Rechtsstaat', p. 717.

138 Schmitt, 'Kodifikation oder Novelle?' p. 924.

139 Ibid., p. 925. In new laws there were precepts, which included concrete guidelines ordering the spiritual posture and persuasion of jurists. 'They give judges a new bond and a new freedom.' These precepts were 'immediately and in most intensive way the positive law'. Ibid., pp. 922–3.

140 Schmitt, *Staat*, pp. 44–5.

141 Schmitt, 'Der Führer schützt das Recht.' p. 947.

142 Schmitt, *Staat*, p. 44.

143 The dominant position of positivism during National Socialism and the positivism of National Socialist legal thinking and praxis has been turned down by a number of writers: see Bernd Rüthers, *Die unbegrenzte Auslegung. Zum Wandel der Privatrechtsordnung im Nationalsozialismus*, Tübingen: Mohr, 1968; Ingo Müller, *Hitler's Justice. The Courts of the Third Reich*, trans. Deborah Lucas Schneider, Cambridge, MA: Harvard University Press, 1991; Stolleis, *The Law under the Swastika*, pp. 8–22; Rottleuthner, 'Substantieller Dezisionismus'. Actually, the legal positivism and formalism which predominated during the German Empire had already lost its predominant position in the Weimar Republic as the anti-liberal judiciary attempted to water down legal reforms.

144 Hannah Arendt, *The Origins of Totalitarianism*. New York: Harcourt, 1973, p. 472.

145 Dana Villa, *Politics, Philosophy, Terror. Essays on the Thought of Hannah Arendt*, Princeton, NJ: Princeton University Press, 1999, p. 17.

146 Philippe Lacoue-Labarthe and Jean-Luc Nancy, *Le Mythe nazi*, Tour de Aigues: Éditions de l'Aube, 1996, p. 22.

147 Ibid., p. 25.

148 Ibid., p. 58–66.

149 Cf. Emmanuel Levinas, 'Reflections on the philosophy of Hitlerism', trans. Seán Hand, *Critical Inquiry*, 17, 1990, pp. 63 71; Josh Cohen, *Interrupting Auschwitz. Art, Religion, Philosophy*, London: Continuum, 2003, p. 7.

150 Lacoue-Labarthe and Nancy, *Le Mythe nazi*, p. 68.

151 Lepsius, 'The problem of perceptions of National Socialist law', p. 24.

152 Cf. Jean-Luc Nancy, *La Communauté affrontée*, Paris: Galilée, 2001, p. 15.

153 Arendt, *The Origins of Totalitarianism*, p. 462.

154 Cited in ibid., p. 325.

155 Jean-Luc Nancy, *The Inoperative Community*, trans. Peter Connor, Minneapolis, MN: University of Minnesota Press, 1991, p. 4. Hubert Rottleuthner has described National Socialist legal philosophy as substantial decisionism: on the one hand there was the substantial natural law, on the other hand the decision and the Führer principle, and in the final analysis the substance could be decided by the Führer, which led to the instrumentalization of the law. Rottleuthner, 'Substantieller Dezisionismus', pp. 29–31.

156 Alfred Rosenberg, *The Myth of the Twentieth Century*, trans. Vivian Bird, Newport Beach, CA: Noontide Press, 1993, p. 344.

157 Ibid., p. xlvi.

158 According to Giorgio Agamben, National Socialism determined the bare life, *zoē* (which differs from *bios*, the mode of life proper to individuals and groups) of

homo sacer in a biological and eugenic key and made it into the site of an incessant decision on value and non-value in which biopolitics turned into thanatopolitics and in which the camp became the absolute political space. Giorgio Agamben, *Homo Sacer. Sovereign Power and Bare Life*, trans. Daniel Heller-Roazen, Stanford, CA: Stanford University Press, 1995, p. 153.

159 Cf. Lacoue-Labarthe and Nancy, *Le Mythe nazi*, pp. 57–8.

160 Ibid., pp. 68–9.

161 Ibid.

162 Sarah Kofman, *Paroles suffoquées*, Paris: Galilée, 1987, p. 36.

163 Nancy, *The Inoperative Community*, p. 60.

164 Nancy, *Being Singular Plural*, trans. Robert D. Richardson and Anne O'Byrne, Stanford, CA: Stanford University Press, 2000, pp. 20–1.

165 Cf. Arendt, *The Origins of Totalitarianism*, p. 445.

166 Carl Schmitt, 'Amnestie oder die Kraft des Vergessens', in *Staat, Grossraum, Nomos. Arbeiten aus den Jahren 1916–69*, Berlin: Duncker & Humblot, 1995, p. 218. It was published on 10 November 1949 in *Christ und Welt* as an anonymous essay under the title 'Amnestie. Urform des Rechts'.

167 Stolleis, *The Law under the Swastika*, p. 183.

168 Hannah Arendt, *Eichmann in Jerusalem. A Report on the Banality of Evil*, London: Penguin Books, 1994, p. 135.

169 Arendt, *Eichmann in Jerusalem*, p. 136.

170 Ibid., p. 49.

171 Ibid., p. 290.

172 Ibid., p. 252.

173 Ibid., p. 26–7.

174 Cf. Fabio Ciaramelli, 'From radical evil to the banality of evil. Remarks on Kant and Arendt', in Alan Milchman and Alan Rosenberg (eds), *Postmodernism and the Holocaust*, trans. Thomas A. Carlson, Amsterdam: Rodopi, p. 102.

175 Arendt, *Eichmann in Jerusalem*, p. 293.

176 Gustav Radbruch, *Grundzüge der Rechtsphilosophie*, Leipzig: Quelle & Meyer, 1914, p. 3.

177 Ciaramelli, 'From radical evil to the banality of evil', p. 102.

178 Schmitt, 'Nationalsozialistisches Rechtsdenken', p. 225.

179 Arendt, *The Origins of Totalitarianism*, p. 470.

180 Ibid., p. 469.

181 Ibid., p. 472.

182 Ibid., p. 470.

183 Ibid.

184 Cf. Avital Ronell, 'The differends of man', *Diacritics*, 19, 1989, pp. 63–75, p. 65.

185 Paul Celan, 'Speech on the Occasion of receiving the Literature Prize of the Free Hanseatic City of Bremen', trans. John Felstiner, in *Selected Poems and Prose of Paul Celan*, New York: Norton, 2001, p. 395.

186 Immanuel Kant, *Kritik der Urteilskraft. Werkausgabe* X, Frankfurt am Main: Suhrkamp, 1990, §40.

187 Hannah Arendt, *The Life of the Mind* I, *Thinking*, New York: Harcourt Brace, 1978, p. 193; Cf. Arendt, *Lectures of Kant's Political Philosophy*, Chicago: University of Chicago Press, 1989.

188 Cf. Nancy, *The Inoperative Community*, p. 35.

189 Immanuel Kant, *Religion within Boundaries of mere Reason*, in *Religion and Rational Theology*, trans. Georgi di Giovanni, Cambridge: Cambridge University Press, 2005.

190 Hannah Arendt and Karl Jaspers, *Hannah Arendt–Karl Jaspers Correspondence*, New York: Harcourt Brace, 1992, p. 166.

191 Here I follow Richard J. Bernstein, *Radical Evil. A Philosophical Interrogation*, London: Polity Press, 2002, p. 38.
192 Ibid., p. 39.
193 Arendt and Jaspers, *Hannah Arendt–Karl Jaspers*, p. 62.
194 Alenka Zupančič, *The Ethics of the Real. Kant, Lacan*, London: Verso, 2000, p. 90.
195 Ibid., p.163.
196 Ibid.
197 Joan Copjec, *Imagine there's no Woman. Ethics and Sublimation*: Cambridge, MA: MIT Press, 2002, p. 144.
198 Arendt refers also to Hans Frank's formulation: 'Act in such a way that the Führer, if he knew your action, would approve it.' Arendt, *Eichmann in Jerusalem*, p. 136. See also Slavoj Žižek, *The Plague of Fantasies*, London: Verso, 1997, p. 235.
199 Hannah Arendt, 'Letter to Scholem', in *The Hannah Arendt Papers at the Library of Congress. Correspondence: Scholem, Gershom Gerhard, 1963–1964*, pp. 33–38. Available online: http://memory.loc.gov/ammem/arendthtml/arendthome.html.
200 Arendt, *The Origins of Totalitarianism*, pp. 447–57.
201 Cf. John Silber, 'Ethical significance of Kant's religion', p. civ, in Immanuel Kant, *Religion within the Limits of Reason Alone*, New York: Harper Torchbooks, 1960; see also Bernstein, *Radical Evil*, p. 14.

Chapter 9

The birth of terrorism out of the spirit of the Enlightenment

The subject of Enlightenment and the terrorist sensorium

Artemy Magun

Terrorism today

Perhaps the most puzzling and pressing form in which the question of evil surfaces for us today is the phenomenon of terrorism. While terrorism may be understandable and rational as an efficient strategy in a mediate way, in its immediacy it appears as an action directly aimed at doing evil: not evil against a particular person or group, but evil as such. Unlike the acts of a regular war, which do evil *to* someone in particular, contemporary terrorist acts seek to do something monstrous or catastrophic *in itself*. Only in the second turn, their action could serve an expressive purpose (to express one's despair) or an instrumental purpose, to do harm to the world hegemony or to a regional hegemony, and/or provoke it into an adventurous and destabilizing military action. Hence, apart from the natural anger and hatred of the terrorists, their acts evoke the age-old question: how can humans will such a thing; how can such a diabolical evil, evil for the sake of evil, be a 'maxim' of someone's behaviour?

Contemporary 'terrorism' is one of the main military strategies of unprivileged groups across the world, used both to achieve direct military goals and to make symbolic statements of opposition and dissent against the global hegemony of liberal capitalism. Terrorism against the indeterminate civilian population came to a dominance in the last decades, following the rise of fundamentalist Islamic radicals after the Iranian revolution, and particularly after the end of the Cold War, which turned the bilateral frame of the local conflicts (allies of the United States against the allies of the Soviet Union) into the asymmetrical frame (rebels and radicals against the rest of the 'civilized world'). The disappearance of the symmetry in status and in the Enlightenment-based ideology (communism versus liberalism), the position of lonely partisans in the face of an all-powerful hegemony, facilitated the transition of many rebellious groups, particularly in Islamic countries, to the terrorist acts as purely negative self-manifestations.

While violence against the civil population and hostage-taking have always existed in wars, today's radicals use them abundantly, sometimes as their *only* strategy, and their acts of violence produce an enormous impact due to their dissemination through the world media, mainly television. The 'terrorist' acts are shocking in their use of violence and in the relatively arbitrary choice of victims. Therefore, they are not only shown on television worldwide, but they also attract the exceptional attention both of news agencies and of their audience. One other crucial factor in the efficiency and spread of terrorism is democracy, existing *de jure* and in some ways *de facto*, and thus making the whole population symbolically responsible for state policy and capable, through election or public opinion, to change that policy. The blind violence of terrorism, addressed from nobody to nobody, corresponds to the idea of modern democracy as of impersonal, post-regicide rule, as the classical professional war corresponded to the absolutist, personified states.

I suggest, at least for the sake of this chapter, to limit the meaning of the word 'terrorism' to the strategy of intimidation with regard to *civil population.* This definition differs from most definitions adopted in international and US law[1] in that it narrows the 'intimidation' down to the civil population, instead of considering any intimidation to be a sign of terrorism. In the latter case, violence against soldiers or government officials, meant to intimidate other soldiers or officials, would count as terrorism, and then almost any act of war could be considered as such. Although, historically, 'terrorism' from below started in Russia, from violence against officials, such use of the term makes it entirely ideological, subjective and lacking historical specificity: any violence not recognized by the state, any breach of the peace would be considered as terrorism. The intimidating violence against civilians is, on the other hand, if not entirely new, at least objectively characteristic for the civil warfare of our times.

Historically, the concept of 'terrorism' made a long journey, from the pejorative title of the violent politics linked with the Jacobin Terror of the French revolutionary government, then to the revolutionary violence against the officials as practised by the nineteenth-century Russian *narodniks*, but also by the Red Brigades and RAF of the late twentieth century, to terrorism against the arbitrarily taken civilian population, practised in the twentieth century by the Algerian rebels, Palestinian liberation fighters, and currently by many clandestine groups in the historically Muslim region. What is common among these three different phenomena is their democratic character, the use of intimidation, and the recourse to the merely negative affirmation of sovereignty. But otherwise, these are three completely different concepts. The first two 'terrorisms' are not really unique: the policy of intimidation against enemies of the state and the war against the ruling class are not that special or surprising. Moreover, the identification of the addressed violence of the Russian nihilists and of the violence against arbitrary victims, in the case of, say, Al Qaeda, is an ideological statement which depends on belief in the state's monopoly on legitimate violence. Which, again, is not to say that there can be no drift between these two concepts, as we will further see in reading Dostoyevsky.

Terrorism and the subject of Enlightenment.

In what follows I will try to show that the contemporary terrorism is the crisis of the Enlightenment subject. This subject is, first of all, characterized by self-control and self-mastery. But the task of mastering oneself sets the further task of auto-affectation. As Heidegger rightly maintained, the true origin of subjectivity (as conceptualized by Kant) is the auto-affectation, or the affectation with nothing, a sphere where the activity of the subject coincides with its passivity, and this indeterminate affective moment provides a foundation for the mutual determination of subject and object.[2] The new subject needs to feel itself, to make sure of itself and of its surroundings. Therefore, Enlightenment consists, literally, in the desire to know. Moreover, this desire is practically expressed by the drive, to *feel*: to know with empirical certainty, and to add the feeling of self to the feeling of an object. This is why the Enlightenment, as a historical movement, brings about not just the emancipation of the subject and the victory of reason over prejudice, but equally the anxiety and the vulnerability.

It is in today's world, the world of mediatized terrorism, that this ambivalence of Enlightenment has reached its culmination. I will start with a brief discussion of the last film by Michael Haneke, *Le Caché.*[3] The protagonist, George (played by Daniel Auteuil), works in a television show. His family is terrorized by someone who keeps sending them the tapes from a video camera that is directed at their yard and records everything that goes on there. These camera shots are subtly integrated into the visual line of the movie, so that we often confuse this spying camera with the camera shooting the movie we are watching. (The movie is shot in a very prosaic, 'realistic' style.) We thus find ourselves in the position of a spy. George starts an inquiry, which turns into a psychoanalytic search of his past, and ends with the discovery of a cruel injustice he has committed on someone in his early childhood. Following the clues left by the perpetrator, George finds the victim of this early injustice, a middle-aged Arabic guy living in an HLM (the French economy housing project). After several meetings and mutual accusations, the latter cuts his throat in front of him. At the end of the movie we see the hero 'hiding' (*caché*) from anyone's gaze in a room with closed curtains. Thus he passes from hiding one's past to hiding oneself, from the gaze of the media, of terror, and of his conscience (which all make one). In the end, the camera gives us a long gaze at the schoolyard, where, on the margin, with our peripheral vision, we can observe the sons of the protagonist and of the victim talking to each other in a friendly way – which suggests they might have planned the whole thing together.

The meaning of the movie is quite straightforward. It is an allegory of present-day terrorism and its complicity with the media: terrorist acts are efficient only as long as the media are obsessively showing them, and because television spectators are fascinated by these acts that horrify them.

Thus the gaze of the media and of the spectators bears terror in itself, and the terrorists return it to them by fulfilling their expectations. What is additionally interesting here, however, is the play between the two functions of the media: that of exposing, making something public, and that of anxiously watching and gazing. The character of Auteuil is a television anchor, but while his exposure in public (in a stupid talk show) is a source of pride and enjoyment, his exposure in his private life is the source of anxiety and terror, which induces him to 'analytic' self-questioning.

Haneke's movie alludes to some contemporary theoretical reflections on the link between the media, society and terror. Thus Paul Virilio defines our time as that of 'universal voyeurism'.[4] Patricia Mellencamp, in her analysis of US television since 9/11,[5] notes the images of anxiety, of 'pure gaze', that dominate the depiction of contemporary wars, such as the picture of an empty parking lot which was shown, for most of the time, during the operation in Baghdad in 2003. Such images, says Mellencamp, both arouse anxiety and play the role of psychological shield against the traumatic knowledge of violence (which is not shown, but feared). Thus the mediatic 'terror' is an ideological phenomenon which raises concerns of security and legitimates states' use of violence and repression but which, at the same time, makes the situation tolerable by concealing the violence itself and showing only its *expectation.*

Terror, both chronologically and logically, is a child of Enlightenment – the age when the famous 'public sphere' and the first modern media were born.[6] This is the sequence we find already in Hegel's *Phenomenology of Spirit.*[7] (The section on freedom and terror during the French revolution follows right after the section dedicated to the Enlightenment.) For Hegel, however, the fault of the Enlightenment consisted in failing to conceive a thing as it is, and, instead, in deriving value only from external utility. The analysis by Haneke in his movie suggests that we might need to take Enlightenment literally, seeing it primarily as the will to light, to vision and knowledge of things as they *are.* This will to light is at the same time tightly connected to anxiety. Here we might need to go back from Hegel to Kant.

Kant continued the rebellion of Rousseau against the vulgar Enlightenment as described by Hegel, against the Enlightenment that wanted to subjugate humans to the calculation of Understanding. Instead, as we know, Kant spoke of the primacy of practical reason over theoretical reason[8] – not in the sense that a hu/man must use his/her knowledge for a noble purpose, but in the sense that s/he has already been in advance active in this *seemingly passive* knowledge. The most famous application of this principle is the famous 'force of imagination', this 'hidden art' that works productively when we think that we just passively process the sensory data.[9]

However, in the short text from 1784, 'An answer to the question: What is Enlightenment?',[10] Kant presents the activity of reason in another form, that of the motto, coming from Horace: *Sapere aude* ('Dare to know!'), 'Have the courage to make use of your *own* understanding!'[11] This 'public use of one's reason'[12] is in itself an act, the praxis of courageous exposure which, according to Kant, prepares and even already embodies the process of Enlightenment. One exercises it in texts, *Schriften* – public writings. Kant mentions the danger that accompanies those texts, as it follows any exposure – this time, danger probably coming from the Prussian police.

In the same text, Kant repeatedly defines the Enlightenment as the 'exit out of the state of immaturity' which is achieved when we learn to live by our own reason, without trusting the state's officials in matters of knowledge and belief. This immaturity, says Kant, we owe to ourselves. And yet we have to exit from this state in order to be truly autonomous, truly obliged only to ourselves – truly subjects, as we would now say.

Thus the motive of *being active in the very passivity* is joined here with two other definitions of Enlightenment: that of a passage or promotion to *recognition*, almost a rite of passage to dignity, and that of subjectivity: of self-relation or self-affection. The media perfectly embody these three sides of Enlightenment: they publish and expose knowledge and opinion; they keep our attention through the constant expectation of something new and breaking through (they speak of the 'news', of the 'new'), thus routinely enacting a collective rite of passage into a new life or a new world; and they also provide an excellent instrument of self-control and self-monitoring of society – a mediation necessary for a finite being to refer to itself, to be a subject.

The French revolution was the explosion of the internal contradictions in the Enlightenment. It was a decisive step forward to 'extricate himself from [his] minority' (one more task of Enlightenment, according to Kant), to build a self-governing, republican nation-subject – and, last but not least, to increase the transparency of society, the rationality of its government. Unexpectedly for most, this laudable project, which seduced almost everyone in Europe in 1789 and 1790, turned into a burst of violence culminating in the September 1792 prison murders and the law against suspects in 1794. This turn received the name of 'terror'. This word was coined in 1793 by the Montagnard fraction of Jacobins who explicitly wanted to terrify their hidden and dissimulated enemies by ruthless repression, but who also accused those enemies of terrifying the people, in their turn. Let us note the strangeness in the use of the very word 'terror' for the phenomenon of modern political violence. This is a word which actually means the *feeling* of someone who experiences fear, but whose political meaning means, contrarily, *the imposition of this feeling.* Clearly, the French terrorists felt and exercised terror at the same time, and it was for them a kind of *negative auto-affection.*

Now, Kant, as we know, reacted to the revolution in a way that one usually understands as 'ambiguous'. Indeed, in the second division of *The Conflict of the Faculties* (1795, published 1798), he writes about it in an enthusiastic tone, and in the *Metaphysics of Morals* (1797) he vigorously denounces it. What exactly could have happened there? We'll understand it better if we consider these texts in some detail.

In the second part of *The Conflict* Kant points at the experience that could both show and guarantee the irreversible progress, in spite of the finitude of our perspective on time.

> There must be some experience in human kind which, as an event [*Begebenheit*], points to the disposition and capacity of the human race to be the cause of its own advance toward the better ... An event [*Begebenheit*] must be sought which points to the existence of such a cause and to its effectiveness in humankind, undetermined with regard to time, and which would allow progress toward the better to be concluded as an inevitable consequence.
>
> The conclusion then could also be extended to the history of the past (that it has always been in progress) in such a way that the event [*Begebenheit*] would have to be considered not itself as the cause of history, but only as an intimation [*als hindeutend*], a historical sign demonstrating [*beweisen*] the tendency of humankind viewed in its entirety.[13]

Kant finds this event happening 'in our time': in the time of the French revolution. But he finds it in a curious way – with a negation: the one which Freud called *Verneinung*,[14] 'denegation'. The event in question, says Kant, does not either depend on whether the 'revolution of the spiritual people' will succeed or fail. Instead:

> It is simply the mode of thinking of the spectators which reveals itself publicly in this game of great transformations, and manifests such a universal yet disinterested sympathy for the players on one side against those on the other, even at the risk that this partiality could become very disadvantageous for them if discovered.[15]

What he means here is the enlightened German audience expressing support for revolution in the journals and in the cafés. A curious argument that locates the event, not in a political occurrence, but in the reflexive turn from this occurrence to the subject. The event is reduced to a gaze at this event. And, of course, these German spectators exemplify the *sapere aude*, being active in their very (political and epistemological) passivity.

This constellation, says Kant, 'is not to be forgotten' and thus, through the memory of humanity, it guarantees the slow but sure progress.

> For that event is too important, too much interwoven with the interest of humanity, and its influence too widely propagated in all areas of the world not to be recalled on any favourable occasion by the nations which would then be roused to a repetition of new efforts of this kind.[16]

Thus the turn from the essentially negative event away to the subject is further reproduced in the repetitive returns to the site of this turn: these returns precisely constitute *subjectivity*. This is possible precisely because the event is unaccomplished, not quite real, so that it is a sign that constantly requires interpretation. ('Ein Zeichen sind wir, deutungslos,' we are a sign with no meaning or interpretation, said famously Friedrich Hölderlin, Kant's reader and follower, in his 'Patmos'.) The 'progress' builds upon the memory of a trauma.

Similar things go on in Kant's text on the regicide, from *The Metaphysics of Morals*.[17] But there the 'unforgettable,' mnemotechnical character of the event is expressed as 'a crime that remains for ever and can never be expiated (*crimen immortale, inexpiabile*), and it seems to be like the sin that cannot be forgiven either in this world or the next'.[18] The subjectivation is accomplished also through the repeated return: through the '*shudder* [*Schaudern*] that one repeatedly feels as soon as and as often as one thinks of this scene, like the fate of Charles I or Louis XVI'.[19]

However, the good news is that no such event has ever happened! A human being, says Kant, is incapable of the diabolical evil, because the latter is a contradictory idea. A formal execution of Louis XVI would embody precisely this idea. Thus it is impossible. Therefore, says Kant, the only conclusion that we can derive is that the king was killed for the very pathological reasons, out of fear, but the actors disguised their actions as an act of law. 'As far as we can see, it is impossible for a human being to commit a crime of this kind, a formal diabolically evil (wholly pointless) crime; and yet it is not to be ignored in a system of morals.'[20]

Thus we see the stakes of the whole discussion and realize the true content of the event – the self-destructive moment of subjectivity. This content is the fantasy of self-foundation, which quite logically coincides with self-annulment. The new man kills the old man, that is, himself. The 'ambivalence' with which Kant reacts to the revolution is explained by the contradictory nature of the impossible idea of revolution: as self-annulment, it is an inexpiable crime, as self-foundation, it is an eternal promise.

Now let us pass to the third division of *The Conflict of Faculties*. This section does not speak about politics at all. However, it is this text that most vividly describes the terrorist constitution of subjectivity – not from the point of view of the event that affects the subject but from the point of view which actively constructs its own destruction and only thus is able to achieve self-mastery.

The third *Conflict*, which is dedicated to *medicine*, namely to the force of the subject 'to become a master over his morbid feelings merely by a firm resolution'. Although the title emphasizes positive self-mastery, the essay is dedicated, primarily, to the negative version of it: to the self-inflicted diseases (hypochondria and insomnia) that the subject is able to inflict upon itself via the force of imagination (*Einbildungskraft*). A person subject to this state 'finds in himself every disease he reads about in books'.[21] The disease appears therefore as that of *reading*, or of imagination induced by signs. This imagination presents something fearful and catastrophic – an *imaginary foe* that the organism has to resist – and thus actualizes the disease. The indeterminacy of the symptoms drives the subject into a compulsive probing activity. Thus, through the medium of imagination, the mind manages to work upon itself (inflicting damage to itself), but in a manner diametrically opposed to the self-mastery of the autonomous will.

> The opposite of the mind's self-mastery, in other words, is faint-hearted brooding about the ills that could befall one, and that one would not be able to withstand if they should come. It is a kind of insanity; for though some sort of unhealthy condition … may be the source of it, this state is not felt immediately, as it affects the senses, but is projected back [*vorgespiegelt*] as an already impending illness by poetic imagination [*dichtende Einbildungskraft*]. And then the self-tormenter (*heautontimoroumenos*), instead of pulling himself together, summons the doctor's help.[22]

The capacity and tendency of the subject to overturn oneself (the landscape is similar with the footnote to *The Metaphysics of Morals*) are analysed along with the subject's capacity to heal oneself. As one could guess, the capacity of self-torment does not arrive to full self-annihilation, but the subject cannot directly heal him/herself either. It has to use signs: for example, the name of Cicero, which, if repeated many times, loses its meaning and is reduced to a sheer sign. Kant's remedy, like Hölderlin's, is to limit the interpretation and to destroy meaning, searching for a sheer *sign*.

The self-relation, or self-affection, of the subject is mediated here by the imagination, which presents the activity as passivity, and the spontaneity as receptivity. Now this is not exactly the same kind of practising knowledge as in the case of *Sapere aude*. Here you also dare to know, but this daring leads you into very serious trouble. If, in the first case, you performed the passive, receptive function in an active way, in the second you actively try to control and overturn yourself, only in order to paralyse yourself, to become extra-sensitive to the slightest stimulus, and to passively experience your activity.

This 'hypochondriac' or 'insomniac' anxiety of a subject who reads too many newspapers and books is the *anxiety of Enlightenment*. (Further below we will discuss the curious 'popularity' of hypochondria, as a disorder of imagination, in the late eighteenth century.) Enlightenment does not only *expose* its knowledge, but it also *penetrates* the whole world with its media. It does this in order to control the world, to keep it in check, to inform it and lead 'out of the state of minority'. But, in fact, through this very activity it *exposes* itself in the most passive or receptive manner to anything that can test its staunchness, to anything that can tempt it by suicide.

But we do not have to forget that Enlightenment *promises*, puts the subject on the brink of a new epoch, of an irreversible step. This promise is, however, also a threat of losing oneself, the danger of the tearing power of time which turns the subject back to him/herself and makes him/her look for a totality; for history in its entirety. And here precisely they construct themselves the diabolical evil, which is impossible – says Kant – but which, structurally, must have a place in the system. The totality will always have a place for an element that would annul it.

Terrorism and the sensorium of Enlightenment.

The Enlightenment *qua* historical epoch is characterized not only by the cult of experience and understanding, not just by the affirmation of an autonomous subject, but also by the discovery of the public sphere and by the discovery of 'sentiment' and 'sensibility'. The eighteenth century – 'the century of Enlightenment', as Kant calls it – was the birth of the sentimentalist style in literature and of the general culture of sensibility. Recent scholarship[23] has persuasively demonstrated the extent to which the value of the sentiment, the sentimental narrative (usually based upon the suffering of a virtuous bourgeois person, mostly a woman, from the conspiracies and humiliation of an aristocratic villain), and the exaggerated emotional expression in letters and in oral discourse, permeated eighteenth-century culture. This image of the epoch of Enlightenment is an important correction to the earlier depiction of it by Jürgen Habermas, who, particularly in his works of the 1970s and 1980s, interpreted the 'public sphere' as that of a rational and non-rhetorical discussion. While it is seductive to see the sentimental as a reaction against the narrow rationalism of Enlightenment, it is now common to view it as an inherent aspect of Enlightenment, which gives body and content to reason and allows the organic development of a person.[24]

The two most important ideological roots of sentimentalism were, first, the empiricism of Locke and the Scottish moral philosophy (Shaftesbury, Hutcheson) that elaborated the notion of 'sentiment' and 'emotionalized' it; second, German pietism (this influence, however, was mostly important in Germany). These influences met with the developing institutions of public media and mass literature (novels), on the one hand, and with the ideological opposition of bourgeoisie to the aristocracy, to produce sentimentalism as a literary genre and a cultural phenomenon. Indeed, the sentimental novels were touching and popular, newspapers required 'sensation' to better impress and interest their audience, and the sentimental novels usually depicted poor virtuous girls of the Third Estate offended by powerful aristocratic villains.

An important aspect of the sentimentalist wave was the aforementioned *hypochondria*. This concept was widely popular in the second half of the eighteenth century: it was both a cultural fact and a medical diagnosis. It was therefore probably prominent as an actual phenomenon, although as Gerhard Sauder[25] notes, in the second half of the century they often diagnosed as *hypochondria* what would have been designated as *melancholia* in the first half. Kant, writing about hypochondria, followed an established cultural and medical tradition[26] which, like him, treated hypochondria as a disease of the imagination,[27] hesitated between its physiological and psychological explanations and associated it with the artistic and intellectual state of mind[28]

What is important in our context is the clear association of hypochondria with sentimentality. Gerhard Sauder, in his study of German sentimentalism,[29] gives examples of such association, for instance the words of Christian Franz Timme: 'Sentimentality is hypochondria of the soul. … All those excesses that evoke hypochondria cause also the sentimentality.'[30] And of Carl Friedrich Pockels: 'hypochondria is not seldom a consequence of a sensuously perceptive character … but even without this bodily weakness hypochondria is often a daughter of the sensibility [*Empfindelei*, a pejorative parallel of *Empfindsamkeit*, sentimentality. – *A.M.*] which has its seat in the force of imagination'.[31] Johann Christoph König, late eighteenth-century German author, contrasts *Empfindsamkeit* (good sentimentality) and *Empfindelei* (bad sentimentality or sensibility), comparing an overly sentimental person with a hypochondriac who is anxious about everything and who unnecessarily complicates his own life. He tells a moralistic story exemplifying the troubles of a hypochondriac and makes a nice reflexive trope suggesting the complicity of literature in the hypochondria:

> The two lovers had a terrible number of scary punishments and significant dreams. If I knew if you, my dear, were already hypochondriac, I would tell you a couple of examples, but since I don't, I'll drop this idea. For otherwise it could happen that I would make you thus into a hypochondriac.[32]

Sentimentalism, once born, has remained important up to our own day and is, for instance, dominant in the mass literature ('love novels') and mass television productions ('soap operas' and many talk shows). As David Denby persuasively argues, sentimentalism was also instrumental in elaborating the progressive social programme which is still present today in the institutions and values of the welfare state, in human rights protection, etc.[33]

'Sentiment' meant, for the eighteenth century, an experiential access to truth, as well as the emotion that engaged the subject in a practical way. The concept went back to the British moral philosophy of Shaftesbury and Hutcheson. Thus, it was not a 'pre-romantic' alternative to the rationalist Enlightenment, but rather its complementary aspect, combining desire of knowledge with a project of emotional intersubjectivity.[34]

Thus in the conclusion of Richardson's *Pamela*, that paradigmatic sentimentalist novel, the narrator praises his heroine, who 'publishes' her sentiments in her touching letters, not just of her sensibility and of her moral sentiment, but also, very much in the spirit of the Enlightenment, of her 'signal veracity', that is, accuracy in the communication of facts.[35]

What is noteworthy about the accent on *sentiment* rather than on knowledge and truth *per se* is the *existential* and *abstract* character of affect. Indeed, when we privilege sentiment, we mean that the very fact of knowing something and experiencing *something*, of being torn out of our solitude by an outside stimulus, is more important to us than what actually has happened. Thus, against the appearance, sentimentalism is the reflexive form of Enlightenment, it is the form of Enlightenment that values light itself, as a medium of communication *and* knowledge, over this or that objective truth.[36] Moreover, we will see that the form comes here into a contradiction with its content.

The sentimentalist literary genre is based on the depiction of sentiment and pursuing the purpose of 'touching' the reader. As I have mentioned there is an obvious link between the sentimentalism and the much discussed 'public sphere' of the eighteenth century – the open space of free communication, mediated by proliferating newspapers and journals.

Lawrence Sterne, author who stood at the origin of the very concept of sentimentality, writes in his *Sentimental Journey* (1768):

> It is an age so full of light, that there is scarce a country or corner of Europe, whose beams are not crossed and interchanged with others – Knowledge in most of its branches, and in most affairs, is like music in an Italian street, whereof those may partake, who pay nothing.[37]

By making this observation (which would be many times repeated in the twentieth and twenty-first centuries)[38] Sterne early notices the tendency towards establishing a worldwide common *sensorium*, which would make information accessible, and make everyone vulnerable to this information, if s/he wants it or not. Towards the end of his work Sterne returns to this thought:

> [A]ll comes from thee, great – great SENSORIUM of the world! which vibrates, if a hair of our heads but falls upon the ground, in the remotest desert of thy creation.[39]

In this sensorium, what becomes crucial for information is its 'penetrating force', its 'sentimentality'. The fantastic physical image refers to an actual fact – the development of the mediatic public sphere which literally makes the world shrink. The capitalization by Sterne of the word 'sensorium' additionally points at the rhetorical reinforcement, amplification which goes together with a sentiment and by which a sentimental author, who seeks to penetrate the attention of the public and to leave an imprint on it, himself contributes to the shrinking of the world.

While Sterne himself mostly concentrates on the erotic sentiments and does not abuse the tear-extracting techniques, other sentimental writers tend mostly to privilege the sentiment of compassion: torturing a character is an even easier way to touch the reader and to penetrate his/her soul than the erotic descriptions.

Moreover, the 'negative' character of emotion is well adapted to the social message of a sentimental narrative which usually connoted the class opposition between the poorer part of the bourgeoisie and the aristocracy. Besides, the 'passions' of the characters express the violence of exteriorization and expropriation that the public sphere, the media, and the need of civilization impose on the subject. The sentimentalist literature did not only *express* the violence of Enlightenment but also accustomed its readers to the world that was becoming increasingly dynamic and rich in information.[40]

In *Pamela*, by Samuel Richardson, the protagonist retells her sufferings with an innocence and lack of foresight that reinforce the compassion of the reader. It is this narrative genre that the Marquis de Sade so brilliantly parodies in his *Justine*, touching the sentiments of his readers even more through a combination of torture and eroticism, but at the same time exposing and thematizing the cruel 'terrorism' hidden in the sentimental show.

The self-contradiction of Enlightenment from Rousseau to Dostoyevsky

Jean-Jacques Rousseau, a key thinker of sentimentalism, was, as is well known, a fierce critic of the rationalist and progressivist Enlightenment, but an apologist of sentiment. Jean Starobinski emphasizes, in his work on Rousseau,[41] the absolute value of *transparency* (honesty, directness, true communication), which, however, is obscured by the artifice of representation. In this preoccupation of his, Rousseau stands right at the centre of his epoch – the value of transparency is the very value of Enlightenment, and of the universal sociability emerging in the new media and social gatherings. However, Rousseau sees the obvious fact that the enlightened sociability, so far as it is institutionalized and stable, remains a fake universal, an exclusive and hypocrite public. The true universal interconnectedness involves a rebellion against the very civilization that had brought the public sphere into being, and requires recourse to emotion, not representation. Transparency requires a powerful penetrating force.

Rousseau develops a doctrine of *pity*, a passion which is inherent in humans but which risks being obliterated by society. At the beginning of his 'Discourse on the Origin and Foundation of Inequality among Men' Rousseau describes the supersensibility of a natural man. This man, says Rousseau, is always 'ready for any event', 'he is always trembling and ready to flee at the slightest noise he hears, at the slightest movement he perceives'.[42] Here is the indeterminate affectability, the natural vulnerability of the man, which Rousseau treats as a reason to flee (to escape the public sphere towards solitude). The man is so fearful, it seems, that he hardly likes to experience sentiments. However, when Rousseau subsequently speaks of *pity*, 'a disposition that is appropriate to beings as weak and subject to as many ills as we are',[43] he himself has recourse to the literary terrorism with which he is in his turn contaminated by another author:

> One sees with pleasure the author of the *Fable of the Bees* forced to recognize man as a compassionate and sensitive being, departing from his cold and subtle style in the example he gives in order to offer us the pathetic image of an imprisoned man who sees outside a wild beast tearing a child from his mother's breast, breaking his weak limbs in its murderous teeth, and ripping apart with its claws the palpitating entrails of this child. What horrible agitation must be felt by this witness of an event in which he takes no personal interest![44]

Thus, in our epoch, it seems necessary to exaggerate and magnify an evil in order for the reader to be touched, while for a natural man this sense of pity must not require such artificial agitation. 'Pity' is here a movement of subjectivation which searches for a free and open subject behind the Enlightenment's cult of clear knowledge but can find such a subject only at the price of shock or terror. The free and open subject appears as a passive and suffering one, paralysed by pity and terror. (These two tragic passions are here inseparable.) But this stoppage is both a critical diagnosis of the modern condition and a way to turn and return to the subjective origin of the rationalist Enlightenment.

A Russian writer, and one of the leading figures of the Russian Enlightenment, Alexander Radishchev, wrote, in 1790, a book entitled *A Journey from Petersburg to Moscow*,[45] for which he was immediately arrested and exiled. The book was written in imitation of Sterne, but it contained a sentimental depiction of the horrible life of the Russian serfs. Apart from the enlightened emancipatory views, the book was a document showing that the nobility could no longer ignore, could not afford not to notice, the life of their compatriots of another estate. The changing optics made the serf holders vulnerable to the suffering of their peers. Radishchev, even more directly than Rousseau, and anticipating the rhetoric of the Montagnard Jacobins, uses the sentimentalist optics to denounce the tyrannical social order.

Thus, in the central scene of the *Journey*,[46] he describes a dream where he sees himself as a self-satisfied monarch. A wanderer comes to this monarch, in spite of ever-vigilant guards, saying that she is 'Truth', and removes walls from his eyes, so that he comes to see the horrible condition of his subjects. The leitmotif of the book is the need to penetrate the blind, deaf, and petrified souls of the power holders, to awaken them 'with a hammer on the head, if necessary',[47] so that they give way to the others' sufferings. Emotions, even though they are valued positively, are seen as violent, shock-like intrusions. As all other sentimentalist writers, Radishchev directly links the need for such sensibility with the question of the freedom of the press.

However, in the 'Dedicace' of the book Radischev writes:

> I said to myself, that nature has been so miserly with her children as to hide the truth forever from him who errs innocently? Is it possible that this stern stepmother has brought us into the world that we may know only calamities, but never happiness? My reason trembled at this thought, and my heart thrust it far away. I found a comforter for man in himself. 'Remove the veil from the inward eye – and I shall be happy' ... I arose from the despair into which sensitivity and compassion had plunged me; I felt within me strength enough to withstand this delusion, and – unspeakable joy – I felt that it was possible for anyone to strive for the well-being of his fellows.[48]

Thus, in spite of the accent on suffering, Radishchev sees the source of positive emotion, not even in the practical overcoming of suffering, but in the very fact of compassion as a basis of the egalitarian sociability, and of truth as a basis of publicity. Such is the formulation of the Enlightenment programme, which redeems the proto-terrorism in the joy derived from the very fact of affectation (which here equals affection).

In another scene of his *Journey*, describing a shipwreck where the narrator, a nobleman, shares his destiny with the simple men who are the oarsmen of the boat, Radishchev writes: 'At the last hour ... all the distinctions invented by men's minds begin to disappear. Man becomes simply man: thus as we saw our end drawing near, we all forgot our rank and station ... '[49] The emotions of fear and suffering are egalitarian, they subvert the existing order by their violence.

To draw a tentative philosophical conclusion, we can say that the Enlightenment, by insisting on the veracity of representation and on the existential facticity of experience, runs into a problem. David Denby, in his analysis of sentimentalism, rightly points out that this genre emerges in response to a problem of mediating the singularity of personal experience with the universality of the abstract reasoning which comes to dominate everyday life with the development of the state and capitalism.[50] It must be added that sentimentalism not just attempts to mediate, but also *expresses* the contradiction between the two, and this contradiction is an internal one. Indeed, the existential singularity is the very definition of experiential truth which the rationalist Enlightenment seeks to establish and to spread about. But the ideal of science, *à la* Descartes or Locke, as a sum and system of facts is put into question by the infinitely continual nature of the world, in which every singular experience has, in fact, vanishingly small significance in the light of the universal totality. However, it is this singular experience which is considered the only true foundation of truth and has a *right* to claim the attention of the subject. The claim of this right by the tiny singularity which is, by definition, on the verge of nothing, which does not *fully* exist in the sense of an objective fact, takes a hyperbolic, terrorist form, and attacks the *subject* of experiential reason, who, on his/her part, is violently overwhelmed by the excessive factual information but who is at the same time paralysed and settled, in its passive openness, by the inescapable identification with a victim, so that the hypochondriac curiosity appears as a moral duty or as hypnotic blackmail. (You ignore the suffering of the other, and then suffer yourself.)

In the nineteenth century, the literary genres and the literary audience itself changed drastically, but the sentimentalist strategies of writing only gained force, and were joined with the critical realist tradition by such writers as Charles Dickens and Fyodor Dostoyevsky.

Dostoyevsky is the author who is directly relevant for our topic, since he was a contemporary of the Russian populist and socialist 'terrorists' – a movement which, as mentioned above, was not yet 'terrorist' in the contemporary sense of terrorizing the civil population, but focused on the political and administrative leaders (although there were occasional 'collateral' civilian victims). This movement was the first non-state violent group to obtain (from its opponents) the name of 'terrorists'. Dostoyevsky, who was familiar, from newspapers, with a case where an innocent victim had been murdered by the revolutionaries (led by Serguey Nechayev) for the sake of the movement's victory, attributed to them the projects of the media-based, provocative terrorism in the contemporary sense of the word. Thus, in a hostile manner, he interprets the political 'terrorists' of the nineteenth century in the way that reminds us of today's terrorist strategies.

In *The Possessed* Dostoyevsky depicts the kind of a suicide terrorist, Kirillov, who wants to commit suicide, just so as to affirm the absoluteness of one moment of being. This obsession with facts is definitive for Dostoyevsky's terror topic. The socialist conspirators use Kirillov's suicide for their purposes and organize a catastrophe, a large-scale fire which is meant to destabilize the situation and provoke a revolution. Lizaveta, the female character of *The Possessed*, wants to publish a book that would neutrally combine stories from different newspapers and journals.

> Her literary scheme was as follows. Numbers of papers and journals are published in the capitals and the provinces of Russia, and every day a number of events are reported in them. The year passes, the newspapers are everywhere folded up and put away in cupboards, or are torn up and become litter, or are used for making parcels or wrapping things. Numbers of these facts make an impression and are remembered by the public, but in the course of years they are forgotten … Yet if all the facts for a whole year were brought together into one book, on a definite plan, and with a definite object, under headings with references, arranged according to months and days, such a compilation might reflect the characteristics of Russian life for the whole year.[51]

Thus, Dostoyevsky ties up terrorism with the mediatic obsession with sensational facts and, moreover, with the Enlightenment obsession with *facts* as such. Terror, or the sheer destruction of one's being, is correlative, in modern times, with the care and interest of the sheer being and the facticity of things.

The main development of this topic by Dostoyevsky is to be found in *The Karamazov Brothers*, namely in the famous presentation by Ivan Karamazov of the case of a 'tear of a single tortured child', because of which Ivan is 'returning his ticket' to the reign of universal harmony (which he seriously considers, both in the socialist and Christian versions). Look how he starts, on what sounds (anachronistically) like a Nietzschean note:

> I could never understand how one can love one's neighbours [*blizhnikh*, the close ones]. It's just one's neighbours, to my mind, that one can't love, though one might love those at a distance. I once read somewhere of John the Merciful, a saint, that when a hungry, frozen beggar came to him, he took him into his bed, held him in his arms, and began breathing into his mouth, which was putrid and loathsome from some awful disease. I am convinced that he did that from 'self-laceration,' from the self-laceration of falsity, for the sake of the charity imposed by duty, as a penance laid on him. For anyone to love a man, he must be hidden, for as soon as he shows his face, love is gone.[52]

Clearly, what is at stake is the force of presentation and representation: the new media culture, the sentimental literature bring things too close to the subject, so that their very spectacle (spectacle of *any*thing!) becomes as intolerable as it is fascinating. Sentimentalist literature draws on a rhetoric of emotional reinforcement and amplification. Ivan questions the very terrorist rhetoric that he, and the author, practise: the rhetoric of vivid and intolerable pictures of suffering.

In a next move, Ivan clarifies the connection of this problem with the world of the media:

> You see, I'm a collector of certain little facts that appeal to me and, would you believe it, I note down and save anecdotes of a particular kind from newspapers and stories, wherever I find them, and I already have a good collection.[53]

Thus a sentimental story of the poor murderer Richard is found in 'a nice pamphlet' translated from French into Russian by 'some aristocratic Russian Lutheran philanthropists and was distributed free with newspapers and other publications for the edification [*prosvestchenie*, lit. 'enlightenment'] of the Russian people.[54]

Of the poor girl whose 'one little tear'[55] he does not want to sacrifice for the sake of the 'higher harmony', Ivan says, 'I understand nothing, and now … I don't want to understand anything. I want to stick to facts.'[56] This argument of Ivan is a paraphrase of an argument by Russian critic Vissarion Belinsky who, in his letter to Botkin, wrote, 'but if I could mount the highest step of the ladder of development I would ask you to give me account of all victims of the life and of history, otherwise I would jump from this highest step head-first.'[57] Thus Belinsky's argument is directed not against Christianity, as in Dostoyevsky, but against Hegel: in both cases, however, the Enlightenment vision of future harmony is involved.

A good enlightened subject, Ivan wants to see the girl avenged with his own eyes, not entrusting this to the future: 'I want to be here when everyone suddenly finds out the why and the wherefore of the being.'[58] Ivan describes the suffering of the child in detail, trying to persuade his interlocutor, Alyosha. Dostoyevsky uses the 'terrorist' tools of sentimentalist literature in order to expose here, so to say, the sentimentalist condition of the Enlightenment and of the public sphere, as such.

Enlightenment means the *overexposure*[59] of the subject who 'dares to know' and to imagine. This exposure is an autodestructive, autoimmune drive of a subject who feels the breath of transcendence but who wants to bring him/herself to the new world in its entirety, to enlighten the totality with the transcendent light. Here, the subject suffers a failure: his erudition, armed by imagination, always finds in the totality something that would bar access to the supposed new epoch of Enlightenment. And it is here that terrorism, as a rhetorical and military strategy, emerges. 'Terrorists', as we saw in 'Le caché', are complicit with their public, those who show – with those who look. The former believe in progress but are too anxious if they have not forgotten anything, attentively following the news. The latter, tired of their sensible passivity, want to be publicly recognized, to manifest themselves in the most touching manner possible, that is, in the manner that would best correspond to the anxieties of the public.

Following Rousseau and Radischev, but also arguing against them, Dostoyevsky formulates the self-contradiction of Enlightenment: the enlightenment of the world throws light also on the things that are incompatible with the utopia of universal harmony that the Enlightenment, even in its sentimental version, projects upon the world. Or, in other words, the Enlightenment enters into contradiction with what it throws light on. (Thus Dostoyevsky goes against Radischev, for whom the light itself redeems its terrible object.) The terrorist strategy works in the space opened up by this contradiction and does not resolve it, but reaffirms it by its paralysing spasm.

Conclusion

To conclude, one has to return to Kant and to his 'An answer to the question: What is Enlightenment?' As mentioned above, this text calls for the 'courage, to know', states that we live in an epoch of Enlightenment, that this Enlightenment consists in the 'exit out of the state of minority', and that it requires 'a free public use of one's understanding' on the condition of obedience to the authorities in practical matters.

Thus the understanding, normally a receptive faculty, is reinterpreted as praxis, but this praxis is then in its turn reinterpreted as relatively passive: consisting mostly in discussions. The subject of Enlightenment is active–passive, active in its passivity and passive in its activity. One can even say that the active voice and the passive voice are here inseparable one from another.

As we have seen above in the second *conflict of the faculties*, the enlightened observers are fully enlightened when they courageously *manifest* their observations in public. Moreover, for Kant, Enlightenment is not just the imperative of learning and knowing, but it is also an 'exit of the state of minority' – a metaphor suggesting a rite of passage, a promotion, a recognition of an individual. Similarly, in the sentimental novel, for instance in Goethe's *Werther*, the theme of the (lost) struggle for recognition and promotion is parallel and complementary to the theme of the exalted erotic sensibility (equally frustrated, in the case of Werther).

In the sensorium of Enlightenment, self-presentation is therefore inseparable from self-knowledge and self-control. The subject of Enlightenment searches for self-affectation, but it can reach it only by actively *affecting itself*. Terror, as the word itself shows, is a moment of indistinction between passivity and activity, manifestation and attention. The 'courage to know' as invoked by Kant is required by the sadistic autoaffective and autodestructive urge that the subject of Enlightenment bears in itself. A contemporary terrorist affirms his or her 'majority' in the light of the Enlightenment, by presenting a counter-argument against the Enlightenment, or against the passage to the majority for the whole of humanity. Thus the terrorist and its public (with its ubiquitous video cameras) hypnotize each other in a deadlock of subjectivity – of a subject who can neither decisively step forward to the good, nor secede from the Enlightenment into the absolute evil.

The current upsurge of terrorist violence as a strategy is a symptom of a deep crisis of the Enlightenment. If, in the eighteenth century, the sentimental openness and the public sphere which depended on it were in many ways liberatory, if not revolutionary, today the resistant terrorist strategies, as well as the corresponding strategies of repression and control on the part of the state, have a paralyzing, disempowering effect. The violence of identification with excessive suffering is used by terrorists to shock the viewer and to burn out the public sphere by organizing its short-circuit. Today's terrorism, like today's charitable sentimentalism, does not question the hegemony of the enlightened subject of the West. Therefore, the terrorists play the ontologically dependent figure of evil, and the Western enlightened subject (whose mirror image they are), in the care of its goodness, sees its main purpose in identifying and helping the poor victims across the world. The illegitimate intervention of terrorists into the television picture does not subvert the essential division of representation into the passive public and the active representatives, even though it expresses the pain of their separation. But, this said, we need to perceive the revolutionary *potential* of the terrorist form – its subversion of the established structure of the public sphere through a mimetic explosion. Even now, the so-called 'Stockholm syndrome' (the growing sympathy of hostages for their takers) is a symptom of the egalitarian potential of terrorism. However, to become revolutionaries and not the military moralists that they are now, terrorists, without adhering to the mere good, should stop aspiring to mere evil.

Notes

1 For a good survey of these definitions, see online: available at: http://en.wikipedia.org/wiki/Definition_of_terrorism.
2 On the notion of the subject's pure self-affection see Immanuel Kant, *Critique of Pure Reason*, trans. P. Guyer and A. Wood, Cambridge: Cambridge University Press, 1997, B 68–69; his *Opus Postumum*, ed. Eckart Förster, Cambridge: Cambridge University Press, 1993; and Martin Heidegger, *Kant and the Problem of Metaphysics*, trans. J. S. Churchill, Bloomington, IN: Indiana University Press, 1962.
3 *Les Films du Losange*, 2005.
4 Paul Virilio, *The Information Bomb*, New York and London: Verso, 2005, p. 16. See also Bernard-François Huygues, *La Quatrième Guerre mondiale*, Paris: Rocher, 2004, and his other writings, on the link between terror and the media.
5 Patricia Mellencamp, 'US television since 9/11', in Andrew Martin and Patrice Petro (eds), *Rethinking Global Security. Media, Popular Culture, and the 'War on Terror'*, New Brunswick, NJ: Rutgers University Press, 2006, pp. 117–31.
6 On the 'public sphere' as the constitutive institution of Enlightenment sociability and of its ideology see Jürgen Habermas, *The Structural Transformation of the Public Sphere*, Cambridge: Polity Press, 1989. Habermas particularly emphasizes the proliferation of paper media in the eighteenth century and their role as conveyors of news and of public opinion.
7 Georg W. F. Hegel, *The Phenomenology of Spirit*, trans. A. V. Miller, Oxford: Oxford University Press, 1977.
8 Immanuel Kant, 'Critique of Practical Reason', in Mary Gregor (ed. and trans.), *Practical Philosophy*, Cambridge: Cambridge University Press, 1996, p. 236.
9 See Kant, *Critique of Pure Reason*, the second chapter of the 'Transcendental Analytic', Doctrine of elements, A pp. 86–130; B pp. 118–68.
10 Immanuel Kant, 'An answer to the question: What is Enlightenment?', *Practical Philosophy*, pp. 16–22.
11 Ibid., p. 17.
12 Ibid., p. 18.
13 Immanuel Kant, *The Conflict of the Faculties*, bilingual edn, trans. Mary Gregor, New York: Abaris Books, 1979, II.5, p. 87. (I use the original pagination as it is reproduced in the quoted edition.)
14 Sigmund Freud, 'Negation', in *The Standard Edition of the Complete Psychological Works of Sigmund Freud* XIX, trans. and ed. James Strachey, London: Hogarth Press, 1956–74, pp. 235–40.
15 Kant, *The Conflict of the Faculties*, p. 88.

16 Ibid.
17 Immanuel Kant, 'The Metaphysics of Morals', *Practical Philosophy*, pp. 353–605.
18 Ibid., p. 464.
19 Ibid.
20 Ibid.
21 Kant, *The Conflict of the Faculties*, p. 103.
22 Ibid.
23 David Denby, *Sentimental Narrative and the Social Order in France, 1760–1820*, Cambridge: Cambridge University Press, 1994; William Reddy, 'Sentimentalism and its erasure. The role of emotions in the era of the French revolution', *Journal of Modern History*, 72, 2000, pp. 109–52.
24 See Gerhard Sauder, *Empfindsamkeit* I, Stuttgart: Metzler, 1974. Sauder cites Roland Mortier: 'sensibilité et lumières vont dans le meme sens et tendent vers la réalisation d'un type humain complet, dont le bonheur consiste non à se mutiler d'une part de soi-même, mais à assumer pleinement tous les aspects de son moi' (ibid., p. 235).
25 Ibid., p. 151. On the parallel between melancholia and hypochondria see also Johnson's *Dictionary*, note 27 below.
26 On the place of hypochondria in Kant see Mary Shell, *The Embodiment of Reason. Kant on Spirit, Generation, and Community*, Chigaco: University of Chicago Press, 1996.
27 See, for instance, Samuel Johnson, *A Dictionary of the English Language*, facsimile of the original 1755 edn, New York: Classic Books, 2005. See also Shell, *The Embodiment of Reason*, p. 426.
28 Ibid., p. 267.
29 Sauder, *Empfindsamkeit* I.
30 Christian Friedrich Timme, *Der empfindsame Maurus Pankrazius Ziprianus Kurt, auch Selmar genannt. Ein Moderoman*, Erfurt, 1781/82, p. 43, p. 59, cited in Sauder, *Empfindsamkeit*, p. 151; my translation.
31 Karl Friedrich Pockels, 'Über die Verschiedenheit und Mischung der Charactere', *Beitrage zur Beforderung der Menschenkenntnis, besonders in Rücksicht unserer moralischen Natur*, Berlin, 1788, pp. 41 ff., cited in Sauder, *Empfindsamkeit*, p. 151; my translation.
32 Johann Christoph König, *Versuch eines populäres Lehrbuchs des guten Geschmacks für Mädchen und Junglinge*, Nuremberg, 1780, p. 126, cited in Sauder, *Empfindsamkeit* III, pp. 102–3.
33 Denby, *Sentimental Narrative*, pp. 1–8.
34 Cf. Sauder, *Empfindsamkeit* I, p. xvi, where he points out that sentimentalism was a response to the seventeenth-century picture of a *homo clausus* – the issue is the possibility of *communication*.
35 Samuel Richardson, *Pamela, or, Virtue Rewarded*, facsimile of the 1769 edn, Berwyn, PA: Oak Knoll, 1929, p. 163.
36 Thus Sauder, *Empfindsamkeit*, p. 170, drawing on Lothar Pikulik (Lothar Pikulik, *Bürgerliches Trauerspiel und Empfindsamkeit*, Cologne: Graz, 1966, p. 290), understands the sentimental sensibility (*Empfindsamkeit*) as a reflection on feeling, which is itself a feeling, and which does not have the first feeling as an object. *Empfindsamkeit* is thus close, according to Sauder, to what Novalis meant when he defined feeling (*Gefühl*) as 'non-positional self-consciousness'. The reflexive, but not objectifying, character of the sentimental is beyond doubt, but I would insist also on the *abstract* character of the sentimental culture: the sentiment to have sentiments as such.
37 Lawrence Sterne, *A Sentimental Journey to France and Italy*, Florida Edition of the Works of Lawrence Sterne, Gainesville, FL: University Press of Florida, 2002, VI, pp. 3–167. 'Preface – in the désobligeant', pp. 16 17.

38 See, for instance, Martin Heidegger, 'The thing', in *Poetry, Language, Thought*, trans. Albert Hofstadter, New York: Harper & Row, 1971, pp. 174–82; Virilio, *The Information Bomb.*

39 Sterne, *A Sentimental Journey*, 'The Bourbonnois', p. 155. See also the chapter entitled 'A fragment' (pp. 45–6), where Sterne explicitly compares this 'sensorium' of sympathy to the tragic theatre: in the city of Abdera, he says, during a presentation of Euripides' play, everyone was taken over by the fire of love.

40 One cannot fail to notice the proximity of this sentimental condition with what Walter Benjamin describes, with regard to the nineteenth and twentieth centuries, as the 'shock'-like experience which characterizes a mass subject. A shock, in Benjamin, is a quick and strong impression in which the fact of being affected is more important than the content of experience, and which excludes concentration. See, in particular, 'On some motives in Baudelaire' and 'The work of art in the age of its mechanical reproduction' (Walter Benjamin, *Illuminations*, ed. Hannah Arendt, trans. Harry Zohn, New York: Schocken Books, 1969, pp. 155–200; pp. 217–51). It is possible that Benjamin's analysis should be extended into the eighteenth century and the shock-like experience seen as a conscious reflexive programme, not just a socio-technological process.

41 Jean Starobinski, *Jean-Jacques Rousseau. La transparence et l'obstacle*, Paris: Gallimard, 1971.

42 Jean-Jacques Rousseau, *The First and Second Discourses*, trans. R. Masters, New York: St Martin's Press, 1964, p. 107.

43 Ibid., p. 130.

44 Ibid., p. 130–31. Mandeville was not only an apologist of crude capitalism but also the author of 'A Treatise of the Hypochondriack and Histerick Passions, Vulgarly call'd the Hypo in Men and Vapours in Women'.

45 Alexander Radishchev, *A Journey from St Petersburg to Moscow*, trans. Leo Wiener, Cambridge: Cambridge University Press, 1958. Russian original: *Puteshestvie iz Peterburga v Moskvu*, Moscow: Pravda, 1978.

46 Ibid., p. 67–76.

47 Ibid., p. 56.

48 Ibid., p. 4.

49 Ibid., p. 51.

50 Denby, *Sentimental Narrative*, p. 139.

51 Fyodor Dostoyevsky, *The Possessed*, trans. Constance Garnett, Part 1, chapter 4, online: http://ebooks.adelaide.edu.au/d/dostoyevsky/d72p/chapter4.html.

52 Fyodor Dostoyevsky, *The Karamazov Brothers*, trans. Ignat Avsey, Oxford: Oxford University Press, 1994, p. 296.

53 Ibid., p. 299.

54 Ibid., pp. 300–1.

55 Ibid., p. 307.

56 Ibid., p. 305.

57 Cited in V. V. Zenkovsky, *Istoria russkoy filosofii* I, Leningrad: EGO, 1991, p. 69.

58 Dostoyevsky, *The Karamazov Brothers*, p. 306.

59 Cf. Virilio, *The Information Bomb*, p. 57.

Chapter 10

The catechism of the citizen

Politics, law and religion in, after, with and against Rousseau[1]

Simon Critchley

In a letter to Voltaire dated 18 August 1756 Rousseau writes:

> I would wish, then, that in every State there were a moral code, or a kind of *civil profession of faith*, containing, positively, the social maxims everyone would be bound to acknowledge, and negatively, the fanatical maxims one would be bound to reject, not as impious, but as seditious.[2]

This, of course, is the germ of the argument for civil religion that Rousseau would go on to elaborate in 1762 in *The Social Contract.*[3] In the letter to Voltaire – and one knows that whatever fellow feeling might have existed between these two was rapidly turning to enmity during these years – the context is Voltaire's response to the Lisbon earthquake of 1755, about which he had published a poem in March 1756. Rousseau goes on: 'In your *Poem on Natural Religion* you gave us the Catechism of man: give us now, in the one I am suggesting to you, the *Catechism of the Citizen*.'[4]

Voltaire, of course, would do no such thing, and went on to write his *Candide* in 1759, which Rousseau in his paranoid megalomania saw as the true response to his 1756 letter, which received only a brief, conciliatory reply. However, in this chapter I want to explore the idea of a catechism of the citizen or a civil profession of faith as a way of thinking about the relation between three interconnected terms: politics, law and religion.

My argument will continually cut in two directions at once in a way that I hope will not bifurcate too egregiously.

1. On the one hand, I want to follow closely at the textual and conceptual level Rousseau's claim that what is required to solve the problem of politics and law is a civil profession of faith, a civil catechism. I want to show how the problem of politics in Rousseau – the very *being* of the political, understood as the act by which a people becomes a people – is articulated around what we might call a paradox of sovereignty that draws it ineluctably towards a religious solution. To borrow Althusser's word – and his extraordinarily intelligent reading of *The Social Contract* will be constantly on my mind as I write, as will that of Badiou[5] – the functioning of Rousseau's

thought is possible only because of the play of a series of *décalages*, displacements or dislocations. Althusser claims that it is the play of these *décalages* that make possible what Rousseau calls his 'sad and great system'[6] and make it impossible at the same time. Rousseau's thought is a self-conscious play of dislocations and displacements, a reflexive series of contradictions, and his text is thus a sort of *machine à décalage* of which he was utterly conscious and which makes him, in my view, along with Nietzsche, the supremely *fictive* philosopher. This play of *décalages* is one explanation of the multiplicity of possible, plausible and deeply contradictory interpretations of Rousseau, whether Kantian or Hegelian, liberal or communitarian, not to mention totalitarian.[7] To be more specific, if the problem that Rousseau is trying to solve in *The Social Contract* is the problem of politics, then the solution to that problem requires religion.[8] Rousseau's purportedly purely *immanentist* conception of the being of politics requires a dimension of *transcendence* in order to become effective; or again, a conception of the political based on the absolute primacy of *autonomy* seems to call for a moment of *heteronomy* for its articulation and authorization.

2. However, on the other hand, I want to use Rousseau's thought in order to show how his conception of the political can throw some light on the present situation, that is, on the darkness of our times. What I mean is that if Rousseau's sad system is a *décalage* machine, then I wonder whether something analogous might be said of our world, defined as it is by a series of nightmarish intrications of politics and religion: we have entered nothing less than an epoch of new religious war. Thus my hunch or hope is that following Rousseau's thinking on politics and religion will somehow allow us to think through and think against our present.

This leads me to the following series of general questions. Is politics conceivable without religion? The answer is obviously affirmative as the evidence of various secular political theories testifies. But is politics *practicable* without religion? That is the question that Rousseau's thinking of politics faces. Can politics become effective as a way of shaping, motivating and mobilizing a people or peoples without some sort of dimension that is religious, that is without some sort of appeal to transcendence? I do not think so. Or rather, I no longer think so. Thus the exemplarity of Rousseau, to my mind, consists in the fact that he gives us the definitive expression of the modern conception of politics: politics is the break with any conception of nature and natural law and has to be based on the concepts of popular sovereignty, association, rigorous equality and collective autonomy understood as the self-determination of a people. And yet, in order for this modern conception of politics to become effective it has to have a religious dimension, a moment of what the Romans used to call *theologia civilis,* civil theology. The *secularization* that seems to define modern politics has to acknowledge a moment of what Emilio Gentile calls *sacralization,* the transformation of a political entity like a state, nation, class or party into a sacred entity, which means that it becomes transcendent, unchallengeable and intangible.[9] So can a political collectivity maintain itself in existence, its unity and identity, without a moment of the sacred, without religion, rituals and something that we can only call *belief?* Once again, I do not think so. Might we not at least conceive of the possibility of redefining the secularization that is believed to be definitive of modernity with the idea of modern politics as a *metamorphosis of sacralization*, where modern forms of politics, whether liberal democracy, fascism, Soviet communism, National Socialism and the rest have to be grasped as new articulations and, indeed, mutations of the sacred?

Before continuing, it should be noted that I have come to this conclusion with no particular joy, as someone with little enthusiasm for religion, whether organized or disorganized. And I say this not simply in response to the chronic re-theologization of politics through which we are living, which makes this time certainly the darkest period in my lifetime. At the heart of the horror of the present is the intrication of politics and religion, an intrication defined by violence, and this is what I would like to begin to think through. I want to do this not in order to break the connection between politics and religion, but to acknowledge the limitations of any completely secular leftist politics. It seems to me that the left has all too easily ceded the religious ground to the right and it is this ground that needs to be regained in a coherent, long-term and tenacious political war of position.[10] As we will see presently, the relation of politics to religion and their intrication raises for me the question of the necessity of *fiction*, of both the seeming necessity for a divine fiction at the basis of politics and the possibility of what Wallace Stevens would call a *supreme* fiction in politics.

The being of politics, or the misnomer of the social contract

As everyone knows, Rousseau begins *The Social Contract* with the following words:

> Man is born free, and he is everywhere in chains. One believes himself the other's master, and yet is more a slave than they. How did this change come about? I do not know. What can make it legitimate? I believe I can solve that question.[11]

Now, the most obvious way of reading these words is to imagine that Rousseau is recommending that we throw off our chains and return to a state of original freedom, what he elsewhere calls natural freedom. This is the romantic or indeed anarchist reading of Rousseau, where revolutionary political activity is justified in so far as it returns us to the allegedly free and original condition of humanity without the shackles of law and government.

However, to read Rousseau in this manner is to misread him. Let's look at those words more closely: man is everywhere in chains, that is, everyone everywhere is in chains, not just the oppressed, the exploited and the poor. Rousseau is clear, 'One believes himself the others' master, and yet is more a slave than they.' Thus – and this is the dialectical logic that Hegel will develop to full effect – the master who believes himself free because of his ability to oppress the poor and disadvantaged and bend them to his will is mistaken in his belief. On the contrary, his very being as master is utterly dependent upon recognition from the slave from whom he believes himself independent and superior. The master is paradoxically less free than the slave because the former's entire being is constituted through his purported superiority to the latter. Rousseau's point is everyone is a slave, especially the master who believes that he is free.

Rousseau goes on, 'How did this change come about?' That is, how is it that human beings all ended up wearing chains? How did we lose our natural freedom, or our natural equality? In other words, what are the origin and foundations of inequality among human beings? Rousseau curtly responds, 'Je l'ignore', 'I do not know,' or 'I am ignorant or unaware of the reason for this transformation.' Now, this is a peculiar thing to say, as seven years earlier Rousseau had given a quite breathtakingly original answer to the question in the *Discourse on the Origin and Foundations of Inequality among Men* (1755), the so-called Second Discourse. Either Rousseau is being inconsistent, or what is going on in *The Social Contract* is not of the order of knowledge or epistemic certainty but something else. We can see here an intriguing and important separation of the realm of knowledge from the realm of legitimacy. The political question of the transformation from freedom to bondage is not an epistemic or empirical question that can be resolved with reference to the state of nature or natural law. It is rather a question of the *legitimacy* of this transformation that presupposes a break between the orders of nature and politics. This means that the order of politics, to paraphrase Rousseau, begins by 'setting aside all the facts', that is, by disregarding the realm of being, and establishing a domain where a new political subject comes into existence, a domain of fiction in the strong sense, the realm of what Badiou calls the event.

With the question of legitimacy we arrive at the problem of politics as conceived by Rousseau. Slightly later in *The Social Contract*, in words set apart in the text with quotation marks, he states the problem in the following terms:

> 'To find a form of association that will defend and protect the person and goods of each associate with the full common force, and by means of which each, uniting with all, nevertheless obey only himself and remain as free as before.'[12]

That is, how can human beings live according to a law that they recognize as equally binding on all citizens, as legitimate for the collective as a whole, and yet at the same time being a law to which they freely submit because they see it as the expression of their own freedom? If there is no question of a return to nature, to an original freedom where we are finally free of our chains, the anarchist dream of society without the state, then the problem is: how can those chains be made legitimate? Or, how can citizens wear legitimate chains? The problem of politics is the relation and transition from forms of non-consensual to consensual bondage. How can we organize society so that freedom and equality could exist in some sort of equilibrium? As Rousseau writes, 'This is the fundamental problem to which the social contract provides the solution.'[13]

But what do the words 'social contract' mean for Rousseau? Is it, indeed, a misnomer for what he imagines as the being of politics? First, the matter of politics is about the establishment of the form of *association* spoken of above. This requires a convention or covenant, Rousseau thinks, but one that is not based on the family or any form of patriarchy *à la* Filmer, or the right of the strongest where the conqueror simply enslaves the conquered *à la* William the Conqueror. Importantly, it also excludes the possibility of a primary covenant between a people and a king:

> Hence before examining the act by which a people elects a king, it would be well to examine the act by which a people is a people. For that act, being necessarily prior to the other, is the true foundation of society.[14]

Thus the essence of politics consists in an act whereby a people becomes a people, an original covenant that presupposes that there has been at one time unanimity.

Althusser usefully illuminates this issue with an opposition between *obstacles* and *forces*; the obstacles that stand in the way of such a form of association and the forces which might enable it, a distinction which echoes Marx's distinction between relations and forces of production. This is also where we are obliged to consider the relation between *The Social Contract* and the Second Discourse. Part Two of the Second Discourse gives an extraordinarily powerful account of the obstacles that stand in the way of legitimate politics, namely the vicious state of war described in its final pages, which it is tempting to translate as the present state of the world, what Agamben in characteristically understated manner describes as 'global civil war'.[15] In this state of war, human beings exist in a state of total alienation and the previous history of humanity is the history of the growth of that alienation. The force that can face and possibly overcome these obstacles is the combined bodily power of alienated individuals, working not for particular interests but for the common interest. This is the force that is described in *The Social Contract,* a force that can take effect only as a transformation of human beings' manner of existence, what Rousseau refers to as a 'change of nature'.

This entails that the relation between the Second Discourse and *The Social Contract* is complementary but radically disjunctive: the radically unequal state of the world in the former, the possibility of a legitimate politics in the latter. Politics, then, is about the creation of a force that can overcome obstacles, which requires an act of aggregation or what Denis Guénoun calls 'pure assembly' where a people unites and decides to act.[16] Let me leave to one side the vast question as to where this force might come from. We can say for sure that it is not given in the situation, but in excess of the situation as a vital but fleeting supplement, a fictional force, perhaps. Yet Rousseau is crystal-clear – and such is his pessimism – this force is rare and can exist only in very few places: Geneva for a while, Corsica for a while, Poland as a theoretical possibility, and so on. I feel certain that he would not find it in the contemporary regimes that go by the misnomer of democracy. True politics is rare, the obstacles are vast and the force required to bring it about is exceptional.

Is this act of association a contract? If it is, then it is a very strange contract. To begin with, there is the first party of the contract, which exists in the state of total alienation described in the Second Discourse, which is to say that it is not free at all but totally enmeshed in systems of social inequality. Yet this radically unfree, alienated individual still possesses the force to give itself in an act of association with others, that is, with others who also exist in a radically alienated state. Yet in giving himself to others the subject contracts with no one except the generality, the imagined association, which is the expected outcome of such self-giving. Rousseau is crystal-clear on this point: 'each, by giving himself to all, gives himself to no one'.[17] Thus there is no contract; I give myself to no one. Indeed, there is no self to give, as it exists in a state of total alienation and becomes a subject only through an act of force where it associates with others. The act of association that is the essence of politics is what I would like to call *the fiction of an alienation from alienation*. In other words, the essence of politics is an act and a fiction. Rousseau is clear: 'These clauses [i.e. of the social contract. – *S.C.*], rightly understood, all come down to just one, namely the total alienation of each associate with all of his rights to the whole community.'[18]

The so-called 'social contract' begins with the *fact* of total alienation, which is overcome by an *act* of total alienation where I give myself to the community, to an imagined generality, to a people *which does not in fact exist.* That is, I totally alienate myself in the name of a fiction of association that would allow me to overcome the total alienation of social inequality. As Althusser rightly underlines, *total alienation is the solution to the state of total alienation.*[19] Thus Rousseau's 'social contract' does not correspond to its concept: it is not a contract based on an exchange between parties, but an act of constitution, of fictive constitution, where a people wills itself into existence. That such a people exists, that it might exist, that the fictional act might become fact, is what Althusser calls Rousseau's 'dream'.[20] One of the important issues towards which this chapter is trying to grope its way is the necessity of such dreams, such supreme fictions, in the political realm. Let me now turn to law.

The general will, law and the necessity for patriotism

Let's ask, very generally: what is the problem to which law is the solution? As we have seen, the problem that Rousseau is trying to solve in *The Social Contract* is the problem of legitimacy. How can we imagine a form of association that would balance the claims of freedom and equality, between individual freedom, and the interests of the collective?

How can my freedom be just one among many freedoms? If I am free, then any law to which I submit must be my law, it must be a law that I give myself. It must be consistent with my autonomy, that is it is a question of a law to which I freely bind myself. So how is my autonomy compatible with equality, namely with the demand that the laws that I freely choose should be binding on myself and other free agents? Rousseau elegantly solves the problem by simply denying that there is an opposition between freedom and equality and making a distinction between the *general will* and the *will of all*.

The will of all is the sum of private interests, of particular freedoms, the interests that can be aggregated together, for example, in the mechanism of a vote in a liberal democracy. The entire problem of liberal democracy from a Rousseauian perspective consists in the fact that one is asked to vote or exercise one's freedom on the basis of one's private interest as an individual rather than the public interest which might well simply conflict with one's private interests, depending upon one's wealth, class, status, property, etc. This entails that Rousseau has an entirely negative relation to what we might call 'actually existing liberal democracy' and *The Social Contract* should not be read, as is sometimes the case in the English-speaking world, as an apologia for a liberalism which is supposedly based on a social contract. On the contrary, I see *The Social Contract* as a radical critique of liberal individualism, which is what is called in the Second Discourse *le faux contrat*[21] based on radically unequal private interests and property ownership and which culminates in a state of war.

The general will, by contrast, is not private interest but the common interest that tends towards the public good. To choose in accordance with the general will is not to choose in relation to my particular, private interest, but in line with what I see as good for the form of political association as a whole. In passing from the state of nature to society I give up my natural freedom, which has no limitation other than my physical power, and I gain civil liberty. The latter is a notion of moral freedom that is acquired only in society with others and consists in obedience to a law that I give myself, i.e. which is consistent with my autonomy. As Rousseau writes, 'For the impulsion of mere appetite is slavery, and obedience to a law one has prescribed to oneself is freedom.'[22] The same argument goes for equality, where I give up the rough natural equality of the state of nature and the vicious social inequality of the state of war for the political equality of all with all. To choose freely is to choose in accordance with the general will, which means that one chooses for all. Therefore, there is no conflict between freedom and equality and the latter is the expression of the former when it is rightly understood. Collective autonomy is the only legitimate political expression of individual autonomy.

To approach matters in this way also solves the problem of sovereignty, because the only being who is sovereign in a legitimate polity is the people itself. The core of *The Social Contract* is a defence of popular sovereignty. Popular sovereignty consists in acts of legislation by the general will, where the people determine themselves by themselves and not through the mediation of any monarch, prince, aristocracy or unrepresentative body. For Machiavelli, the true citizen loves the city more than his own soul. Rousseau's hyper-Machiavellian twist to this wisdom is to add that the city is nothing else but the expression of one's own soul, it is the civic incarnation of the animate. One is a political subject only by virtue of the association of which one forms a part. For Rousseau, there exists a sheer transparency between my freedom and those of my fellow citizens; freedom and equality are two sides of the same coin. But the metal that melds the two sides of the coin is love of one's city, of one's *patrie,* and Rousseau vigorously defends the need for civic patriotism.

For Rousseau, the most important maxim of legitimate government is following the general will, and this means that all private, particular interests have to be excised from the body politic. But how, then, do citizens freely subjugate their freedom to the general will? And how can citizens take an *interest* in the law? For Rousseau, unlike Kant or indeed Habermas, rationality is not a sufficient nor even reliable guide. Citizens have to be *formed*: 'Therefore, form men if you want to command men: if you would have the laws obeyed, see to it that they are loved.'[23]

Citizens must be formed, that is, they must be taught to *love* the law and that requires virtue. By the word 'virtue' Rousseau simply means that which enables the particular will to conform with the general will. Virtue is the becoming-general or becoming-generic of the particular will. How can this be achieved? The answer is simple: love of the *patrie*, the fatherland.[24] *Patriotism* is the key to making people virtuous, love of the fatherland is the passion that forms citizens and teaches them to love the law. This is why the issue of public education is of such political importance for Rousseau, for without it there would be no way of constituting and maintaining a legitimate polity.

Any project of constitution writing must, for Rousseau, be guided by the following question: 'No constitution will ever be good and solid unless the law rules the citizens' hearts. But how can men's hearts be reached?'[25] And the answer is shocking. The only way of getting citizens to love the law and the *patrie* is 'With children's games; with institutions which appear trivial in the eyes of superficial men, but which form cherished habits and invincible attachments.'[26]

These games would be what we might call *ceremonies of nationhood:* spectacles, games and festivals which are always conducted 'in the open',[27] like the public festivals described in Rousseau's denunciation of theatre in his 1758 'Letter to D'Alembert'.[28] In such spectacles nothing would be represented, as in conventional theatre. On the contrary, spectacles would be the pure presence to itself of the people through the games or ceremonies which the people enact. Rousseau recommends horsemanship as 'an exercise well suited to Poles', which could play a similar role to bullfighting, whose role in maintaining 'a certain vigour in the Spanish nation is not negligible'.[29]

It is not difficult for non-bullfighting, post-Kantian metropolitan, cosmopolitan metrosexuals like ourselves to ridicule such ideas. But the issues that they raise are more serious. If human rationality is fallible, to say the least, if it cannot be assumed that citizens will always will the good, then this requires a political account of formative passions that might force citizens to love the law, that is to overcome the obstacles of alienation and inequality through an act of association. Now, is such a thing practicable without fairly robust notions of civic patriotism and public education? I have my doubts.

The authority of the law

Let me return to the argument about law in *The Social Contract* and see how the relation between politics and law comes up in Book II. Rousseau writes, 'By the social pact we have given the body politic existence and life: the task now is to give it motion and will by legislation.'[30] If the social contract, understood as the coincidence of freedom and equality in the general will, is what breathes life into a legitimate polity, then it is law that gives that polity the motivation and legs to get up and walk. Rousseau defines law in the following fascinating paragraph:

> But when the whole people enacts statutes (*statue*) for the whole people it considers only itself, and if a relation is then formed, it is between the entire object from one point of view and the entire object from another point of view, with no division of the whole. Then the matter with regard to which the statute is being enacted is general, as is the enacting will. It is this act which I call law.[31]

In French, the verb that is doing the work here is *statuer*, to decree, ordain, rule or enact; in short, to make law. For Rousseau, laws are acts of the general will. If one accepts Rousseau's analysis then it becomes immediately clear that we can longer ask who makes the laws, because laws are the expression of the general will. Laws are acts by virtue of which a people legislates for itself and where sovereignty is entirely popular. It is clear that this conception of law stands opposed to Hobbes's conception of the monarch as he who legislates for a society, but who stands outside the social order in a kind of state of nature. If the total alienation of the state of war requires the *externality* of the monarch, Hobbes's 'mortal god', then Rousseau has a purely *internalist* conception of law and sovereignty where a people contracts with itself in the act of association or assembly. But the obvious difference between Hobbes and Rousseau disguises a deeper similarity in their logic of sovereignty. Althusser is quite right in saying:

> Rousseau's theoretical greatness is to have taken up the most frightening aspects of Hobbes: the state of war as a universal and perpetual state, the rejection of any transcendental solution and the 'contract' of total alienation. But Rousseau's defence against Hobbes is to transform total alienation in externality into total alienation in internality.[32]

If Rousseau's logic of sovereignty is entirely immanent, then Hobbes's monarch is the factual transcendence of the sovereign. But the important point here is that the political opposition between monarchical sovereignty and popular sovereignty is a transformation of the *modality* of the Hobbesian logic: God the monarch becomes God the people. As we will see presently, the paradox of sovereignty in Rousseau is that his avowedly immanentist conception of politics is also drawn towards transcendence in two instances: the person of the legislator and the doctrines of civil religion.

For Rousseau, no one in the political realm stands outside the law, for law is willed by everyone in that realm. This line of thinking has the peculiar consequence that subjects of the general will can no longer ask 'whether the law can be unjust, since no man can be unjust towards himself; nor how one is both free and subject to the laws, since they are merely records of our wills'.[33] In this conception of law there is a perfect transparency or mirroring of my will in the general will. If, in Hobbes, the authority of the monarchical sovereign lies in their being both inside and outside the society for which they legislate, for Rousseau sovereignty is purely internal, purely immanent, perfectly narcissistic. This is why sovereignty cannot be represented in an external body: a monarch, the state or even parliament. Sovereignty is the pure presence to itself of the body politic animated by the general will. Rousseau writes, in an extraordinary passage from Book III of *The Social Contract* that seems to anticipate Schopenhauer:

> Sovereignty cannot be represented, for the same reason that it cannot be alienated; it consists essentially in the general will, and the will does not admit of being represented: either it is the same or it is different; there is no middle ground.[34]

What we find in Rousseau is the source of the modern critique of representation whose *locus classicus* is Plato's critique of *mimesis* and which extends into thinkers like Heidegger and Guy Debord: the true 'subject' cannot be the subject of representation and all forms of representation conceive of the subject as subject *to* the spectacle and its theatre of war and inequality.[35] We see this at work already in the 1758 'Letter to D'Alembert', where the critique of theatre is essentially a critique of representation and where, by contrast, in the public festivals that Rousseau recommends, nothing gets represented and there is no spectacle. What takes place in the festival is just the presence to itself of the people in the process of its enactment.

As such, politics is not about representation, but is rather, as Badiou writes, the manifestation of 'the "collective being" of citizen militants'.[36] If it is asked: how does this being show itself? Then the answer is: as nothing, if you please.[37]

As Rousseau tirelessly points out in his tirades against England,[38] this is the error of parliamentarianism:

> The English people thinks it is free; it is greatly mistaken, it is only free during the election of Members of Parliament; as soon as they are elected, it is enslaved, it is nothing. The use it makes of its freedom during the brief moments it has it fully warrants its losing it.[39]

As Edmund Morgan points out, the idea of political representation is a magical enigma: in a representative government, so the story goes, the people are not just the governed, they are also the government, which somehow happens through the miracle of representation. But how exactly can a few be said to *represent* the many? They cannot. The truth of the situation, rather, is that the spurious legitimacy of representative government rests on the simple fiction of the few *believing* that they represent the many and, if the fiction is believed, vice versa.

Sovereignty cannot be represented because it is the people alone who have legislative authority and who make the law: 'the instant a People gives itself Representative, it ceases to be free; it ceases to be'.[40] The only representation that is possible in a legitimate polity is at the level of executive power, namely the magistrates who are elected by the people to carry out its will. But the executive does not make the law, as in representative government; it only carries it out. Yet this move in Rousseau's argument establishes the distinction between sovereignty and government, which opens a further *décalage*: the distinction between generality and particularity.

How is government instituted? It can be instituted only through an act of the general will which flows from the sovereignty of the people. How does the sovereign, who is by definition general, become government, which is particular, particularly when those people chosen to govern also, of necessity, form part of the sovereign people? Rousseau faces the contradiction head-on:

'The difficulty is to understand how there can be an act of Government before the Government exists'.[41] The answer is quite astonishing: it is through the *sudden conversion of sovereignty into democracy.* It should be recalled that democracy was described earlier in Book III as 'a Government without a Government' and rejected as being suited to a nation of gods, but not human beings:

> Here again is revealed one of those astonishing properties of the body politic by which it reconciles apparently contradictory operations. For this reconciliation is accomplished by a sudden conversion of Sovereignty into Democracy; so that without any perceptible change, and simply by a new relation of all to all, the Citizens having become Magistrates pass from general to particular acts, and from the law to its execution.[42]

Thus, without any visible change, the sovereign people transforms itself into a government. That is, each of the individuals that constitute the body of the people becomes a magistrate, if only temporarily. Having refused democracy as being too god-like, Rousseau acknowledges that the establishment of legitimate government necessarily requires a passage *through* democracy and from there into the elective aristocracy that he recommends as the most felicitous form of government. Thus the passage from the general to the particular requires a sudden god-like moment of transfiguration.

This opens up a fault line in Rousseau's argument. Having insistently argued that the only legitimacy possible in a polity is through acts of generality, the passage from sovereignty to government, from the general to the particular, means that we have to speak of a *qualified generality* or a *divided and particularized universality.* This is nowhere clearer than in the enigma of voting procedures outlined in Book IV. Rousseau is forced to the contradictory conclusion that the general will has to be manifested in the majority, that is, generality finds expression only in particularity, which entails that there is no political room for the minorities which also make up the sovereign body of the people. We will come back to this contradiction in relation to Rousseau's account of dictatorship, which is nothing less than the suspension of the sovereign authority of the people by the very agency that claims to speak in its name.

The paradox of sovereignty

For Rousseau, the problem that law appears to solve is that of the relationship between freedom and equality. If he is right, then he has solved the problem of politics, which is a problem akin to 'squaring the circle in geometry'.[43] However, my view is not that Rousseau succeeds in squaring that circle, but rather that his text is articulated around a series of conceptual *décalages* of which we are the inheritors. Rousseau's thinking enacts a series of paradoxes that any serious thinking of the being of politics is obliged to confront. This is nowhere clearer than in the problem of the authority of the law.

The problem is: if the only law that I can follow is a law that I give myself, a law that is the expression of the general will, a law that is consistent with my autonomy yet binding on all members of the social group, then by virtue of what does this law have *authority*? The obvious answer is that if the law is nothing else but the act of the general will, then authority becomes self-authorship. That is, there can be no higher court of legal authority than autonomy. Yet, if authority becomes self-authorship, then doesn't a legitimate polity end up as a form of *collective narcissism*?[44] Despite the immanentist logic of Rousseau's argument, isn't there a need for a moment of transcendent authority in law in order to bind subjects to the law, a moment of radical externality or heteronomy like the function of the monarch in Hobbes? If Rousseau also seems to need a mortal god to animate his politics, then is such an authority conceivable without religion? I think these problems will take us to the very heart of the paradox of sovereignty that forces Rousseau into his argument for the legislator and from there into the dependence of politics and law on religion.

Rousseau, of course, being the most supremely fictive and self-conscious of philosophers, recognizes precisely the problem that I have raised. On the one hand, in Book II he writes, 'The People subject to the laws ought to be their author.'[45] Yet, on the other hand, he goes on seemingly to contradict himself. 'How will a blind multitude, which often does not know what it wills because it rarely knows what is good for it, carry out an undertaking as great, as difficult as a system of legislation?'[46] That is, how can an uninformed and ignorant multitude will the good? How can they learn to act not simply on the basis of private interest but on the basis of common interest, not the will of all but the general will? Rousseau concludes, 'By itself the people always wills the good, but by itself it does not always see it.'[47] Therefore, Rousseau claims, the people needs a guide, it requires something or someone that will, in the fatefully misunderstood words of Book I of *The Social Contract*, force the people to be free.[48]

This leads Rousseau to the beautiful fiction of what he calls the 'legislator' or 'lawgiver', an 'extraordinary man' or 'genius'.[49] The legislator is described by Rousseau as the engineer of the state machine. He is the person who legislates for society, but who has to stand apart from society. The legislator belongs neither to the order of nature, as he intervenes in politics by establishing the constitution, nor to the political order, because he is not subject to the laws that he declares. The office of the legislator is strictly paradoxical, because 'this office which gives the republic its constitution has no place in that constitution'.[50] That is, in order for the internalist laws generated by the general will to have authority, they have to be decreed or 'statuted' by a quasi-external lawgiver who belongs neither to the realm of politics nor to that of nature, but who exists in a 'no place'.[51] It is by occupying this quasi-external, quasi-divine 'no place' that the lawgiver gives a fictional majesty to the law. Rousseau writes:

> When Lycurgus gave his fatherland laws, he began by abdicating the Kingship. It was the custom of most Greek cities to entrust the establishment of their laws to foreigners. The modern Republics of Italy often imitated this practice: the Republic of Geneva did so as well and to good effect. Rome in its finest period witnessed the rebirth of all the crimes of Tyranny in its midst, and found itself on the verge of perishing, for having united the legislative authority and the sovereign power in the same hands.[52]

Of course, if we lived in a society of gods and not human beings – a democracy – then this problem would not arise. Although, as we have just seen, there is a miraculous god-like moment in the transition from sovereignty to government; we are not gods, at least not for more than a moment. Therefore, what is required is a separation of sovereign power, which resides in the people, from legislative authority, which belongs to the lawgiver. Here we approach the paradox of sovereignty: it is only through the strangeness of the foreigner that the laws are seen to have authority and to be binding on an autochtonous people. On the one hand, the law is and has to be the free expression of the general will, the perfect interiority of a people to itself, but on the other hand, there has to be a lawgiver, that is someone who stands outside society and by virtue of which the law has authority beyond the self-authorizing acts of the general will. The only legitimate law is one that we give ourselves, yet the law has to be given to us.

As we know, Rousseau – the troubled Genevan, the internal exile and the foreigner in France – wrote fascinating and revealing projects for the constitutions of Poland and Corsica. One has to invent the fiction of a legislator from outside in order to lend authority to the law, even if that law is legitimate only if it is a law that society gives to itself. Such is the paradox of sovereignty at the heart of political legitimacy. Rousseau confesses the point, and reading the text here is like watching an iceflow break up: 'So that one finds at one and the same time two apparently incompatible things in the work of legislation: an undertaking beyond human force, and to execute it an authority that is nil.'[53]

As Groucho Marx might have said, don't let appearances deceive you, these 'two things' do not just look contradictory, they *are* contradictory. The authority of the law whose essence is the general will requires the fiction of a lawgiver who overrides the will of the people. The people cannot give the law to itself without the fiction of the law being given to it by an outside agency. Political self-authorship has to be underwritten by a ghost author, a quasi-divine legislator.

The vast question that this raises is the relation of politics, law and legal authority to religion and religious authority. This is the problem that Rousseau tackles in the final, fascinating pages of *The Social Contract* that deal with civil religion. To say that this is a contemporary political problem is to risk considerable understatement. If it is the fiction of the legislator that provides the necessary authority for a people to self-authorize itself through the general will, then can we have such authority without religion? That is, can we have law without religion, without some moment of sacralization? Rousseau puts the problem much more sharply: in order to establish a legitimate political order, there would need to exist 'a superior intelligence who saw all of man's passions and experienced none of them, who had no relation to our nature yet knew it thoroughly'.[54] In short, 'It would require gods to give men laws.'[55] In an intriguing footnote Rousseau cites Machiavelli when the latter writes:

> The truth is that there has never been in any country a lawgiver who has not invoked the deity; for otherwise his laws would not have been accepted. A wise man knows many useful truths which cannot be demonstrated in a way that will convince other people.[56]

Every legislator has to authorise the law with reference to the beautiful fiction of a divinity.

Rousseau's reasoning at this point is subtle and revealing, involving a further *décalage,* this time an inversion of the order of cause and effect:

> Each individual, appreciating no other scheme of government than that which bears directly on his particular interest, has difficulty perceiving the advantages he is supposed to derive from the constant privations required by good laws.[57]

In order for the individual to understand the beneficial effects of submitting to the general will, he or she would *already* have to live in the legitimate polity which those effects bring about. That is, 'the effect would have to become the cause … men would have to be prior to laws what they ought to become by means of them'.[58] It is only the effect of the law that might bring the privately interested individual to will the cause, that is, to will generally. In order for this conundrum to be solved, the lawgiver must appeal:

> to an authority of a different order, one which might be able to compel without violence and to persuade without convincing. … This is what has at all times forced the fathers of nations to resort to the intervention of heaven and to attribute their own wisdom to the Gods.[59]

If the privately interested citizen can be compelled to believe that the laws which govern political life have the same divine source as those which govern the universe – in, for example, the fiction of natural law – then he or she might be persuaded to assume the yoke of the general will without being in a position to be rationally convinced by it, for this rationality will follow only from entering a legitimate political association. That is, the beneficial effects of a subject submitting to the law can lead that subject to will the cause only when appeal is made to a divine cause.

Of course, this contains also the seeds of what Rousseau sees as the Caligula solution to political authority: one declares oneself a god at the same time as declaring that the people are animals. The exquisite historical irony of *The Social Contract* is that Rousseau asks at a certain point, 'which people, then, is fit for legislation?'[60] He assembles a characteristically Rousseauesque list of criteria, '[a people] whose every member can be known to all … one that can do without all other peoples and without which every other people can do'.[61] A people fit to receive laws should live on the edges of history and not at its centre, possessing customs that are solid but also malleable. This sounds very nice, but where might one find such a place? Rousseau casts around and declares that Corsica is the one country in Europe fit to receive laws: 'I rather suspect that this small island will one day astound Europe.'[62] Of course, not too many years later something came out of Corsica that did astonish Europe, namely Napoleon, who drastically limited the legislative power of the French Republic in order to allow a massive expansion of imperial, executive power which culminated in his breathtakingly narcissistic self-coronation as emperor in 1804. It would seem that there is little to prevent the legislator from becoming a tyrant, from believing that he is a mortal god that incarnates the general will. Such is the risk that is always run when politics is organized around any economy of the sacred, where the deeper and more searching question is whether politics is practicable without a moment of sacralization.

In this regard, Rousseau's argument for dictatorship in Book IV is extremely revealing. Rousseau asserts that the legislator should not frame the constitution and establish political institutions with such rigidity 'to the point of depriving oneself of the power to suspend their effect'.[63] That is, the laws which issue from the sovereign authority of the people must be able to be suspended, what Roman jurists called *iustitium*, and which Agamben has interestingly analysed.[64] Such *iustitium*, a suspension or literally a standstill, is permitted only in the case of an emergency, which arises when the safety of the *patrie* is at stake. That is, when national security is threatened by external attack or internal dissent, then the sovereign authority of the general will can be suspended: 'If, however, the peril is such that the laws as an instrumentality are an obstacle to guarding against it, then a supreme chief [*chef*] is named who silences all the laws and provisionally suspends the Sovereign authority.'[65]

This supreme chief is the dictator, who does not have the power to make laws, but can suspend their operation. What Rousseau is envisaging here is the state of exception when *iustitium* is required in order to preserve the security of the political order of the *patrie.* The obvious questions that this raises are: who decides on the state of exception, for how long and what is permitted or, more accurately, forbidden in such a state? Rousseau turns once again to Roman history for guidance, where the senate decided upon the choice of the dictator and the period of dictatorship did not exceed six months, otherwise it would become tyrannical. The fascinating corollary of this position, particularly for contemporary devotees of so-called 'civic republicanism', is the necessary co-implication of republicanism and dictatorship. For Rousseau one cannot have one without the other; the sovereign authority of law cannot exclude the possibility of its suspension; no justice without *iustitium.*

Of course, the contemporary dilemma is whether, as Agamben thinks, following Benjamin, in modern bio-politics 'the state of exception ... has become the rule'.[66] If this is the case – and Agamben provides compelling, if partial, legal evidence to justify his claim – then dictatorship is the generalized form of contemporary government. This entails that in a situation of declared danger or peril to the 'homeland' – after a 'terrorist' attack, say – the executive power of a president can override the legislative authority of the other organs of government, not to mention international legal institutions like the United Nations and niceties like the Geneva Conventions. In a time of war, particularly something as vague and indefinite as a 'war on terror', justice becomes *iustitium* and the republic slides into dictatorship.[67]

When Agamben speaks of the contemporary geo-political situation as a 'global civil war', this can, I think, be heard as an echo of Rousseau's analysis of inequality culminating in a state of war in the Second Discourse. It is hard to disagree with such a diagnosis at the present time.[68] For Rousseau, the necessity for the passage from popular to dictatorial sovereignty arises when there is a purported threat to national security. At such moments the dictator can declare *iustitium* and legitimately banish or put to death those who threaten the nation: the internal or external enemy. It is at this point that the entire sacred underpinning of sovereign power turns on the determination of the figure of *homo sacer,* as he who can be legitimately killed without being sacrificed. It is curious to note that, as part of a critique of theocracy in the final pages of *The Social Contract,* Rousseau writes that 'Then to die for one's country is to become a martyr, to break the laws is to be impious, and to subject the guilty man to public execration is to deliver him to the wrath of the Gods: *sacer estod,* be accursed.'[69]

The problem of civil religion

The conclusion to Rousseau's argument for the legislator is clear: there can be no legal authority, and hence effective political legitimacy, without an appeal to religious authority. There can be no legitimate polity, and legitimacy implies immanence, without an appeal to transcendence, ultimately transcendence in the form of the sacred. It is this problem that leads Rousseau towards the issue of civil religion with which *The Social Contract* concludes. But these extraordinary pages are not, as might appear on a cursory reading, an addendum to the main argument about politics, but its transcendental condition of possibility. However, it is my contention that Rousseau's argument about civil religion is also the condition of *impossibility* for his conception of politics. His text wavers between the paradoxes or *décalages* which make its articulation possible. Once again, I am not suggesting that Rousseau was unaware of this. On the contrary – self-conscious fictor that he was – he was acutely aware of what he was doing.

Civil religion can be thought of as a profession of faith that is paradoxically both transcendent and subordinate to the immanentism of popular sovereignty.[70] What Rousseau tackles with alarming directness, much more radically than in his other writings on religion, and more than a century before Nietzsche, is the problem of Christianity and politics, namely the Christian separation of theological and political authority. In the religions of antiquity there was an identity of theological and political authority. One need only read the *Oresteia* or the tragedies of Sophocles to realize that the gods of the Athenians were gods of the city, civic gods without universal jurisdiction: the gods of Sparta were not the gods of Athens, Corinth or Thebes. Oddly, this relativity of belief never seems to have led to religious war. Christianity, by contrast, which requires universality of belief, has led to little else but religious wars for the past couple of millennia. Christianity divides political and theological authority, declaring that the kingdom of God is not of this world but of the next. It is, for Rousseau, an essentially anti-political religion. He declares, 'far from attaching the Citizens' hearts to the State, it detaches them from it as from all earthly things. I know of nothing more contrary to the social spirit.'[71]

The task of a civil religion is that of 'reuniting the two heads of the eagle',[72] that is, bringing together political and theological authority. Rousseau's critique of the political utility of Christianity, in my view, is compelling, but it leads him to construct a conception of civil religion that is at best syncretic and at worst cynical. He declares that 'the dogmas of civil religion ought to be simple, few in number, stated with precision, without explanations or commentary'.[73]

The positive dogmas include belief in an omnipotent and provident deity, the happiness of the just and the punishment of the wicked, the sanctity of the social contract and the laws, without forgetting the necessity of a belief in the afterlife. It would not, I believe, be an exaggeration to describe this miscellany of dogmas as somewhat opportunistic. What's more, if someone is found to be a social hypocrite by publicly acknowledging the authority of the laws but behaving as if he did not believe them, then 'let him be punished with death; he has committed the greatest of crimes, he has lied before the laws'.[74] *Sacer estod* – the sacredness of civil religion requires the execution of the *homo sacer*. If the purpose of civil religion is to provide a transcendent, sacred underpinning to the immanence of the general will, then it does not require much imagination to see how such sacredness might be violently employed to legitimate the most ugly forms of state repression and state terror, particularly when we link them together with Rousseau's argument for dictatorship. In the period of the National Convention in France after 1792, pacific invocations of the *Être Suprême* in civic festivals found their echo in the bloody violence with which blasphemers were executed. The general will can become murderous.

And yet ... *must* the general will be murderous? If Rousseau's conception of civil religion amounts to little more than a cynical amalgam of neo-pagan dogmas, then does this discredit the whole idea of civil religion? I don't think so, for at least two reasons, one diagnostic and descriptive, the other more normative or perhaps simply hopeful. I will develop the more hopeful reason in conclusion, so let me begin descriptively. It is my belief that there is no way of understanding contemporary political reality without a clear understanding of the nature, history and force of civil religion, by which I mean the sacralization of politics in its diverse and contradictory forms, which arises when a political unit transforms itself into a sacred entity as a way of buttressing its claim to legitimacy.

This is most obviously the case in American civil religion, which finds banal but compelling empirical confirmation in the weird symbolism of the $1 bill, complete with the words 'In God we trust', although they were added by Eisenhower only in 1956.[75] In addition to the Roman eagle of the Great Seal of the United States, we find two allusions to Virgil, the inscription *Novus ordo seclorum*, 'a new order of ages' and *Annuit coeptis*, 'he has approved our undertaking'. These allusions bring together the divine source for the polity with a prefiguration of the idea of Manifest Destiny. It is the divine source whose radiant sun-like eye stares out at us at the top of the incomplete Masonic pyramid, with its thirteen steps symbolizing the number of the original colonies and the Roman numerals MDCCLXXVI. It is the God of American civil political religion who underwrites the act of republican association, the unification of a disparate plurality, *E pluribus unum*. Beyond the materiality of the greenback, the articles of American civil religion find expression in the pledge of allegiance, the worship of the flag, the cult of the war dead and entire culture of war.

To move far too quickly, the presence of civil religion can be seen in various European nationalisms, but it can be seen most strikingly in the extraordinary symbolism of the European flag, with its crown of twelve yellow stars on a blue background. The flag was adopted by the Council of Europe on 8 December 1955 and was based on a design by Arsène Heitz. It seems innocent enough, with the stars representing the diverse European peoples (at least, 'the Europe of the Twelve') on a background of the blue western sky. It is apparently a simple symbol for European integration. However, Heitz was a pious and devoted Catholic and his design was directly inspired by the history of the apparitions of the Blessed Virgin in the rue du Bac in Paris. In the summer of 1830 the Virgin Mary appeared to Catherine Labouré, a novice in the Sisters of Charity in the rue du Bac. The Virgin went on to demand that Catherine have a medal struck, the 'Miraculous Medal'. On this medal the Virgin is depicted with a halo of twelve gold stars around her head in an allusion to the Revelation of St John (12:1). Now, if all this seems like a flight of fancy, then one might simply note that the day the European flag was adopted by the Council of Europe, 8 December, is also the Feast of the Immaculate Conception, adopted by Pius IX on 8 December 1854, exactly 101 years earlier. I am not suggesting that the European Union is a covert Catholic conspiracy, but there is at the very least a story to tell and a history that requires uncovering.

Without an understanding of the intrication of politics and religion we have little hope of comprehending the present through which we are all too precipitously passing. Ours is a time of new religious war, what an as yet unpublished report by the Rand Corporation calls a time of 'cosmic war' where political actors are religious believers or 'cosmic warriors' with a Manichean opposition between Good and Evil. It seems to me that any attempt to understand politics at the present time has to begin from the datum of *sacred violence*, of political violence carried out in the name of the divine: 'Religious contestation in Europe before the age of nationalism and Marxism is a better guide to the future than the secular conflict of the Cold War.'[76]

It is in relation to a triangulation of politics, religion and morality that the present is playing itself out, and I see little sign of this changing in the foreseeable future. For example, the much discussed factoid about the presence of moral values in the exit polls from the US presidential elections of November 2004, which caused a minor panic among American liberals, is deeply interesting to a humble philosopher. Citizens are making political decisions that are really moral judgements and these judgements flow from a religious metaphysics, to be precise the alleged will of God. Although one may argue that such a religious morality is pernicious, in either its US Christian version or its Jihadist obverse, there is no doubt that the triangulation of faith, morality and politics is a powerful framework of intelligibility that makes powerful sense and motivates subjects in a way that far outstrips its secular opponents. Any political movement in the United States or elsewhere ignores this connection between faith, morality and politics at its peril. This, it seems to me, is what the religious right in the United States has powerfully and with ever-growing hegemony understood since the late 1970s. In my view, there can be no leftist, egalitarian politics without an acknowledgement of the motivational force of religion and an attempt to harness that force for progressive ends. This entails facing up to issues like civic patriotism, moral education and the necessity for populism, even ceremonies of nationhood. Once again, to be clear, I say this with reluctance and little enthusiasm, but these are dark times.

Such is what we might call the 'actuality' of Rousseau, and this is the reason why I have sought to follow closely the intrication of three terms in Rousseau's text: politics, law and religion. We have followed a series of conceptual *décalages* around which Rousseau's 'sad system' is staged, where the condition of possibility for any legitimate form of political association requires the externality of the legislator for its authorization and the transcendence of civil religion for its sacralization. Sadly, this condition of possibility is also the system's condition of impossibility, and we have seen Rousseau's political argument result in a rather improbable conception of civil religion. But it might lead elsewhere. With that in mind, let me turn to my conclusion and to my more hopeful reason for focusing on the theme of civil religion.

Conclusion: the politics of the supreme fiction

There is a double miracle at work in politics. On the one hand, politics requires a willing suspension of disbelief. It requires that the many believe in the fictions told to them by the few who govern them. That is, government requires make-believe, whether the belief is in the divine right of kings or the quasi-divinity of the people that is somehow meant to find expression through the magic of representative government, the organ of the party, the radiant sun-like will of the glorious leader, or whatever. But, on the other hand, the extraordinary thing about politics is that it not only *requires* a willing suspension of disbelief, it also *receives* it. The force in any polity always lies with the many, yet somehow, for most of history the many submit to the will of the few who claim not only to be working in their interest, but to embody their collective will. Of course, it might be pointed out that political power is always possessed by the people with the 'guns and sticks', usually the police and the military, and if the many don't possess them, then they are powerless. That is, of course, incontrovertible, but it doesn't begin to explain what we might call the *fictional force* whereby the many submit to the few without the constant threat of physical violence. Considered closely but disinterestedly, politics is a very curious matter. In order to understand its operation all we possess is history, which is what makes the work of historians of politics so essential.

With that in mind, I'd like to turn briefly to Edmund Morgan's *Inventing the People. The Rise of Popular Sovereignty in England and America.* The central theoretical category in this fascinatingly rich historical account of the transition from monarchical to popular sovereignty in England and America during the seventeenth and eighteenth centuries is *fiction.* The main concern of Morgan's book is to explain how it is that the fiction of the divine right of kings gave way to that of the sovereignty of the people. The interesting thing about this conjunction of fictions is that whereas it is difficult from this end of history to see the idea of the divine right of kings as anything more than an absurdity based on the idea of the king as the visible god, the overwhelming majority of people and politicians are attached to, or at least ventriloquize, some version of the idea of popular sovereignty: that all human beings are equal or indeed created equal, that government should be by the people and for the people, that government embodies and enacts the will of the people, blah, blah, blah. Morgan's point is that *historically* one fiction succeeds the other in the extraordinary years of the 1630s and 1640s in England and in a different but strongly related way in the American colonies in the 1760s and 1770s. But, more important, perhaps, *conceptually* one fiction resembles the other much more closely than we might like to imagine: God the king becomes God the people.[77] Morgan notes:

> The sovereignty of the people was not a repudiation of the sovereignty of God. God remained the ultimate source of all governmental authority, but attention now centred on the immediate source, the people. Though God authorized government, He did it through the people, and in doing so He set them above their governors.[78]

Indeed, it might be said that the fiction of popular sovereignty is a more fictional fiction than divine right.[79] A king is a visible presence with a crown and sceptre and usually a large family with expensive tastes, but where might one *see* the people? One can see people, but where exactly is *the* people to be found? The fact that most of us might happen to believe in the fiction of popular sovereignty and the idea or ideal that legitimate government is the expression of the will of the people in no way diminishes its fictional status. A moment's thought reveals that it is based on a series of logical *décalages*, namely that the people are the governed, but also the government, and that this identity of government and the governed somehow happens through the miracle of *representation*, which is truly the central shibboleth of liberal democracy. But how exactly can a few be said to *represent* the many? How can a particularity speak for a generality when the latter is not actually present? Of course, it cannot. What is the case, however, is that the *legitimacy* of the few rests on the fiction of *believing* that they represent the many. At which point a number of opposing possibilities arise: either politics and politicians are entirely cynical or they actually believe that they incarnate the will of their voters and the people as a whole through the magic of representation. Similarly, either the electorate believe that their politicians are a group of cynical, self-interested, money-grabbing crooks or they actually believe that their will is miraculously represented through the mechanism of the vote. Representative government prevents the inconveniencies of democracy, namely the genuine sovereign authority of a people. In my opinion the United States of America is the *least* representative of the Western democracies.

Politics, then, is a kind of magic show, where we know that the rabbit has not miraculously appeared in the empty hat and the magician's lovely assistant has not been sawn in half, but where we are willing to suspend disbelief and go along with the illusion. This is where Rousseau is so instructive, as he is the most fictively self-conscious of philosophers.[80] The concise, near-geometrical abstraction of *The Social Contract* is a political fiction, the fiction of popular sovereignty understood as association without representation, which is, for Rousseau, the only form of politics that can face and face down the *fact* of gross inequality and the state of war. The being of politics is the act of association without representation. This fiction requires, in turn, other fictions, those of law and religion. The fiction of politics has to be underpinned by the authority of a quasi-divine legislator and the dogmas of civil religion. For Rousseau, the binding of a political collectivity has to be the self-binding of the general will and this requires the ligature of *religio*. Such a religion has to be inculcated through shared beliefs, civic values and what can only be described as political rituals, such as pledges of allegiance, national anthems, honouring the war dead, the sacredness of the flag, or whatever. Such is the necessary armature of any *theologia civilis*.

So, is my conclusion simply that we cannot and should not enter into discussions of politics without acknowledging the dimension of fiction, particularly religious fiction, in legitimating political life? That would seem to be what lies behind the skeptical, rather Humean, historical approach adopted by Morgan. Politics requires fictions of the sacred and rituals of sacralization for its legitimation and these fictions need to be exposed for what they are. Any empire's new clothes need to be stripped away in order to see the old, rotting flesh of the state.

However, let me push my argument a little further and speculate. It should not be thought that I am opposing fiction to fact here. I do not think that a general critique of political fictions is a mere sacrifice on the altar of empiricism to the god of political realism. In my view, in the realms of politics, law and religion there are *only* fictions, but I do not see this as a sign of weakness but as a signal of *possible* strength. The distinction that I would like to advance in closing is not between fiction and fact, but between fiction and *supreme fiction*. In saying this, I allude to Wallace Stevens, and the dim possibility of a fructive collision between poetry and politics. For Stevens, poetry permits us to see fiction as fiction, that is, to see the fictiveness or contingency of the world. It reveals in his terms 'the idea of order' which we imaginatively impose on reality.

Such is what we might think of as the *critical* task of poetry, where I understand critique in the Kantian sense as demystifying any empiricist myth of the given and showing the radical dependency of that which is upon the creative, ultimately imaginative, activity of the subject. The critical task of poetry is to show that the world is what you make of it. But that does not exhaust the category of fiction. Paradoxically, a supreme fiction is a fiction that we know to be a fiction – there being nothing else – but in which we nevertheless believe. For Stevens, it is a question here of final belief: 'The final belief is to believe in a fiction, which you know to be a fiction, there being nothing else. The exquisite truth is to know that it is a fiction and that you believe it willingly.'[81]

As he writes elsewhere, 'final belief/ Must be in a fiction' and the hope of a supreme fiction is to furnish such final belief.[82] In his most important and difficult poem, 'Notes toward a Supreme Fiction', Stevens attempts to articulate the conditions for such a fiction, but only offers notes towards it, something indeed like musical notes. He writes of the supreme fiction that it is not given to us whole and ready made, but that,

It is possible, possible, possible. It must
Be possible.[83]

My hope here is that we might begin to transpose this possibility from the poetical to the political realm, or indeed to show that both poetry and politics are realms of fiction and that what we can begin to envision in their collision is the possibility of a supreme fiction. What is to be hoped for in politics is the possibility of a supreme fiction, the fiction of political association, the fiction of politics *as such*. This requires that we begin to start thinking about politics as radical *creatio ex nihilo,* as bringing something into being from nothing. This is what Marx attempted in his 1843 'Introduction' to the *Critique of Hegel's Philosophy of Right* where, it seems to me, he gets close to the idea of a supreme fiction. For Marx, the logic of the political subject is expressed in the words: '*I am nothing and I should be everything*' (*'Ich bin nichts, und ich müßte alles sein'*).[84] That is, beginning from a position of nothingness or what we called above with Althusser 'total alienation', a particular group is posited as a generality, which requires 'the total alienation of this total alienation', in the act of political association. Marx's name for the supreme fiction is 'the proletariat', which he qualifies as communist, that is, as rigorously egalitarian.

To borrow a line of thought from Badiou, what is lacking at the present time is the possibility of such a name, a supreme fiction of final belief around which a politics might organize itself.[85] What is lacking is a theory and practice of the general will understood as the supreme fiction of final belief that would take place in the act by which a people becomes a people. What is lacking is an understanding of how the fiction of political association requires the fictions of law and religion for its authorization and sacralization. In the absence of a new political name, the political task is the poetic construction of a supreme fiction, what Stevens also calls 'the fiction of an absolute'. Such a fiction would be a fiction that we *know* to be a fiction and yet in which we believe nonetheless. All we have at the present time are some notes towards this fiction and the open question with which we began: the question that Rousseau asked Voltaire exactly 250 years ago. A catechism of the citizen would be a supreme fiction, a fiction of final belief. It should be remembered that what Rousseau asks from Voltaire in the 1756 letter is a *poem*:

> This work, done with care, would be the most useful book ever composed, it seems to me and perhaps the only one needful to men. Here, Sir, is a subject for you. I passionately wish you might be willing to undertake this work and adorn it with your Poetry.[86]

Is the fact that we are still asking for this poem a sign of hope or a symptom of despair? It is possible, possible, possible it is the former, but the paralyzing prospect of the latter causes me to hesitate, and I suddenly see the fancy of a supreme fiction breaking up like an ice-flow. At that point, to be honest, I am not sure what to think. What can I hope?

Notes

1 This is a newly edited version of 'The Catechism of the Citizen: Politics, Law and Religion in, after, with and against Rousseau', published in *Law and Humanities*, 1, 2007, pp. 79–110.

2 Jean-Jacques Rousseau, *The Discourses and other early Political Writings*, ed. and trans. V. Gourevitch, Cambridge: Cambridge University Press, 1997, p. 245; emphasis mine.

3 The literature on civil religion is immense and I cannot begin to do it justice here. For a very useful recent historical account of the emergence of civil religion from the Rome of Numa Pompilius to the French revolution see Mark Silk, 'Numa Pompilius and the idea of civil religion in the West', *Journal of the American Academy of Religion*, 2004, 72, pp. 863–96. For a discussion of American civil religion see Michael Angrosino, 'Civil religion *redux*', *Anthropology Quarterly*, 2002, 75, 239–67.

4 Rousseau, *The Discourses*, p. 246; emphasis mine.

5 See Louis Althusser, 'Rousseau: the social contract (the discrepancies)', in *Montesquieu, Rousseau, Marx*, trans. Ben Brewster, London and New York: Verso, 1972; Alain Badiou, *Being and Event*, trans. Oliver Feltham, London and New York: Continuum, 2005. A formal similarity between Althusser's and Badiou's interpretations of Rousseau can be noted, although it conceals a vast difference at the level of the ontologies that are driving the two interpretations. They both display a similar formalism in picking out the contradiction between particularity and generality that both defines and divides Rousseau's text, but they take this in very different directions. For Badiou, the originality of Rousseau consists in thinking the being of politics in terms of category of the *event*, understood as a subjective act of creation whose radicality consists in the fact that it does not originate in any structure supported within being or the situation, such as the realm of the socio-economic. On the contrary, for Althusser, this is precisely the failure of Rousseau's politics, and it leads Rousseau towards an entirely ideological politics which has no way of facing up to the savage potentiality of capitalist relations of production. Obviously, the key figure behind both of these interpretations is Marx and my own interpretation of Marx is very much on my mind as I read Rousseau. (See my *Infinitely Demanding. Ethics of Commitment, Politics of Resistance*, London and New York, Verso, 2007.)

6 Althusser, 'Rousseau: the social contract (the discrepancies)', p. 107.

7 I am thinking in particular of Arendt's influential and deeply misguided critique of Rousseau. See Hannah Arendt, *On Revolution*, London: Penguin, 1963.

8 I owe this insight on the relation of politics to religion to conversations with Joe Tinguely, PhD student, New School for Social Research.

9 Emilio Gentile, *Politics as Religion*, trans. G. Staunton, Princeton, NJ: Princeton University Press, 2006.
10 As Gramsci once famously wrote, 'socialism is the religion that is needed to kill off Christianity'.
11 Rousseau, *The Social Contract and other later Political Writings*, p. 41.
12 Ibid., pp. 49–50.
13 Ibid., p. 50.
14 Ibid., p. 49.
15 Giorgio Agamben, *State of Exception*, trans. Kevin Attell, Chicago: University of Chicago Press, 2005, pp. 2–3; see also pp. 85–8.
16 Cf. Denis Guénoun, *L'Enlèvement de la politique*, Paris: Circé, 2002, p. 15.
17 Rousseau, *The Social Contract*, p. 50.
18 Ibid.
19 Althusser, 'Rousseau: the social contract (the discrepancies)', p. 127.
20 Ibid., p. 147.
21 Rousseau, *The Discourses*, p. 173.
22 Rousseau, *The Social Contract*, p. 54.
23 Ibid., p. 13.
24 'This gentle and lively sentiment, which combines the force of *amour propre* with all the beauty of virtue, endows it with an energy which, without disfiguring, makes it into the most heroic of all the passions' (ibid., p. 16).
25 Ibid., p. 179.
26 Ibid., p. 179.
27 Ibid., p. 186.
28 See Jean-Jacques Rousseau, *Politics and the Arts*, trans. A. Bloom, Ithaca, NY: Cornell University Press, 1960.
29 Rousseau, *The Social Contract*, p. 186.
30 Ibid., p. 66.
31 Ibid., p. 67. The final sentences are much more precise and interesting in French than in English: 'Alors la matière sur laquelle on statue est générale comme la volonté qui statue. C'est cet acte que j'appelle une loi.'
32 Althusser, 'Rousseau: the social contract (the discrepancies)', p. 136.
33 Rousseau, *The Social Contract*, p. 67.
34 Ibid., p. 114.
35 See Alain Badiou, *Logiques des mondes*, Paris: Seuil, 2006, p. 575.
36 Alain Badiou, *Being and Event*, p. 347.
37 'But what then will be the object of these entertainments? What will be shown in them? Nothing, if you please.' (Rousseau, *Politics and the Arts*, p. 126.)
38 And I self-hatingly love him all the more for this reason: 'I have never liked England or the English.' (Jean-Jacques Rousseau, *Confessions*, trans. J. M. Cohen, London: Penguin, 1953, p. 547.)
39 Rousseau, *The Social Contract*, p. 114.
40 Ibid., p. 115.
41 Ibid., p. 117.
42 Ibid., pp. 117–18.
43 Ibid., p. 179.
44 I discuss this in my *Continental Philosophy. A Very Short Introduction*, Oxford: Oxford University Press, 2001, chapter 2.
45 Rousseau, *The Social Contract*, p. 68.
46 Ibid., p. 68.
47 Ibid., p. 68.
48 Ibid., p. 53.

49 Ibid., p. 69.
50 Ibid., p. 69.
51 Like Augustine's God in Book X of *The Confession of St Augustine*, trans. J. K. Ryan, New York: Doubleday, 1960, p. 254.
52 Rousseau, *The Social Contract*, p. 70.
53 Ibid., p. 70.
54 Ibid., p. 68.
55 Ibid., p. 69.
56 Ibid., p. 71.
57 Ibid., pp. 70–1.
58 Ibid., p. 71.
59 Ibid., p. 71.
60 Ibid., p. 77.
61 Ibid., p. 77.
62 Ibid., p. 78.
63 Ibid., p. 138.
64 See 'Iustitium', Agamben, *State of Exception*, pp. 41–51.
65 Rousseau, *The Social Contract*, p. 138.
66 Benjamin, quoted in Agamben, *State of Exception*, p.6.
67 It is difficult to think of a more plausible interpretation of the novel category of 'unlawful combatant' in the case of detainees in Guantanamo Bay, where the legal framework of the Geneva Conventions that protect the rights of prisoners-of-war was suspended by the invention of a new legal category that permitted the extension of executive power.
68 However, what I say should not be interpreted as political agreement with Agamben's position. Although I find Agamben's work diagnostically very powerful, particularly at the level of philology and the history of law, particularly Roman law, Agamben has very little to offer politically other than making some Benjaminian noises about 'divine violence' and a 'politics of pure means' or Arendtian noises about praxis. (See Agamben, *State of Exception*, p.88.) What Agamben lacks is precisely what can be found in Rousseau: a conception of the being of politics understood as the act of association.
69 Rousseau, *The Social Contract*, p. 147. On this point, see Gourevitch's helpful elucidation, '*Sacer estod*, "be accursed": the ancient Roman formula uttered upon delivering someone to public execration and the Gods' (ibid., pp. 305–6.)
70 In Robert Bellah's formulation, civil religion is that religious dimension that is arguably found in the life of every people through which it interprets its historical and social experience in the light of some transcendent reality, usually God. (See Robert N. Bellah, *The Broken Covenant. American Civil Religion in Time of Trial*, Chicago: University of Chicago Press, 1992.)
71 Rousseau, *The Social Contract*, p. 147. In an eerie anticipation of Nietzsche's argument in *On the Genealogy of Morals*, Rousseau writes that Christianity is slave morality: 'True Christians are made to be slaves; they know it and are hardly moved by it; this brief life has too little value in their eyes' (ibid., p. 149).
72 Ibid., p. 146.
73 Ibid., p. 150.
74 Ibid.
75 I borrow here from Gentile, *Politics as Religion*, pp. xi–xii *et passim*.
76 'Analyzing Religious Politics and Violence', Rand Corporation, September 2006, unpublished typescript. I'd like to thank Jack Miles for letting me see a copy of this document.

77 As Rousseau writes, 'the voice of the people is indeed the voice of God.' (Rousseau, *The Social Contract*, p. 8.)
78 Edmund Morgan, *Inventing the People. The Rise of Popular Sovereignty in England and America*, New York: Norton, 1988, p. 37.
79 Ibid., p. 153.
80 Whichever genre he works in: the theatrical comedy of manners (*Narcisse*), the sentiment-soaked epistolary novel (*La Nouvelle Héloïse*), the didactic treatise in moral education (*Emile*), the quasi-scientific hypothetical history of humanity (*Discourse on Inequality*), the creation of a sexualized subjectivity defined and divided by intimacy (*The Confessions*) or meditative *askesis* (*Reveries*).
81 Wallace Stevens, *Opus Posthumous*, ed. M. J. Bates, New York: Knopf, 1989, p. 189.
82 Wallace Stevens, *The Palm at the End of the Mind*, New York: Vintage, 1967, p. 187.
83 Ibid., p. 230. I'd like to thank Todd Kronan for persuading me that the roots of Stevens's idea of the supreme fiction lie in his reading of Santayana.
84 *Marx-Engels Werke* I, Berlin: Dietz, 1988, p. 389; *Marx. Early Political Writings*, ed. J. O'Malley, Cambridge: Cambridge University Press, 1994, p. 67.
85 Alain Badiou, 'Politics: a non-expressive dialectics', online: http://blog.urbanomic.com/sphaleotas/archives/badiou-politics.pdf.
86 Rousseau, *The Social Contract*, p. 245.

Part III

Desire

Chapter 11

What's so funny about Infinite Justice?

Janne Porttikivi

'Infinite Justice' was the name initially given to the Bush government's offensive launched against that multifaced enemy called 'terrorism'. And as we know, this name was quickly abandoned and replaced by the more descriptive and perhaps more neutral term 'war against terrorism'. There are, of course, several good reasons for the change, but I think the name 'Infinite Justice' is a better expression for the Bush government's spontaneous reaction to the destruction of the World Trade Center towers: international terrorism is the absolute evil, and so in Bush's idealistic rhetoric the only way to fight back at the same level is 'Infinite Justice'. In this light it was only consistent that Bush also declared that Osama Bin Laden was wanted 'dead or alive' in the good old spirit of the wild west.

Why the new name? I think there were important and essential strategic reasons for this. Justice, which is indifferent to human life, or justice, which has absolute power over human life or over life in general, refers more to divine law than to human law. Although there is a powerful truth in Carl Schmitt's thesis that all political and juridical concepts are secularized theological concepts,[1] it wasn't politically wise in that sensitive political-religious situation to declare or bring forth openly that there is an intimate connection between politics and theology.

The aim of the US government was to form the largest possible coalition, to form allied forces against international terrorism and the states which are supporting it, so called rogue states or the 'axis of evil'. There was a fear that reference to God would not only alienate the secularized Western countries but also those Islamic countries which also condemned terrorist attacks, rather than get them to join the coalition. There is a consensus for one thing, perhaps for different reasons but a consensus anyway, between the secularized Western countries and the not so secularized Islamic countries: only the divine law is eternal and thus infinite; human law is linked to place and time and thus finite. Perhaps Infinite Justice happens at the end of time, if God will, in some sort of messianic time, but at least one thing is certain: the Last Judgement is not the business of any earthly courtroom, not even that of the US Supreme Court, and George W. Bush was surely not directly expressing God's will.

The problem with the Infinite Justice is then, as Jacques Rancière has pointed out,[2] that it means justice without limits. It's justice that ignores all the distinctions by which its practice is traditionally delimited: it is impossible to distinguish any more legal punishment from the vengeance of individuals, when all the barriers which were separating the law from politics, ethics or religion have been erased.

That's why, for Rancière, there was no language excess: '"Infinite justice" states exactly what's at stake: the assertion of a right identical to the omnipotence hitherto reserved for the vindictive God. All traditional distinctions end up being abolished with the erasure of international forms of law.'[3] Of course this erasure is already the principle of terrorist action itself, but fighting back in the same terrain as your enemy as it has already been determined, leads easily to the vicious circle in which you are beginning to look more and more like your enemy.

This current international political situation is characterized by what Rancière calls 'the excess of ethics over law and politics'.[4] For some time now this rise of ethics to the detriment of justice has characterized the forms by which the Western powers have intervened abroad. This blurring of the limits between ethics and politics has taken on the form of the humanitarian military intervention. The principle behind this is revealed by the figure of the absolute victim, a victim of infinite evil. Not only are there nowadays suffering victims everywhere – 'everybody is somebody's victim' is a good motto for our politically correct time – but there has to be also the absolute victim of infinite evil which grounds this whole edifice and legitimizes every military action taking place in any corner of the world:

> The obligation of attending to the victims of absolute Evil has become identical to the fight without limits against this evil. And this is identified with deploying unlimited military power, acting like a global police force in charge of restoring order to every part of the world where Evil can find shelter.[5]

In this weird 'coincidence of oppositions' any military action is always presented as a means to guarantee the peace or safe delivery of humanitarian aid. As Slavoj Žižek says, the fundamental irony of this situation is that we are living in a world where the old Orwellian motto 'War is peace' has finally become reality:

> [A]s Tony Blair said, perhaps we will have to bomb the Taliban in order to secure food transportation and distribution ... Thus we no longer have the opposition between war and humanitarian aid: [when] an American plane is flying above us one never knows what it will drop, bombs or food parcels.[6]

In this situation the denunciation of communist crimes and the Nazi Holocaust has also acquired a whole new meaning. Not only have the crimes been transformed into the monstrous effects of regimes that have to be fought against (because then we would be still in the political field), but into the forms whereby an infinite, unthinkable and unforgivable crime was made manifest: the work of an Evil power exceeding all legal and political measures. As Rancière says, '[e]thics has become the way to think this infinite or absolute evil, which has created an irremediable break in history'.[7]

The ultimate consequence of this contemporary ethical ideology is the paradoxical constitution of an individual's absolute right whose rights have, in fact, been absolutely negated. These individuals actually appear as the victims of 'an infinite Evil against which the fight is itself infinite. This is the point at which the one defending the victims' rights inherits absolute right.'[8] And this absolute or sovereign power creates a zone of indistinction where law and non-law are absolutely inseparable, because the absolute right is the same as the non-right.[9] This is the reason for the total indeterminacy of the law as it deals with the prisoners held captive at Guantanamo Bay. In this zone of indistinction or juridical and political black hole, victims and culprits alike fall into the abyss of 'infinite justice'.

As Rancière says, Hegel already ridiculed such a night of the absolute or the abstract and immediate infinite in which 'all cows are grey'. That's because for Hegel the one who wants to find himself beyond and immediately within the absolute has before himself nothing but that of the empty negative, the abstract infinite.[10] The lack of ethical distinctions or, rather, the excess of ethics over the law and politics has transformed the prisoners of Guantanamo Bay into captives of this type of infinite, the only difference being for Rancière that now in this night all cows are not grey but orange.[11]

Is it possible to find some way out of these political and ethical deadlocks? Surely it is; it only needs firm (axiomatic and universal) political decision and courage to make this decision actual through meticulous transformation of the current situation point by point.[12] (And the first step has been already taken: almost right away at the beginning of his presidency Barack Obama announced that Guantanamo Bay will be closed in the near future.)

But of course on the level of thought one can ask many questions concerning these universals and how to make them concrete. For example, it is clear that this type of infinity which Rancière speaks of refers to something which Hegel called 'bad infinity', which is mired with abstract universals and empty rhetorics (although the consequences of this infinity have been nearly catastrophic). In my chapter there is a kind of parallax view which is focused on two kinds of thinking of ethics and politics. There are two divergent lines which I try to follow: Hegel, comedy and politics, and Kant, tragedy and ethics. But as was expected there occurs some kind of short-circuit between these divergent lines of thought, and both thinkers are read closely together from the perspective of Lacanian psychoanalysis.[13]

But the Hegelian question is, concerning infinite or finite justice, what would the justice be if it had limits which are external to it? Finite and limited justice, precisely. Against this limited and finite conception of justice (and of politics and ethics) I will argue that the true Hegelian infinite refers, as Alenka Zupančič says, to the very contradiction at the heart of human being which can precisely not be qualified as finite.[14] In the Hegelian perspective you cannot get around the fact that, if there's going be any kind of justice or valid concept of universal human rights in this world, it has to, of course, concern our limited and finite being but in such a way that it is still attending the infinite. Only infinite justice can be truly universal, and in the same way human rights have to be the rights of the infinite. If this justice has its limits, these limits are not external but internal to this justice itself. But this means also that if this justice and these rights are going to be truly universal, they have to be made concrete, because, as we shall see, for Hegel, the abstract and empty universals are not truly universal at all.

One can argue that the whole Hegelian speculative philosophical edifice, his infamous 'system', is directed against the basic premises of Kantian philosophy. Kant is very much the philosopher of 'bad infinity', and Kantian ethics seems to be overwhelmed with goals and ideals (moral law, for example) which we are bound to seek but can never realize. And it is this Kantian horizon of thinking which Hegelian philosophy tries to transcend or leave behind. This is, of course, only partial truth, but it is instructive to see how the same kinds of arguments which Hegel marshals against Kant can be directly applied when we want to attack or go against our contemporary ethical ideology, whose dominant trait is, as Rancière said, 'the excess of ethics over law and politics'.

First before I go on to Kant's moral philosophy I will argue, following Zupančič's analysis of Hegel's thought that one way to attain this 'true infinity' and make it, as Hegel demands, the concrete universal is, perhaps surprisingly, through comedy. Through reading what Hegel and Lacanian psychoanalysis has to say about comedy and its paradoxical relation to the human finitude I try to argue that perhaps the answer to the impasses of international politics is not to refer our constitutive finitude as in tragedy but our paradoxical finitude that is revealed by the fundamental structure of the comedy to be actually infinite. It's not a question of the finite being which encounters its tragic end in breaking its limits and will never reach its desired goal other than in infinite approximation, but the kind of immanent transcendence which breaks through every limitation and barrier to become truly infinite.

The tragic mode of representation

Hegel's discussion of comedy in *Phenomenology of Spirit* is not exactly what we would today call an immanent approach to art.[15] For Hegel art is not the immediate subject of discussion; it comes alive in the process of discussion of something else, namely religion and the relationship to the Absolute. The actual framework of this discussion is that of self-representation of Absolute Spirit through art and religion. But on the other hand Hegel does not, either, simply apply his pre-established concepts to different forms of art, he introduces the latter as cases of concretely existing moments of the concept, and this indirect approach allows him to propose some surprising insights about the nature of comedy. And as Zupančič argues these insights could function as a very productive starting point for a philosophical discussion of comedy and its relation to ongoing ethical and political problems.[16]

In the section called 'The spiritual work of art' Hegel is actually dealing with a very narrow and precise segment of (Greek) art, represented by the names of Homer (the epics), Aeschylus and Sophocles (tragedy), and Aristophanes (comedy). But Hegel is not here interested in some individual works of art and their authors, or even some all-encompassing theory of comedy. He is looking for something which could be called the movement of the comic spirit or the comic subjectivity, which is not tied to any specific work of art. If this comic subjectivity has any universal validity, we should be able to discern its movement not only in different works of art from different historical periods but also in the different forms of art.

How, then, does Hegel conceive of art in the *Phenomenology*? As Zupančič emphasizes, the representation is the key issue of the Hegelian analysis. The central question is how the spiritual work of art is representing the absolute. According to Hegel in the world of the spiritual work of art there exists a pre-established division or duality in which one term stands in immediate opposition to another:

> We are thus dealing with a rather brutally divided world where such notions as essence, substance, necessity, universality (and the corresponding entities – gods) stand opposed to those of appearance, subjectivity, contingency, individuality (and the entities that correspond to these notions – human beings).[17]

And in Hegel's analysis the gradual transformation of representation, i.e. different ways in which this duality is mediated, puts the three genres of epic, tragedy and comedy in a not only historical but also dialectical succession.

In the universe of the epic these two domains, that of human beings and that of the gods, are linked together in an external way, as a 'mixture' (*Vermischung*) of the universal and the individual. The epic representation is thus nothing but 'a synthetic combination of the universal and the individual'.[18] But the principle of this combination remains external. The weakness or the limitation of this kind of universal is for Hegel that it is not really limited by its own concrete individuality, but remains above it. The universal powers (gods) have in epic the form of individuality, and their actions are identical to those of men; they simply act like humans, but at the same time they actually withdraw from the connection with the concrete and remain unrestricted in their own specific characters.[19] 'As such,' Zupančič writes, 'this universal and its powers remain a "void of necessity" that floats above the heroes and everything else.'[20]

With tragedy Hegel moves forward in his attempt to conceptualize this constitutive division of the Greek world. In tragedy the language is no longer simply a universal medium of representation, that is a simple narrative: the heroes now speak for themselves. On the stage there are now standing conscious characters that exist as actual human beings. They impersonate the heroes and portray them in the actual speech and action of the actors themselves. The tragic performance displays to the audience 'conscious human beings who *know* their rights and purposes, the power and the will of their specific nature and now know how to *assert* them'.[21] Through actors, the universal itself now starts to speak. And, as Zupančič says, tragedy is indeed the form of art which *(en)acts* the universal.[22]

In this way we come to a new mode of representation, in which the actors put on their masks and thus represent the essence with the help of the mask. But then the actor is no longer himself, he only brings to life the (universal) essence he represents. 'The mask as such has no content, it is more like the pure surface ... that separates the self of the actor from his stage character as (represented) essence.'[23] But, for Hegel, in this gap between the actor and the character lies also the flaw in the tragic mode of representation.

In tragedy 'the essence ultimately exists only as the universal moment, separated by the mask from the concrete and actual self, and as such this essence is still not actual.'[24] The supposed union of the actor and the character, the concrete individual and the universal essence, remains thus external, and, in fact, hypocritical: 'the hero who appears before the onlookers splits up into his mask and the actor, into the person in the play and the actual self'.[25] For the tragic mode of representation this split between actor and character is unbridgeable, and in the end the actor, who is there to represent the essence, tries in vain to make us forget his actual self, and to see through his mask only the sublime character as the universal essence.

In the tragic mode of representation the actor thus tries to reach through his mask the universal essence which is represented by his character, but ends up in failure, and this failure is also now reflected in the content of the tragedy. Usually in tragedy its hero or heroine is longing for some supersensible, universal essence – this is his *hubris* – but is violently thrown against his own limits, his ineradicable human finitude, and is in this process himself destroyed. For the proof of his essential freedom – in willingly submitting to his fate, the hero is a negative proof of human freedom; in him necessity turns into subjective freedom – he has to pay a high price: for the tragic hero or heroine there is reserved only one place or end: that of death. For Zupančič, the 'tragic paradigm' means precisely that this endless movement of contradiction is directly subjectified or individualized: 'By choice or play of circumstances, the tragic hero comes to embody and to be the playground of this endless contradiction, which cannot but tear him or her apart, destroy him or her (as an individual).'[26] This tragic movement is essentially negative, and the metaphysical 'grandeur' of tragedy consists precisely of the fact that only through its failure can it be successful.

This means that tragedy has exactly the same structure as the Kantian sublime: only at the price of his or her material destruction can the subject represent the non-representable, 'infinite', which in this process turns or becomes visible and is elevated into a sublime figure through which some super-sensible, eternal idea shines. In tragedy 'the acting subject, via the various ordeals that befall her, has to let – often at the price of her own death – some universal idea, principle or destiny shine through her'.[27] In tragedy representation succeeds only by its very failure: an individual tries to become universal, but ends up being only a sublime character with a particular end, death.[28]

In this way opens up also the Lacanian perspective to the tragedy. For Lacan every tragedy is ultimately tragedy of desire. In tragedy there is always some kind of difference or gap between demand and its satisfaction, and desire inhabits this gap. And as Zupančič says, 'tragedy is the pain of this difference'.[29] Through the relation between the objective circumstances (chance or fate) and the subjective singularity (which is constitutive to hero or heroine) tragedy explores the domain of this dialectics of desire. But this gap between the different levels of being is not that which separates tragedy and comedy from each other or makes them different genres. On the contrary, it is their common trait.[30] Lacan remarks in Seminar VII that although ethics, as properly conceived, always implies that dimension of life that can be called tragic, we must not forget that in the comic 'too, it is question of the relationship between action and desire, and of the former's fundamental failure to catch up with latter'.[31] Comedy has also its dialectics of desire, but it is also something else, and there must be at least minimal difference between the comic and tragic failure.[32]

Comedy at work

There is a powerful tradition which sees in comedy the emphasis on the human side of representation. This other side of representation is a remainder of the physical residue that the symbolic mask can never completely sublimate or absorb, an irreducible remainder of the symbolic representation.[33] From this perspective comedy is a genre that strongly emphasizes our essential humanity, its joys and limitations. It forces us to recognize and accept the fact that we are *finite* beings. And the lesson of comedy is that 'we are only human, with all our faults, imperfections and weaknesses, and it helps us to deal affirmatively and joyfully with the burden of human finitude'.[34]

As Zupančič remarks, this kind of conception of comedy is both simplistic and ideologically problematic. For example, from this perspective the comic characters are often opposed to tragic heroes and heroines, who are then considered as 'extremists' seeking to transcend the human limitations and realize the impossible at any costs, which cannot but end up in (political or ethical) catastrophe.[35] There is indeed the same sort of politics or ethics of human finitude, whose corollary is, as Žižek points out, 'that the ultimate source of totalitarian and other catastrophes is man's presumption that he can overcome this condition of finitude, lack and displacement, and "act like God", in a total transparency, surpassing his constitutive division'.[36]

Although one could argue that Hegel goes rather a long way in this same direction in his analysis of comedy, he however makes an essential qualification. Unlike those who see comedy as giving voice only to the human side of representation, Hegel goes further and introduces an important shift of perspective, which Zupančič formulates as follows: 'the comic character is not the physical remainder of the symbolic representation of essence; it is this *very essence as physical*'.[37] How is that possible? In tragedy abstract universality and fate was opposed to its other, the individual self that represented this fate as a stage character, but in comedy, Hegel says, 'the actual self of the actor coincides with what he impersonates (with his stage character), just as the spectator is completely at home in the drama performed before him and sees himself playing in it'.[38] In other words, unlike tragedy it does not try to go beyond the representation, to reach some transcendent beyond, but, on the contrary, it eliminates from its world this supposed transcendental realm altogether and returns to this side of representation. In this sense, for Hegel, the comic work of art indeed does away with (a tragic mode of) representation. More precisely, a theatrical performance is still, of course, a performance, but what loses the form of representation (the form of being separated from the actual self) is universal powers, gods, fate and essence.[39] In comedy, 'the individual self is the negative power through which and in which the gods, as also their moment … vanish'.[40] Through this disappearance the individual self is now the sole actuality and the universal powers have lost their form of something (re)presented to consciousness, something altogether *separate* from consciousness and utterly alien to it (as was still the case in the epic and tragedy).[41]

In other words, in comedy absolute powers lose their form of representation by appearing themselves as subjects or as concrete beings. This is according to Zupančič the crux of the Hegelian comedy, and she comments on it as follows:

> When comedy exposes to laughter, one after another, all the figures of the universal essence and its powers (gods, morals, state institutions, universal ideas, and so on) it does so, of course, from the standpoint of the concrete and the subjective; and, on the face of it, we can indeed get the impression that in comedy the individual, the concrete, the contingent, and the subjective are opposing and undermining the universal, the necessary, the substantial (as their other) … Hegel's point, however, is that in this very 'work of negative' (through which comic subjectivity appears) comedy produces its own necessity, universality, and substantiality (it is itself the only 'absolute power'), and it does so by revealing the figures of the 'universal in itself' [i.e. abstract universal – *J.P.*] as something that is, in the end, utterly empty and contingent.[42]

And consequently comedy is not the undermining of the universal, but its own reversal into the concrete, the labour or work of the universal itself. For Zupančič, '*comedy is the universal at work*'.[43]

Let us pause here for a moment so that we can expose fully just how radical Hegel's position is. At first sight it seems that in comedy all that is concrete, and belongs to the content, refutes the universal-formal. There is no sacred thing or solid belief that comedy could not shake to its foundations. Hegel says it explicitly:

> Pure thoughts of the Beautiful and the Good thus display a comic spectacle: through their liberation from the opinion which contains both their specific determinateness as content and also their absolute determinateness … they become empty, and just for that reason the sport of mere opinion and the caprice of any chance individuality.[44]

Yet Hegel's point is that this movement of revealing the universal as a play of 'the caprice of chance individuality' is possible only through a radical shift in the fundamental structure: 'the comic movement, its "negative power", is *the movement of the universal itself* (and precisely as *movement*, this universal is also the subject)'.[45] And this same movement is at work when we move from epic to comedy via tragedy.

From this Hegelian ground Zupančič makes an important distinction between *true* and *false* comedies (or subversive and conservative comedies). This does not depend on what content is subjected to comical treatment; it is a question of the mode of the comic processing itself. 'False, conservative comedies are those where the abstract-universal and the concrete do not change places and do not produce a short circuit between them.'[46] The concrete remains in them external to the universal, and they only invite us to recognize and accept it as the indispensable companion of the universal, its necessary physical support:

> The paradigm of these comedies is simply the following: the aristocrat (or king, or judge, or priest, or any other character of symbolic stature) is *also* a man (who snores, farts, slips, and is subject to the same physical laws as other mortals).[47]

The great wisdom, as we already noted, of those comedies which, as Zupančič says, actually get stuck half-way down the path to the comical is: 'we have to consider and accept the material, physical, concrete, and human aspect of things, otherwise we will be carried into dangerous abstract idealism, extremism, if not even fanaticism'.[48]

As Zupančič explains, this mechanism leaves all the universals fundamentally untouched in their abstract purity, since the dirt is absorbed by the human side, which is then forgiven as part of the 'necessary evil'. This kind of comedy remains caught in an abstract dualism of the concrete and the universal, and its conservatism springs from the fact that it offers the audience, via the 'human' aspect, identification with this symbolic character as ego-ideal. In this process the function of ego-ideal remains not only untouched, but even reinforced: 'We identify with the heroes' weaknesses, yet their higher calling (or universal symbolic function) remains all the more the object of respect and fascination (instead of being the object of comic laughter).'[49]

Zupančič's example of this false comedy and how it works is, not surprisingly, now already half forgotten, and for a good reason: ex-President of the United States George W. Bush and his media strategy of mocking his own presidential self, which, of course, aimed precisely at portraying the inflexible war President as a fallible individual who is aware of his faults and imperfections.[50] But the real comedy of George W. Bush, as Zupančič rightly emphasizes, was seen at times when he did not make any effort to be specially funny, but solemnly appeared as an American President who believed that he really was an American President and seriously pronounced some of his famous 'Bushisms', like this one: 'Our enemies are innovative and resourceful, and so are we. They never stop thinking about new ways to harm our country and our people, and neither do we.'[51] These 'Bushisms' displayed always clear signs of self-relating negativity, which is a distinctive mark of true Hegelian comedy. Contrary to this, the other kind of Bush humour, with which he liked to demonstrate his ability to laugh at these miracles of wit, easily transformed his comedy, as Zupančič says, simply 'into a conservative way of accepting and tolerating sheer stupidity'.[52] And in this case, the best way to counter this tendency is the good old wisdom of the Marx Brothers: 'This man looks like an idiot and acts like an idiot; but this should not deceive you – he *is* an idiot!'

In true comedy, instead, substance, necessity and essence all lose their immediate, and thus abstract, self-identity and coincidence with themselves. It is important to remember that the comic 'mode of representation does not imply a return to immediacy or to an organic fusion of opposites'. In comedy 'the substance becomes subject in the moment when, through a split in itself, it only starts relating to itself'.[53] In contrast, tragedy can appear as an organic fusion or synthesis of the actor-subject and the character precisely because it is relaying on the classical mode of representation, in which the subject still represents the character (and the better the representation the more powerful will be the feeling of fusion of these two) but is at the same time strictly separated from it. For the tragic mode of representation this gap in representation is constitutive; it is something which is impossible to overcome in it and which it constantly stumbles upon. Only through failure in the representation itself can tragedy get a glimpse of something which is constitutively beyond its reach, and it is only in death that the split between subject and (symbolic) character, between individual and universal essence, is abolished.

As Zupančič says, the problem is that this supposed fusion of two is exactly that: a fusion of two different things, an individual representation of the universal, and it does not reach 'the point where one of the two terms would generate the other from itself, and become this other'.[54] But in contrast in true comedy this coincidence of the self (the actor) and his character means that the split between these two now inhabits that character itself (the essence). It is precisely this inner split or self-relating negativity that constitutes the place of the subject in the symbolic character.[55] In comedy 'we cannot say that the subject-actor represents a (comic) character for the spectator, but that the subject-actor appears as that gap through which the character relates to itself,' and through this self-relating negativity it 'represents' itself.[56]

It is precisely this relating of the 'universal essences' (character) to themselves and to other 'universal essences' that creates the movement in which the universal becomes concrete, and becomes the subject. In different kinds of comedies the 'stereotypical' characters, 'abstract universalities', are set in motion and, through flow of events, the concrete, subjective universality is produced.[57] In comedy we often start with an abstract universality, or a stereotypical character which usually even has a generic name (tramp, shrew, miser, idiotic master, cunning servant, etc.) and move through trials and errors of comedy towards the self-relating negativity of the concrete universality. 'In comedy, some universality ("tramp", "worker", "misanthrope" ...) has to let a subject in all his concreteness shine through it – not as the opposite of this universal (or as its irreducible support), but as its own inherent truth, its flexibility and life'.[58] As Zupančič reminds us it would be hard to find something more concrete, subjective and universal (and full of life) all at the same time, for example, as Chaplin's character, the tramp.

This generally acknowledged materialism of comedy is, however, very paradoxical materialism. The comic universe is, as a rule, the universe of the indestructible life. (This feature is brought to climax in cartoons, but is present in most comedies.) As Zupančič notes, 'regardless of all accidents and catastrophes (physical as well as psychic or emotional) that befall comic characters, they always rise from the chaos perfectly intact, and relentlessly go on pursuing their goals, chasing their dreams, or simply being themselves'.[59] It seems that nothing can really happen to them, which somehow contradicts the supposed realism of comedy, that it should celebrate the human finitude and its limitations and deficiencies. There is indeed a strange immortality that pertains to comic figures, analogous almost to the ability of Sadean victims to survive all their misfortunes. Zupančič comments:

> The reason for which comedy is profoundly materialistic is not simply that it reminds us of, and insists upon, the mud, the dirt, dense and coarse reality as our ultimate horizon (which we need to accept), and as a condition of our life. Comedy is materialistic because it gives voice and body to the impasses and contradictions of this materiality itself.[60]

The body or the matter is not the limit of a 'pure intellect' or some ideal, but the very point of its origin. This is comedy's materialism. Comedy is not materialistic because it sets in opposition to some abstract and universal ideality, or some idealistic passion which is then ridiculed or laughed at through a comic procedure, it is materialistic because 'it sees the turning of materiality into pure spirit and of pure spirit into something material as *one and the same movement*, driven by a difficulty inherent to materiality itself'.[61] The materialism of comedy is the materialism of the spirit.

So when in the archetypical scene of comedy some dignified symbolic character (a king, a judge, a priest, etc.) stumbles from one human misfortune to another, and still always rises up as if nothing has happened, we should not overlook the fact that, as Lacan reminded us, what is really funny and makes us laugh is not that some dignitary falls (that is, in contrast, rather pathetic) but that he rises from it and goes about his business as if nothing has happened.[62] The space of the comic is the space between the dignified symbolic mask and the ridiculous vulgarity of ordinary life, but the properly comic procedure means not simply that this dignified mask (or some sublime passion) is undermined through the intrusion of everyday reality. On the contrary, as Slavoj Žižek points out there happens a kind of structural short-circuit or exchange of places: the very dignified mask or passion appears now more like a pathetic idiosyncrasy, an utterly human weakness, and it is this very attachment to some excessive passion which makes these comic characters human.[63]

The 'materiality of spirit' is the real comic object, and comedy produces it in its self-relating negativity as the aspect of the universal itself:

> This is why, for Hegel comedy is not simply a turn from the universal (from universal values of the beautiful, the just, the good, the moral ...) towards the individual or particular (as always and necessarily imperfect and limited [...]), but corresponds instead to the very speculative passage from the abstract universal to the concrete universal. For Hegel, it is the abstract universal itself that is, by definition, imperfect and limited, because it lacks the moment of self-consciousness, of the self, of the concrete; it is universal and pure only at the price of being ultimate empty ... The turn towards the individual is the turn of the universal itself, it is the risk and the trial of the universal.[64]

Comedy is thus full of assertion of universality, the immediate coincidence of universality with the character's or actor's singularity. The individual, the hero, is indeed a negative force that undermines all the elevated universal values, but *at the same time* this self-relating negativity itself is the only true remaining universal force; it is the very movement of concrete universality, which contains all that is indestructible or immortal, that is infinite, in comedies and the comic characters. For Zupančič this universal that does not go through this (comic) process is not a true universal: 'It is only with the concrete that we come to real spirit of the universal, and that is the reason why the materialism of comedy is precisely the materialism of spirit.'[65]

The true comic spirit is not thus reducible to the contemporary metaphysics of finitude; on the contrary, for Zupančič, in comedy there is always the question of the 'physics of infinite'. And Zupančič argues that this is also a point where Hegelian and Lacanian perspectives meet.[66] The predominant contemporary concept of human finitude does not only refer to the fact we are all mortal and sooner or later we will drop dead, more essentially it refers to limits and limitations of *living* human beings. In this context finitude appears to be a Master Signifier of human limitations, incompleteness, division, out-of-jointness, antagonism, exposure to others, 'castration', etc. Moreover, according to Zupančič, the ethical part of this appears when this description mutates into prescription, from 'We are limited, divided, exposed' to 'Be limited, divided, exposed!' The ethics of this contemporary 'metaphysics of finitude' thus consists of 'a paradoxical injunction of the possible'.[67] And this imperative of the possible blocks right away any kind of attempt to break away from this closure of finitude and create something innovative in any domain of politics and ethics.

In contrast to that, Lacanian ethics, which is located at the level of the real, is not, however, simply that of an imperative of the impossible, of going beyond the limits of what is humanly possible. Real as impossible does not mean that the real is something that cannot possibly happen; on the contrary, 'the whole point of the Lacanian concept of the real is that the *impossible happens*.'[68] And indeed the concept of the real can help us find a way out from the deadlocks of our contemporary ethical ideology and the impasses of its politics. As Alain Badiou argues:

> First, the distinction he makes between the real and reality … and in particular [Lacan's] conception of the real as being, in a situation, in any given symbolic field, the point of impasse, or the point of impossibility, which precisely allows us to think the situation as a whole, according to its real. … [E]mancipatory politics always consists in making seem possible precisely that which, from within situation, is declared to be impossible.[69]

And next I try to find traces of new ways to think about our political and ethical impasses in going through Kantian philosophy from the Lacanian perspective.

Moral law and its vicissitudes

Among the classical philosophers Kant is without doubt the one who has most influenced the way we even today understand the problem of ethics and moral law and especially the question of evil. One could argue that Kant's practical philosophy opened the way for a truly modern conception of ethics, and in that sense we are all post-Kantians. Kant firmly asserted the primacy of 'pure practical reason', over its speculative-empirical counterpart. His moral philosophy is nothing other than a sustained affirmation of universally binding subjective 'truth', i.e. moral law, made in the absence of any reliable knowledge as such.[70] Kant's moral philosophy rests on a kind of ultimately axiomatic prescription known as the 'categorical imperative', which is based on purely 'subjective' or practical awareness of moral obligation and its formal-universal character. Now, our question concerns the implications of Kantian ethics when it is seen from a Hegelian and Lacanian perspective.

The Kantian idea of ethics is simple and revolutionary, it means a clear-cut break with any traditionally conceived ethics which attempts to provide for it a direct ontological foundation via some substantial or essential notion of supreme Good, or what Jacques Lacan calls the service of goods (*service des biens*).[71] Lacan praises Kant for banishing the notion of supreme Good from the field of ethics and through that making for the first time possible a truly modern conception of ethics. But this Kantian breakthrough has its price, and it has been argued that Kantian ethical rigourism makes morality as such impossible, or, at least, that it demands from the ethical subject that it should accomplish impossible things. If commentators have often criticized Kant for demanding the impossible in his ethics, Lacan attributes an incontestable theoretical value to this demand, because according to him it introduces a whole new dimension to the field of ethics, a dimension which traditional ethics has almost completely ignored, namely that of desire.[72] Taking the maximum distance to any consequentialist ethics by insisting on the fact that the moral imperative is not concerned with what may or may not be done, Kant, according to Lacan, discovered the essential dimension of ethics: the dimension of desire, which circles around the real *qua* impossible.

For Lacan, Kantian ethics, as an ethics grounded in desire, has to be situated at the level of the real, not that of the reality. It is necessarily beyond the pleasure principle and its corollary, the reality principle. Everything hinges here, of course, on the difference between reality and the real and how it is conceived. As Žižek points out, if real could be understood as some kind of ultimate point of reference, as finally true, or 'real', reality beneath all the false appearances of which our everyday reality consists, then the Lacanian 'ethics of the real' would be no more than a badly covered new version of the good old substantialist ethics.[73]

However, for Lacan the real is something that resists symbolization. The symbolic order is constitutive to the human reality, but that order is not everything (not-all, *pas-tout*), there is always a gap, a leftover, a remainder – or, if we change the perspective slightly, an excess, a surplus, something that sticks out. So the real is not something external to the symbolic order, but, precisely because it is on the contrary something internal to it, it is its inherent limit. The real is the internal stumbling block of the symbolic order on account of which it can never become 'itself', achieve its self-identity or totality. And Kantian moral law is for Lacan related to this impossible real:

> The breakthrough is achieved by Kant when he posits that the moral imperative is not concerned with what may or may not be done. To the extent that it imposes the necessity of a practical reason, obligation affirms an unconditional 'Thou shalt'. The importance of this field derives from the void that the strict application of the Kantian definition leaves there. … [W]e analysts are able to recognize that place occupied by desire. Our experience gives rise to a reversal that locates at the centre an incommensurable measure, an infinite measure, that is called desire.[74]

In other words Lacan's point is that Kantian moral law, in its strictly formal-universal character – it is without content or any determinable referent which could be assigned to it – introduces a void or a hole in our symbolic world, that is, to our reality. There is in the midst of our universe a gap or inconsistency, which Lacan designates as the real of our being.[75] Following this Lacanian insight Žižek remarks, 'There is ethics – that is to say, an injunction which cannot be grounded in ontology – in so far as there is a crack in the ontological edifice of the universe; at its most elementary, ethics designates fidelity to this crack.'[76]

Kantian moral law has no determinate content, it doesn't specify anything you should or should not do. It's not the Ten Commandments or any other imaginable collection of legal rules or norms. All content of the law disappears, and we have only a formal criterion of morality. A formal law is a law which does not specify its object – on the contrary, its universality demands that it is a purely subjective maxim, necessarily subtracted from every order of objectivity. That's why what Kantian moral law makes, presents or brings forth is only a void. This void is according to Kant a void of all that is pathological in the subject: this means to Kant all the objects which are linked to sensibility or the subject's sensory interest, everything which can be located in the empirical domain, everything which gives pleasure or makes the subject happy.[77]

What remains? Only the criterion of morality which consists of its universalizability. For Kant the fundamental law of pure practical reason, i.e. the categorical imperative, is the 'act that the maxim of your will could always hold at the same time as a principle in a giving of universal law'.[78] As Gilles Deleuze has remarked, in this radically new conception of the law, 'the law is no longer regarded as dependent on some predetermined concept of the good but, on the contrary, the good itself is made to depend on the law.'[79] This means also that the moral law has no longer its foundation in some higher principle from which it would derive its authority, but it is self-grounded in the act in which subject (as noumenal, free being) itself posits law to itself.

From this crucial aspect of Kantian ethics it follows that the formal structure of an ethical act does not presuppose any (notion of the) good but, rather, defines it: 'The good is nothing but the name for the certain formal structure of action.'[80] It is here that we can conceive a move from the abstract universality of the (traditionally interpreted) Kantian ethics, in which the ethical subject is tragically condemned to endlessly or infinitely repeat his failure to conform to the moral law, towards ethics which is tied more to the concrete universal and which is perhaps more attuned to the (Hegelian) model of comedy than to the tragic vision of man's original finitude.

But what is this formal structure of action, and is it happening also in this world and not only in the supposed noumenal domain of being? This is, of course, the crucial problem of Kant's moral philosophy: how is a pure and accomplished ethical act possible? In other words, how to individuate the free and autonomous (transcendental) self and 'how to situate this self in the empirical world in which it acts?'[81] Because, without this, it will remain totally empty and formal abstract universality without any real consequences in this world. According to standard Hegelian criticism of Kantian moral philosophy this is of course impossible: Kantian ethics fails to take into account the concrete historical situation in which the ethical subject is embedded, and which provides the determinate content of the good. In other words, what is wrong with Kantian formalism is precisely its formalism, its inability to offer any concrete or positive conception of good. But this criticism misses the whole point of Kantian ethics and is at the same time totally incapable of noticing where the true radicality of it lies. One could, on the contrary, as Žižek forcefully does, argue that:

> the unique strength of Kant's ethics lies in this formal indeterminacy: moral Law does not tell me what my duty is, it merely tells me that I should accomplish my duty. That is to say, it is not possible to derive the concrete norms I have to follow in my specific situation from the moral law itself – *which means that the subject himself has to assume the responsibility of 'translating' the abstract injunction of the moral Law into series of concrete obligations.* In this precise sense, the point of Kant's ethics is (to paraphrase Hegel) 'to conceive the moral Absolute not only as Substance, but also as Subject': the ethical subject bears full responsibility for the concrete universal norms he follows – that is to say, the only guarantor of the universality of positive moral norms is the subject's own contingent act of performatively assuming these norms.[82]

Its precisely Kant's formalism which makes possible the break with any kind of traditional ethics based on the self-enclosed substance of a particular life world: 'I can no longer simply rely on the determinate content provided by the ethical tradition in which I am embedded; this tradition is always already "mediated" by the subject; it "remains alive" only in so far as I effectively assume it.'[83] The only way to undermine ethical particularism is not via reference to some more universal positive content (like 'universal values shared by all humanity') but by accepting that the ethical universal is in itself indeterminate, empty, and that it can be translated into a set of positive explicit norms only by means of my active engagement, for which I take full responsibility. '[T]here is no determinate ethical universality without the contingency of the subject's act of positing it as such.'[84]

According to Kant's ethics we have to draw the radical conclusion that duty is only that which the subject makes his duty, and the subject has to answer for it. What is inadmissible in it is for the ethical subject to claim that his 'duty was imposed upon him, that he could not act otherwise, that he only followed the commandment of the law.'[85] This brings us to the core of the relation between the subject and the law. As Zupančič says, the crucial problem of the moral law is the subject's place in its constitution, i.e. in the constitution of the universal.[86] The reason why it is impossible to efface the subject from the ethical act is not particular but universal. For the gesture by which every subject, by means of his action, posits the universal, performs a certain operation of universalization that is a necessary but at the same time contingent condition of ethics: the subject is nothing other than this moment of universalization. According to Zupančič, 'the ethical subject is the point where the universal comes to itself and achieves its determination'.[87]

This is also according to Žižek the whole point of Hegel's critique of Kant, which is, as we have seen, however, quite explicit already in Kant's thought: there is no moral law which would free me of the responsibility for its determinable content: 'actual universality is not only the abstract content common to all particular cases, but also the "negative" power of disrupting each particular content'.[88] The subject of ethics cannot rely on some determinate content which would fix the co-ordinates of his ethical activity in advance. The only way for him to reach the universal is to accept the objective indeterminacy of his situation and at the same time hold on to the point of the real of his situation, i.e. its void: 'I become universal only through the violent effort of disengaging myself from the particularity of my situation: through conceiving this situation as contingent and limiting, through opening up in it a gap of indeterminacy filled in by my act.'[89] This means also that subjectivity and universality are strictly linked to each other, without subject there is no universality, and vice versa.

As Žižek emphasizes one important consequence of this is that we have to reject any reference to duty as an *excuse*. In the domain of ethics, at least in ethics worthy of the name, you cannot say, for example: 'I know this is difficult, and perhaps painful, but what can I do? The moral law imposed the act on me as my unconditional duty!' Contrary to what is thought 'There is no excuse for not accomplishing one's duty!' is *not* the true motto of Kantian ethical rigour, but its much more uncanny inversion: '*There is no excuse for accomplishing one's duty!*'[90] Without the subject's active act of universalizing it the reference to duty is profoundly hypocritical, and in fact is linked to that which psychoanalysis calls perversion or perverse attitude. The subject's position to law is reversed to a passive, or even masochistic position: from the subject of law to the subject which is totally subjected to law ('just follow the orders, don't worry anything else'):

> What we encounter here is the properly perverse attitude of adopting the position of the pure instrument of the big Other's Will: it's not my responsibility, it's not me who is effectively doing it, I am merely an instrument of the higher Historical Necessity … [I]sn't it nice to be able to

inflict pain on others in the full awareness that I am merely fulfilling the Other's will.[91]

Žižek's examples of this perversion of moral law are the proverbially severe and sadistic teacher who subjects his pupils to merciless discipline, from duty, of course, and the Stalinist politician who loves mankind, but none the less carries out horrible purges and executions. It breaks his heart, but what can he do? It's his duty to the progress of humanity. This is what the Kantian ethics ultimately prohibits.[92]

Endless progress or sharp break?

Is then the purely ethical act possible in Kantian practical philosophy? I think that it is, but it is possible only on condition that we drop out from the Kantian edifice Kant's two most important postulates of pure practical reason, that of the immortality of the soul and the existence of God.

Kant defines the notion of the highest good as complete conformity of the will to the moral law: Kant calls this *holiness*, a perfection of which according to him no rational sensible being is capable at any moment of his existence. A little contradictorily Kant claims that the highest good is, however, practically possible only on the presupposition of the immortality of the soul, because it requires endless progress towards that complete conformity.[93]

The notion of the highest good demands that the moral subject is at the same time both finite and infinite (endless), mortal and immortal. But even that's not enough, for the infinite existence of the subject does not in itself make possible the highest good. Something else is also required, and that is another postulate of the practical reason: the existence of God. As Zupančič says, 'it is only God's point of view that makes access to the highest good possible, since it is only from the point of view of God that this (infinite) duration appears as a whole, as a unity.'[94] The subject is directly engaged and immersed in the (infinite) process of improvement, which is why he can never see its totality. It is possible only from God's point of view.

But what complicates things in relation to the possibility of accomplished ethical act is that this access to the noumenal being, or this God's point of view, which could give us access to the noumenal domain of being, is in fact not only impossible but also prohibited for the subject in Kantian ethics. The reason for this is that if we had access to it, the whole basis of our subjectivity, our morality and freedom, or indeed, our moral freedom would collapse. That's because our freedom and morality persist only in a space in between the phenomenal and the noumenal: 'We are free only in so far as our horizon is that of the phenomenal, in so far as the noumenal domain remains inaccessible to us.'[95] In a paradoxical way for Kant the highest good, the complete fitness of the will to the moral law, or the accomplished pure ethical act, would mean also for the subject the ultimate moral catastrophe, losing all his moral worth.

For Kant direct access to the noumenal domain would reduce us to mere mechanical puppets or lifeless automata and deprive us of the very freedom which forms the core of our subjectivity and moral dignity.[96] For this reason this possibility, direct access to the noumenal domain, is no less catastrophic than the highest evil, for which Kant reserves the name 'diabolical evil'. Diabolical evil would be situated at the same level as the moral law. Diabolical evil would actualize itself if we were to elevate opposition to moral law to the level of a maxim (a principle or law) and do evil deeds purely for the sake of duty and without any pathological (egoistical or pleasure-seeking) reasons. But as Zupančič says, if 'opposition to the moral law were elevated to a maxim or principle, it would no longer be opposition to the moral law, it would be the moral law itself.'[97] For Kant this is simply absurd, and he concludes that diabolical evil cannot apply to human beings.

In a paradoxical way both the supreme Good and the diabolical Evil are banished from the Kantian ethical edifice. (Try to imagine a religion in which there is no God or Devil, religion without God.) That's because he introduces the diabolical evil and the highest good in a strictly symmetrical way: for him 'they are both "ideals" in which will would coincide entirely with the law, and they are both excluded as cases which cannot apply to human beings.'[98]

But this means also that in the Kantian ethical system the highest good is structurally the same as the highest evil. Kant is forced to describe evil in the same terms as he would describe a pure ethical act. For Kant, it is in no way easier to realize Evil than it is to realize Good. So Alenka Zupančič can assert that '*diabolical evil, the highest evil, is indistinguishable from the highest good, and that they are nothing other than the definitions of an accomplished* (*ethical*) *act*.'[99] At the level of the structure of the ethical act, the difference between good and evil does not exist, evil is formally indistinguishable from good.

So, if we can no longer accept this reference to God or to the immortality of soul, how do we stand in relation to the ethical act and its accomplishment? According to our current ethical ideology, or metaphysics of finitude, accomplished supreme good is already the same thing as diabolical evil, because it forces human beings towards the impossible and ends up in catastrophe. There is a limit which human beings should not cross without serious consequences. But we should accomplish here the Hegelian move and posit that this limit is not between finite and infinite beings, or between immanence and transcendence. There is no Other World which would limit our being, every human situation is therefore actually infinite: a true ethical act only universalizes it and makes it into something concrete.

For Zupančič this means also that one cannot attain the realm of the ethical by means of gradual elevation of will, by pursuing more and more refined, subtle and noble goals, by gradually turning away from one's 'base animal instincts'. To move from the pathological to the ethical we need a sharp break, a 'paradigm shift'.[100] This goes against the usual image of Kantian ethics according to which these ethics demand a perpetual 'purification' (from everything pathological) and an asymptotic approach to the ethical idea. Infinite progress towards moral perfection is not Kant's only answer to what seems to be the inherent structural impossibility of accomplishing a pure ethical act. As Zupančič argues it is possible to discern another concept of the ethical act which goes in the opposite direction: in Kant the genuine ethical act, the 'act of freedom', is always subversive, it is never simply the result of an 'improvement' or a 'reform':

> If man is to become not merely *legally*, but *morally*, a good man ... this cannot be brought about through gradual *reformation* so long as the basis of the maxims remains impure, but must be effected through a *revolution* in the man's disposition ... He can become a new man only by kind of rebirth, as it were through a new creation.[101]

Notes

1 See Carl Schmitt, *Political Theology*, trans. George Schwab, Cambridge: MIT Press, 1985.
2 Jacques Rancière, 'Prisoners of the infinite', trans. Norman Madaradz, online, available at: http://www.counterpunch.org/Rancière0430.html (accessed 30 April 2002); Jacques Rancière, 'Les prisonniers de l'infini', *Chroniques des temps consensuels*, Paris: Seuil, 2005, pp. 127–31.
3 Ibid.
4 Ibid.
5 Ibid.
6 Slavoj Žižek, *Welcome to the Desert of the Real*, London and New York. Verso, 2002, p. 94.
7 Rancière, 'Prisoners of the infinite'.
8 Ibid.
9 It's not difficult to discern here the same mechanism which according to Giorgio Agamben inevitably produces the twin figures of sovereign power and its obverse, Homo Sacer, the absolute victim. See Giorgio Agamben, *Homo Sacer*, trans. Daniel Hellen-Roazen, Stanford: Stanford University Press, 1998.
10 See G. W. F. Hegel, *Science of Logic*, trans. A. V. Miller, Armherst, MA: Humanity Books, 1999, p. 122.
11 Rancière, 'Prisoners of the infinite'.
12 Reference is here obviously to Alain Badiou's conception of politics.
13 This Kantian-Hegelian parallax view has of course from the beginning been a constant reference of Slavoj Žižek's thought.
14 I will rely here extensively on Alenka Zupančič's excellent analysis of Hegelian comedy in *The Odd One in. On Comedy*, Cambridge, MA: MIT Press, 2008.
15 Ibid., p. 20.
16 Ibid., p. 21.

17 Ibid., p. 23.
18 G. W. F. Hegel, *Phenomenology of Spirit*, trans. A. V. Miller, London: Oxford University Press, 1977, p. 441.
19 For Hegel this kind of universal effaces 'through the invincible elasticity of its unity ... the atomistic singleness of the doer and his constructions, preserves itself in its purity and dissolves everything individual in its fluid nature'. Ibid., p. 442.
20 Zupančič, *The Odd One in*, p. 24.
21 Hegel, *Phenomenology of Spirit*, p. 444.
22 Zupančič, *The Odd One in*, p. 25.
23 Ibid.
24 Ibid.
25 Hegel, *Phenomenology of Spirit*, p. 450.
26 Zupančič, *The Odd One in*, p. 55.
27 Ibid., 37.
28 As Lacan reminds us, the fundamental character of all tragic action is that it leads to a triumph of death: 'the relationship between action and the desire which inhabits the space of tragedy functions in the direction of a triumph of death'. *The Seminar of Jacques Lacan* VII, *The Ethics of Psychoanalysis, 1959–1960*, ed. Jacques-Alain Miller, trans. Dennis Porter, London and New York: Routledge, 1992, p. 313.
29 Zupančič, *The Odd One in*, p. 129.
30 Ibid.
31 Lacan, *The Ethics of Psychoanalysis*, p. 313.
32 Zupančič, *The Odd One in*, p. 129.
33 Ibid., p. 26.
34 Ibid., p. 47. As one author puts it, 'when we wish to be pure disincarnate spirit or pure disincarnate intellect, the comedian asks us to remember the objective, material conditions of life with which we must make our peace, if we are to retain our sanity and survive. He will not let us forget that we are men, that we are finite and conditioned creatures – not angels.' Nathan A. Scott, 'The bias of comedy and the narrow escape into faith', in Robert W. Corrigan (ed.), *Comedy: Meaning and Form*, San Francisco: Chandler, 1965, p. 113, cited in Zupančič, *The Odd One in*, p. 46.
35 Ibid.
36 Slavoj Žižek, 'From "passionate attachments" to dis-idenfication', *Umbr(a)*, 1, 1998, p. 16.
37 Zupančič, *The Odd One in*, p. 26.
38 Hegel, *Phenomenology of Spirit*, p. 452.
39 Zupančič, *The Odd One in*, p. 26.
40 Hegel, *Phenomenology of Spirit*, p. 452.
41 Zupančič, *The Odd One in*, p. 27.
42 Ibid.
43 Ibid.
44 Hegel, *Phenomenology of Spirit*, p. 452.
45 Zupančič, *The Odd One in*, p. 28.
46 Ibid., p. 30.
47 Ibid.
48 Ibid., p. 31.
49 Ibid.
50 Ibid., p. 33.
51 Bush, Washington, DC, 5 August 2004. Ibid., p. 34.
52 Ibid., p. 34

53 Ibid.
54 Ibid., p. 35.
55 Ibid. Slavoj Žižek relates an incident which proves that such an ontological comedy can occur also in real life: '[I]n December 2001 in Buenos Aires … Argentinians took to the streets to protest against the current government, and especially against Cavallo, the economy minister. When the crowd gathered around Cavallo's building, threatening to storm it, he escaped wearing a mask of himself (sold in disguise shops so that the people could mock him by wearing his mask). It thus seems that at least Cavallo did learn something from the widespread Lacanian movement in Argentina – the fact *that a thing is its own best mask*. What one encounters in tautology (the repetition of the same) is thus pure difference – not the difference between the element and the other elements, but the difference of the element from itself.' Slavoj Žižek, *Parallax View*, Cambridge, MA: MIT Press, 2006, 28–9.
56 Zupančič, *The Odd One in*, p. 36.
57 Ibid., pp. 36–7.
58 Ibid., pp. 37–8. In tragedy we are in fact dealing with an opposite movement: we always start with a very concrete and strong personality, with a hero, with whom we are supposed to identify, a significant individual with a proper name that often gives the tragedy its title. As Zupančič says, it would be hard to imagine universal or generic names as titles of tragedies – *Othello* as *The Jealous Husband* or *Hamlet* as *The Prince who Knew too Much* – and still remain in the territory of tragedy. Ibid., p. 37.
59 Ibid., pp. 28–9. There is indeed some kind of excess of life or life's constitutive too-muchness which essentiallly appears in comedy. Lacan links this feature of comedy to its phallic character: 'One must simply remember that the element in comedy that satisfies us, the element that makes us laugh, that makes us appreciate it in its full human dimension, not excluding the unconscious, is not so much the triumph of life as its flight, the fact that life slips away, runs off, escapes all those barriers that oppose it, including precisely those that are the most essential, those that are constituted by the agency of the signifier. The phallus is nothing more than a signifier, the signifier of this flight. Life goes by, life triumphs, whatever happens. If the comic hero trips up and lands in the soup, the little fellow nevertheless survives.' Lacan, *The Ethics of Psychoanalysis*, p. 314.
60 Zupančič, *The Odd One in*, p. 47.
61 Ibid.
62 Ibid., p. 30.
63 See Žižek, *Parallax View*, p. 43.
64 Zupančič, *The Odd One in*, p. 38.
65 Ibid., p. 38.
66 Ibid., p. 50.
67 Ibid., p. 51.
68 Ibid.
69 Alain Badiou, *Ethics*, trans. Peter Hallward, London and New York: Verso, 2001, p. 121.
70 See Peter Hallward, *Badiou. A Subject to Truth*, Minneapolis, MN: University of Minnesota Press, 2003, p. 167.
71 See Lacan, *The Ethics of Psychoanalysis*, pp. 311–24.
72 '[T]hat is nothing less than the impossibility in which we recognize the topology of our desire.' Lacan, *The Ethics of Psychoanalysis*, p. 315; see also Alenka Zupančič, *Ethics of the Real*, New York and London: Verso, p. 3.
73 Slavoj Žižek, *The Plague of Fantasies*, London and New York: Verso, 1997, p. 214.

74 Lacan, *The Ethics of Psychoanalysis*, pp. 315–16.
75 It is precisely this void or gap, or, more precisely, this formal void of Law that sustains our desire, which means that the greatest sin that one can be guilty of, according to the ethics of psychoanalysis, is to fill this void with some content and saturate it with some substantial good or, which means the same thing, some lethal enjoyment, *jouissance:* 'one is faithful to one's desire by maintaining the gap which sustains desire'. Žižek, *The Plague of Fantasies*, 1997, p. 239. This is the whole point of Lacan's famous ethical maxim of psychoanalysis: 'The only thing of which one can be guilty is having given ground relative to one's desire.' Lacan, *The Ethics of Psychoanalysis*, p. 319.
76 Žižek, *The Plague of Fantasies*, 1997, p. 214.
77 Jacques-Alain Miller, 'A discussion of Lacan's "Kant with Sade"', *Reading Seminars I and II*, ed. Richard Feldstein, Bruce Fink and Maire Jaanus, Albany, NY: SUNY Press, 1996, p. 226.
78 Immanuel Kant, 'Critique of Practical Reason', *Practical Philosophy*, ed. and trans. Mary Gregor, Cambridge: Cambridge University Press, 1996, p. 164.
79 Gilles Deleuze, *Coldness and Cruelty*, New York: Zone Books, 1991, p. 82.
80 Zupančič, *Ethics of the Real*, p. 92.
81 Hallward, *Badiou*, p. 168.
82 Slavoj Žižek, *The Plague of Fantasies*, p. 221.
83 Ibid.
84 Ibid.
85 Zupančič, *Ethics of the Real*, p. 60.
86 Ibid., p. 61.
87 Ibid., pp. 61–2.
88 Žižek, *The Plague of Fantasies*, p. 222.
89 Ibid.
90 Ibid.
91 Ibid., pp. 222–3.
92 Ibid.
93 See Kant, 'Critique of Practical Reason', p. 238.
94 Zupančič, *Ethics of the Real*, p. 77. 'The Infinite Being, to whom the temporal condition is nothing, sees in what is to us an endless series the whole of conformity with the moral law. … [A man] cannot hope, either here or in any foreseeable future moment of his existence, to be fully adequate to God's will … he can hope to be so only in the endlessness of his duration (which God alone can survey)'. Kant, 'Critique of Practical Reason', p. 239.
95 Žižek, *Parallax View*, pp. 23.
96 Kant says this explicitly in a section of his 'Critique of Practical Reason' entitled 'Of the wise adaptation of man's cognitive faculties to his practical vocation,' where he endeavours to answer the question of what would happen to us if we were to gain access to the noumenal domain, to the *Ding an sich*. '[I]nstead of the conflict which now the moral disposition has to carry on with the inclinations, in which, though after some defeats, moral strength of soul is to be gradually acquired, *God and eternity in their awful majesty* would stand unceasingly *before our eyes*. … [H]ence most actions conforming to the law would be done from fear, only a few from hope, and none at all from duty, and the moral worth of actions, on which alone in the eyes of supreme wisdom the worth of the person and even that of the world depends, would not exist at all. As long as human nature remains as it is, human conduct would thus be changed into a mere mechanism in which, as in a puppet show, everything would *gesticulate* well but *no life* would be found in the figures.' Kant, 'Critique of Practical Reason', p. 258.

97 Zupančič, *Ethics of the Real*, p. 90.
98 Ibid., pp. 91–2.
99 Ibid., p. 92.
100 Ibid., pp. 10–11.
101 Immanuel Kant, *Religion within the Limits of Reason Alone*, New York: Harper Torchbooks, 1960, pp. 42–3, cited in Zupančič, *Ethics of the Real*, p. 11.

Chapter 12

Moralization interrupted

On Lacan's thesis of 'the supreme good as radical evil'

Marc de Kesel

> At least we can learn from them that absolute goodness is hardly any less dangerous than absolute evil ...
>
> Hannah Arendt[1]

> The signifier ... is what represents ... the subject for another signifier.
>
> Jacques Lacan[2]

The Good in the extreme twentieth century

'Actualizing the supreme good in a supreme way.' Is this not an adequate title for the general socio-ethical programme of the twentieth century? Were the numerous revolutions of that time not all inspired by the highest ethical values – at least by what each revolutionary programme considered as such? And, once in power, were these programmes not able to remove all the obstacles barring the implementation of their social and ethical ideas? At times, however, it did not hold off the most disastrous results. The more such programmes were in the optimal condition of getting actualized, the more they were fated to turn into straight oppression and terror. The ideals of the communist project, for instance, were highly noble and social, but the regimes of that name ended up being responsible for a totalitarian violence that ruined millions of human lives. Today, in a similar way, America's intention to bring democracy all over the world rather seems to turn into the opposite. The question of whether the so-called 'war on terror' is itself not responsible (or at least co-responsible) for raising the quantum of terror in our global village is unfortunately all too legitimate.[3]

Though, of course, each one of these examples requires a detailed analysis, in a general perspective one can say they all illustrate, in the domain of the political, the experience of radical finitude which is so typical for modernity and its technical condition. Modernity supposes to have limitless capability of solving all problems faced, till all at once, it is forced to face the limits of this very limitlessness. Then, in some symptomatic events, it unexpectedly faces the inherent boundaries of its technical all-powerfulness. It more precisely faces *the limits being the very effect of its limitless omnipotence.* Able to dominate whatever it met, at times, modernity's technical power realizes how unable it is to dominate precisely its limitless capacity to dominate. Here, the clearest example to be put forward is the twentieth-century experience of the nuclear threat: as if, creating nuclear weapons, we had remained blind to their capability to destroy the entire world, including ourselves.

This kind of omnipotence's impotence which is characteristic of late modernity's technical condition can be observed in the field of the political as well. Capable of creating a totally new society, modern man forgot to notice *himself* in this very creation and ran the risk of ending up with a totalitarian political order in which none of its citizens was able to have a properly free and creative life.

And why not apply this condition of 'finite infinity' to our modern *ethical* capacities, to our moral and social intention to make this world a better place to live? We are technically able to actualize the global good, but we are capable as well of using the same ability as a weapon of terror and destruction. How often did the twentieth-century programmes of reorganizing society in a more just and ethically better world not turn into oppression and other kinds of social disaster?

Modernity's technical, ethical and socio-political experiences force us to question the most basic suppositions underlying our relation to the world (including to ourselves). The question we face is: given the fact that we are technically able to manipulate or even create whatever we want, what, then, does it mean that we do not see we are at the same time enabling the destruction of all there is, including ourselves?

In that sense, it is far from being senseless to ask what the 'we' underlying the omnipotent self-destructive capacity exactly means. Or, to put it in a more formal way: *from which point* do we, moderns, relate to reality, including ourselves? What makes this point to be the point from where we, at the same time, could make *and* destroy ourselves? In other words, what is the *subject* of that finite/infinite power of ours? What is the subject of that capacity to blindly destroy itself, i.e. the subject it is? Or, which amounts to the same thing, what is the subject/bearer of that power that meets its finitude in its very infinite?

A forgotten question

Nowadays the question of the subject, if mentioned at all, is perceived as outdated or even senseless. This was not the case along the twentieth century. Although, then, the *notion* of 'subject' was severely criticized, the *question* of the subject was at the top of the agenda, if only because the paradigms of our relation to reality (including to ourselves) were profoundly questioned. Phenomenology, existential philosophy, anthropology, psychoanalysis and many of the other social sciences: each of them, in their own way, tried to reconsider and to reformulate the basic assumptions of our relation to reality. And the most basic question was the one of the 'support', the 'ground' or 'subject' of that relation. Is there a grounding *subjectum* to it, and what is its precise status?

It is an abysmal question, for *it questions at the same time the very condition of questioning*. Does the question of the subject proceed from a 'point' which is itself unquestionable? Can it suppose itself being based in an unquestionable ground, or is this question's own subject to be put endlessly into question? In other words: is, at the end, the subject of that question more than a mere *supposition*? And what if the subject of science and of modern consciousness in general is, in the last resort, a mere supposition as well? What if the supposedly unshakable 'ground' of modernity's relation to the world is indeed a mere assumption, a fiction, an imagination?

That question cannot be treated by scientific methods. Although modern science cannot but assume itself to be based in a solid point of departure, in a point of scientific 'certainty' (as already Descartes put it), this very point cannot be scientifically proved. Defining itself to be an 'objective' knowledge, it cannot make its own starting point – the point hiding its 'subject' – the 'object' of its scientific research, not to mention scientific certainty. And yet this is nonetheless the way we commonly deal with the question of the subject nowadays. Since the last decade of the twentieth century, we are driven back on science in our discussions on that issue. We again believe we can find a scientifically sustained answer to the question of the subject of science or, more generally, the subject of our consciousness.[4]

Since Descartes, the subject of modern science is the supposed 'point' *outside* its object. It is from that very point we organize our 'objective' inquiries and experiments. Yet, unlike Descartes, we no longer consider this 'point' to be a substantial 'soul'. Eighteenth-century materialism taught us to give up any belief in the existence of such independent 'cogito' or 'subject'. As a merely abstract point, however, it remained indispensable for modern science. Without a point 'outside' the object, an 'objective' observation – and, thus, knowledge – of this object is simply impossible. Though since La Mettrie[5] the Cartesian dualism has been declared invalid, yet the split between the 'subject' and the object of science remained a condition *sine qua non* for this very science.

Nonetheless, it has always been – and is still – modernity's dream that, one day, science will succeed in doing the impossible, i.e. in having *scientific* knowledge of the very 'outside point' from where it operates; to have objective knowledge of the point that by definition cannot be objective at all. To explain the subject of science scientifically, i.e. to give a fully scientific explanation of the ground science rests upon and of the 'point' it operates from: this is what science is not able to do *precisely because of its modernity*. It is modernity's most basic experience that our knowledge lacks such a ground. It is no longer based in being as such, in *das Ding an sich*, as Kant puts it. Then, we are ourselves the 'ground' of our knowledge, as Descartes had already put forward. But not as a substantial ground but as a mere supposition, as eighteenth-century materialism correctly had replied. And this is how things still are now: the ground upon which our relation to reality is based, the 'point' from where we relate to that reality – is an imaginary one, a fictitious supposition. Not only do we ignore reality's ontological ground, we also ignore the ontological ground of the 'point' from where we relate to reality.

Transferred to the ethical sphere, the consequences of this modern condition come even more clearly into the light. For what to think if the 'subject' or 'ground' of moral values is merely supposed, imagined, fantasized? And when we indeed have to be *ourselves* that subject, what then if this, too, is an invention? What if our so-called 'self', being the subject of morality, is the result of imagination? What if both the good and the human subject of that good are mere fantasy?

Put in an ethical perspective, we understand maybe better why the abysmal question of the subject nowadays has lost the popularity it had in the twentieth century. In the revolutionary atmosphere of these times, the abyss of that question was still bearable, if only because it was tempered by the promising new times everyone was passionately expecting. Now, however, the time of 'dreaming' is over. In a way, we all have become 'conservatives', at least in the *formal* sense of the word. We would rather behold what we have than take the risks of radical change. Anyway, it is one of the reasons why the all too *open* question of the subject has lost its appealing effect on us. In fact, we can no longer stand this kind of unbearable openness underlying our very relation to the word as well as to ourselves – which is why science, more than ever, is asked to comfort us, and to give us a solid base. No wonder then that, in such times of science, religion has made its comeback. It fulfils a similar function as antique and medieval science did and as modern science is supposed to do according to an increasing number of people. Better than science is able to, religion can give back a stable and fixed subject. Longing for an unshakable ground underneath their feet, moderns are not abhorrent of sticking to religion.

However, this idea of a fixed, unquestioned subject is not without danger. Even in its shape of mere supposition or imagination. In order to face the problems our late modernity has to deal with, the question of the subject, however abysmal it may be, is as inevitable as indispensable. I will argue that it is necessary to retake once again that old, *unzeitgemäss* question of the subject, of the 'ground' that we suppose we rest on, and which, indeed, is nothing else than a *supposed* one, a *supposition* or *hypothesis.* The ancient Greek word for *subjectum*, *hypothesis*, names in fact the very status of the modern subject: it is the fantasized, supposed, imagined point our relation to the world rests upon.

The Lacanian subject

This is at least the radical conclusion Jacques Lacan draws in his conceptualization of the modern human condition. Lacking any ontological ground, the human relation to reality takes its starting point from – and, in this sense, is based upon – simple supposition. And what is this supposition based upon? From a certain perspective, it is based on 'itself', i.e. on the human capacity to suppose, to imagine, to dream, to invent things out of nothing. It rests on what Kant called the *reine Einbildungskraft*.[6] Or, referring to the Freudian paradigm Lacan entirely assumes: it is a matter of wishing – a wishing which *precedes* what is wished and even 'who' is wishing. It is an autonomous imagination or wishing which, as such, is *not* based in any self. In this, Lacan differs from Kant. For according to Lacanian theory, human wishing has to long even for a 'self', for a 'ground' to be based on. Man's imagination has to create (i.e. to imagine) even its own 'self'; it has to suppose itself to be the ground of his imagination and that, contrary to what is the case, the human 'self' is therefore *not* the product of imagination, of wish and supposition.

So is it us who have invented us a 'self'? Of course not. We found that 'self' in the others: in the ones around us with whom we identified and still identify. Consciousness or thought is not primordially an individual but a *social* affair. Thought is based in identification with others, and even there it has still to invent (to imagine) its base, its subject. The ground – the bearer or subject – of my imagination or my wishing is an image, not of me but of the other. And by denying that procedure I act as if that image is mine. That 'acting as if' results in the only real 'me' I have. So, indeed, my identity's origin is social. For Lacan, 'psychology' *is* 'sociology':[7] my *psyche* – that which I think I am, my subject, the point from where I relate to reality as 'me', as an identity – is the result of identification with the other, with the *socius, le semblable*. Social identification with others precedes – and, in that sense, grounds – my identity.

In a first phase of his thought, Lacan defines identity as a *Gestalt*, referring to the then popular *Gestalt* psychology. In the next phase, Lacan redefines the scene in which the 'self' invents itself as the specific scene Freud refers to as *die andere Schauplatz*: the scene of the unconscious representations (*Vorstellungen*).[8] Here again, the social field in which the libidinal being has to invent its identity (its subject) is a field of images. Yet, now, Lacan considers these images as what Freud calls *Vorstellungen*. The field of these representations forms an autonomous structure with a particular logic, described in Freud's *Traumdeutung* and (as Lacan has put it) similar to the linguistic structures described in Ferdinand de Saussure's famous *Cours de linguistique générale*. This representational (fictional) field in which the libidinal being has to invent its identity is, more precisely, the cultural field as described by Claude Lévi-Strauss: a field organized by the materiality of the signifier – *signifiants* – and governed by linguistic logic.[9]

So I live in and by – and *only* in and by – representations or signifiers. This is to say that *the ground of my identity – my subject – is itself* not *a representation or signifier.* Signifiers only *represent* it. The subject is that 'which a signifier represents for another signifier', as Lacan puts it in one of his most basic formulas.[10] *As such*, it has no proper existence; it exists only *through* representation, *through* the signifier, whose existence is not real but fictional.

This is crucial. The subject as such is not a signifier among signifiers, it is the insisting 'absentee' every signifier refers to, an 'absentee' who exists only through the never-ending game of references. The subject is the bearer of a fictional world in which, as such it remains missing. This is the case for the human subject or, more exactly, for the subject *of* human being's 'supposed' identity.

So any identity, i.e. anything that pretends to be what it is, is not what it is; it 'is' only this pretension, thus the basic thesis of Lacanian theory. Any 'self' 'is' solely to the extent it is represented. It exists only *by means of* – *in* or *as* – this representation, i.e. *in* or *as* the signifiers that represent it, not for us or others like us, but for other signifiers. The stuff we are made of is signifiers, but the point in which we constitute ourselves as being the bearer/subject of that stuff is a void, a kind of 'nothing' sustained only by the signifiers referring to it. This void, this 'nothing': this is 'us' in our quality of subject.

Lacan's formulation of the modern condition not only tells that we relate to things in so far as they are signifiers endlessly referring to other signifiers, but that even this signifying reality has no ground in itself, that it is itself based not in a signifier but in what exists only by being represented by signifiers. In other words, the identity of signifiers is based in the signifier's 'unsublatable' lack.[11]

Good ...

And so is the good. Is the good what it is? Is it *identical* to itself? If it is, then, only in the way it *signifies* itself as such – which is possible solely by means of signifiers. In the final analysis, the good is but a signifier. No thing or act is good *in itself.* It is good only in its quality of signifier, i.e. in its quality of representing the subject to another signifier. What does this mean? And what is the position of the subject in this? What is its function?

Good is good in so far as it refers to another good, in so far as it is part of a signifying system of goods borrowing their quality of goodness from their mutual reflecting effect. This makes the realm of the good comparable – if not structurally similar – to that other realm of often *less moral* goods which is our modern capitalist economy. With a term borrowed from Karl Marx, one can say that the good is a fetish,[12] a commodity that takes its value no longer from what it really means in the eyes of someone. It is no longer taken for its use value, but for its exchange value, its reference to other fetishes, to other commodities, i.e. signifiers. We are thus dealing with an autonomous system of goods, of which the effect on us is not necessarily *morally* good, as many of capitalism's vicissitudes show all too well. And so is an ethical system too: its values are based not in themselves but in their mutual reference. And, as we will discuss further on, that system of ethical values can also flourish when its effect on the people is not good at all or even disastrous.

The question, then, is: does a system of goods – of fetishes, of values – rest in itself? Is it its own *subject*? Not at all. Ethics is not based in 'values', so the basic line of Lacan's moral insight suggests. Values function as signifiers, and these do not rest in themselves but are representative of something else. They represent the *subject*, and they do this not for other subjects, but for other signifiers, other values. To paraphrase Lacan's formula: an ethical value represents the subject for another ethical value. So, ethical values form a relatively autonomous system in which each of them refers to the realm of other ethical values. Yet they do not *simply* represent one another, nor are they *based* in that mutual representation: they represent *the subject*, and it is that subject which they are based in. This is to say that ethical values represent *us* and that this is the way (and the only way) in which we are involved in the good(s)[13] we live by. It is *us* that are the subject of those goods.

So does this mean that *we* decide about what is good or not? Not exactly. For there is no 'we' independent from the good and capable of sovereignly deciding about it. The realm of the good or good*s* precedes us, they are that which we live in and by, which we identify with, which gives content to our life and our identity. They are, however, not to be considered as what satisfies our *needs*. The goods we live by do *not fill up* our lack. On the contrary, they *grant* us our lack, they affirm and consolidate it. Values are used, not to satisfy our needs, but to sustain our 'need of needs', i.e. our unsatisfiable desire. This is the core of Lacan's ethical theory.

For indeed, we *are* desire: unfulfilled and unfulfillable desire. The values ethics provides us with, the good and good*s* we live by, they do not satisfy our desire, they only stimulate that desire and make us *long* for satisfaction. Values and goods do not rest in themselves but in their very lack, and it is precisely there, on the locus of that lack, that we locate ourselves as their subject, as their ground and *raison d'être.*

In our quality of subject, we make the difference between the ethical value and 'itself', between the good and 'itself'. *In* that difference, we ourselves are located as desire. There, we are constituted as the bearer, the subject of those values, or, more exactly, as the subject of desire supported by those values. We 'are' the place where those values occur, where they *take place*; and this is why they never take place in a definite and exhaustive way. Being the subject of the good, we occupy the place where that good is on the verge of geting fully actualized, where it is near to becoming entirely real. Our function as subject, however, is to *not* let this happen. To be the subject of the good means to prevent it from getting *real*. This is the way the good is in the service of desire and this is what it means that we are the subject of the good (or, which amounts to the same thing, of the desire for the good).

... and evil

And what is evil? It is the good become real. It is the accomplished fullness of a value, it is a value no longer resting in its lack. It coincides with a situation where the ethical is completely actualized, or desire *really* satisfied. Evil is a good so 'extreme' that it has become its own subject, i.e. that its subject is no longer a void (for it is only that void which can give us a free rein to be its bearer/subject).

However strange these definitions may sound, they are the logical consequences of Lacan's axiom: the primacy of desire. Since we *are* desire, the satisfaction of that desire coincides with its extinction and, thus, with the extinction and death of 'us' who live by that desire. Life is never full life; it is basically nothing else than desire to live. So, full life or satisfied desire means death to the subject of that life and that desire. Since the good is good only in so far as it rests in its lack, and, on the very locus of that lack, represents the subject to another good, the extreme good – the good as resting finally in the completion of itself – is radical evil. It implies the death of the subject, for the subject existed only in so far as it longed for it.

Is full satisfaction of desire, then, simply not possible? Here it is crucial to notice that it is not impossible *as such*. It is only impossible *for a subject*. This is what the Lacanian concept of enjoyment – *jouissance* – is about. *Jouissance* tells the situation in which the libidinal being enjoys its ultimate object of desire and in which, thus, his desire is entirely satisfied. This situation is possible, Lacan argues, but not without a fading of the subject. In the moment of *jouissance*, the subject cannot be present with its own experience. At that moment, his entire libidinal economy (i.e. the desire he *is*) is supported by a small set of signifiers that form the 'phantasm'.[14] The phantasm gives a last – imaginary – consistency to the libidinal economy when its subject fades away, as for instance is the case in the moment of *jouissance*. So what is at stake in the concept of *jouissance* is that, in moments of full satisfaction, the subject keeps on occupying the place of the lack and keeps on affirming this lack. Only it does so by fading away.

Is *jouissance* a good thing? Is it the good *par excellence*? The answer to both questions is negative. *Jouissance* is not to be considered as a signifier and, thus, not as a good. It names the *enjoyment* – the usufruct – of the ultimate object, the 'object a' or *das Ding*, which is to be located *beyond* the realm of signifiers (so Lacan explains in his seminar on ethics).[15] *Jouissance* is the transgressive move in which the libidinal being leaves the realm of the signifier behind. In that moment it passes the borders limiting the realm of values and ethical norms, and loses itself – read: loses its subject – in the domain of *das Ding*. So, at the very place where Aristotelian and other traditions locate the Supreme Good, there, we must locate *jouissance*. In that perspective, enjoyment is to be considered as radical evil. For it implies the annihilation of all good(s), including even the subject of those goods.

Human ethics is orientated, not towards the Supreme Good, but towards radical evil. This is the strange conclusion Lacan, in his seminar on ethics, draws from his insight that human life is basically desire, unfulfilled desire. Ethics must provide both framework *and* freedom to desire. Therefore, it must prevent desire from getting fully satisfied, just like it must prevent ethical rules to be fully fulfilled.

Ethics is not about the attempt to fasten down human behaviour on a series of fixed values and rules that culminate in the dignity of the Supreme Good. Ethics is about desire and, thus, about us, because we 'are' desire or – as, more exactly, Lacan put it – because we are the subject of the desire of the Other. Since our condition has become modern, we *are* radical openness – 'radical' in the sense that it is no longer supported by a God who embraces and encloses that openness and gives it an ultimate protection, a divine home. Our house is the one of an open and infinite desire that has no fixed ontologically based co-ordinates.

However, it belongs to our modern condition as well to deny or repress the open desire we 'are'. We can but remain blind to the lack on which our libidinal constitution is based. It is only in a fleeting moment we can face the truth telling we 'are' unfulfillable desire. Acknowledging this desire *as such* is inevitably at odds with the certainty of consciousness we spontaneously want. That is why, against all spontaneous inclinations, ethics must put the unconscious openness of desire at the centre of its interest. The purpose of the ethical law is to give human desire a framework of limits, without which it is not able to maintain itself. The ultimate function of that framework, however, is to provide free space to desire and to make *jouissance* possible.

This is to say that ethics must make clear it is not able to give us what we expect from it, i.e. the satisfaction of our desire. So, for highly ethical reasons, ethics must not give us what it (necessarily) promises. If it would try to do so, if it would give us the desired satisfaction, it would certainly be unable to really do so, but it would nonetheless be able to do *as if* it does so. This 'as if' offers the disposition of terror and totalitarianism – also of the ethical type. An ethical authority, pretending to bring full satisfaction to us, can only oblige us to do *as if* we were in the full possession of it. And in that case, we can only do *as if* we were like this by detecting the lack of satisfaction *with others* – in fact by projecting our own lack on to them – accusing them of undermining the ethical standard we all are supposed to have reached.[16] So communist society, pretending to have overcome all the shortcomings of the old bourgeois society, ended up in a situation of paranoid social control where everyone was suspecting anyone else of being responsible for the 'bourgeois lack' that prevented communist society from getting actualized.

Fighting the 'enemy of the people', they in fact transported their own lack on to these alleged enemies in order, there, to deny it – i.e. to destroy it, and – which is one of the consequences – to destroy the people who were marked by it.

The latter were forced to deny what it means to be the *subject* of communism. The place where communism 'took place', the locus where it touched 'ground', is not the one where it got actualized, but where it met its own lack, or, more precisely, where it met itself as *desire* (i.e. as *longing* for its supposed 'self'). Here, evil was caused by denying desire or, what amounts to the same thing, by denying the true subject of desire. Pretending to be its own subject, claiming to be the answer to desire, the good turned into radical evil.

How to interrupt evil?

How to avoid evil? It is not an easy question, if only because of the more basic question preceding this one: is evil avoidable at all? Is a world conceivable without evil? Or, more precisely, is it a good thing to suppose that such a world is possible? Of course, we *want* to avoid evil, we *want* a world freed from it, but since 'evil' is ultimately that which our wanting – our desire – is orientated towards, the question is more complex than one may think at first sight.

Let us be more precise. The fact of desire's orientation towards evil does not mean that we really and consciously want evil to be materialized or actualized. At the *unconscious* level we want to lose ourselves in *jouissance*, which, being located beyond the good, must be characterized as evil. But the unconscious level is meant to *stay* unconscious, which implies that, at the conscious level, we suppose the satisfaction of desire to be something good. Here, we face what it really means to live at the same time on the two levels of the conscious and the unconscious. Consciously we rightly condemn evil and try to ban it from our world. But this does not prevent us from consuming our daily portion of evil, it is true not in its *real* but in its *fictitious* state. What else do we consume on television and other mass media? We enjoy the same evil, which ethics fights against, time and again on the screen. And, what is more, we even do so while morally condemning it. For this is what happens while watching television, from news programmes to weekend movies: we perform evil in order to show, to ourselves and to others, how bad this is; but in the meantime we enjoy it and give way to our desire's unconscious point of ultimate orientation. This is how 'evil' *jouissance* is at work in good moral consciousness. Fighting for the good(s) on the conscious level, on the unconscious one, we secretly give way to our desire's intention to lose ourselves (i.e. our 'subject') in a domain that leaves all good(s) behind.

Is this kind of evil avoidable? Is human culture conceivable without dealing with evil in an imagined, fictional way? I don't think so. Since time immemorial, human beings have imagined evil things and have enjoyed those images, including the evil they show. All ancient legends, epics, tragedies, even comedies seem to confirm this. So is, then, this kind of evil innocent and harmless? Should we, then, not worry about it? Certainly we should. For if we do not bother about it, we cynically collaborate with it and stimulate the evil of 'moralizing ethics', i.e. the ethics of the 'beautiful soul', as Hegel puts it in his critique on Kantian morality.[17] In such a moral mind, the focus on evil is not so much meant to fight it, but to promote the own moral 'soul' as being itself free from evil or other ethical incorrectness. Its constant obsession with evil is but a veil for a narcissistic preoccupation in its own 'soul'. This is why such moral consciousness does not realize that, in fact, it *sustains* the evil in the outside world. Instead of fighting evil, it makes use of it in order to persuade the own soul that all evil is with others. This kind of moral consciousness does not realize that it basically transfers its own evil on to others.

This is the dominant immorality of current moralizing ethics, as perfectly sustained by contemporary visual culture. How comfortable it is to transfer our own evil fascination with evil to others locked up behind a television screen. Dumping our own evil in that little box, we can pretend to be ourselves untouched by any evil at all. In this perspective, television and the mass media in general are the way *par excellence* to install all over the planet the moralizing ideology of the 'beautiful soul'. It is time to realize that precisely this worldwide-practised moralizing ethics is at least co-responsible for the evil in the world that it pretends to fight against.

Can we avoid this? Can we avoid the evil of misusing human evil and moralizing it? The problem is that, if we pretend we can, we almost inevitably fall into the trap of moralizing ethics, since we, then, suppose the world conceivable without any evil. In that case, we presume that our desire to get rid of all evil can fully be satisfied. And, as has become clear now, this is the trickiest way to deny what ethics is about: desire, unfulfillable desire. In the name of desire, in the name of desire's orientation towards *jouissance*, we always will have to deal with evil. At least as something we deal with in our imagination, evil is unavoidable.

But all this is not to say we should not *interrupt* the evil of the moralizing misuse of human evil. Not able to definitely clear up that evil (since it is involved in the human condition defined as desire), we can – and must – *disrupt* it and at least temper its pernicious effects. We must do so for the sake of ethics. It is the aim of ethics to stop the misrecognition of humans' basic reality, i.e. their desire. The aim of ethics is not to give us the good we expect from it (it is exactly this, which it cannot give us), but to sustain our desire and to make *jouissance* possible. It is crucial to realize that desire's misrecognition cannot be stopped once and for all. Such misrecognition belongs to desire's very condition. For no man can consciously stand the void he – i.e. his desire – is based on. That is why we cannot but repress and deny what we, at the most basic level, are: desire. However, since this denial can be ethics' own evil, we must have an eye for it, detect it and interrupt it.

Here we face the core of non-moralizing ethics. Its main target is to interrupt again and again the never absent, spontaneous misrecognition of human desire. That is why ethics, first of all, has to be critical about itself, about its hidden inclination to deny its very *raison d'être*, i.e. human desire. Ethics' shape is that of a law, i.e. of a set of commandments limiting desire and prohibiting *jouissance*. But the subject of that law is to be located not in the good it contains or in the values it supports, but in the point where all good and all values lack. This is to say that the ethical law rests in its lack; that its subject is to be located in that very void. This is the precise place the human subject occupies, as subject of the law in the double sense of the word: in the sense that he is subjected to the law and passively thrown under it, *and*, at the same time, as active subject/bearer of the law, as the one who gives ground and *raison d'être* to that law. Within the gap between both, between the passively subjected one and the active subject, there, desire moves to and fro. This gap makes the law a support of desire; and it is the same gap which makes man both the law's and desire's subject. Or, which amounts to the same thing: in the distance or difference between the law and the law 'itself', there, the law found its ground, a ground coinciding with both its own lack and the lack we 'are' in our quality of libidinal being.

The evil that threatens ethics from within is to misrecognize its lack as being its very base, its subject. This is the evil at work within contemporary moralizing ethics as well as in the great ethical and social ideologies of the last century. Without retaking the question of the subject, we will never be able to interrupt that evil. And, for the sake of ethics, we have to interrupt the evil, which is inherent to ethics as its very condition.

Notes

1 Hannah Arendt, *On Revolution*, Harmondsworth: Penguin Books, 1981, p. 82.
2 'Le signifiant, à l'envers du signe, n'est pas ce qui représente quelque chose pour quelqu'un, c'est ce qui représente précisément le sujet pour un autre signifiant.' Jacques Lacan, *Séminaire IX, L'identification 1961–1962*, 6 December 1961, unpublished.
3 Bob Woodward, *State of Denial. Bush at War*, Part III, New York: Simon & Schuster, 2006.
4 See, among so many publications, Daniel C. Dennet, *Consciousness Explained*, Boston, MA: Little Brown, 1991.
5 Julien Offray de La Mettrie, *Machine Man and other Writings*, trans. Ann Thomson, Cambridge: Cambridge University Press, 1996.
6 *Rein*, here, means 'only', 'exclusive', 'autonomous'. For Kant's critical philosophy, the imagination must never operate in a *rein*, autonomous way. It has to be connected with the 'object' perceived by the *Anschauung*. Stating that the 'subject' is a mere supposition, a mere product of the *reine Einbildungskraft*, is a provocative claim, even in relation to Kantian theory.
7 Sociology, interpreted in the original meaning of the term: not as defining a proper object in reality, but as a specific point of view on reality. This is sociology as seen by its 'founding fathers', or as deployed by Georges Bataille, ex-husband

of Lacan's wife, in his famous 'Collège de sociologie'. Markos Zafiropoulos has written a remarkable book about sociology's (specifically Durkheim's) decisive influence on the early Lacan: Markos Zafiropoulos, *Lacan et les sciences sociales*, Paris: Presses Universitaires de France, 2001.

8 Jacques Lacan, *Écrits*, Paris: Seuil, 1966, pp. 548, 685, 689, 799.

9 Markos Zafiropoulos, *Lacan et Lévi-Strauss, ou, le retour à Freud 1951–1957*, Paris: Presses Universitaires de France, 2003.

10 Lacan, *Écrits*, pp. 819, 835, 840. Lacan uses this formula for the first time in his seminar on transference: Jacques Lacan, *Le séminaire, Livre VIII, Le transfert 1960–1961*, ed. Jacques-Alain Miller, Paris: Seuil, 1991, pp. 286, 307.

11 Here 'unsublatable' refers to the Hegelian notion of 'sublation', *Aufhebung*.

12 See the famous section 4 of the first chapter in *Capital*, 'The fetishism of commodities and the secret thereof'. Karl Marx, *Capital* I, *A Critique of Political Economy*, London: Penguin Books, 1992).

13 As already mentioned, there is a formal equivalence between the ethical good and the economic goods. See Jacques Lacan, *Le séminaire, Livre VII, L'éthique de la psychanalyse 1959–1960*, ed. Jacques-Alain Miller, Paris : Seuil, 1986, pp. 255–6, 269 ; *The Seminar of Jacques Lacan, Book VII, The Ethics of Psychoanalysis 1959–1960*, ed. Jacques-Alain Miller, trans. Dennis Porter, New York and London: Routledge, 1992, pp. 215–17, 228–9.

14 Lacan elaborates the concept of 'phantasm' in his seminar on 'desire and its interpretation'. Jacques Lacan, *Le Séminaire VI, 1958–1959*, unpublished.

15 For the concept of *das Ding* see Lacan, *Le Séminaire VII*, pp. 55–86; *The Ethics of Psychoanalysis*, pp. 43–70. See also Chapter 4 of: Marc de Kesel, *Eros and Ethics – Reading Jacques Lacan's Seminar VII*, Albany: SUNY Press, 2009, pp. 83–104.

16 This 'as if' attitude typifies 'perversion', which Lacan distinguishes from the two other possible attitudes *vis-à-vis* the lack constituting us as *beings* of desire, namely 'neurosis' and 'psychosis'. 'Neurosis' – which names the attitude of normal people – represses the lack (*Verdrängung*), passing it constantly to other signifiers, while 'psychosis' rejects it (*Verwerfung*), building up an entirely imaginary world (a delusion, *ein Wahn*). In 'perversion' the lack is both acknowledged and denied: projecting his own lack (i.e. his finitude, pain, shortcomings, fears, etc.) on to the other, the sadist (who is a typical example) recognizes the lack constituting human desire, but at the same time denies it, doing *as if* the lack carved into the body of the other only shows absence of lack, fullness, *jouissance*. Lacan elaborates this concept of 'perversion' in his famous essay 'Kant avec Sade', Lacan, *Écrits*, pp. 765–90. See also Chapter 6 of: Marc de Kesel, *Eros and Ethics* pp. 121–162.

17 For this Hegelian concept see, among other passages, Hegel's *Phenomenology*: G. W. F. Hegel, *Phänomenologie des Geistes*, Hamburg: Meiner, 1988, pp. 433, 439–40.

Chapter 13

When psychoanalysis meets Law and Evil

Perversion and psychopathy in the forensic clinic

Jochem Willemsen and Paul Verhaeghe

Introduction: the polymorphous perversity of every subject versus Law and Evil

Since Freud, the discourse on sexual deviations has made a full circle. Before Freud, sexual aberrations were considered to be rare, sinful and criminal. In a word: Evil. Freud himself demonstrated that sexual deviations are not that rare and can even be understood as part of normal psychosexual development. It is only in cases where fixation and regression were apparent that he considered them to be pathological. As a result, the pre-Freudian criminal sinner was reinterpreted as a patient who had to be treated. After Freud, and largely due to his theory, Western society became much more liberal. Furthermore, the Kinsey Reports of 1948 and 1953 empirically demonstrated that almost nobody fits the norm, i.e., heterosexual coitus in the missionary position with orgasm for both participants. The explanation can be found in Freud's study of infantile sexuality, as elaborated in the still magisterial *Three Essays on the Theory of Sexuality* and further developed in a number of later texts.

In short, Freud discovered what every nanny long knew, namely, that sexuality begins from childhood onwards, if in a very unique manner. There is no such thing as a genital instinct that irresistibly thrusts man toward woman and vice versa right from the start. It is a question not of human instincts, but of drives. The life of the drive develops through the component drives that are only later gathered under the coordinating flag of so-called genital sexuality. These drives are both partial and autoerotic. Partial means that they concentrate on certain bodily areas (oral, anal, genital …) rather than on the body in its entirety. Autoerotic means that these drives focus first on parts of the *subject's* body, not on that of the other. On the basis of these readily observable data, Freud concludes that our sexuality is grounded in a polymorphously perverse predisposition. Moreover, this polymorphously perverse predisposition is the basis of the original and universal predisposition of the human sexual drive.[1] Almost any 'adult' perverse trait can be observed in the child, putting perversion in a completely different light.[2]

Consequently, according to Freudian theory, the distinction between 'normal' perverse traits and the perverse structure is not easy to make.

The combination between Kinsey and Freud provided a secure base to the sexual revolution and the accompanying liberalization in Western society. The net result is that almost every sexual interaction has become acceptable as long as there is mutual consent between the partners. Strangely enough, this means that we have returned to a society in which sexual deviation has become again synonymous with a crime! The nineteenth century sinner/criminal who was turned into a twentieth-century patient has now become a twenty-first-century perpetrator. The so-called liberalization has made things very unclear, because the 'diagnostic' criterion for sexual deviation has become more or less synonymous with the absence of informed consent between the partners. Hence the two main contemporary categories of sexual deviancy: rape and paedosexuality. Yet again, in a word: Evil.

A similar reduction shows its effects on another important concept in the forensic field: psychopathy. Throughout its history, this concept was often on the verge of being reduced to antisocial behaviour. When Prichard launched the term of moral insanity in 1835, he designated a group of patients with deficiencies in the affective faculty. To Prichard the term 'moral' referred primarily to the emotional and conative aspects of the psyche, as in 'moral treatment'. Nevertheless, this diagnostic label owed much of its success to the systematic misinterpretation of the word 'moral' as referring to antisocial.[3] In the second half of the nineteenth century, synonyms such as constitutional inferiority and degenerative insanity became very popular, expressing the idea that psychopathy is associated with innate evil. Although subsequent psychiatrists developed a more comprehensive concept of psychopathy, its judgemental undertones never disappeared. Popular media have taken over this narrow interpretation and continue to portray an image of the psychopath as a thoroughly bad criminal. This image, however, does not correspond with the current scientific notion of psychopathy, in which a set of personality features are defined that can be applied in a non-forensic context. Indeed, an eminent scholar in this area advanced Oskar Schindler, the saviour of hundreds of Jews, as a psychopath.[4]

The question we are facing now is *how to understand perversion and psychopathy independently of this contemporary reduction, while at the same time acknowledging the link with the Law.* Below we will address the description of the criminal behaviour of the pervert and the psychopath. But instead of focusing on the nature and frequency of this behaviour, and the chance of relapse, we will study the psychic dynamics that lead to such behaviour. Following this, the problem of perversion and psychopathy will be approached in separate steps, in which the Oedipal situation, and the relation to the Law and to language are described through Freudian-Lacanian theory. Where possible, we will use fragments of interviews conducted during our own ongoing research among male detainees. Yet, before we start, we must clarify our use of the concepts of perversion and psychopathy.

In psychoanalytic literature, psychopathy is often sided with perversion. In this chapter, however, we will advocate that perversion and psychopathy are two clearly distinct clinical *tableaux*, each having relevance in the forensic field.[5] Perversion in the context of this chapter refers to the clinical structure as defined by Lacan, implying a specific relation towards the Other and a specific way of regulating the drives. We use the term of psychopathy in the way Robert Hare has conceptualized it. In the 1980s Hare began to lift this concept from a swamp of misconceptions and popular ideation by making a *retour à* Hervey Cleckley's original work on the topic.[6] In contrast to the common idea that a psychopath is simply a mad criminal, Hare's elaboration consists of a specific constellation of interpersonal, affective, and lifestyle characteristics. On the interpersonal level, psychopaths are grandiose, arrogant, callous, dominant, superficial, and manipulative. Effectively, they are short-tempered, unable to form strong emotional bonds with others, and lack empathy, guilt, and remorse. These interpersonal and affective characteristics are associated with a socially deviant (although not necessarily criminal) lifestyle that includes irresponsible and impulsive behaviour and a tendency to ignore or violate social conventions.

Hare developed an instrument to assess psychopathy. The Psychopathy Checklist – Revised (PCL-R) consists of twenty items that have to be scored 0, 1, or 2 by a trained clinician.[7] Zero means that a certain feature of psychopathy is absent, 2 means that it is definitely present, while 1 is scored in cases when the feature is somewhat present. This assessment has to be based on a semi-structured interview in combination with a thorough study of the forensic dossier (containing interrogations, investigations, etc.). Collateral information is indispensable in order not to be conned by a psychopath. This assessment procedure results in a score between 0 and 40. The most rigorous and most frequently used cut-off point for psychopathy is a score equal to or greater than 30, although a cut-off point of 25 has been advocated for Europe.[8] The PCL-R is at present considered the gold standard for the assessment of psychopathy.[9] During the last decade, the concept has gained tremendous importance in forensic psychology, and has been described as 'what may be the most important forensic concept of the early twenty-first century'.[10]

The forensic clinic meets classic psychoanalytic theory

It is by no means coincidental that the perverse subject is rarely found in the normal consultation room, contributing to the difficulty of the theoretical formulation of perversion. The most important descriptions of perversion come from compulsory treatment, that is to say, the forensic clinic. The same goes for psychopathy. The first documented encounter between a psychoanalyst and a psychopath was in the context of the forensic clinic.[11] This introduces an important bias: here we are always dealing with 'perpetrators'.

This must be taken into account, because it clearly concerns a selective group. Research concerning the so-called sub-criminal or 'successful' psychopath is as scarce as research about exhibitionists or sadomasochists.[12]

Let's start with perversion. What do these forensic descriptions teach us about perversion, particularly with the Freudian criterion 'deviations with respect to the goal'?[13] Three characteristics emerge:

- the enactment in reality of a rigid pre-genital scenario
- that compulsively imposes itself on the pervert subject, and
- establishes a relationship of power.

The first characteristic is fairly classical: it is not enough just to have perverse fantasies; they must also be carried out in a 'hands on' manner (with the exception of voyeurism and exhibitionism). Nevertheless, this requires further clarification. Ever since the sexual revolution, neurotic subjects have also performed their fantasies, with the result that this criterion becomes considerably more blurry. Moreover, the perverse character must not be sought in the specific content of the sexual scenario – any paraphiliac scenario can be enacted in a normal-neurotic context. The specifically perverse aspect lies in its rigidity, combined with its unfree character. Any deviation causes anxiety and tension. From a psychoanalytic perspective, what we are dealing with here is repetition compulsion rather than repetition as such. Indeed, the presence of repetition in neurotic sexuality always introduces something new into the proceeding dialectic of desire.[14] Repetition compulsion, in contrast, as Freud discovered in his study of the traumatic neuroses, is indeed compulsive and always fails in its repeated attempt to symbolize the traumatic Real. This indicates a link between perversion and a traumatic anamnesis.

The second characteristic stands in stark contrast to the neurotic ideal: the perverse subject is not the liberated erotic connoisseur of the neurotic's wet dream, quite the opposite. Empirical research into the basic unconscious convictions and cognitive schemes of paedophiles found five convictions, including the sense that the tension cannot be controlled, and this occurring within the larger context of an uncontrollable world.[15] The pervert is fundamentally unfree, compulsively driven to repeat the same thing. It is, moreover, frequently experienced as bizarre; its completion will bring relief but sometimes also shame, disgust, guilt, and depression.

The implication is that the perverse subject is pre-eminently divided. Note that even perverts don't know what drives them; here the subject division is total. In the forensic context, this causes difficulties because the forensic clinician wants to know what is driving the behaviour, and expects to get confessions. The 'perpetrator' cannot give them, however, for the simple reason that he barely knows his own motives. This has the clinical consequence that in day-to-day life the perverse subject often presents a banal normality. In neurotics, the division is less extreme and more 'dynamic', thus presenting combinations of normal and abnormal behaviour.

The third characteristic is the most interesting, for a number of reasons. Clinical descriptions show how the perverse subject always directs its scenario towards the other in an explicit relationship of power, that is: the power of the pervert. The exhibitionist, for example, succeeds only if the other is shocked, the masochist will explicitly instruct the other what to do, etc. The above-mentioned empirical research reveals the paedophile's second basic unconscious conviction: the idea that the world is divided into superior and inferior creatures, the latter being forced to submit themselves to the former.[16] Immediately following from this is the conviction of the need to control the other and the world in general.

This last point shows how the power relationship is not restricted to perverse acts – the pervert is also frequently the priest of a challenging new 'ethic of pleasure' that needs an audience that has to be controlled as well. Here, power is not necessarily synonymous with brute violence; it has to do with the relational aspect, the need to have the situation under control. It is important to stress this, because it means that not every pervert inevitably comes into contact with the police.

A different picture emerges from the forensic study of the criminal psychopath. Psychopathy is associated with an earlier onset of delinquent behaviour, faster recidivism, more excessive use of violence, and more violence in institutions.[17] The prototypical psychopath, as described by Cleckley, is an incorrigible thief and swindler who does not refrain from using threat or violence. We do not adhere to the image, propagated by popular media (and some researchers), of the psychopath as a cruel or sadistic criminal, preeminently a serial killer. Although the psychopath has little consideration for the rights and emotional life of other people, it is not common for him to derive sexual excitement from dominating and tantalizing his victims. The psychopath's criminal attitude seems mainly directed towards material gain.

However, the psychopath's criminal tendencies cannot be reduced to a purely instrumental orientation. Cleckley noted that many antisocial acts of the psychopath are inadequately motivated, in the sense that crimes are committed even when the material gain is not needed or ridiculously small. Moreover, psychopaths commit crimes at moments or in situations in which the chance of being caught is all too evident. As Greenacre noted, '[s]kill and persuasiveness are combined with utter foolishness and stupidity'.[18]

This does not mean that the psychopath commits his crimes in a compulsive way. The compulsiveness that can be noted in the neurotic (e.g., kleptomania, pyromania) and in the pervert's sexual praxis, is absent in the psychopath. The psychopath misses the rigidity and stereotypy of such compulsions; he is a versatile criminal who commits a broad range of different crimes.[19] Take for instance psychopaths' sexual offences: instead of being fixated on one type of victim, they are able to abuse anyone they can, minors as well as adults. Their choice of victimizing minors is often inspired by the simple reason that they are more easily controllable. Another motive can be their thrill-seeking: abusing a child out of curiosity. Or otherwise, a minor is just the first person they can get their hands on, for instance their own children. All possible motives for psychopaths seem to have in common that they are not guided by some fundamental fantasy or fixation on a particular libidinal object. In contrast to the pervert, the psychopath who commits sexual offences is never a specialized offender.

This lack of fundamental fantasy can also be found in the sexual life of psychopaths, typified by Cleckley as 'impersonal, trivial, and poorly integrated'.[20] The psychopath seems to regard sex very casually, without any desire to explore or to ravish the partner in a shared experience. Sexual activity with a prostitute or casual pick-up is experienced at the same level as sexual activity with their partner, because what they feel is not about to bring out loyalty or love. In Robert Hare's Psychopathy Checklist, the psychopath's sexuality is characterized as promiscuous sexual behaviour, referring to frequent impersonal, casual, or trivial sexual activities. Homosexuality and heterosexuality can co-occur, mainly motivated by thrill-seeking. 'Evidence of consistent, well-formulated deviation was extremely rare in a large group of male psychopaths personally observed in a closed psychiatric institution.'[21]

The pervert and the Law: disavowal

It's now an open secret that yesterday's victims of sexual abuse run the risk of becoming today's perpetrators. However, the link between the victim and the abuser is considerably more complex than a simple black-and-white picture. The connection between a PTSD based on sexual abuse and the perverse structure does not mean that every victim of sexual abuse becomes a perpetrator, let alone perverse. Within Lacanian theory, a subject's specific structure will depend on the specific relational structure between it and the Other.[22] The combination of a chronic traumatic anamnesis and a neurotic structure is also very well possible, and results in *Borderline*.

Hence the question is: what sort of original relation between the subject and the Other is necessary for perversion to occur, and where does trauma fit into this process? The forensic descriptions all point towards an abusive Other, traditionally anticipated to be the father or his replacement – fitting well with our phallic-patriarchal expectations. The idea that a mother might abuse her child is incompatible with our conventional myths of motherly love. At least three women were necessary to explode this myth.[23] Empirical research has meanwhile shown that sexual delinquents are significantly less securely attached than other delinquents and, moreover, that this insecurity has to do in particular with attachment to the mother rather than the father.[24]

Let us first return to normal development. The infant's inevitable starting point is the passive position, that is to say, it is reduced to being the passive object of the mother's desire and acquires the basis of its own identity through a mirroring alienation coming from the (m)other. Once this basic identity is sufficiently stable, the next step will see the child attempting to take the active position. In-between is a transitional phase where the child still clings to the secure relationship through the use of a 'transitional object' (classically the pacifier). In this way, the anxiety about losing the mother can be managed. In a normal, Oedipal situation, the father's function is to create a situation where the child's further development can take place, if only by the fact that the mother's desire is channelled towards him.

In the psychogenesis of perversion this doesn't happen. The mother reduces the child to her passive object, to the thing that makes her whole. Because of this mirroring, the child remains under her control, a part of herself.[25] The child thus gains no representational entry into its own drive, let alone to any subsequent elaborations of its own desire. In structural terms, it is reduced to the phallicized object *a*, through which the mother fills in her own lack, the process of separation never taking place.[26] As a third figure, the father is reduced to a powerless observer defined as insignificant by the mother. This banalizing of the Other of authority will return later on when the pervert takes the Law into its own hands as regards *jouissance*.[27]

In this manner, the child finds itself in a paradoxical position: on the one hand, it is the imaginary phallus of the mother – a win for the child. On the other hand, the price the child pays for this is high: there is no separation; any further development into its own identity will be blocked. In response, the child will perform a characteristic reversal in the attempt to safeguard its gain. The child will try to exchange its passive position for the active, taking the reins in its own hands whilst at the same time maintaining the privileged position. In clinical terms, this is most evident in masochism. The masochist presents him or herself as an object of enjoyment for the other, albeit in such a way that s/he has created the whole scenario and directs it – this is the instrumental aspect that clearly shows the passive–active reversal, on condition that 'active' is interpreted as 'leading'. The pervert may appear passive, but is not.

In Lacanian theory, subjectivity is considered as an enduring structure between the subject and the Other, focusing on drive and desire. This explains why every structure entails mechanisms of defence as well. The perverse subject formation has its own distinctive mechanism. Defence is always directed towards an underlying anxiety, beginning with the subject's own drive tension and subsequently elaborated through exchanges with the first and second Others and their desire. With this, we have reinterpreted Freud's castration anxiety in terms of an anxiety either about being unable to satisfy the Other's phallic desire, or about being *too* able to satisfy it.[28] In perversion, we are dealing with a particular manifestation of the second situation: the subject is defined as the perfect answer to the phallic desire of the first Other. In Freudian terms, this implies *the lack of* castration, that is to say, the mother's castration (Freud), the Other's castration (Lacan). At the same time, the phallic lack *beyond* the mother–child dyad is indeed recognized, particularly in the form of the powerless and insignificant second Other.

This equivocalness is grounded in the typically perverse defence mechanism: disavowal.[29] Through disavowal, the pervert adopts a double stance. He disavows the phallic lack (for himself and for the mother), while at the same time recognizing its existence (for the rest of the world in general and for the father in particular). The result is a clear-cut split: the pervert lives in a divided world where lack and the regulating law are both recognized and disavowed at the same time.

We found an example of this split in the statements of a pervert priest who was convicted for sexually molesting dozens of minors. During the first interrogation immediately after his arrest, he admitted the following:

> I admit that some twenty or thirty years ago I first discovered that I got sexually aroused by touching minors. I felt that my penis got into an erection. At that moment, I decided for myself that I had to be careful, all the more because I already observed that a certain child was looking at my crotch when I touched him. Although I tried, it wasn't easy to suppress these feelings. I admit that I looked for children in swimming pools. But I still insist that I did not have sexual contacts with them.

At the start of the second interrogation, he asked for a psychiatrist, and he admitted that he might have 'repressed' certain things:

> In my mind, there might be a split between 'the priest' who by definition wouldn't do such things, and me as a 'person', who might have got up to something without the priest knowing it.

Despite this defence mechanism the underlying anxiety persists, since in this particular situation it involves anxiety about being reduced to the passive object of the Other. Hence the pervert's typical reversal of positions: the perverse subject compels others to assume the passive position of the object, while taking the active position for himself. In this way, the underlying anxiety can be mastered. In practice, this means that not only will the pervert turn himself into the instrument of the Other's enjoyment; he will also submit this other to his own system of rules *à propos* enjoyment.

Perverse anxiety is often understood as an Oedipal anxiety, i.e., an anxiety about the castrating father. This is wrong; the anxiety is about the maternal super-ego. It was the first Other who was in control, and the perverse scenario is explicitly aimed at reversing this situation. This is the main reason why behavioural treatments based on the 'paternal' super-ego usually fail: they are beside the point, that is, they fail to address the maternal super-ego of the pervert. The anxiety lies at a much deeper level, closer to the psychotic anxiety about being devoured by the Other. The reaction against the imposition of the paternal law will frequently be aggression.

Disavowal is not restricted to the sexual relationship. It determines the pervert's entire relation to the symbolic Other, that is, towards authority and *jouissance.* In the pervert's own world there is no lack, and his own laws are imposed on the Other. In the conventional world the law will apparently be followed, that is to say, the pervert acts on the assumption that *others will follow the conventional rules* and he will make full use of that knowledge.

Indeed, the original relation will repeat itself with the successors to the first and second Others in adult life albeit with a passive–active reversal. The perverse subject will assume an instrumental position towards the subsequent 'first' Other, in order to ensure that Other's enjoyment. This is the paradox from a neurotic point of view: the pervert is firmly convinced that he works himself to death for the Other's enjoyment.[30] Hence the persistent ideas that the victims 'asked for it', that they 'do enjoy it, you know', etc., ideas that were certainly true for the original first Other. This conclusion may similarly be found – in a reduced version – in the so-called 'cognitive distortions', testifying time after time to the conviction that the victim was 'cooperative', or even that it was the victim who took the initiative.[31] This can be illustrated by an episode of an interview with a pervert who was convicted for raping his five-year old son.

> *Interviewee.* In the morning, I hear that Jeffrey is awake at seven-thirty. I say, 'Jeffrey, it's a bit early,' and he responds, 'But I have to go to the toilet.' I agree and I hear him going to the living room and turning on the television. I say, 'Jeffrey, it is too early for *Sesame Street*. Come in bed with Daddy. But you have to be good and sleep.' What I always used to do with him when he was little was this … [He sings a child's song while acting as if he is handling the ears of the child.] And by doing that, he gets excited and he starts bouncing on me. I say, 'No, Jeffrey, you can't do that.' [He says what the child would have said:] 'Yes, yes, Mammy and Daddy do the same,' and he starts to bounce, he pulls down my pyjama trousers and he takes my genitals. [He says what the child would have said:] 'Eat up.' But I say, 'No, don't eat that up.' [He says what the child would have said:] 'Eat pick.' I explained it like that to child protection services and they distort it completely. [He sounds angry and astonished.] Now honestly, that's why I am angry with them, those bastards. They say I allowed him to do it. Oh, come on, he asked for it. They say I also asked for it. Don't give me that! They blew up the whole thing.

In its adult manifestation the re-edition of the original relation has one important advantage, i.e., the passive–active reversal. Despite his instrumental position in ensuring the Other's total enjoyment, the pervert will feel he has succeeded only if he provokes anxiety in this Other.[32] This is the pervert's proof that he escaped being totally reduced to the Other's desire, and proof of the turnaround in the relation. It is the Other who has been reduced to the object of enjoyment, the anxiety testifies to this.

The stance is even more equivocal, if that is possible, in the pervert's relation to the replacements of the second Other, the Other of law and authority. The Other's law is not only challenged and unmasked as an insipid convention, appropriate only for the little people. In all the relations where the perverse subject truly participates, the law is completely swept aside. In its place, the pervert will substitute its own law, i.e., a pseudo-ethos preached with abundant conviction to which the Other is obliged to submit. Any book by the Marquis de Sade illustrates this characteristic, which is never absent from the perverse structure. Pages of meticulous descriptions of perverse scenarios alternate with chapters that outline the Sadean ethos of *jouissance* in an attempt to convince the other of the rightness of its justice in comparison to the wishy-washy nature of conventional law.

This relation to the Law – challenge, ridicule, and replacement – results in the pervert's focus on the gaze of the second Other, intended to make it clear to this Other that he is powerless. This means that there is indeed a triangular structure in the perverse structure, albeit in the equivocal way we saw above. The neurotic, on the other hand, will always experience the gaze of such a third figure as a censure, and for precisely that reason will try to avoid it as much as possible.

The psychopath and the Law: retraction

In contrast to the perverse structure, the psychopath's father does not emerge as a powerless observer defined as insignificant by the mother. On the contrary, a significant number of the psychopaths we interviewed spoke with veneration of their father. The Belgian psychoanalyst and psychiatrist Léon Cassiers has made some interesting statements from a structural point of view that will guide us in the exploration of this problem.[33] His central proposition is *that the psychopath puts into question the legitimacy of the lack that is created by the Symbolic order.* He points out that the Oedipus complex of the psychopath is characterized by an ambiguous discourse on the side of the mother: on the one hand she recognizes the Law, but on the other hand she considers its representant in the family, the father, as being capricious and violent. The Law is adopted by the psychopath, not foreclosed, and separates the child from the mother. But at the same time the Law cannot function as a safeguard, because its point of reference has a threatening quality. As a consequence, the psychopath's strategy will consist of denouncing the legitimacy of the Law and the lack it entails through cunning or through force.

In our discussion of Cassiers, we want to stress that violence may not be confused with aggression. Colette Soler makes the distinction between different kinds of violence.[34] First there is the violence that consists in a transgression of the Law. This violence often takes the form of aggression: physical or sexual aggression, neglect of children, bullying, criminality, etc. Second, there is a form of violence that marks the establishment of a Law, and more generally a social discourse. The violence here lies in the fact that the establishment of a social discourse – as democratic as it can be – requires the subjection of the individual to a given order. In order to obtain a position in the discourse, the individual has to assent to certain norms and ideals and he has to pay the price of his freedom. This second kind of violence is also present in the Oedipus complex: the passage from the dual relation with the mother towards the triangular structure of the Oedipus complex is marked by alienation and castration.

Returning to Cassiers, we claim that the Oedipus complex of the neurotic does not differ that much from the Oedipus complex of the psychopath, since they are both marked by the second kind of violence. However, the difference lies in the way the father handles the violence that is structurally implied in the establishment of the Law. In the neurotic, the violence of the Law is obscured by the desire of the father. The neurotic's father can be divided into a Symbolic father and a Real father.[35] The Symbolic father is the father in as much as he fulfils his function as referent to the Law, while the Real father is the man of flesh and blood. The Real father does not coincide with the Symbolic father: referring to the Law is a function he fulfils, a job that he does. Moreover, the Real father is himself subjected to the Law he refers to. Besides this function, he is also a subject of desire – a desire in which the mother somehow plays a role. In other words, the father himself is not all Law, he is divided between Law and desire and is marked by a lack. In as much as the father ties together Law and desire, he obscures the fact that the Law is based on violence.

Characteristic for the psychopath's Oedipus complex is the absence of a tie between Law and desire. Several psychoanalytic authors have described the typical familial constellation in which psychopathy emerges. Greenacre was the first to describe the typical situation of 'a stern, respected, and often obsessional father who is remote, preoccupied, and fear-inspiring in relation to his children; and an indulgent, pleasure-loving, frequently pretty but frivolous mother who is often tacitly contemptuous of her husband's importance'.[36] Lacan also refers to the psychopath's father as being *le monstre sacré:* 'They are often characters strongly marked by a style of radiance and success, but in a unilateral manner, in the register of unbridled ambition or authoritarianism, sometimes of talent, of genius. They don't necessarily have to be a genius, have merit, or be mediocre or nasty, it's sufficient that this be unilateral and monstrous'.[37] In our own research we find this typical constellation (indulging mother–idealized father) in a sufficient enough proportion of the sample interviewed for it not to be coincidental. In structural terms this constellation consists of a father who, himself not being subjected to the Law, applies the Law to his own liking and as a means of dominating the Other, rather than a means to gain recognition and love from the Other. This father is not marked by the lack, so the mother does not function as an object *a*, cause of desire, for the father. Since the structural violence implied in the establishment of the Law is not hidden by desire, as in the neurotic, the violent and threatening dimension of it remains all too evident. Therefore, for the psychopath the Law is based on violence instead of desire. The Law functions in a contradictory way in the psychopath: he will refer to the Law, *but the Law will always have an illegitimate character to him because it is based on violence.*[38]

When a psychopath is asked about his ethical viewpoints, he will not hesitate to invoke great principles such as Politeness (as one psychopath said, 'politeness goes a long way') or Tolerance (as another claimed, 'I think you must accept everyone the way they are'). However, in the larger scope of their lives, these principles seem rather virtual than real. The sincerity with which these principles are invoked contrasts strongly with the lack of impact they have on their actions. A similar contradiction can be observed when they speak about their criminal actions. The psychopath will present his criminal action as a righteous one or even as a moral obligation. For instance one psychopathic drug dealer claimed that to him 'dealing drugs was a matter of conscience'. He added that he was addressing the demands of the market, so he was right to do so. These statements are not just *a posteriori* justifications of behaviour. They testify to the psychopath's *a priori* conviction that something illegitimate has happened to him and that he has the right, and even the obligation, to correct this initial injustice. This injustice is the lack that the subject has to bear once he identifies with the Law.

This *a priori* feeling of entitlement reminds us of those who declare themselves to be the 'exceptions'.[39] Freud refers to people who feel exempt from the most common rules and obligations, and who refuse to be subjected to the general displeasures of life. When asked to make a temporary sacrifice for the sake of a better end, they affirm that they have renounced enough, suffered enough and have a claim to be spared any further demands. This typical relation towards the Law and the lack is 'connected with some experience or suffering to which they had been subjected in their earliest childhood, one in respect of which they knew themselves to be guiltless, and which they could look upon as an unjust disadvantage imposed upon them'.[40]

It seems that the psychopath is caught in a double and contradictory movement: the movement in which he identifies with the Law will confront him with the illegitimate nature of the lack, and in order to correct this illegitimacy he has to break the Law and retract the lack (e.g., by stealing or swindling the object from the Other). To the psychopath, invoking and breaking the Law are part of one reality and the psychopath is blind to this contradiction. The contrast with perversion can be made at this point, since the pervert lives in two split realities: one in which the lack and the regulating Law are recognized and another where the lack is disavowed and a new Law is installed.

This contradiction is also notable in the speech of the psychopath. A detailed study of video-tapes and interviews with psychopaths revealed that the narratives of psychopaths contain more negations, contradictory statements, fewer cohesive ties, frequent skipping from topic to topic, and plots that are less likely to be resolved.[41] In our experience this is the typical defensive style of the psychopath, and we suggest coining it as *retraction* in order to differentiate it from neurotic repression and perverse disavowal. It appears that psychopaths frequently use retractors,[42] i.e., a word, phrase, or clause which detracts from the statement preceding it. Freud denoted a similar mechanism, namely kettle-logic in his book about *Jokes and their relation to the unconscious.*[43] This logic goes as follows. A. borrowed a copper kettle from B., and after he had returned it, was sued by B. because the kettle now had a big hole in it which made it unusable. A's defence was: 'First, I never borrowed a kettle from B. at all; secondly, the kettle had a hole in it already when I got it from him; and thirdly, I gave him back the kettle undamaged.' Each of these defences is valid in itself, but taken together they exclude one another.

Let's take two examples, one from Rieber and Vetter,[44] and another from our own research project:

> *Example 1.* 'John is an honest person. Of course, he has been involved in some shady deals!'
> *Example 2* is a fragment of an interrogation of a man who provided the weapon for a murder. After admitting that he gave the killer a weapon, he claimed to be ignorant about its purpose: 'I assure you that I never knew that this weapon would be used for the murder. I would never provide a weapon that is to be used for a murder, and even if I did, I would never give a pistol but a revolver: a revolver never jams and doesn't throw out a shell.'

In these examples, the psychopath is unable to perceive the contradiction in his statement. This inability has nothing to do with lack of intelligence. (The man from the second example had an IQ of about 130.) Rather, it seems that the psychopath identifies with the first part of the statement (in example 1 about honesty; in example 2 about moral objections to deliver a weapon for a murder) enough to place himself in that position (example 1, the position of honesty; example 2, the position of good intentions). The fact that he occupies this position makes it impossible for him to see that the second part of his statement corresponds to a different position (example 1, shady deals; example 2, delivering an efficient murder weapon). The signifier corresponding to the first position is juxtaposed to the signifier corresponding to the second position, without dialectical relation. The psychopath identifies completely with the first signifier, pretends to correspond with it, so the signifiers that follow are arbitrary or even contradictory: *ex falso sequitur quod libet*. We consider this way of operating the chain of signifiers a mode of defence. The selective identification with one signifier without dialectification through a second signifier preserves the psychopath from the confrontation with the illegitimate and threatening gap between the signifiers.[45]

However, this lack of dialectical relation between signifiers makes it impossible for the psychopath to express a desire through signifiers, since desire resides precisely in the gap signifiers. It is the neurotic's dividedness between a first and a second signifier that allows him to express a desire in signifiers addressed to the Other. The psychopath does not seem to be marked by this division and is unable to assume the position of a subject of desire.

The inability to take the position as a subject of desire also means the inability to take responsibility, because responsibility refers to the degree to which one assumes one's own desire. Indeed, the psychopath can admit what he did, but at the same time he is unable to acknowledge the true nature of his act, his intention to do it and the consequences of his act. He will invoke circumstances, coincidence, and provocation by the victim, etc., all to avoid the idea that he, as a subject, stands at the origin of the act.

Take for instance the following fragment from a psychopath who was convicted of robbery and murder. He admitted to the murder, but described it as an accident:

> *Interviewee.* I think he [the future victim] had seen a shadow, because he yelled 'Is anybody there?' while entering. So I stood behind the wall and thought: I will surprise him, he will run away, so we [he and his two companions] can escape. As I jump up in front of him, he yells, 'Hmmm, you bastard!' [imitates the yell of the victim] and grabs me. You know, I have much respect for that, and if someone broke into my house, I think I would have the same reaction. I think that this man's mentality was so young in his mind that he did not know any better ... He grabs me, I panic at that moment and we enter a struggle in which he trips over my shoes. He pulls me along in his fall, and in that fall I make a swinging move. Now, I myself can believe what I tell you – although you might look at it in an objective way – but nobody else believes what I say now. And I understand that, because it is not very credible when they find a corpse with a hammer stuck in its head. Nonetheless, this man pulls me down, and I make a swinging move in order to keep my balance. When I get back up, I see that my hammer stuck in his skull and everywhere was blood.

Interviewer. So there was only one blow? [I knew that the coroner had counted thirteen blows.]
Interviewee. No, that's another thing. [Irritated.] Of course, according to the court, the definition of a blow is rather unclear. That man grabbed me, in a state of panic we shove around, left and right, and he got small cuts on his head. They counted nine of those cuts. Excuse me, but according to me those are not blows. A blow from a hammer is something completely different from little cuts from a fight. But I leave aside the forensic evidence. At the time of my trial, I made a forensic enumeration of all possible angles and bloodstain patterns and how they didn't accord with what the prosecutor would say, but my lawyers told me: 'Don't do it, because if you do, the jury will think that you want to talk yourself out of it.' And that was not what I wanted, because I am guilty.

Notice the retraction in his attitude towards the victim ('much respect' versus 'this man's mentality was so young'), and the psychopath's relative freedom to change the meaning of the words 'blow' and 'guilt'.

The psychopath's inability to endure the division between signifiers has important consequences on the development of identity and the psychopath's relation towards the lack of the Other. The psychopath does not have the ability to develop an identity through the concatenation of signifiers. The possibility of depression is always present. Furthermore, unable to bear his own lack, the psychopath will not tolerate the lack of the Other, either. At this point anxiety can arise. We will develop these two points.

First, the development of identity. The psychopath is structurally inclined to narcissism. Unable to define himself as a particular subject, different from all others, he presents himself as exceptional, better than all others. Here again, the psychopath reminds us of the character type described by Freud as the 'exception', because, independent from any real achievement, he thinks very highly of himself, resulting in the magnification or even the invention of his virtues.[46] They may identify with 'very "high" ideals' that are 'especially expansive, and utterly detached from reality'[47] but they might also turn to external reality to gratify their narcissism.[48] However, this narcissism is only a makeshift for his inability to apply the dialectical operation of signifiers that is required for identity formation.

An important part of identity formation is the installation of an Ego-ideal. The Ego-ideal is a signifier that organizes the subject's position in the Symbolic order and forms an important part of his conscience. This signifier contains the promise of the possibility to neutralize the division of the subject between Law and desire: when the subject lives up to the expectations of the Other, he will gain recognition and even love of the Other. Of course, no neurotic ever completely complies with the ideals, but the tendency towards them is more or less present. In the psychopath the Ego-ideal does not function at all. This is obvious from his lack of conscience.[49] However, this also means that the psychopath lacks the possibility to gain recognition and love of the Other by living up to certain standards and ideals. The psychopath will often complain about this, in a sense that he feels misunderstood and mistreated. The psychopath has no other possibility to gain recognition and love than by manipulation or force. Here we see two typical figures of the psychopath: those who gain respect by being 'strong personalities', ruthless, uncompromising and dominant, and those who gain love by sweet-talk, charm, and pitiful drama. However, when they succeed social recognition will not lead to personal dignity and love will not lead to mutual engagement.

In the case where these strategies fail, the psychopath finds himself in a difficult situation. Here depression can arise, with most of the symptoms we meet in neurotic depression. However, one symptom is always absent, notably a lack of self-esteem and self-reproach. The depressive psychopath is demanding, dominant, moaning, peevish, manipulative and often violent. A suicidal gesture cannot be excluded. Suicide often appears very impulsive and without the typical neurotic fantasy about the reaction of the Other ('Will they miss me?'). One psychopath claimed that suicidal thoughts did come up once in a while, but just as a sudden thought that stayed only for a few seconds. In the following fragment another psychopath comments on his suicide attempt:

> *Interviewer.* In that depressive period, were you often thinking about death, or making a plan to commit suicide?
> *Interviewee.* No, it was all of a sudden. I stopped taking my medication, I was tired of it, and I always put the pills aside. Then all of a sudden I made the decision. There was no plan … I just wanted to stop medication because I felt bad about it. But I kept on receiving my pills, and I saved them. No, I just put them aside, not to save them. I put them in a box. In the evening, while going to my closet, I saw them and I thought: why not? No, I didn't reflect on it one single moment. If there would have been a revolver, I just would have put it to my head. I didn't think about the fact that I would leave behind my mother and my daughter. I just said: why not? No farewell note, nothing.

The negations and the retractions in this fragment all concern the question why he kept his medication. It seems impossible for him to conceive of his death wish, just as the earlier cited murderer was unable to conceive of his intention to kill.

Second, the relation towards the lack of the Other. To the psychopath, the father must seem like a fraud and an imposture: the father claims to incorporate something that he cannot incorporate, he takes a position that cannot be the position of a subject, so he must be a fraud. The neurotic considers the lack of the Other as legitimate and he feels obliged to it. The hysteric and the obsessional subject each try to fill in the lack of the Other in their own way: respectively by identifying with the Other's phallic desire and by offering phallic objects.[50] The psychopath, however, will not accept the lack of the Other because it refers to violence. The psychopath cannot think of the lack of the father in terms of his cause of desire (the mother), he thinks of it in terms of deceit. This will be the basic attitude of the psychopath towards the Other: the lack of the Other is a fraud. Any demand the Other addresses to him is therefore considered illegitimate.

During the interviews we conducted, we found this attitude over and again in the psychopath's attitude towards his victims. Consider the following fragment in which a swindler talks about having conned his girlfriend, and others:

> *Interviewer.* Do you find it embarrassing towards your girlfriend that you conned her?
> *Interviewee.* No, I have little problem with emotions.
> *Interviewer.* So you do not feel ashamed or guilty?
> *Interviewee.* No, my sense of guilt is very small, or in fact … nil. … I never feel guilty about financial scams because you cannot con someone who has got no money. Those who have no money are impossible to con. The people I con are themselves so greedy that they are looking for more on a very short term. This is something that is normally impossible. Therefore, these people are not honest with themselves. So I have no problems afterwards. When I put up a fraudulent system and a foolish peasant is willing to invest €400,000 in an illegal system … I put this money in my pocket and don't bring it back and I disappear with €400,000. Once I step into my car I forget about this peasant.
> *Interviewer.* So in fact you misuse the greed of other people?
> *Interviewee.* Yes, that's the definition of fraud.

The psychopath is unable to interpret the motives of others in terms of lack and desire. This results in a basic distrust and suspicion towards the motives of other people. During the research project we conducted, we frequently encountered psychopaths who reported feeling distrustful under the gaze of the Other. However, this distrust does not develop into shame or social phobia as in the neurotic. Rather, it tends to result in periods of social withdrawal, fugues and paranoid ideation. Several psychopaths reported that the use of a narcissistically invested object such as beautiful women or an impressive car made them feel more at ease in the interaction with others. Others maintain a 'close' relation with their indulgent mother or girlfriend, who demonstrates astonishing endurance towards the caprices of their child/partner: she has no Demand towards him. Others grow old in solitude.

Conclusion: law and evil

Our main argument in this chapter is that psychopathy and perversion are two distinguishable clinical diagnoses, each of which has relevance within the forensic field. In perversion the partial drives are elaborated into a fixated sexual praxis in which the castration of the first Other is disavowed. In psychopathy, however, sexual praxis is marked not by a specific phantasmatic structure but by opportunism and absence of emotional attachment. While the pervert structure is primarily organized in relation to the first Other (i.e., the subject's relation to *jouissance*), psychopathy demonstrates a particular organization in relation to the second Other (i.e., the subject's relation to authority). In psychopathy the father's authority is founded on violence rather than on desire, so the Law and the lack have an illegitimate and threatening statute. The psychopath's mode of defence is *retraction*, by which he identifies with the Law or a given signifier and at the same time denounces its legitimacy. In the forensic clinic, this results in different attitudes towards crime. The pervert sexual offender is unable to assume responsibility due to the belief that he sacrifices himself for the Other's enjoyment. The psychopath, on the other hand, is unable to assume responsibility because he feels *a priori* justified in his actions.

Once the difference between psychopathy and perversion is made, many new questions arise. The first question is how psychopathy should be considered in relation to the three structures of classical psychiatry: neurosis, perversion, and psychosis. Is psychopathy a fourth structure? Can we speak of a psychopathic subject in the same way we speak of a pervert subject? In this chapter we substantiated that psychopathy differs fundamentally from the structure of perversion. Another important question is the differential diagnosis between psychopathy and psychosis, which in some cases requires a sophisticated clinical approach.[51] Although we did not pay attention to this question, we join the long-established consensus in psychiatry that psychopathy and psychosis are separate diagnoses.[52] During the historical development of the concept, psychopathy has scarcely been connected with psychosis, and more frequently with neurosis.

Based on our analysis of the psychopath's relation towards the Other, we are inclined to see some correspondence with the neurotic structure. In common with the neurotic, the psychopath is not the object of the mother's desire because he identified with the Symbolic father. However, the differences lie in the way the psychopath's father appears in the Oedipus complex, in the way the psychopath relates to the Symbolic order, and in the way the psychopath handles the lack. Therefore it can be argued that psychopathy is a different structure, a fourth structure, next to neurosis, perversion, and psychosis. The conceptual benefit of having this clear-cut distinction would be to reduce the risk of confusion between neurosis and psychopathy. One of the main reasons why the concept of psychopathy became outdated in Continental psychiatry was precisely the lack of differentiation between neurosis and psychopathy: psychopathy was often used as a generic term to designate the broad area of psychopathology that floats between clear madness and normality.[53]

A clear demarcation between psychopathy and neurosis would also have the benefit of making it evident that the treatment model for neurosis should not be transposed unaltered to the treatment of psychopathy. Although conclusions are advanced with caution, the general consensus is that the traditional treatment programmes for offenders are not suitable for psychopathy.[54] Although Wong and Hare proposed guidelines for the treatment of psychopaths, they affirm that the goal of this treatment is damage control, and not changing the personality: 'it is unrealistic to try to effect fundamental changes in the psychopath's personality structure'.[55] In our understanding, these words echo Freud's repeated statement that a reliable character is necessary for psychoanalytic treatment: 'Deep-rooted malformations of character [*Ausgeprägte Charakterverbildungen*], traits of an actually degenerate constitution, show themselves during treatment as sources of a resistance that can scarcely be overcome'.[56] In his paper *On narcissism* Freud even acknowledges narcissism as a limit in the treatment of neurotics: 'it seemed as though this kind of narcissistic attitude in [neurotic patients] constituted one of the limits to their susceptibility to influence'.[57]

In contrast to this pessimism, Lösel and Schmucker found very reassuring evidence for the treatment of sexual offenders.[58] In a meta-analysis involving 22,181 sexual offenders, they found that treatment succeeded in reducing sexual recidivism by 37 per cent in comparison with sexual offenders who receive no treatment. This reassuring conclusion might inspire optimism about the treatment of perversion.[59] The diagnostic confusion between psychopathy and perversion might have made some psychoanalysts conclude that perversion is untreatable, while in fact it is psychopathy that is untreatable.

Notes

1 Sigmund Freud, 'Three essays on the theory of sexuality', *The Standard Edition of the Complete Psychological Works of Sigmund Freud* VII, trans. and ed. James Strachey, London: Hogarth Press, 1978 [1905], pp. 171–2, p. 231.

2 This is why the question of perversion has to be reformulated. Not, why did someone become perverse? But, why didn't we all remain perverse? Freud's answer is well known: the Oedipus complex is the developmental phase that takes care of normalization. The combination of somatic immaturity of the genitals and anxiety about the father causes the child to take its distance from its pre-genital desire for the mother and identify with the normative image presented by the father. Later, with the somatic maturity of puberty, the child will address itself to other others. At that point, the early pre-genital drives will be submitted to the genital drive as such and reduced to what precedes coitus.

3 Henry Werlinder, *Psychopathy. A History of the Concepts*, Stockholm: Uppsala Universitet, 1978.

4 David T. Lykken, 'Psychopathic personality. The scope of the problem', in Christopher J. Patrick (ed.), *Handbook of Psychopathy*, New York: Guilford Press, 2006.

5 In this text, we will not pay attention to the diagnostic problem in differentiating psychosis and psychopathy. Interesting clinical remarks on this topic are made by

Hervey Milton Cleckley, *The Mask of Sanity*, St Louis, MO: Mosby, 1976; Helene Deutsch, 'The impostor. Contribution to Ego psychology of a type of psychopath', in J. R. Meloy (ed.), *The Mark of Cain. Psychoanalytic Insight and the Psychopath*, Hillsdale, NJ: Analytic Press, 2001; and in the case study of F. Declercq, M. Vandenbroucke, and I. Storme, 'Un cas « mixte » de meurtre sexuel sadique avec incendie criminel nocturne. Psychopathie ou psychose?' *Annales Médico-psychologiques*, 166, 2008.

6 Cleckley, *The Mask of Sanity*.

7 Robert D. Hare, *Manual for the Revised Psychopathy Checklist*, Toronto, ON: Multi-health Systems, 2003.

8 Robert D. Hare, Danny Clark, Martin Grann, and David Thornton, 'Psychopathy and the predictive validity of the PCL-R. An international perspective', *Behavioral Sciences and the Law*, 18, 2000, pp. 623–45.

9 All cases of psychopathy cited in this chapter have a score on the PCL-R of 30 or more in order to have clear-cut examples.

10 John Monahan, on the cover of Christopher J. Patrick (ed.), *Handbook of Psychopathy*, New York: Guilford Press, 2006.

11 Karl Abraham, 'The history of an impostor in the light of psychoanalytical knowledge', *Psychoanalytic Quarterly*, 4, 1935 [1925], pp. 570–87.

12 In field research on sadomasochism, Weinberg et al. found that the contract of the pervert forms an obstacle for criminal behaviour. Although 'pushing the limits' was an acceptable violation of the original contract, transgression of the rules was not. One homosexual man involved in sadomasochism said, 'Once in a while there is a top who really wants to hurt someone. Word gets around and no one goes near him.' Martin S. Weinberg, Colin J. Williams, and Charles Moser, 'The social constituents of sadomasochism', *Social Problems*, 31, 1984, pp. 379–89, p. 386. This might explain why few if any sadomasochists are found in jail.

13 Freud, 'Three essays on the theory of sexuality'.

14 Jacques Lacan, *The Seminar of Jacques Lacan* XI, *1964, The Four Fundamental Concepts of Psycho-analysis*, trans. Alain Sheridan, London: Vintage, 1998, pp. 42–53.

15 Tony Ward and Thomas Keenan, 'Child molesters' implicit theories', *Journal of Interpersonal Violence*, 14, 1999, pp. 141–57.

16 Ibid.

17 E.g. Stephen Porter, Angela R. Birt, and Douglas P. Boer, 'Investigation of the criminal and conditional release profiles of Canadian federal offenders as a function of psychopathy and age', *Law and Human Behavior*, 25, 2001, pp. 647–61; Michael Woodworth, and Stephen Porter, 'In cold blood. Characteristics of criminal homicides as a function of psychopathy', *Journal of Abnormal Psychology*, 111, 2002, pp. 436–45.

18 Phyllis Greenacre, 'Conscience in the psychopath', in J. R. Meloy (ed.), *The Mark of Cain. Psychoanalytic Insight and the Psychopath*, Hillsdale, NJ: Analytic Press, 2001, p. 364.

19 Porter et al., 'Investigation of the criminal'.

20 Cleckley, *The Mask of Sanity*, p. 359.

21 Ibid.

22 Paul Verhaeghe, *On being Normal and other Disorders. A Manual for Clinical Psychodiagnostics*, New York: Other Press, 2004.

23 Elisabeth Badinter, *L'Amour en plus. Histoire de l'amour maternel XVIIe–XXe siècle*, Paris: Flammarion, 1980; Estela Welldon, *Mother, Madonna, Whore. The Idealization and Denigration of Motherhood*, New York: Guilford Press, 1998; E. Welldon, 'Female perversion and hysteria', *British Journal of Psychotherapy*, 3,

1995, pp. 406–14; Estela Welldon, 'Contrasts in male and female perversions', in C. Cordess and M. Cox (eds), *Forensic Psychotherapy*, London: Jessica Kingsley, 1996; Anna Motz, *The Psychology of Female Violence. Crimes against the Body*, Hove: Brunner Routledge, 2001.

24 Tony Ward, Stephen M. Hudson, William L. Marshall, and R. Siegert, 'Attachment style and intimacy deficits in sex offenders. A theoretical framework', *Sexual Abuse. A Journal of Research and Treatment*, 7, 1995, pp. 317–55; Stephen Smallbone and Mark R. Dadds, 'Childhood attachment and adult attachment in incarcerated adult male sex offenders', *Journal of Interpersonal Violence*, 13, 2004, pp. 555–73.

25 'This creates in the perverse person the deep belief that she is not a whole being, but her mother's part-object, just as she experienced her mother when she was a very young infant.' Welldon, *Mother*, p. 9.

26 Lacan expresses it as follows: 'The whole problem of the perversions consists in conceiving how the child, in its relationship with its mother – a relationship that is constituted in analysis not by the child's biological dependence, but by its dependence on her love, that is, by its desire for her desire – identifies with the imaginary object of her desire in so far as the mother herself symbolizes it in the phallus.' Jacques Lacan, 'On a question prior to any possible treatment of psychosis', trans. Bruce Fink, in *Ecrits*, New York and London: Norton, 2006. See also Serge André, *L'Imposture perverse*, Paris: Seuil, 1993.

27 This forms the basis for what are today called 'cognitive distortions'. Kurt M. Bumby, 'Assessing the cognitive distortions of child molesters and rapists. Development and validation of the MOLEST and RAPE scales', *Sexual Abuse. A Journal of Research and Treatment*, 8, 1996, pp. 37–54. These distortions are assumed to comprise part of the aetiology and, moreover, to sustain the continuation of perverse behaviour. L. Stermac and S. Segal, 'Adult sexual contact with children. An examination of cognitive factors', *Behavior Therapy*, 20, 1989, pp. 573–84. In the cognitive-behavioural approach, it is now accepted that these distortions contain basic *unconscious* convictions. Dan Van Beek and Jules Mulder, 'De rol van cognitieve vervormingen in het plegen van pedoseksuele delicten en hun plaats in de behandeling', *Tijdschrift voor seksuologie*, 26, 2002, pp. 79–86. From our perspective, such 'cognitions' are taken over during subject formation through the mother's perverse mirroring. The most important subsequent 'distortion' in perversion is that the other enjoys the scenario, with the pervert as the instrument of this enjoyment – this is the kernel of the perverse subject formation.

28 Verhaeghe, *On being Normal and other Disorders*, pp. 351 ff.

29 Sigmund Freud, 'Fetishism', *The Standard Edition of the Complete Psychological Works of Sigmund Freud* XXI, trans. and ed. James Strachey, London: Hogarth Press, 1978 [1927].

30 'Perversion adds a recuperation of the Φ that would scarcely appear original if it didn't interest the Other as such in a very particular way. It is only my formulation of fantasy that enables one to see here how the subject makes itself the instrument of the Other's *jouissance*.' Jacques Lacan, 'The subversion of the subject and the dialectic of desire in the Freudian unconscious', trans. Bruce Fink, in *Ecrits*, New York and London: Norton, 2006, p. 697.

31 Gordon Hall, 'Sexual offender recidivism revisited. A meta-analysis of recent treatment studies', *Journal of Consulting and Clinical Psychology*, 63, 1995, pp. 802–9; H. Kennedy and D. Grubin, 'Patterns of denial in sex offenders', *Psychological Medicine*, 22, 1992, pp. 191–6; Tony Ward, Stephen M. Hudson, Lucy Johnston, and William Marshall, 'Cognitive distortions in sex offenders. An integrative review', *Clinical Psychology Review*, 17, 1997, pp. 479–507.

32 Judith Feher-Gurewich, 'The philanthropy of perversion', in J.-M. Rabaté (ed.), *Lacan in America*, New York: Other Press, 2002.
33 Léon Cassiers, 'Psychopathie et légitimité de la castration symbolique', *Topique. Revue freudienne*, 16, 1975, pp. 65–79.
34 Colette Soler, 'Je vous dirai le titre à la fin', paper presented at I colloque de psychanalyse de l'Association des Forums du Champ Lacanien de Wallonie (Belgique), 2003, online: www.lacanw.be/archives/violence/030503%20Je%20vous %20dirai%20le%20titre%20a%20la%20fin … %20(C.%20Soler).pdf.
35 Jacques Lacan, *Le Séminaire* IV, *1956–1957, La Relation d'objet*, Paris: Seuil, 1994.
36 Greenacre, 'Conscience in the psychopath', p. 48.
37 Jacques Lacan, *The Seminar of Jacques Lacan* III, *1955–1956, The Psychoses*, trans. Russel Grigg, London: Routledge, 1993, pp. 204.
38 Cassiers, 'Psychopathie et légitimité de la castration symbolique'.
39 Sigmund Freud, 'Some character-types met with in psycho-analytic work', *The Standard Edition of the Complete Psychological Works of Sigmund Freud* XIV, trans. and ed. James Strachey, London: Hogarth Press, 1978 [1916].
40 Ibid., p. 313.
41 S. E. Williamson, 'Cohesion and Coherence in the Speech of Psychopathic Criminals (Communication Disorders)', unpublished doctoral dissertation, Vancouver: University of British Columbia; Chad A. Brinkley, Amit Bernstein, and Joseph P. Newman, 'Coherence in the narratives of psychopathic and non-psychopathic criminal offenders', *Personality and Individual Differences*, 27, 1999, pp. 519–30; Chad A. Brinkley, Joseph P. Newman, T. J. Harpur, and M. M. Johnson, 'Cohesion in texts produced by psychopathic and nonpsychopathic criminal inmates', *Personality and Individual Differences*, 26, 1999, pp. 873–85.
42 R. W. Rieber and Harold Vetter, 'The language of the psychopath', *Journal of Psycholinguistic Research*, 23, 1994, pp. 1–28.
43 Sigmund Freud, 'Jokes and their relation to the unconscious', *The Standard Edition of the Complete Psychological Works of Sigmund Freud* VIII, trans. and ed. James Strachey, London: Hogarth Press, 1975 [1905].
44 Rieber and Vetter, 'The language of the psychopath'.
45 This identification is not to be confused with the 'as if' identification in psychosis. Helene Deutsch (Deutsch, 'The impostor') addressed this question and noted two differences. First, the psychopath identifies only with objects which correspond to his Ego-ideal. While the 'as if' personality searches for a stable but often dull object of identification (e.g., housewife, factory worker), the psychopath especially searches for identifications that mark his grandiosity. Second, the 'as if' personality is not aware of his disturbance, while the psychopath, firmly pretending that he is what he pretends to be (e.g., a successful salesman), knows that he does not correspond with it. When he gets exposed, he laughs it away.
46 Freud, 'Some character-types met with in psycho-analytic work'.
47 Greenacre, 'Conscience in the psychopath'.
48 Deutsch, 'The impostor'.
49 The psychopath and the neurotic live in a different time frame. The intermingling of past, present, and future that is introduced into the life of the neurotic by the Ego-ideal ('When you will have lived up to these standards and reached these goals, you will be … ') is completely absent in the life of the psychopath. Indeed, the psychopath never feels encumbered by unfavourable circumstances (e.g., being in prison). One of their typical expressions goes like this: 'I'm an optimist. I don't look back to the past, I always look into the future.' Of course, this is not true: the psychopath does not look into the future, he does not make many mid

to long-term plans; he is guided by the spur of the moment and does not possess the determination and patience to realize goals in life.

50 Verhaeghe, *On being Normal and other Disorders.*

51 Declercq et al., 'Un cas « mixte » de meurtre sexuel sadique'.

52 Werlinder, *Psychopathy.*

53 Ibid.

54 Robert D. Hare, 'Psychopathy. A clinical and forensic overview', *Psychiatric Clinics of North America*, 29, 2006, pp. 709–24.

55 Stephen Wong and Robert D. Hare, *Guidelines for a Psychopathy Treatment Program*, Toronto, ON: Multi-health Systems, 2005, p. 10.

56 Sigmund Freud, 'Freud's psycho-analytic procedure', *The Standard Edition of the Complete Psychological Works of Sigmund Freud* VII, trans. and ed. James Strachey, London: Hogarth Press, 1975 [1904], p. 254.

57 Sigmund Freud, 'On narcissism. An introduction', *The Standard Edition of the Complete Psychological Works of Sigmund Freud* XIV, trans. and ed. James Strachey, London: Hogarth Press, 1978 [1914], p. 73.

58 Friedrich Lösel and Martin Schmucker, 'The effectiveness of treatment for sexual offenders. A comprehensive meta-analysis', *Journal of Experimental Criminology*, 1, 2005, pp. 117–46.

59 See also the case study of Franco De Masi, 'The paedophile and his inner world. Theoretical and clinical considerations on the analysis of a patient', *International Journal of Psychoanalysis*, 88, 2007, pp. 147–65.

Chapter 14

'That which in life might prefer death ... '

From the death drive to the desire of the analyst

Véronique Voruz

> What the analyst has to give, unlike the partner in the act of love, is something that even the most beautiful bride in the world cannot outmatch, that is to say, what he has. And what he has is nothing other than his desire, like that of the analysand, with the difference that it is an experienced desire.
>
> Jacques Lacan[1]

From the death drive to the desire of the analyst: the title of this chapter names the trajectory of the formation of an analyst. The formation of the analyst must include the metamorphosis accomplished in the analytic experience – from *that which in life might prefer death* to a pacified subjective position indexed on the symptom, condition of possibility of the desire of the analyst.[2]

Freud may have invented the concepts necessary to structure the analytic process, but Lacan is the one who truly elaborated the question of the formation of the analyst;[3] and he did so in the very terms elicited by the analytic experience. With Lacan, the formation and definition of the analyst differ radically from the practice of other human institutions. Lacan's pragmatic reflection on what constitutes a 'good' analyst, and on the ways in which the position of a given subject as analyst could be 'guaranteed', impelled him to produce a series of extremely lucid developments on the love of one's neighbour, ethics and desire.[4] His rigorous analyses fundamentally reinterpreted – and so irreversibly displaced – the age-old philosophical questions of self, morality, conscience and responsibility.

This chapter will map a few of these displacements in the perspective chosen by Lacan himself: that of the possibility of 'guaranteeing' something of the position of the analyst through the analytic experience itself, and not through an empty reference to the Other of knowledge, of Law or social institutions. The first step on this journey starts from the Freudian invention of the concept of the death drive, initially as a tendency towards inorganicity. Rapidly, Freud deployed his concept to also account for the will to destruction (of self or other) in civilization – or *evil*. Lacan drew the consequences of Freud's once scandalous claim – that 'delight in evil'[5] is not the privilege of perverts – for the position of the analyst: if the paramount concern of human life is to secure appropriate pathways for drive satisfaction (*jouissance*),[6] how can anyone be entrusted with the position of analyst? It is in order to extract analytic practice from this conundrum that Lacan turned to Kant, and so formulated his first – and now axiomatic – ethical principle: not to give up on one's desire.[7] In 'Kant with Sade' Lacan pursues the reasoning initiated in *Seminar VII* and provokingly affirms the complementarity of Kant's and Sade's positions: both are structured on the model of a universal absolute, both extol the beyond of the pleasure principle, and the one reveals the truth of the other. In this fundamental – if mystifying – text Lacan also reveals the obscene jouissance of the object-voice enduring beyond the formalist screen of the Kantian moral law. In this respect, 'Kant with Sade' is Lacan's 'de-Oedipalized' response to Freud's discreet intimation[8] of a direct relationship between the categorical imperative and the superego. Since the universal is structurally superegoic, Lacan seeks to counterpoise the ethics of psychoanalysis to all universal absolutes. In the analytic process the subject encounters the possibility of isolating the 'axiom' of his or her own *singular* jouissance – or the fantasy:[9] the 'universal' law of one's singularity. The chapter will close with an assessment of Lacan's successive conceptualizations of the end of analysis, which he consistently used as a compass for his theorization of an ethics of psychoanalysis.

The death drive – a Freudian name for 'evil'

> [T]he field of Das Ding is rediscovered at the end, and ... Freud suggests there that which in life might prefer death. And it is along this path that he comes closer than anyone else to the problem of evil or, more precisely, to the project of evil as such.[10]

Despite its mythical name of *Thanatos*, despite being, in Lacan's words, a notion which is 'very suspect in itself',[11] the death drive is the first concept to name something of 'evil' without resorting to the mystical, the religious, the demonic or the otherworldly[12] – tautological causalities that substantiate phantasmatic interpretations of the Other as malevolent. In naming the death drive – in naming what, precisely, resists nomination in so far as it is not fully of the order of language – Freud also began circumscribing a hitherto secret logic, starting with the fact that, in Lacan's words, there is that which in life might prefer death. This very precise formulation goes straight to the heart of what Freud had to accept at the end of his life – that there exists a form of satisfaction which goes against the grain of the subject's good, perceived in the classical sense of well-being, self-preservation; that the appeal of 'perversions'[13] may be more potent that 'normal genital' love; and that people are undeniably far more attached to such a satisfaction than to pleasure. To this day, Freud's 'metapsychological imagining',[14] his 'creationist sublimation',[15] remains infinitely relevant to understanding the human condition – though Lacan's sober ciphering of the death drive in the formula of the fantasy makes it a less dramatic, more operative concept. For what human institution but psychoanalysis still takes seriously the affirmation that there is happiness in evil/suffering?

Beyond the pleasure principle

What is the pleasure principle, and how does Freud introduce its beyond? A central tenet of Freudian psychoanalysis is that mental life is regulated through the combined operation of the pleasure and reality principles.[16] After Lacan's demonstration in *Seminar VII*, we can assert that 'the opposition between the pleasure principle and the reality principle is not founded … since the latter is merely a modification of the former, destined to ensure its success'.[17] The pleasure principle, whose aim is also furthered by the reality principle, occupies centre-stage in psychoanalytic theory until 1920. In *Beyond the Pleasure Principle* Freud is forced to recognize that there also exists a compulsion powerful enough 'to disregard the pleasure principle'[18] in the mental apparatus. Two phenomena, manifest in the analytic experience, had alerted him to the insistence of something disrupting the regulation of psychic life by the pleasure principle in its homeostatic[19] mission: the negative therapeutic reaction,[20] and repetition-compulsion. These phenomena led Freud to substantially modify his theory of the drives.

Developing his reflection through a series of situations in which people are seen to repeat unpleasurable events – such as traumatic neuroses or the *fort-da* play which repeats the separation from the mother[21] – Freud articulates the following hypothesis: 'we shall find courage to assume that there really does exist in the mind a compulsion to repeat which overrides the pleasure principle'.[22] This leads him to redefine '*an instinct* [as] *an urge inherent in organic life to restore an earlier state of things*'.[23] All instincts therefore tend towards this aim, and the aim of all life is death. Life is an ever-lengthening detour on the way to death.[24] In turn, self-preservation is accounted for by the want to return to inorganic life in the way and state that suits the organism. So death commands the pathways of life: 'the organism wishes to die only in its own fashion'.[25] On the other hand, sexual instincts seek to prolong life, so the dynamic of life arises from the struggle between these two instincts: tendency to inorganicity versus survival of the species via the individual (*Eros*). Later on in the text, Freud supposes that death and life instincts are 'associated from the first',[26] a key point for his subsequent elaboration. Finally, Freud concludes that since the pleasure principle is actually 'a tendency operating in the service of a function whose business it is to free the mental apparatus entirely from excitation',[27] the 'pleasure principle seems actually to serve the death instincts'.[28]

The dualism of the drives: fusion/defusion

Freud's drive theory is consistently dualistic, which is logical, since he situates this dualism as the economic root cause of all psychical conflicts. Freud first divided the drives into 'ego instincts' and sexual libido, and then into ego instincts and object instincts (to account for the libidinal investment of the ego). In *Beyond the Pleasure Principle* he once again reconfigures this supposed dualism to account for the subject's obdurate repetition of unpleasurable experiences, his obscure attachment to his symptoms:

> The opposition between the ego-instincts and the sexual instincts was transformed into one between the ego-instincts and the object instincts, both of a libidinal nature. But in its place a fresh opposition appeared between the libidinal (ego- and object-) instincts and others, which must be presumed to be present in the ego and which may perhaps actually be observed in the destructive instincts. Our speculations have transformed this opposition into one between the life instincts (Eros) and the death instincts.[29]

However, this new dualism is tempered by the theory of the fusion of instincts, which Freud returns to in section IV – entitled 'Two classes of instincts' – of *The Ego and the Id*:

> This hypothesis [of the dualistic answer to the problem of the goal and purpose of life] throws no light whatever upon the manner in which the two classes of instincts are fused, blended, and alloyed with each other, but that this takes place regularly and very extensively is an assumption indispensable to our conception.[30]

By fusing with the libido, the death instinct can be diverted away from the individual and on to the outside world, where it manifests itself as an '*instinct of destruction*'.[31] In this text Freud also suggests that if there is the possibility of fusion, there can also be a 'defusion'.[32] Thus Freud makes of sadism the 'representative'[33] of the death instinct in situations of both fusion and defusion:

> The sadistic component of the sexual instinct would be a classical example of a serviceable instinctual fusion; and the *sadism* which has made itself independent as a perversion would be typical of a defusion, though not of one carried to extremes. ... we perceive that for purposes of discharge the *instinct of destruction* is habitually brought into the service of Eros.[34]

In other words, in a 'normal' individual, Eros and Thanatos are fused in roughly equal proportions: the death drive is integrated in the sexual relation as a sadistic component securing the discharge of the tension that it represents. Sheer sadism, in the form of the instinct of destruction exerted on to another person outside of a sexual relation, would be indicative of a defusion – though not a complete one – between Eros and Thanatos.

A paradoxical satisfaction

One year after *The Ego and the Id*, Freud takes the fusion between life and death instincts to its logical conclusion in *The Economic Problem of Masochism* (1924) – namely, that self-destruction can be 'enjoyable' because discharge of the death drive can be sexualized and so provide a libidinal satisfaction.

This dense, technical text warrants a close reading: not only does it provide Freud's final position on the organizing principles of psychic life; it also develops a fine classification of the various manifestations of masochism – no longer as a mere vicissitude of the drive, but also as accounting for a satisfaction which the subject values over and above his or her own life: in this text, Freud accepts the existence of a primary masochism.[35]

The principles of psychic life

Since it is not possible to understand masochism in terms of the pleasure principle – in instances of masochism, the pleasure principle, supposed watchman over our lives, is paralysed – Freud investigates the relationship of the pleasure principle to life/death instincts. He had previously argued that the principle governing all mental processes was a tendency towards stability, or the 'Nirvana principle',[36] and equated the Nirvana principle with the pleasure principle, stating that it was in the service of the death instincts:[37] its function is to guard against the demands of the life instincts, which 'disturb the peace'. But in *The Economic Problem of Masochism* Freud changes his position, because not all of pleasure and unpleasure can 'be referred to an increase or decrease of a quantity' (as in *Beyond the Pleasure Principle*): thus there can be 'pleasurable tensions and unpleasurable relaxations of tension'.[38] Pleasure and unpleasure depend, 'not on a quantitative factor', but on a relevant qualitative characteristic (e.g. 'rhythm' or 'sequence'). Although the Nirvana principle, 'belonging as it does to the death instinct', may have become the pleasure principle in living organisms, they are not to be regarded as one. And the source of this modification can only be 'the life instinct, the libido, which has thus, alongside of the death instinct, seized upon a share in the regulation of the processes of life'.[39]

As a result, Freud reformulates his psychic principles as follows. 'The *Nirvana* principle expresses the trend of the death instinct' (the aim of which is 'quantitative reduction'); 'the *pleasure* principle represents the demands of the libido' (the aim of which resides in 'the qualitative characteristic of the stimulus'); and the '*reality* principle represents the influence of the external world' (by organizing the 'postponement of discharge').[40] These principles coexist, as they have different aims, but the pleasure principle remains the watchman over our lives. The Nirvana and pleasure principles, respective organizing principles of death and life instincts, are, for most intents and purposes, as one. It is the Oedipus complex that will disturb this 'natural' harmony by prohibiting aggression and inducing a defusion of instincts via the desexualization of the parental figures.

A metapsychological account of masochism

Freud then considers the puzzling phenomenon of masochism, of which he distinguishes three forms: 'as a condition imposed on sexual excitation' or *erotogenic* masochism; 'as an expression of the feminine nature' or *feminine* masochism;[41] and 'as a norm of behaviour' or *moral* masochism. The most 'incomprehensible' form, *erotogenic* masochism (pleasure in pain), lies 'at the bottom of the other two forms' and so is the form that requires elucidation.[42] To explain the mysterious confluence of pleasure and pain, Freud refers to his *Three Essays on the Theory of Sexuality.* In the *Three Essays* Freud had argued that sexual excitation was produced 'economically', once a certain threshold of tension due to pleasure was passed.[43] By analogy, here he suggests that beyond a certain threshold, the tension due to pain/unpleasure produces sexual excitation. This analogy provides 'the physiological foundation on which the psychical structure of erotogenic masochism would afterward be erected'.[44]

But Freud is also after a *metapsychological* explanation, accounting for the 'regular and close connections of masochism with its counterpart in instinctual life, sadism'.[45] So erotogenic (or primary) masochism is explained by reference to the dualism of the drives: the libido must render the death instinct sufficiently 'innocuous' to prolong life. To that effect a portion of death instincts is diverted to the outside world under the form of destructiveness, mastery, will to power and aggression. Another portion is placed directly in the service of the sexual function as sadism. Yet another portion is not taken outwards; with the help of the accompanying sexual excitation, it becomes libidinally bound there as primary masochism:[46] it is the residuum of 'the phase of development in which the coalescence ... between the death instinct and Eros took place'.[47] So all is 'well' prior to the formation of the superego. It is Freud's analysis of moral masochism that exposes the instinctual impasse of civilized life.

Moral masochism appears to have lost all connection with sexuality. In other forms of masochism, the command of the loved one is essential to the fantasy. Here 'the suffering itself is what matters ... the true masochist always turns his cheek whenever he has a chance of receiving a blow'.[48] Is this just defused death drive? To answer this question Freud distinguishes moral masochism from 'unconscious' guilt (evidenced by a need for punishment) and conscious guilt, where 'the ego reacts with feelings of anxiety (conscience anxiety) to the perception that it has not come up to the demands made by its ideal, the superego'.[49] The superego is crystallized by introjection into the ego of the parental figures, entailing a defusion of instincts, desexualized through the incest prohibition installed by the Oedipus complex. This defusion produces the severity of the superego and it is at this point that Freud states, without further ado, that 'Kant's Categorical Imperative is thus the direct heir of the Oedipus complex'.[50] By contrast, moral masochism is a re-sexualization of conscience and morality,[51] and the moral masochist is caught between the sadism of the superego towards the ego and the masochism of the ego: 'in order to provoke punishment from this last representative of the parents, the masochist must do what is inexpedient, must act against his own interests, must ruin the prospects which open out to him in the real world and must, perhaps, destroy his own real existence'.[52]

The Freudian impasse

The Economic Problem of Masochism evidently prefigures *Civilization and its Discontents*, a text in which Freud argues that the Oedipus complex produces an instinctual impasse for the subject:[53] the condition of civilization is incest prohibition, which produces a defusion of the drives through the desexualization of the parental figures. When desexualization fails, the subject is the hapless seat of moral masochism. When it is successful, the subject's ego is the object of the superego's sadism in the guise of the – conscious or unconscious – sense of guilt, for the death drive can rarely manifest itself outwards in destruction, mastery etc., at least in times of peace. The double renunciation upon which civilization is premised produces aggression which either feeds the superego or is deployed in sublimation.[54] In this perspective, ethics is a cultural solution to the aggression produced, then repressed by the Oedipus:

> The cultural super-ego has developed its ideals and set up its demands. Among the latter, those which deal with the relation of human beings to one another are comprised under the heading of ethics. People have at all times set the greatest value on ethics, as though they expected that it in particular would produce especially important results. And it does in fact deal with a subject which can easily be recognized as the sorest spot in every civilization. Ethics is thus to be regarded as a therapeutic attempt – as an endeavour to achieve, by means of the command of the super-ego, something which has so far not been achieved by means of any other cultural activities.[55]

Conversely, the death drive is the condition of possibility of civilization; once desexualized it provides the instinctual force necessary to sustain ethics.

But in the Freudian configuration, happiness can exist only in suffering/evil, as we substitute sadism towards the self (in the guise of the categorical imperative) for sadism towards others (destruction, mastery, etc.).

Lacan's monism of the drive

What are we to make of Freud's complex typology of 'enjoyed' suffering? First, we note that Freud had to hypothesize the fusion of instincts in order to account for the 'happiness in evil' experienced by the subject beyond the pleasure principle. I won't much develop this point here but it is worth noting that the dualism of the drives is strikingly artificial in Freud's work, since so many phenomena are only understandable in terms of their fusion. Lacan remarked upon it in *Seminar II*:

> Note that the tendency to union – Eros tends to unite – is only ever apprehended in its relation to the contrary tendency, which leads to division, to rupture, to a redispersion, most especially of inanimate matter. These two tendencies are strictly inseparable. No notion is less unitary.[56]

This is why, to quote Miller's characterization, Lacan substituted a *monist* concept of the drive for Freud's strained dualism. In the monist perspective Lacan used the term 'fantasy' to 'concentrate everything that pertains to libidinal satisfaction in Freud'.[57] All modalities of libidinal satisfaction (including masochism and sadism) are thus referred to the imaginarized versions of object *a* organizing the oral, anal, scopic and invocatory drives. This is why Lacan's reflection on ethics in 'Kant with Sade' takes the fantasy as axiom of the subject's satisfaction.

Second, when Freud apprehends the ethical concepts of conscience and morality, he does so in connection with the beyond of the pleasure principle. In so doing, he demonstrates the equivalence between the superego and the moral law, which are modalities of jouissance. In *Lakant*, Miller summarizes the import of *The Economic Problem of Masochism* as follows:

> We recall the thesis according to which moral masochism has no erogenous zone because moral conscience itself is erogenized. Moral conscience, a product of so-called renunciation, cannot impose renunciation to the drive, which enjoys its very renunciation. I therefore had to demonstrate that the superego, the law, is nothing other than a strategy of the drive, a concealment of the drive.[58]

In the last analysis, *The Economic Problem of Masochism* demonstrates that the rationalization intrinsic to moral law acts as a 'concealment of the drive'.

'Love thy neighbour' and the position of the analyst

> Man tries to satisfy his need for aggression at the expense of his neighbour, to exploit his work without compensation, to use him sexually without his consent, to appropriate his goods, to humiliate him, to inflict suffering on him, to torture and kill him.[59]

The Economic Problem of Masochism is Freud's metapsychological contribution to the question of ethics and morality. In *Civilization and its Discontents* Freud describes human relations in very Sadean terms. And in *Reading Seminars I and II*, Miller argues that Lacan's 'Kant with Sade' is a 'rewriting' of *The Economic Problem of Masochism*.[60] The very titles of the great psychoanalytic writings on ethics signal clearly enough the surprising connection, first voiced by Freud, between ethics and sadism/masochism, and so between ethics and perversion. Thus Roudinesco, in her book on perversion, phrases the Freudian contribution as follows:

> [Freud] conferred an essentially human dimension on the perverse structure – [as] jouissance in evil/suffering, the eroticization of hatred, but not as a defect, degeneracy, an anomaly … This is how Freud introduced what one could call a universal of the perverse difference in the psyche: every human being is inhabited by crime, sex, transgression, madness, negativity, passion, *égarement*, inversion etc. … By showing that the perverse disposition is specific to man, that each subject carries a potential for it within himself – and so that pathology clarifies the norm – Freud affirmed that the only limit to the abject deployment of perversion came from a sublimation incarnated in the values of love, education, Law and civilization.[61]

So morality is sustained by a sublimation of the attraction for sin/fault. For Lacan this connection between sublimation and perversion, between ethics and desire, is more than sufficient to question the very possibility of a psychoanalytic ethics. If ethics is of the order of desire, then what could its object-cause be?

The fallacy of moral satisfactions

Until Lacan, the post-Freudian doctrine of counter-transference[62] was considered sufficient to deal with the position of the analyst, problematized only as an occasional entanglement with the patient's unconscious. However Lacan, taking Freud seriously, started to push the question of the analyst's position as early as in his *Seminar I*. To provide a quick characterization of what is at stake here, we must distinguish psychoanalysis from other forms of social bond. According to Brousse,[63] and unlike in other modalities of the social bond (i.e. other modalities of *transference*), the analyst eventually unveils the mechanism of the transference itself, as this is the only way to free the analysand from the repetition of his or her pattern of alienation in the Other. The analyst's direction of the treatment is thus devised to disable the root cause of the Other's power on the analysand – which, with Lacan, we know to be the fantasy.

So what could possibly lead anyone to want to occupy such a 'selfless' position, a position in which there should be nothing to gain at the level either of narcissism or of perverse jouissance? Indeed, since Freud, we can no longer be blind to the 'fallacy of the satisfactions said to be moral', as Lacan put it in his *Seminar* on transference (a year after the *Ethics*):

> If we are to take seriously Freud's denunciation of the fallacy of the satisfactions said to be moral, in so far as there is aggressiveness hidden there which succeeds in stealing the jouissance of the one who exercises it at the same time as it inflicts the consequences of its misdeed on his social partners [... then] we have to wonder in what ways we can operate honestly with desire. That is to say – how to preserve desire in the act, the relation between desire and the act?[64]

So the superego, under the guise of morality, steals the jouissance of whoever seeks to be moral. And the 'satisfactions' at stake consist in 'finding satisfaction in aggression for the sake of aggression. That is what the death drive and the Freudian superego are all about.'[65] Clearly then, the 'moral' analyst is not to be trusted.

The analyst beyond the Good

Lacan's first, now obvious rejoinder to traditional moralists, who operate on the assumption that the Good and pleasure are equivalent, is that already with Freud's first formulation of the pleasure principle we see that its only function is to keep us away from what Lacan calls *Das Ding* in *Seminar VII:* 'Freud's use of the good can be summed up in the notion that it keeps us a long way from our jouissance.'[66]

In *Seminar VII* Lacan ciphers the beyond of the pleasure principle in the equation *jouissance* = *mal* (the French term *mal* means both evil and suffering).

> [I]f we continue to follow Freud in a text such as *Civilization and its Discontents*, we cannot avoid the formula that *jouissance* is evil [*mal*]. Freud led us by the hand to this point: it is evil [*mal*] because it involves suffering [*mal*] for my neighbour.[67]

This is why Freud is 'literally horrified' by the command to love one's neighbour, whose 'fundamental nature is bad'.[68] But if fundamental evil dwells within this neighbour:

> [t]hen it also dwells within me. And what is more of a neighbour to me than this heart within which is that of my jouissance and which I don't dare to go near? For as soon as I go near it, as *Civilization and its Discontents* makes clear, there rises up the unfathomable aggressivity from which I flee, that I turn against me, and which in the very place of the vanished Law adds its weight to that which prevents me from crossing a certain frontier at the limit of the Thing.[69]

And Lacan, opposing altruism to love of the neighbour, illustrates the former with the famous reference to St Martin, who gives half his cloak to the beggar – altruism, the service of the Good, cloaks the jouissance of the other. By responding to need, St Martin forecloses the beggar's desire: 'perhaps … he was begging for something else, namely that St Martin either kill him or fuck him'.[70] Altruism, which leads me to respond to the needs of the other as mirroring my own, 'becomes the pretext by means of which I can avoid taking up the problem of the evil I desire, and that my neighbour desires also'.[71]

Clearly altruism provides an unsatisfactory basis for the ethics of psychoanalysis: in order to know what it truly means to love one's neighbour, 'one would have to know how to confront the fact that my neighbour's jouissance, his harmful, malignant jouissance, is that which poses a problem for my love'.[72] Not only does altruism come in handy to steer clear of one's own jouissance, but it also generates narcissistic benefits. Pointing to the intimate connection between the good and power (since the power to give implies the power to deprive), Lacan adds that the service of the Good merely sustains the ego ideal, noted I(A) on the graph of desire, the signifier of omnipotence representing 'the power to do good'.[73] To sustain I(A) is a strategy of 'concealment of the drive'.

The Kantian solution: beyond the service of the Good

Lacan's effort to situate the ethics of psychoanalysis beyond the service of the Good takes him to Kant, who moved the age-old debate on ethics away from the Good and on to the terrain of the subject's division and thus *beyond the pleasure principle*. Lacan's resort to Kantian ethics can therefore be understood as follows: the analyst, like one acting in abidance with the categorical imperative, must act out of will and not out of pleasure, interest or personal gratification (the Kantian pathological). It is the question of the foundation of such will that intrigues Lacan, after Kant. On the one hand, the negative therapeutic reaction, like the Kantian concept of radical evil,[74] underlines the possibility of there being 'bad' will, or a will of saying 'no' to the good – what Žižek refers to as being 'evil out of principle'.[75] On the other, the only will there is, is a will to jouissance – but how can a will to jouissance be ethical? And, sure enough, the paradoxical nature of Kantian ethics is made explicit in the opening paragraphs of *Kant avec Sade*:

> *Philosophy in the Bedroom* comes eight years after the *Critique of Practical Reason*. If, after having seen that the one accords with the other, we show that it completes it, we will say that it gives the truth of the *Critique*.[76]

Happiness in Evil

In the opening paragraph of 'Kant with Sade', a text written by Lacan in 1962 as a preface to Sade's *Philosophy in the Bedroom*, we find the expression 'happiness in evil', a reference[77] to a short story by Barbey d'Aurevilly entitled *Happiness in Crime* (1874). The story is that of the undying, all-consuming love between the beautiful Hauteclaire Stassin and M. de Savigny, whose marriage took place after Hauteclaire, posing as her servant, poisoned the ailing Comtesse de Savigny. The family doctor, who narrates the criminal affair, admits to having spent the twenty years following the murder spying for signs of remorse or unhappiness in the couple, signs that would point to the existence of conscience, but is forced to recognize that their happiness knew no bounds. Lacan uses this example to signal the prevalence of the theme of happiness in evil in nineteenth-century literature, numerous other examples of which can be found as in, for instance, Baudelaire's poems *The Flowers of Evil*.

The literary references are used by Lacan to retrace the 'ethical' condition of possibility of psychoanalysis in a sequence nicely logicized by Miller. The emergence of the theme of happiness in evil is a 'formative condition of the possibility of psychoanalysis', and it emerges in the contemporaneous writings of Kant and Sade: 'Happiness in evil means taking pleasure in pain. This formulation is the literary precursor of the death drive ... the superego.'[78] If ethics refers to 'the kind of relationship established between the subject and the other',[79] then 'the way for science is prepared by rectifying the position of ethics'.[80] Namely: once the theme of happiness in evil is profoundly imprinted on the consciousness of the times, it becomes possible for Freud's sadistic superego ('*the voice of the sadistic superego*'[81]) to inscribe itself as the 'scientific' successor to its devilish literary precursors:

> In this respect, Sade did indeed begin the groundwork that was to progress for a hundred years in the depths of taste in order for Freud's path to be passable. ... If Freud was able to enunciate *his* pleasure principle without even having to worry about marking what distinguishes it from its function in traditional ethics, even without risking that it should be heard as an echo of the uncontested prejudice of two millennia, to recall the attraction which preordains the creature to its good, along with the

> psychology inscribed in various myths of goodwill, we can only credit this to the insinuating rise across the nineteenth century of the theme of 'happiness in evil'.[82]

So Kant and Sade are the ethical condition of possibility of psychoanalysis: Kant and Sade's work modified the framework within which the relationship between subject and other was envisaged, introducing the beyond-the-pleasure principle as the root cause of both radical evil and 'pure' moral law. These themes were taken up *aesthetically* in nineteenth-century poetry and literature, and this taste for happiness in evil made Freudian psychoanalysis possible. 'To be able to do something you need a kind of consent from the milieu, from the spirit of the time.'[83] Simply put, the development of the theme of happiness in evil was necessary for psychoanalysis to become an object-cause of desire, it would not have been sufficient for it to be true, therapeutic, efficient, etc. This is no doubt why in *La troisième* Lacan expressed the view that the future of psychoanalysis would depend on the future of the real: the modes of jouissance of the future may not include a *taste* for psychoanalysis. Hence Lacan's interest for Kant, concerned as he is with *judgement*.

Kantian ethics

Why, then, does Lacan turn to Kant[84] on the question of psychoanalytic ethics? Because the Kantian subject is the subject of desire, understood beyond the pleasure principle, and so is 'a void in objective causality, in the scientifically determinable'.[85] To demonstrate this, in 'Kant with Sade' Lacan develops the Kantian distinction between *wohl* and *das Gute*, both translated as *bien* in French:

> The pleasure principle is the law of feeling good [*bien*], which is *wohl* in German and might be rendered as 'well-being' [*bien-être*]. In practice, this principle would submit the subject to the same phenomenal sequence that determines his objects. The objection which Kant raises against this is, in accordance with his rigorous style, intrinsic. No phenomenon can lay claim to a constant relationship to pleasure. No law of feeling good can thus be enunciated that would define the subject who puts it in practice as will. The quest to feel good would thus be a dead end were it not reborn in the form of *das Gute*, the good that is the object of the moral law.[86]

Thus the categorical imperative – the first formulation of which is 'Act only according to that maxim whereby you can at the same time will that it should become a universal law' – arises out of 'a void of all that is pathological in the subject'.[87] Out of this apparent purity emerges a *formal* moral law, a law that does not have an object: or an ethics grounded in desire. In Lacanian terms, the moral law seeks to be a purely signifying formula with no reference to any object whatsoever. In 'Kant with Sade' Lacan, however, will argue that there is an object-cause to the Kantian desire.

In her thought-provoking introduction to the French edition of Kant's *Essai sur les maladies de la tête* (1764) David-Ménard accentuates Lacan's suggestion that it is Kant's distrust for a position reached on the basis of 'pathological objects' which impels him to elaborate his moral formalism. She argues that the moral law is Kant's answer to 'the ontological incapacities [of the things of the world] to give one a hold on rational, that is to say *a priori*, determination',[88] and articulates her assertion with what Kant says of perception in his essay on Swedenborg, *Dreams of a Spirit-Seer*: 'Generally, a coherent illusion of the senses is a much more remarkable phenomenon than the impostures of reason', because rational arguments can be disproved whereas 'illusions of the senses touch to the primary foundation of our judgements'.[89] She argues that Kant's suspicion of perception is in direct correlation with madness:

> Kant privileges, as elementary phenomenon of madness, the internal upheaval of the act of perception which, no doubt, differentiates the madman from the normal man, but in such a way that the inversion of the relative weight of fantasy and perception in the madman evidences the normal phenomenon of the habitual limitation of our phantasmagoria by what we call our real impressions.[90]

Thus for Kant reason, and *a fortiori* the moral law, a purely rational apparatus devised according to a quasi-mathematical logic, is to protect us from errors of judgement.

The return of the voice

The Kantian subject may be free from objective causality, from scientific determinism, but Lacan demonstrates that it is not free from the object-cause of the moral law that it gives itself. Indeed, at the very moment at which Kant evacuates all pathological objects, Lacan points out that the *object*-voice is reintroduced:[91] 'Experience tells us that we make ourselves hear commandments inside ourselves, the imperative nature of which is presented as categorical, in other words unconditional.'[92] It is on the status of the voice that Lacan makes use of Sade to reveal the truth of Kant: 'In coming out of the Other's mouth, Sade's maxim is more honest than Kant's appeal to the voice within, since it unmasks the split [between the enunciating subject and the subject of the statement] that is usually covered up.'[93] Miller develops this point in two parts in his 'Discussion of Lacan's "Kant with Sade"':

> Kant leads us to believe that the subject is speaking to himself, enunciating a law that terrorizes him. Whereas Sade presents us with a formulation in which the distinction between subject and other is explicit.

> He reveals the division of the subject, whereas Kant makes us think it is an auto-, non-divisive affectation.[94]
> Whereas in Kant's work, there is no one else, that is, the subject auto-affects himself with the voice of duty, Lacan reveals a division: there is someone else who enunciates the duty, and *he who enunciates the duty is not dutiful. He who enunciates the duty is not subject to the duty he enunciates.* He is a vicious character.[95]

So the Kantian moral law, originating as it does from a subject defined as a void in objective causality, nonetheless conceals the division of the subject between enunciation and statement, and so the sadistic command of the superego the Kantian subject is prey to. Simply put, *the moral law masks the drive*; just as any universal imperative does.[96]

You can know the axiom of your being

As such the moral law cannot set an example for psychoanalytic ethics, as it falls under the heading of 'the fallacy of the satisfactions said to be moral'. What Lacan truly shows in 'Kant with Sade' is that every speaking being [*parlêtre*] is subjected to the formula of his or her fantasy, which could be translated in mock Kantian terms as 'Act in such a way as to maximize your jouissance'.[97] In the final analysis, the object of the drive is none of the imaginarized forms discussed by Lacan in *Seminar X* as objects *a*, it merely is surplus-enjoyment [*plus-de-jouir*], the final cause of desire,[98] expressed in the categorical imperative of one's singular jouissance. If every subject is subjected to the imperative of having to maximize his jouissance, what is the effect of the analytic experience on this imperative?

In 'Kant with Sade' Lacan creates a Sadean maxim on the basis of the myriad fantasies enumerated in Sade's writings: '"I have a right to enjoy your body", anyone can say to me, "and I will exercise this right without any limit to the capriciousness of the exactions I may wish to satiate with your body."'[99] Miller interprets Lacan's 'construction' of Sade's fundamental fantasy as illustrative of the construction of the analysand's fundamental fantasy in analysis:

> Analysis really is a process of simplification … because analysis involves the shrinking of the libido and the progressive construction of the fundamental fantasy from various fantasies, the construction of the subject's fundamental maxim, to use Kant's term. It is equivalent to the fundamental maxim of one's conduct, that is, the law that it obeys. And it constitutes meanings and signification. That is, the fundamental fantasy is essentially a formula that says, 'Act in such a way that you will always obey the formula.'[100]

An analyst having reached the end of his own analysis will know the axiom of his or her being, and will refuse to act as complement to the analysand's fantasy (as Sade completes Kant's). By positioning him- or herself as object-cause of the analysand's desire, the analyst gets the analysand to recount the multiple versions of his or her fantasy in order to operate the same logical reduction which produced the subject-analyst as analyst. The analyst then can incarnate the object-cause of the analysand's desire,[101] a desire which like all desires is *structurally perverse*, and so expose the jouissance of the analysand: by incarnating the object-cause of the analysand's desire, *and not of his or her fantasy*, the analyst incarnates *castration* in order to separate the analysand from his or her deleterious, mortifying jouissance. (Castration of course is to be understood as *a limit to jouissance*.) As such, the analysand may hope to substitute his or her happiness in suffering/evil for a new modality of satisfaction, involving identification with his or her symptom that will provide a jouissance extracted from the fantasy.[102] We can also see that the core of the fantasy is superegoic – in Lacan's terms the command to 'enjoy' beyond any limit – in the manner illustrated by Sade's infinite – and infinitely tedious – catalogue of perversions. As Foucault once put it, 'To hell with the literary sacralization of Sade, to hell with Sade: he bores us, he is a disciplinarian, a sergeant of sex, an accountant of arses and their equivalents.'[103] Unlike what the neurotic secretly hopes for in analysis, the limitlessness of jouissance is the true horror, not castration, and it is the anxiety generated by that limitlessness that prevents the subject from *acting out of desire*.

The desire of the analyst: a consequentialist ethics

> 'The universal is in the service of the will to jouissance.'[104]

At this point, the moment to conclude, we can provide a more operative definition of the desire of the analyst: the desire of the analyst is distinct from any universal, which our reading of Freud and Lacan leads us to recognize as *structurally* superegoic. Thus the desire of the analyst is to produce singularities:

> [Lacan] logicized Freud's desire to separate it from its particularity, to uproot it from the paternal fantasy, to elicit the form said to be that of the desire of the analyst. This desire is not, for all that, a pure desire. It is the desire to separate the subject from the master-signifiers which collectivize him, to isolate his or her absolute difference, to circumscribe subjective solitude, and also the object [providing] surplus-enjoyment [*objet plus-de-jouir*] which at the same time is upheld by this void but also fills it up.[105]

Kantian ethics – or the 'ethics of the bachelor'[106] of the good intention – are to be opposed to the consequentialist ethics of psychoanalysis,[107] characterized above all by the analytic act and *its always unpredictable consequences.* When in *Television*[108] Lacan refers to Kantian ethics as an ethics of the bachelor, no doubt with reference to Kant's refusal to get married,[109] it is not to have a dig at Kant but to show that psychoanalytic ethics has to involve the Other. It is not sufficient to occupy an 'ethical' position, obtained as far as can be through the construction of the fundamental fantasy, it also involves having to 'make oneself the object of the Other's jouissance, in the irreducible uncertainty of the desire of the Other'.[110] Simply put, the analyst has to act without any guarantee, and to deal with the consequences of his or her act. He or she cannot take comfort in the 'purity' of his or her intentions.

Quoting Lacan in 'Science and Truth' – 'guileless errors are the most unforgivable of all errors'[111] – Miller comments that guileless errors are 'errors that mistake their desires for realities. In psychoanalysis, we say that mistaking one's desires for realities is to be the slave of your fantasy. Behind the error made in good faith, there is jouissance, the enjoyed sense [*sens joui*] of the fantasy.'[112] This echoes Lacan's own position: 'The psychoanalyst's position leaves no escape, excluding as it does the tenderness of the beautiful soul.'[113] Ultimately, Lacanian ethics is more Hegelian than Kantian.

Conclusion: the end of analysis as compass

It is well known that Lacan departed from the Freudian orthodoxy in one absolutely fundamental respect: where Freud recommended a new 'slice' of analysis every five years,[114] Lacan asserted that the analytic experience was very much terminable.[115] The analytic process taken to its end will result in an eventual 'cancelling of one's subscription to the unconscious' [*désabonné à l'inconscient*].[116] And when Lacan had to deal with the repeated crises traversing his psychoanalytic community,[117] he decided to 'give institutional consequences to his teaching'.[118] Specifically, in his 1967 *Proposition on the Analyst of the School,*[119] Lacan suggested organizing the analytic community through the dispositif of the pass and the end of analysis, seeking to *actualize an unprecedented modality of the social bond.*

Lacan's reasoning can be laid out sequentially. Decades of institutional strife had shown, among other things, that no amount of knowledge or clinical experience could provide a guarantee of the position of a subject as analyst. Yet, for reasons that should have become clear in the course of this chapter, Lacan would not give up on the definition of the subject-analyst. In his *Proposition* he recommended indexing the definition of the analyst on the end of analysis, defined at the time in terms of a subjective destitution – a lack-of-being [*manque à être*] produced by the fall of object *a*.[120] As it is object *a* that gives logical consistency to the Other, the end of analysis also implies the evaporation of the Other. And, since there is no Other to 'guarantee' the subject-analyst, 'the psychoanalyst authorizes himself'.[121] An analyst is therefore the product of an analysis taken to its end: 'The termination of the psychoanalysis superfluously said to be didactic is in fact the passage from the psychoanalysand to the psychoanalyst.'[122] As to the dispositif of the pass, it verifies the emergence of the desire of the analyst on a case-by-case basis: not *guarantee but verification*.

Lacan further develops his theorization of the position of the analyst and the end of analysis in subsequent years. First, around the time of the *Proposition* Lacan introduces the concept of the analytic act, developed in his *L'Acte analytique*. In his 'Discours à l'EFP' Lacan famously utters the following: 'my discourse appeases in no way the horror of the psychoanalytic act. Why? Because it is the act ... which does not support the *semblant*.' This statement can be read in conjunction with the elaboration which Lacan makes, a few years later, in *Seminar XX*. Lacan introduces the dimension of love in the question of the position of the analyst, showing that the analyst intervenes from the place of S (Ⱥ), or the place of the lack of guarantee in the Other (see especially chapters III and VII). S (Ⱥ) is produced as an empty place through the extraction of object *a* hitherto saturating it with jouissance through the operation of the fantasy.[123]

We now have a few terms with which to apprehend the end of analysis: the subjective destitution produced by the extraction of the object enables a subject to act in such a way as to confront the absence of guarantee in the Other as to the consequences of his or her act, an act which does not therefore support the *semblant*. *Seminar XX* also gives us the idea that if the act originates in S (Ⱥ), and so is not orientated by the phallus, then it is oriented by love.

This configuration, progressively built by Lacan, does not represent his final word on the question. Later on in his work he returns to the end of analysis in order to *include* jouissance in its definition. There is a very clear, absolutely crucial indication on the place of jouissance at the end of analysis in *Seminar XXIV*: jouissance is obtained through identification with one's symptom.[124] And 'to know how to make do with one's symptom, this is the end of analysis' (16 November 1976).

> So what does it mean to know? To know means to know how to make do with one's symptom, how to disentangle it, how to handle it, to know has something to do with what man does with his image, it is to imagine the way in which one can handle one's symptom. Here I am of course talking about secondary narcissism, radical narcissism, the narcissism that one calls primary being, in the event, excluded. To know how to make do with one's symptom, this is the end of analysis. It has to be said that it's a bit short. It really doesn't go very far. How to practice with this, this is of course what I am trying to transmit in this crowd, I don't know with what result.[125]

The analysed symptom is of course not the same symptom as at the beginning of the analytic experience. It is the symptom after the fall of object *a*, a symptom reduced to its core, ciphering a singular mode of enjoyment.[126]

If, in the perspective of the later Lacan, the end of analysis includes jouissance, then the desire of the analyst can no longer be conceived of as a 'pure desire'.[127] The subject-analyst, like any subject – including analysed subjects – remains the locus of the drive's 'demand' for satisfaction: irrespective of the subjective configuration in which it is taken up, jouissance is always obtained, in one form or another, in the same quantity. *The analyst's jouissance must therefore be included in the desire of the analyst – lest it returns in other guises.* And Lacan explored some such guises in 'Kant with Sade', concluding to a 'neither Kant nor Sade' – at least as far as the ethics of psychoanalysis are concerned. The real question facing psychoanalysis, then, what distinguishes it from other transferential dispositifs, is that of the articulation of the 'constant tension' of the drive[128] with the ethics of the analyst.

Perhaps somewhat controversially, and to leave something to desire, I will conclude by saying that at the end of his life Lacan substituted a politics of psychoanalysis for an ethics of psychoanalysis, which he ended up thinking to be an 'unsustainable' proposition: 'From an ethical point of view our profession is unsustainable, this is in fact why it makes me sick, because I have a superego, like everyone else.'[129] Taking my bearings on *Seminars XX* and *XXIII*, I would say that such politics would involve two principles: not to saturate lack with jouissance, and to keep RSI (Real–Symbolic–Imaginary) as distinct from one another as possible.[130]

Notes

1 Jacques Lacan, *Le Séminaire, Livre VII, L'Éthique de la psychanalyse 1959–1960*, ed. Jacques-Alain Miller, Paris: Seuil, 1986, p. 347; *The Seminar of Jacques Lacan, Book VII, The Ethics of Psychoanalysis, 1959–1960*, ed. Jacques-Alain Miller, trans. Dennis Porter, London and New York: Routledge, 1992, p. 300. For Lacan's texts, and where available, page references will be given first to the French text and second to the English translation.

2 Lacan develops the theory according to which the axis of analysis is the desire of the analyst in *Seminar VIII*. (Jacques Lacan, *Le Séminaire, Livre VIII, Le Transfert 1960–1961*, Paris: Seuil, 2001.) Safouan summarizes Lacan's reflection by stating that this principle 'stems from the principle according to which desire is the desire of the Other'. (Moustapha Safouan, *Lacaniana. Les Séminaires de Jacques Lacan 1953–1963*, Paris: Fayard, 2001, p. 158; my translation.) *A minima*, the desire of the analyst can be defined as 'the refusal to delude oneself with anything that is of the order of the Good'. (Moustapha Safouan et al., *Travailler avec Lacan*, Paris: Flammarion/Aubier, 2007, p. 11; my translation.)

3 For Lacan, Freud had not fully drawn the consequences of his findings with regard to the organization of the transmission and preservation of psychoanalysis. Thus he interpreted the foundation of the IPA as indicative of Freud's conviction that psychoanalysis could be transmitted only through the mechanism

of repression: 'Freud entrusted his message to the IPA, betting on the fact that it would be preserved through the intervention of repression.' (Safouan et al., *Travailler avec Lacan*, p. 22; my translation.) As a result, the IPA was content to parrot Freud, but did not innovate. Lacan castigated the IPA in the following terms in his *écrit* 'The Situation of Psychoanalysis and the Training of Psychoanalysts in 1956': 'For in the use that is made in the psychoanalytic institution of Freud's concepts, how can we fail to see that their signification is in no way taken into account? And yet it is to nothing but their presence that one can attribute the fact that the association has not yet fallen apart and been dispersed into the confusion of Babel.' Lacan concludes his *écrit* by comparing the IPA to M. Valdemar, after Poe's 'The Facts in the Case of M. Valdemar'. M. Valdemar had died while under hypnosis and his cadaver therefore did not decompose. (Jacques Lacan, *Écrits*, Paris: Seuil, 1966, p. 486; *Écrits. The First Complete Edition in English*, trans. Bruce Fink, New York: Norton, 2006, p. 406.) In the same text, and in its Appendix, Lacan suggests that had Freud founded the IPA after having written his *Group Psychology*, he would undoubtedly have been more alert to the 'sterilizing' effects of identification to the image on the group. (Ibid., pp. 474, 489; pp. 397, 409.) Lacan proposed the pass as an alternative to transmission through identification (which entails the repression of desire).

4 This is most evident and comprehensive in *Seminar VII* and the contemporaneous *écrit* 'Kant with Sade'. Yet these questions are present throughout Lacan's teaching. For example, in *Seminar I* Lacan engages in a close reading of Freud's 'Observations on transference-love' and 'The dynamics of transference' in order to extricate the analytic relation from the imaginary order entrenched by the IPA doctrine of counter-transference, insisting on the fundamental asymmetry between analyst and analysand, and so situating the analyst firmly in the locus of the Other. And Lacan returns to the ethics of psychoanalysis as late as 1977 in *Seminar XXIV* and 'Propos sur l'hystérie'.

5 Lacan, *Écrits*, p. 765; p. 655

6 In *Seminar VII* Lacan defines jouissance as the 'satisfaction of a drive'. (Lacan, *Le Séminaire VII*, p. 248; p. 209.) See also Jacques-Alain Miller, 'Contra-indications to psychoanalytical treatment', *Psychoanalytical Notebooks*, 4, 2000, pp. 65–73, for a definition of jouissance as drive satisfaction.

7 'I propose then that, from an analytical point of view, the only thing of which one can be guilty is of having given ground relative to one's desire.' (Lacan, *Le Séminaire VII*, p. 368; 317.)

8 Sigmund Freud, 'The economic problem of masochism' [1924], Penguin Freud Library (PFL) 11, ed. Angela Richards, trans. James Strachey, London: Penguin, 1984, p. 422.

9 In his summary of *La Logique du fantasme* (1966–67) Lacan defines the fantasy as an axiom: 'The fantasy, to take things at the level of interpretation, functions there as an axiom, i.e. it is distinguished from the laws of variable deduction, which specify the reduction of symptoms in each structure, because it figures there under the modality of constancy.' (Jacques Lacan, *Autres écrits*, Paris: Seuil, 2001, p. 326; my translation.)

10 Lacan, *Le Séminaire VII*, p. 124; p. 104.

11 Ibid., p. 252; p. 212.

12 '*Civilisation and its Discontents* concerns the effort to rethink the problem of evil once one acknowledges that it is radically altered by the absence of God.' (Ibid., p. 218; p. 185.)

13 'Perversions are sexual activities which either (a) *extend*, in an anatomical sense, beyond the regions of the body that are designed for sexual union, or (b) *linger*

over the intermediate relations to the sexual object which should normally be traversed rapidly on the path towards the final sexual aim.' (Sigmund Freud, 'Three essays on the theory of sexuality' [1905], PFL 7, p. 62; original emphasis.) In the same text Freud poses that the 'same disposition to perversions of every kind is a general and fundamental human characteristic'. (Ibid., p. 109.) In other words, for human sexuality the norm is perversion. For Roudinesco, 'perversion is specific to mankind: the animal world is excluded from it, as it is from crime. Not only is it specific to mankind, present in all cultures, but it presupposes the existence of speech, language, art, even a discourse on art and sex.' Elisabeth Roudinesco, *La Part obscure de nous-même. Une histoire des pervers*, Paris: Albin Michel, 2007, pp. 13–14; my translation

14 Lacan, *Le Séminaire VII*, p. 341; p. 295.

15 Ibid., p. 251; p. 212.

16 Freud develops this proposition in 'Formulations on two principles of mental functioning'. The pleasure principle and the reality principle 'respectively dominate the primary and secondary mental processes' (Sigmund Freud, 'Formulations on two principles of mental functioning' [1911], PFL 11, p. 33), with the primary processes ('These processes strive towards gaining pleasure; psychical activity draws back from any event which might arouse unpleasure,' ibid., p. 36) referring to unbound energy and the secondary processes to bound energy. Secondary processes take account of the real world, allowing the subject to act on reality in order to obtain pleasure without experiencing unpleasure. It involves the deferral of pleasure.

17 Safouan, *Lacaniana*, p. 139; my translation.

18 Sigmund Freud, 'Beyond the pleasure principle' [1920], PFL 11, p. 308.

19 I.e. keeping the quantity of excitation present in the mental apparatus as low as possible or at least constant.

20 In 'The Ego and the Id' Freud ascribes the 'negative therapeutic reaction' to an unconscious sense of guilt finding satisfaction in the illness. (Sigmund Freud, 'The Ego and the Id' [1923], PFL 11, pp. 390–1.)

21 Freud, 'Beyond the pleasure principle', pp. 281–7.

22 Ibid., p. 293.

23 Ibid., p. 308; original emphasis.

24 Ibid., pp. 310–11.

25 Ibid., p. 312.

26 Ibid., p. 330.

27 Ibid., p. 336.

28 Ibid., p. 338.

29 Ibid., p. 335.

30 Freud, 'The Ego and the Id', p. 381.

31 Ibid.; original emphasis.

32 Ibid., p. 382.

33 Ibid., p. 380.

34 Ibid., p. 382.

35 In 'Instincts and their vicissitudes' Freud thought that masochism was secondary, 'the reversal of an instinct into its opposite … The turning round of an instinct upon the subject's own self is made possible by the reflection that masochism is actually sadism turned round upon the subject's own ego … '. (Sigmund Freud, 'Instincts and their vicissitudes' [1915], PFL 11, p. 124; original emphasis.) See also the discussion and 1924 footnote in 'Three essays' (Freud, 'Three essays on the theory of sexuality', pp. 70 ff.)

36 Freud, 'Beyond the pleasure principle', pp. 276–8.

37 Freud, 'The economic problem of masochism', p. 414.

38 Ibid., p. 414.
39 Ibid., p. 415.
40 Ibid.; original emphasis.
41 Feminine masochism not because it is specific to women, quite the contrary, but because the frequent fantasies in which the subject is bound, whipped, beaten, debased in any way, like a misbehaving child, place the subject in a characteristically female situation: being castrated, copulated with, giving birth. There is also some guilt often present justifying the punishment in the manifest content of the fantasies, so there are connections with infantile masturbation and moral masochism. See also Freud's 'A child is being beaten' [1919] (PLF 10) and Eric Laurent's excellent analysis of this text in 'Feminine positions of being', in Véronique Voruz and Bogdan Wolf (eds), *The Later Lacan. An Introduction*, Albany, NY: SUNY Press, 2007.)
42 Freud, 'The economic problem of masochism', p. 415.
43 Freud, 'Three essays on the theory of sexuality', p. 124.
44 Freud, 'The economic problem of masochism', p. 418.
45 Ibid., p. 418.
46 Ibid., p. 418.
47 Ibid., p. 419.
48 Ibid., p. 420.
49 Ibid., pp. 421–2.
50 Ibid., pp. 421–2.
51 Ibid., p. 424,
52 Ibid., p. 425.
53 Véronique Voruz, 'The logic of exception', *Law, Culture and the Humanities*, 2, 2006, 162–78.
54 Sublimation describes 'a type of creative activity deriving its force from the sexual drive in so far as it invests socially valorized objects.' (Roudinesco, *La Part obscure de nous-même*, p. 20; my translation.)
55 Sigmund Freud, 'Civilization and its discontents' [1929], PFL 12, p. 336.
56 Jacques Lacan, *Le Séminaire, Livre II, Le Moi dans la théorie de Freud et dans la technique de la psychanalyse 1954–1955*, ed. Jacques-Alain Miller, Paris: Seuil, 1978, p. 101; *The Seminar of Jacques Lacan, Book II, The Ego in Freud's Theory and in the Technique of Psychoanalysis, 1954–1955*, ed. Jacques-Alain Miller, trans. John Forrester, Cambridge: Cambridge University Press, 1988, p. 79.
57 Jacques-Alain Miller, 'Biologie lacanienne et événement de corps', *La Cause freudienne*, 44, 2000, pp. 26–9.
58 Jacques-Alain Miller (ed.), *Lakant*, Paris: Collection rue Huysmans, 2003, p. 22; my translation.
59 Freud, 'Civilization and its discontents', quoted in Lacan, *Le séminaire VII*, p. 217; p. 185.
60 Jacques-Alain Miller, 'A discussion of Lacan's "Kant with Sade"', in Richard Feldstein, Bruce Fink and Maire Jaanus (eds), *Reading Seminars I and II*, Albany, NY: SUNY Press, 1996, p. 212.
61 Roudinesco, *La Part obscure de nous-même*, pp. 104–7; my translation.
62 As defined by Laplanche and Pontalis, counter-transference refers to the 'unconscious reactions of the analyst to the person of the analysed party and more specifically to the latter's transference.' (Jean Laplanche and J.-B. Pontalis, *Vocabulaire de la psychanalyse*, Paris: Presses Universitaires de France, 1967.)
63 Marie-Hélène Brousse, 'Le transfert dévoilé', *La Règle du jeu*, 2006, No. 30.
64 Lacan, *Le Séminaire VIII*, p. 14; my translation.
65 Miller, 'A discussion of Lacan's "Kant with Sade"', p. 220.

66 Lacan, *Le Séminaire VII*, p. 218; p. 185.
67 Ibid., p. 217; p. 184; translation modified.
68 Ibid., p. 218; p. 186.
69 Ibid., p. 219; p. 186.
70 Ibid., p. 219; p. 186.
71 Ibid., p. 220; p. 187.
72 Ibid., p. 220; p. 187.
73 Ibid., p. 274; p. 234.
74 Immanuel Kant, *La Religion dans les limites de la simple raison*, Paris: Vrin, 2004.
75 Miller, 'A discussion of Lacan's "Kant with Sade"', p. 215.
76 Lacan, *Écrits*, p. 765; 646.
77 James B. Swenson, 'Annotations to "Kant with Sade"', *October*, 51, 1989, pp. 76–104, p. 78
78 Miller, 'A discussion of Lacan's "Kant with Sade"', p. 220.
79 Ibid., p. 218.
80 Jacques Lacan, 'Kant avec Sade', *Écrits*, Paris: Seuil, 1966, p. 765; *Écrits: The First Complete Edition in English*, trans. Bruce Fink, New York: Norton, 2006, p. 645.
81 Miller, 'A discussion of Lacan's "Kant with Sade"', p. 222; original emphasis.
82 Lacan, 'Kant avec Sade', p. 765; p. 645.
83 Miller, 'A discussion of Lacan's "Kant with Sade"', p. 216.
84 On Lacan's reading of Kant from a more philosophical perspective the reader is referred to Alenka Zupančič's *Ethics of the Real*, London and New York: Verso, 2000.
85 Miller, Lakant, p. 28–9.
86 Lacan, 'Kant avec Sade', p. 766; p. 646.
87 Miller, 'A discussion of Lacan's "Kant with Sade"', p. 226.
88 Monique David-Ménard, 'Présentation', in *Observations sur le sentiment du beau et du sublime*, Paris: Flammarion, 1990, p. 32; my translation,
89 Ibid., p. 15.
90 Ibid.
91 On the voice, see Mladen Dolar's excellent book *A Voice and Nothing More*, Cambridge, MA: MIT Press, 2006, and Jacques-Alain Miller's 'Jacques Lacan et la voix', *Quarto*, 54, 1994, pp. 47–52.
92 Lacan, 'Kant avec Sade', p. 766; p. 646.
93 Ibid., p. 770; p. 650.
94 Miller, 'A Discussion of Lacan's "Kant with Sade"', p. 234.
95 Ibid., p. 222.
96 In his psychological portrait of President Wilson, Freud depicts Wilson's superego in the following terms: 'You must make the impossible possible! You are the beloved son of the Father! You are the Father himself! You are God!' This Freudian version of the superego is much closer to the Lacanian superego as a mad commandment to 'enjoy!' at any cost to the unfortunate host of the cruel injunction to seek limitless jouissance. See Sigmund Freud and William C. Bullitt, *Le Président T. W. Wilson. Un portrait psychologique*, Paris: Payot, 2005.
97 Miller, *Lakant*, p. 64.
98 Ibid., pp. 64–5.
99 Lacan, 'Kant avec Sade', p. 769; p. 648.
100 Miller, 'A discussion of Lacan's "Kant with Sade"', p. 224.
101 See Marie-Hélène Brousse, 'L'Usage de l'objet', *Quarto*, 85, 2005.
102 This is the version of the end of analysis currently developed by Miller (*L'Orientation lacanienne, 2007–2008*, unpublished seminar) in the perspective of the last period of Lacan's teaching.

103 Michel Foucault, 'Sade, sergent du sexe', *Dits et Ecrits* II, Paris: Seuil, 1994, p. 822.
104 Jacques-Alain Miller, 'Théorie de Turin', 2000, online: www.causefreudienne.net/ecole/textes-fondateurs/theorie-de-turin.
105 Ibid.
106 Jacques Lacan, *Autres écrits*, Paris: Seuil, 2001, p. 541.
107 Jacques-Alain Miller, *Politique lacanienne 1997–1998*, Paris: Collection rue Huysmans, 2001, pp. 105–8.
108 Lacan, *Autres écrits*, p. 541.
109 In *Lakant* Miller traces Kant's use of the formula *sic volo, sic jubeo* in the first chapter of the *Critique of Practical Reason* to Juvenal's sixth satire, which debates the question of whether a man should marry or not. Juvenal concludes that in any case a man should never marry a woman. Miller interprets this otherwise cryptic Kantian reference as revealing the truth of Kant's internal debate between his superego, incarnated by the voice of a feminine tyrant, and the voice of reason, which he seeks to oppose to it at all costs. (Miller, *Lakant*, p. 41.)
110 Safouan et al., *Travailler avec Lacan*, p. 61.
111 Lacan, *Écrits*, p. 859; p. 729.
112 Miller, *Politique lacanienne*, p. 109.
113 Ibid.
114 See Sigmund Freud, 'Analysis terminable and interminable' [1937], *The Standard Edition of the Complete Psychological Works of Sigmund Freud* XXIII, trans. and ed. James Strachey, London: Hogarth Press, 1956–74, pp. 211–53.
115 In earlier seminars Lacan developed less radical versions of the end of analysis. For example in *Seminar VII* he states that 'To have carried an analysis through to its end is no more nor less than to have encountered that limit [the inexistence of the Sovereign Good] in which the problematic of desire is raised.' (Lacan, *Le Séminaire VII*, p. 347; p. 300.) In this perspective the end of analysis produces a modality of being-towards-death, and a superegoic doctrine of the ethics of psychoanalysis. (See Miller, 'Biologie lacanienne'.)
116 Lacan coins this expression with reference to James Joyce (Jacques Lacan, *Le Séminaire, Livre XXIII, Le Sinthome 1975–1976*, Paris: Seuil, 2005, p. 166), also stating in 'Lituraterre' that the writer 'went straight for the best that could be expected of an analysis at its end' (Lacan, *Autres écrits*, p. 11; my translation).
117 In a series of five seminars published under the title *Politique lacanienne 1997–1998* (2001), at the time of yet another crisis in Lacan's School, Miller returns to the institutional history of psychoanalysis. In this insightful seminar series Miller presents the invention of the pass – laid out in the 'Proposition of 9 October 1967 on the Analyst of the School' and put to the vote after Lacan's December address, *Discours à l'École freudienne de Paris* (Lacan, *Autres écrits*) – as a response to the failure of all previous institutional models. Miller contrasts the Freudian solution – to secure the existence of the analytic community through the performance of rituals – to the initial Lacanian solution: to organize the analytic community around transference to Lacan's own teaching. Faced with the failure of his own model, Lacan invented the dispositif of the pass, devised to attest to the end of an analysis. The pass 'introduces a new definition of the psychoanalyst' (Miller, *Politique lacanienne*, p. 50; my translation): the analyst is no longer defined in terms of knowledge, age or clinical experience, but in terms of his or her own analysis. An analyst is an analysed subject. And the pass verifies the emergence of the desire of the analyst.
118 Miller, *Politique lacanienne*, p. 70.
119 As Miller reminds us in his 'Théorie de Turin' (2000), for Lacan the Analyst of the School is also the analyst 'who [is] capable to analyse the School as subject.'

The School is a subject in so far as 'it is determined by the signifiers of which it is the effect, for this is what defines a subject, and nothing else.' The School therefore needs 'interpretations of itself as subject'.

120 Miller, *Politique lacanienne*, p, 53. 'La structure ainsi abrégée vous permet de vous faire une idée de ce qui se passe au terme de la relation de transfert, soit: quand le désir s'étant résolu qui a soutenu dans son operation le psychanalysant, il n'a plus envie à la fin d'en lever l'option, c'est-à-dire le reste qui comme determinant sa division, le fait déchoir de son fantasme et le destitue comme sujet.' (Lacan, *Autres écrits*, pp. 251–2.)

121 Lacan, *Autres écrits*, p. 243. ' ... [T]he principle according to which the analyst authorizes himself ... was simply designed to prevent analysts from sheltering in semblance in order [not to have to invest their] desire.' (Safouan, *Lacaniana*, p. 13; my translation.)

122 Lacan, *Autres écrits*, p. 251; my translation.

123 In chapter 3 of *Encore* Lacan defines S (A̶) as the signifier of the locus of the Other in so far as the Other is lacking (Jacques Lacan, *Le Séminaire, Livre XX, Encore 1972–1973*, ed. Jacques-Alain Miller, Paris: Seuil, 1975, p. 31), and situates object *a* as correlated to this lack. In chapter 7, Lacan states that the aim of psychoanalysis is to dissociate A – written as S (A̶) on the tables of sexuation – and *a* (ibid., p. 77): in other words, the direction of the analytic treatment resides in *not* saturating the lack in the Other with jouissance. (This is what, for Lacan, distinguishes psychoanalysis from psychology.) My reading of *Seminar XX* is informed by Marie-Hélène Brousse's 2007–08 seminar 'La clinique du lien social' at Paris 8 University (unpublished).

124 '[The question of identification] is a very interesting question because according to what some have been saying, the end of analysis would be to identify with the analyst. For my part, I don't think so. But still, this is what Balint argues, and it is very surprising. So what does one identify with at the end of analysis? Does one identify with one's unconscious? This is what I don't believe. I do not believe it because the unconscious remains – I say 'remains', I do not say 'remains eternally', since there is no such thing as eternity – remains the Other. It is the Other with a big O that is at play in the unconscious. I can't see how one could give sense to the unconscious if not by situating it in the Other ... So what does an analysis, which is a kind of *repérage*, consist of? Could it, or could it not, be to identify – to identify whilst securing a number of guarantees, taking some form of distance – to identify with one's symptom?' (Jacques Lacan, *Le Séminaire XXIV, L'Insu que sait de l'Une-bévue s'aile à mourre 1976–1977*, unpublished, 16 November 1976; my translation.)

125 Ibid., 16 November 1976; my translation

126 For a theoretical account of the reduction of the symptom to the sinthome at the end of analysis see Jacques-Alain Miller, 'The sinthome, a mixture of symptom and fantasy', in Voruz and Wolf, *The Later Lacan*, pp. 55–72.

127 Miller, *Theorie de Turin*.

128 In 'Instincts and their vicissitudes' [1915] Freud says: 'We thus arrive at the essential nature of instincts in the first place by considering their main characteristics – their origin in sources of stimulation within the organism and their appearance as a constant force – and from this we deduce one of their further features, namely, that no actions of flight avail against them.' (Freud, 'Instincts and their vicissitudes', p. 116.) This is commented on by Lacan in the following terms: 'This articulation [of the drive in terms of a constant tension] leads us to make of the manifestation of the drive the mode of a headless subject, for everything is articulated in terms of tension, and has no relation to the subject

other than one of topological community.' (Jacques Lacan, *The Four Fundamental Concepts of Psychoanalysis*, London: Penguin, 1977, p. 181.)

129 Jacques Lacan, 'Propos sur l'hystérie', *Quarto*, 2, 1981, pp. 5–10; my translation.

130 Marie-Hélène Brousse gave a practical example in her annual seminar (2007–08): Nicolas Sarkozy's motto during the French presidential campaign was 'Travailler plus pour gagner plus', or 'Work more to earn more'. This soundbite is indicative of a collapse between a symbolic dimension, work and an imaginary object, money. In this example the conflation of S and I forecloses lack as imaginary objects saturate the lack in the Other, thereby also foreclosing desire.

Bibliography

Compiled by Jari Kauppinen

Classics

Anselm of Canterbury, 'De conceptu virginali et de originali peccato'. In *Opera Omnia* (1). Edinburgh: Nelson, 1946–61.

Aquinas, St Thomas, *De Malum* in *Quaestiones disputata de Malo. Opera Omnia iussu Leonis XIII edita* XXIII. Rome, 1982.

Aquinas, St Thomas, *Summa Theologica. Cum textu et recensione Leonina*, *Pars I–III*. Rome, 1952–52.

Aristotle, *Ethica Nichomachea* (II:5–6, III:1, V:10, VII:6, 10–11, IX:4). (English translation: *The Nicomachean Ethics of Aristotle*, trans. Sir David Ross, London: Oxford University Press, 1966.)

Aristotle, *Metaphysica* (English translation: *Aristotle's Metaphysics*, trans. W. D. Ross, Oxford: Clarendon Press, 1924.)

Aristotle, *Categoriae* (10). (English translation: *The Categories* in *Book I of Aristotle in Twenty-three Volumes*, ed. and trans. Harold P. Cooke and Hugh Tredennick, Cambridge, MA: Harvard University Press, 1973.)

Augustine, St, *Confessiones*, Corpus Christianorum, Series Latina, 27. Turnhout, 1981. (English translation: *Confessions*, trans. Henry Chadwick. Oxford: Oxford University Press, 1992.)

Augustine, St, *De civitate Dei*, Corpus Christianorum, Series Latina 47–8. Turnhout, 1955. (English translation: *Concerning the City of God against the Pagan*, trans. Henry Bettenson. London: Penguin, 1972.)

Augustine, St, *De natura boni contra Manichaeo* [*Schaff*]. *Documenta Catholica Omnia. Documenti Lineamenta.*

Baader, Franz, 'Über die Behauptung, dass kein übler gebraucht der Vernunft sein kann'. *Morgenblatt* 1807, No. 197.

Baader, Franz, 'Über Starress und Fliessendes' in *Jahrbücher der Medizin als Wissenschaft* III, 2. (1807).

Bayle, Pierre, *Dictionnaire historique et critique* (1697), Part I reproduced as ARTFL project, University of Chicago). (English translation: *Historical and Critical Dictionary*, selections trans. Richard Popkin. Indianapolis, IN: Bobbs-Merrill, 1965.)

Böhme, Jakob, *Aurora, oder Morgenröte in Aufgang*. Frankfurt am Main: Insel, 1992.

Cohen, Hermann, *Religion der Vernunft aus dem Quellen des Judentums*. Leipzig, 1919. (English translation: *The Religion of Reason*, trans. Simon Kaplan. New York: Ungar, 1972.)

Freud, Sigmund, *Das Unbehagen in der Kultur. Studien Ausgabe* IX, *Fragen den Gesellschaft. Ursprung der Religion*. Frankfurt am Main: Fischer, 2000. (SA 9.) (English translation: *Civilization and its Discontents*, trans. James Strachey. SE XX, 1950; Penguin Freud Library 12, *Civilization, Society and Religion*. London: Penguin, 1985.

Freud, Sigmund, *Totem und Tabu*. SA 9. *Studien Ausgabe IX. Fragen den Gesellschaft. Ursprung der Religion*. Fischer, Frankfurt am Main, 2000 (SA 9) (English translation: *Totem and Taboo*, trans. James Strachey. SE XIV, 1950; Penguin Freud Library 13, *The Origins of Religion*. London: Penguin, 1985.)

Freud, Sigmund, *Jenseits der Lustprinzips*, Studien Ausgabe Band III, *Psychologie des Unbewussten*. Frankfurt am Main: Fischer, 2000. (SA 3.) (English translation: *Beyond the Pleasure Principle*, trans. James Strachey, SE XVIII, 1950; Penguin Freud Library 11, *On Metaphsychology*. London: Penguin, 1984.)

Freud, Sigmund and Albert Einstein, *Warum Krieg? A Briefwechsel* (1932). Zürich: Diogenes, 2003. (English translation: *Why are there Wars?* SE XXII.)

Gersonides (Levi Ben Gerson), *The Commentary of Levi Ben Gerson on the Book of Job*, trans. Abraham I. Larsen. New York: Bloch Press, 1946.

Hegel, G. W. F., *Phänomenologie des Geistes*. Hamburg: Meiner, 1999. (English translation: *Phenomenology of the Spirit*, trans. A. W. Miller. Oxford: Oxford University Press, 1977.)

Hegel, G. W. F., *Vorlesungen über die Philosophie der Geschichte*. Stuttgart: Reclam, 1997. (English translation: *Lectures on the Philosophy of World History*, trans. H. B. Nisbet. Cambridge: Cambridge University Press, 1975.)

Hegel, G. W. F., *Vorlesungen über die Historie der Religion*. Hamburg: Meiner, 1993. (English translation: *Hegel's Lectures on the History of Religion* ed. Peter C. Hodgson, trans. R. F. Brown, P. C. Hodgson and J. M. Stewart. Berkeley, CA: University of California Press, 1988.)

Hume, David, *Dialogues concerning Natural Religion*, ed. Norman Kemp Smith. Indianapolis, IN: Bobs-Merrill, 1947.

Kant, Immanuel, *Über das Misslingen aller philosophischen Versuche in der Theodizee*. Werke 6, Akademie Ausgabe, Cologne: Könemann, 1995. (English translation: 'On the failure of all attempted philosophical theodicies' in Michael Despland, *Kant on History and Religion*. Montreal: McGill-Queen's University Press, 1973.)

Kant, Immanuel, *Die Religion innerhalb der Grenzen der blossen Vernunft*. Hamburg: Meiner, 1990. (English translation: *Religion within the Limits of Reason alone*, trans. T. H. Greene and H. H. Hudson. New York: Harper Torchbooks, 1960.)

Kierkegaard, Søren, *The Concept of Anxiety*, trans. Reidar Thoner, Princeton, NJ: Princeton University Press, 1980.

Kierkegaard, Søren, *Sickness unto Death*, trans. Edna Hong and Howard V. Hong, Princeton, NJ: Princeton University Press, 1983.

Kierkegaard, Søren, *Fear and Trembling*, trans. Edna Hong and Howard V. Hong, Princeton, NJ: Princeton University Press, 1983.

Leibnitz, Gottlob, *Essais de théodicée sur la bonté de Dieu. La liberté de l'homme et l'origine du mal*. Paris: Flammarion, 1999.

Machiavelli, Niccolo, *Il Pricipio*, in *Opere*, Milan, 1966. (English translation: *The Prince*, trans. Peter Bondanella and Mark Musa. Oxford: Oxford University Press, 1984.)

Maimonides, Moses, *The Guide to the Perplexed*, trans. Schlomo Pines. Chicago: University of Chicago Press, 1963.

Mandeville, Bernard, *The Fable of the Bees, or, Private Vices, Public Benefits*. Harmondsworth: Penguin, 1970.

Nietzsche, Friedrich, *Zur Genealogie der Moral*. Kritische Studienausgabe 5. Munich: DTV/de Gruyter, 1999. (English translation: *On the Genealogy of Morals*, trans. Walter Kaufmann. New York: Vintage, 1969.)

Nietzsche, Friedrich, *Jenseits von Gut und Böse*. Kritische Studienausgabe 5. Munich: DTV/de Gruyter, 1999. (English translation: *Beyond Good and Evil*, trans. Walter Kaufmann. New York: Vintage, 1968.)

Plato, *Protagoras* (345d–359e), trans. Adam Beresford. London: Penguin, 2005.

Plato, *The Sophist* in *Six Great Dialogues*, trans. B. Jowett. Mineola, NY: Dover Trift, 2007.

Plato, *Laws*, trans. Benjamin Jowett. *The Internet Classic Archive.*

Plato, *The Republic* (II: 359b–379c, X: 612a–621) in *Dialogues of Plato in Four Volumes* I, trans. B. Jowett. Oxford: Clarendon Press, 1953.

Plotin, *Enneades* I, 8 (*Peri tou tina kai pothen ta kaka*). (English translation: *The Enneads*, trans. Stephen McKenna. London: Faber, 1966.)

Pope, Alexander, *An Essay on Man* in *Selected Poetry and Prose*, ed. W. K.Wimsatt, Jr. Austin, TX: Holt Rinehart & Winston, 1951.

Rousseau, Jean-Jacques, *Émile, ou, Education*. Paris: Flammarion, 1966. (English translation: *Emile*, trans. Allan Bloom. New York: Basic Books, 1979.)

Rousseau, Jean-Jacques, *Discourse sur l'origin et les fondements de l'inégalité parmi les hommes*. Paris: Livre de Poche, 1996. (English translation: *A Discourse on Inequality*, trans. Maurice Cranston. London: Penguin, 1984.)

Rousseau, Jean-Jacques, 'Lettre (424) à Voltaire, L'Hermitage. Le 18 âout 1756', in *Lettres philosophiques. Anthologie*, ed. Jean-Françoise Perrin. Paris: Livre de Poche, 2001. (On Lisbon earthquake.)

Saadiah ben Joseph Al-Fayyumi, *The Book of Theodicy. Translation and Commentary on the Book of Job*, trans. L. E. Goodman. New Haven, CT: Yale University Press, 1988.

Sade, Marquis de, *Les Infortunes de la vertu*. Paris: Librio, 1997.

Sade, Marquis de, *La Philosophie dans le boudoir*. Paris: UGE, 1999. (English translation: *Justine, Philosophy in the Bedroom, and other Writings*, trans. Austryn Wainhouse and Richard Seaver. New York: Grove Press, 1968.)

Sade, Marquis de, *Les 120 Journées de Sodome*. Paris: UGE, 1998.

Sade, Marquis de, *Histoire de Juliette*. Paris: UGE, 1976, 1977. (English translation: *Juliette*, trans. Austryn Wainhouse. New York: Grove Press, 1968.)

Schelling, F. W. J., *Philosophische Untersuchungen über das Wesen der Menschlichen Freiheit und die damit zusammenhängenden Gegenstände*. Stuttgart: Reclam, 1999. (English translation: *Of Human Freedom*, trans. James Guttmann. Chicago: Open Court, 1936.)

Schopenhauer, Arthur, *Die Welt als Wille und Vorstellung*. Munich: DTV, 1998. (English translation: *The World as Will and Representation*, trans. E. F. J. Payne. Mineola, NY: Dover, 1966.)

Spinoza, Benedictus de, *Ethics*, trans. G. H. R. Parkinson. Oxford: Oxford University Press, 2000.

Spinoza, Benedictus de, *Tractatus Theologico-politicus*, trans. Samuel Shirley. Leiden: Brill, 1989.

Voltaire, 'Poème sur la Destruction de Lisbonne, ou Examen de cet Axiome, Tout Bien'. (*Journal Encyclopédique)/Poèmes sur la religion naturelle et sur le désastre de Lisbonne* in *Voltaire Intégral en ligne.*

Voltaire, *Zadig, ou la Destinée.* Paris: Livre de Poche, 1999. (English translation: *Zadig, or, Destiny* in *Candide, Zadig and other Stories*, trans. Donald M. Frame. London: Penguin, 1981.)

Voltaire, *Le Monde comme il va. Vision de Babou.* Paris: Gallimard, 2006. (English translation: *The World as it is* in *Candide, Zadig and other Stories*, trans. Donald M. Frame. London: Penguin, 1981.)

Voltaire, *Candide.* Paris: Librio, 2004. (English translation: *Candide* in *Candide, Zadig and other Stories*, trans. Donald M. Frame. London: Penguin 1981.)

Evil in modern times

Adams, Marilyn McCord, *Horrendous Evils and the Goodness of God*, Cornell Studies in Philosophy of Religion. Ithaca, NY: Cornell University Press, 1999.

Adams, Marilyn McCord and Robert Merrihew Adams (eds), *The Problem of Evil.* Oxford: Oxford University Press, 1990.

Adorno, Theodor W., *Negative Dialektik.* Frankfurt am Main: Suhrkamp, 1975.

Adorno, Theodor W. and Max Horkheimer, *Dialektik der Aufklärung.* Frankfurt am Main: Fischer, 1969.

Ahern, M. B., *The Problem of Evil.* London: Routledge & Kegan Paul, 1971.

Alford, Fred, *What Evil means to Us.* Ithaca, NY: Cornell University Press, 1997.

Allison, Henry E., *Kant's Theory of Freedom.* Cambridge: Cambridge University Press, 1990.

Anderson-Gold, Sharon, 'Kant's rejection of devilishness. The limits of human volition'. *Idealistic Studies*, 14, 1984.

Arendt, Hannah, *The Origins of Totalitarism* (1951). New York: Harcourt Brace, 1973.

Arendt, Hannah, *Eichman in Jerusalem. A Report on the Banality of Evil* (1963). Harmondsworth: Penguin, 1992.

Arendt, Hannah, *The Life of the Mind* (1971). New York: Harcourt Brace, 1978.

Ariès, Paul, *Le Retour du Diable. Satanisme, exorcisme, extrême droite.* Villeurbane: Golias, 1997.

Auge, Marc-Hezlich C., *Le Sens du Mal. Anthopologie, histoire, sociologie de malade.* Paris: Archives contemporaines, 1984.

Badiou, Alan, *L'Éthique. Essai sur le conscience mal.* Paris: Nous, 2003.

Bataille, Georges, *L'Érotisme.* Paris: Minuit, 1957.

Bataille, Georges, *La Littérature et le Mal.* Paris: Gallimard, 1957.

Bataille, Georges, *La Part Maudite* précédé par *La Notion de dépense.* Paris: Minuit, 1980.

Baudrillard, Jean, *La Transparence du Mal. Essai sur les phénomènes extrêmes.* Paris: Galilée, 1990.

Bauman, Zygmunt, *Modernity and the Holocaust.* Cambridge: Polity Press, 1989.

Benso, Silvio, *Pensare dopo Auschwitz. Etica filosofica e teodicea ebraica.* Naples: Esi, 1992.

Berkowitz, Elizier, *Faith after Holocaust.* New York: Krav, 1974.

Blanchot, Maurice, *Le Pas au-delà*. Paris: Gallimard, 1973.
Blanchot, Maurice, *L'Écriture du désastre*. Paris: Gallimard, 1980.
Borne, Etienne, *Le Problème du Mal*. Paris: Presses Universitaires de France, 1963.
Braiteman, Zachary, *(God) after Auschwitz*. Princeton, NJ: Princeton University Press, 1998.
Browning, Christopher R., *Ordinary Men*. New York: Harper Perennial, 1992.
Buber, Martin, *Gottesfinsternis*. Zürich: Manesse, 1953.
Buber, Martin, *Good and Evil. Two Interpretations*. New York: Scribner, 1953.
Caloz-Tschopp, Marie-Claire, *Les Sans-Etat dans la philosophie de Hannah Arendt. Les humains superflus, le droit de avoir des droits et la citoyenneté*. Lausanne: Payot, 2000.
Cavalcante-Schuback, Marcia Sà, 'Kant och friheten bortom gott och ont' in Immanuel Kant, *Religionen inom det blotta förnuftens gränser*. Stockholm: Natur och Kultur, 2004.
Chalier, Catherine, *La Persévérance du Mal*. Paris: Cerf, 1987.
Cioran, E. M., *L'Élan vers le pire*. Paris: Gallimard, 1988.
Colpe, Carsten and Wilhelm Schmidt-Biggemann (eds), *Das Böse. Eine historische Phänomenologie des Unerklärlichen*. Frankfurt am Main: Suhrkamp, 1993.
Curley, Edwin M., 'Maimonides, Spinoza, and the Book of Job' in Heidi M. Ravven and Lenn E. Goodman (eds), *Jewish Themes in Spinoza's Philosophy*. New York: State University of New York Press, 2002.
Davies, Brian (ed.), *Philosophy of Religion. A Guide and Anthology*. Oxford: Oxford University Press, 2000.
Deleuze, Gilles, *Spinoza. Philosophie pratique. Les Lettres sur le mal*. Paris: Minuit, 1981.
Deleuze, Gilles, *Le Presentation du Sacher-Masoch*. Paris: Minuit, 1967.
Derrida, Jacques, *Foi et savoir*. Paris: Seuil, 2000.
Derrida, Jacques, *États d'âme de la psychanalyse. Adresse aux États généraux de la Psychanalyse*. Paris: Galilée, 2000.
Derrida, Jacques, 'To forgive: the unforgivable and the imprescriptible', trans. Elisabeth Rottenberg in John Caputo et al., *Questioning God*. Bloomington, IN: Indiana University Press, 2001.
De Vries, Hent, *Religion and Violence. Philosophical Perspectives from Kant to Derrida*. Baltimore, MD: Johns Hopkins University Press, 2002.
Dietzsch, Steffen (ed.), *Luzifer lacht. Philosophische Betrachtungen von Nietzsche bis Tabori*. Leipzig: Reclam, 1993.
Drewermann, Eugen, *Strukturen des Bösen. Die Jahwistische Urgeschichte in exegetischer, psychonalytischer und philosophischer Sicht*. Paderborn: Schöning, 1977–78.
Fackenheim, Emil, *To Mend the World. Foundations of post-Holocaust Jewish Thought*. Bloomington, IN: Indiana University Press, 1994.
Farrer, Austin, *Love Almighty and Ills Unlimited. An Essay on Providence and Evil*. London: Collins, 1962.
Fine, Robert and Charles Turner (eds), *Social Theory after the Holocaust*. Liverpool: Liverpool University Press, 2000.
Finkelstein, N., *The Holocaust Industry. Reflections on the Exploitation of Jewish Suffering*. London and New York: Verso, 2000.
Foucault, Michel (ed.), *Moi, Pierre Rivière, ayant égorgé ma mère, ma soeur, mon frére … un cas de parricide au XIXe siècle*. Paris: Gallimard/Juillard, 1973.

Foucault, Michel, *Surveiller et punir. Naissance de la prison*. Paris: Gallimard, 1975.
Frings, Manfred S., 'Is there room for evil in Heidegger's thought or not?' *Philosophy Today*, 32, 1988.
Gatti, Roberto, *L'enigma di Male. Un'intepretazioni di Rousseau*. Rome: Studium, 1997.
Gatti, Roberto, *Il chiaroscuro del mondo. Il problema del male tra moderno e post-moderno*. Rome: Studium, 2002.
Geach, Peter T., *Providence and Evil*. Cambridge: Cambridge University Press, 1977.
Geddes, Jennifer L., *Evil after Postmodernism*. London and New York: Routledge, 2001.
Geyer, Carl-Friedrich, 'Theodizee oder Kulturgeschicte des Bösen. Anmerkungen zu einem Gegenwärtigen Diskurs', *Zeitschrift für Philosophische Forschung*, 46, 1992.
Girard, René, *Le Sacrifice*. Paris: Bibliothèque nationale de France, 2003.
Goldhagen, Daniel, *Hitler's Willing Executioners. Ordinary Germans and the Holocaust*. New York: Knopf, 1998.
Haag, Herbert, *Vor dem Bösen ratlos?* Munich and Zürich: Piper, 1978.
Haag, Herbert, *Abschied vom Teufel*. Zürich: Benziger, 1969.
Häring, Hermann, *Das Böse in der Welt. Gottes macht oder ohnmacht*. Darmstadt: Wissenschaftliche Buchgesellschaft, 1999.
Häring, Hermann and David Tracy (eds), *The Fascination of Evil*. London: SCM Press; Maryknoll, NY: Orbis Books, 1998.
Heidegger, Martin, *Schelling. Abhandlung über das Wesen der Menschlichen Freiheit*. Tübingen: Niemeyer, 1971.
Heidegger, Martin, 'Blochmann-Brief, 12. September 1929' in Martin Heidegger and Elisabeth Blochmann, *Briefwechsel 1919–1969*, ed. Joachim von Storck. Marbach am Neckar: Deutsche Schillergeschäfte, 1989.
Heidegger, Martin, *Die Metaphysik des deutschen Idealismus. Zur erneuten Auslegung von Schelling. Philosophischen Untersuchungen über das Wesen der Menschlichen Freiheit und die damit zuzammenhängenden Gegenstände* (GA 49). Frankfurt am Main: Klostermann, 1991.
Heidegger, Martin, 'Abendgespräch in einem Kriegsgefangenenlager in Russland zwischen einen Jüngeren und einem Älteren' in *Feldweg-Gespräche* (GA 77). Frankfurt am Main: Klostermann, 1995.
Heidegger, Martin, *Schelling. Vom Wesen der Menschlichen Freiheit* (GA 42). Frankfurt am Main: Klostermann, 1998.
Hermanni, Friedrich, *Die Letzte Entlastung Vollendung. Vollendung und Scheiten der abendländischen Theodizee in Schellings Philosophie*. Vienna: Passagen, 1994.
Hermanni, Friedrich and Peter Koslowski (eds), *Das Wirklichkeit des Bösen. Systematisch-theologische und philosophische Annäherungen*. Berlin: Fink, 1998.
Hick, John, *Evil and the God of Love* (1966). Basingstoke: Palgrave Macmillan, 2007.
Hirvonen, Ari, 'The problem of evil revisited', *NoFo. The Journal of Extreme Legal Positivism*, 4, 2007.
Howard-Snyder, Daniel (ed.), *The Evidential Argument from Evil*. Bloomington, IN: Indiana University Press, 1996.
Irlenborn, Bernd, *Le Pardon*. Paris: Aubier-Montagne, 1967.
Irlenborn, Bernd, *Der Ingrimm des Aufruhrs. Heidegger und das Problem des Bösen*. Vienna: Passagen, 2000.

Irlenborn, Bernd, 'Das Guter ist das Böse. Die Depontenzierung des Bösen in Schellings *Freiheitsschrift* vor dem Hintergrund der abendländischen Privationslehre' *Archiv für Begriffsgeschicte*, 42, 2000.
Jankélévitch, Vladimir, *Le Mal*. Paris: Arthaud, 1947.
Jankélévitch, Vladimir, *L'Imprescricptible. Pardonner? Dans l'honneur et la dignité*. Paris: Seuil, 1986.
Janssen, Hans-Gerd, *Gott-Freiheit-Leid. Das Theodizeeproblem in der Philosophie der Neuzeit*. Darmstadt: Wissenschaftliche Buchgesellschaft, 1989.
Jaspers, Karl, 'Das Radikale Böse bei Kant 1935' in *Rechenschaft und Ausblick. Reden und Aufsätze*. Munich: Piper, 1951.
Jonas, Hans, *Gottesbegriff nach Auschwitz. Eine jüdische Stimme*. Frankfurt am Main: Suhrkamp, 1987.
Jonas, Hans, *Dem bösen Ende näher. Gespräche über das Verhältnis des Menschen zur Natur*, ed. Wolfgang Schneider. Frankfurt am Main: Suhrkamp, 1993.
Jonas, Hans, *The Gnostic Religion. The Message of the Alien God and Beginnings of Christianity*. Boston, MA: Beacon, 2001.
Journet, Charles, *Le Mal. Essai théologique*. Paris: Desclée de Brouwer, 1961.
Kittsteiner, Heinz Dieter, *Naturabsicht und Unsichtbare Hand. Zur Kritik des geschichtphilosophishes Denkens*. Frankfurt: Ullstein, 1980 (1984).
Klossowski, Pierre, *Sade, mon prochain*. Paris: Seuil, 1967.
Kreiner, Armin, *Gott im Leid. Zur Stichhaltigkeit der Theozidee-Argumente*. Freiburg: Herder, 2000.
Lacan, Jacques, 'Kant avec Sade', in *Écrits*. Paris: Seuil, 1966.
Lacan, Jacques, *Le Seminaire. Livre VII. L'éthique de la psychanalyse*. Paris: Seuil, 1986.
Lacoue-Labarthe, Philippe, *La Fiction du politique*. Paris: Bourgois, 1988.
Lacoue-Labarthe, Philippe and Jean Luc Nancy, *Le mythe Nazi*. Tour d'Aigues: Aube, 1991.
Larrimore, Mark (ed.), *The Problem of Evil. A Reader*. Oxford: Blackwell, 2001.
Lavelle, Luis, *Le Mal et la souffrance*. Morin: Bouère, 2000.
Levinas, Emmanuel, 'Transcendance et mal' in *Le Dieu qui vient à la idée*. Paris: Vrin, 1986.
Levinas, Emmanuel, 'Reflections on the Philosophy of Hitlerism. Prefatory Note 28. March 1990' (bilingual), *Critical Inquiry* 17, autumn 1990.
Levinas, Emmanuel, 'La Souffrance inutile' in *Entre nous. Essais sur le penser-à-l'autre*. Paris: Grasset, 1991.
Lévy, Bernand-Henri, *La Pureté dangreuse*. Paris: Grasset, 1994.
Lyotard, Jean-François, *Le Differend*. Paris: Minuit, 1983.
Lyotard, Jean-François, *Heidegger et « les juifs »*. Paris: Galilée, 1988.
Mackie, J. L., 'Evil and omnipotence', *Mind*, 64, 1955.
Madden, Edward H. and Peter H. Hare, *Evil and the Concept of God*. Springfield, MA: Thomas,1968.
Marcel, Gabriel, *Pour une sagesse tragique et son au-delà*. Paris: Plon, 1968.
Maritain, Jacques, *Dieu et le permission du mal*. Paris: Desclée de Brouwer, 1967.
McCabe, Herbert, 'Evil', *New Blackfriars*, 62, 1981.
Miller, Richard Lawrence, *Nazi Justiz. Law of the Holocaust*. Westport, CT: Praeger, 1995.
Mouffe, Chantal, *The Democratic Paradox*. London: Verso, 2000.

Müller, Ingo, *Furchtbare Juristen. Die unbewältige Vergangenheit unsere Justiz.* Munich: Kindler, 1995.

Nabert, Jean, *Essai sur le mal.* Paris: Aubier-Montagne, 1970.

Nancy, Jean-Luc, *L'Impératif catégorique.* Paris: Flammarion, 1983.

Nancy, Jean-Luc, *L'Expérience de la liberté.* Paris: Galilée, 1988.

Nemo, Philippe, *Job et l'éxess du mal.* Paris: Grasset, 1978.

Nicoletti, M., *La politica et il Male.* Brescia: Morcelliana, 2000.

Nino, Charles Santiago, *Radical Evil on Trial.* New Haven, CT: Yale University Press, 1996.

Nussbaum, Martha, *The Fragility of Goodness. Luck and Ethics in Greek Tragedy and Philosophy.* Cambridge: Cambridge University Press, 1986.

O'Connor, D., 'Good and evil dispositions', *Kant-Studien*, 76, 1985.

Ontologie et politique. Actes du colloque Hannah Arendt 'Politque et pensée'. Paris: Tierce, 1989.

Osiel, Marc, *Mass Atrocity, Ordinary Evil and Hannah Arendt. Criminal Consciousness in Argentina's Dirty War.* New Haven, CT: Yale University Press, 2003.

Pareyson, Luigi, *Ontologia della libertà. Il male et la sofferenza.* Turin: Einaudi, 1995.

Peterson, Michael L. (ed.), *The Problem of Evil. Selected Readings.* Notre Dame, IN: University of Notre Dame Press, 1992.

Peterson, Michael L., *God and Evil. An Introduction to Basic Issues.* Boulder, CO: Westview Press, 1998.

Petman, Jarna, 'Fighting the evil with international economic sanctions', *Finnish Yearbook of International Law 1999*, 10, 2002.

Petman, Jarna, 'The Problem of Evil and International Law' in Jarna Petman and Jan Klabbers (eds), *Nordic Cosmopolitanism.* Leiden: Nijhoff, 2002.

Pierretti, Antonio (ed.), *Giobbe et il problema del male nel pensioero contemporanea.* Assisi: Cittadella, 1996.

Pike, Nelson (ed.), *God and Evil. Readings on the Theological Problem*, Contemporary Perspective Philosophy series. Englewood Cliffs, NJ: Prentice-Hall, 1964 (London 1981).

Porée, Jérôme, *La Philosophie à l'épreuve du mal. Pour une phénoménologie de la souffrance.* Paris: Vrin, 1993.

Porée, Jérôme, *Le Mal. Homme coupable, homme soufrant.* Paris: Colin, 2000.

Porée, Jérôme and Alain Verginioux, *Où est le Mal ? Tragique, éthique, politique.* Paris: Harmattan, 2000.

Portinaro, Pier Paolo, *Il male.* Milan: Cortina, 2000.

Portmann, Stephan, *Das Böse. Die Ohnmacht der Vernunft. Das Böse und die Erlösung als Grundprobleme in Schellings philosophischer Entwicklung.* Meisenheim am Glan: Hain, 1966

Reboul, Olivier, *Kant et le problème du mal.* Montréal: Presses de l'Université de Montréal, 1971.

Rella, Franco, *Figure del Male.* Milan: Feltrinelli, 2002.

Revault d'Allonnes, M., *Ce que l'homme fait à l'homme. Essai sur le mal politique.* Paris: Seuil, 1995.

Ricouer, Paul, *Finitude et culpabilité* I, *L'Homme fallible;* II, *La Symbolique du mal.* Paris: Aubier, 1960.

Ricouer, Paul, *Le Mal. Un défi à la philosophie et à la théologie.* Geneva: Labor & Fides, 1986.

Ricouer, Paul, 'Le scandale du mal', *Esprit* 7–8, 1988.

Rogozinski, Jacob, *Le Don de la loi. Kant et l'énigme de l'éthique.* Paris: Presses Universitaires de France, 1999.

Rougemont, Denis de, *La Part du diable.* Neuchâtel: Baconniere, 1945.

Roviello, Anne-Marie, *Sens commun et modernité chez Hannah Arendt.* Brussels: Ousia, 1987.

Rözer, Florian (ed.), *Das Böse.* Göttingen: Steidl, 1995.

Rubinstein, Richard, *After Auschwitz. History, Theology and Contemporary Judaism.* Baltimore, MD: Johns Hopkins University Press, 1992.

Safranski, Rüdiger, *Das Böse, oder Das Drama der Freiheit.* Frankfurt am Main: Fischer, 1999.

Scheler, Max, *Der Formalismus in der Ethik und die Materiale Wertethik. Gesammelte Werke 2.* Bonn: Bouvier, 2005.

Schindler, Pesach, *Hasidic Responses to the Holocaust in the Light of Hasidic Thought.* New York: Ktav, 1990.

Scholem, Gersom, 'Sitra Ahra. Good and Evil in Kabbalah' in *On the Mystical Shape of the Godhead. Basic Conceps in the Kabbalah*, trans. Joachim Neugroschel. New York: Shocken, 1991.

Schuller, Alexander and Wolfert von Rhaden, *Die Andere Kraft. Zur Renaissance des Bösen.* Berlin: Akademie, 1993.

Schulte, Christoph, *Radikal Böse. Die Karriere des Bösen von Kant bis Nietzsche.* Munich: Fink, 1988.

Sentis, Laurent, *Saint Thomas Aquin et le Mal. Foi chrétienne et théodicée.* Paris: Beauchesne, 1992.

Sertillanges, Antonin-Dolmance (A.-G.), *Le Problème du mal.* Paris: Aubier-Montagne, 1951.

Siepmann, Helmut and Kaspar Spinner (eds), *Elf Reden über das Böse.* Bonn: Romanistischer Verlag, 1992.

Smith, Gary, *Hannah Arendt Revisited. 'Eichmann in Jerusalem' und die Folgen.* Frankfurt am Main: Suhrkamp, 2000.

Staten, Henry, 'Radical evil revived', *Radical Philosophy*, 98, 1999.

Steiner, George, *In Bluebeard's Castle. Some Notes towards the Redefinition of Culture.* New Haven, CT: Yale University Press, 1971.

Surin, Kenneth, *Theology and the Problem of Evil.* Oxford: Blackwell, 1968.

Svendsen, Lars H., *Ondskapens filosofi.* Oslo: Universitetsförlaget, 2001.

Swinburne, Richard, 'The problem of evil' in *Reason and Religion*, ed. Stuart C. Brown. Ithaca, NY: Cornell University Press, 1977.

Taylor, Charles, *The Malaise of Modernity.* Toronto: Anansi, 1991.

Todorov, Tzvetan, *Face à l'extrême.* Paris: Seuil, 1991.

Vardy, Peter, *The Puzzle of Evil.* London: Sharpe, 1992.

Vetö, Miklos, *Le Mal.* Paris: Harmattan, 2000.

Villa, Dana R., *Politics, Philosophy, Terror. Essays on the Thought of Hannah Arendt.* Princeton, NJ: Princeton University Press, 1999.

Vogel, Christian, *Vom Toten zum Mord. Das wirkliche Böse des Entwicklungs-geschichte.* Vienna: Hanser, 1989.

Wellmer, Albrecht, 'Der Mythos vom leidenden und werdenden Gott. Fragen an Hans Jonas' in *Endspiele. Die unversöhnliche Moderne.* Frankfurt am Main: Suhrkamp, 1993.

Werle, Gerhard, *Justiz-Strafrecht und polizeiliche Verbrechengbekämpfung im Dritten Reich*. Berlin: De Gruyter, 1995.
Whitney, Barry, *Evil and the Process of God*. New York: Mellen Press, 1985.
Whitney, Barry, *What are they Saying about God and Evil?* New York: Paulist Press, 1989.
Wieviorka, Anne, *Le Procèss Eichmann*. Brussels: Complexe, 1989.
Wirth, Jason, M., *The Conspiracy of Life. Meditations on Schelling and his Time*. Albany, NY: State University of New York Press, 2003.
Wodzinski, Cesary, *Heidegger i problem zla* [*Heidegger and the problem of evil*]. Warsaw, 1994.
Wyschogrod, Edith, *Spirit in the Ashes. Hegel, Heidegger and Man-made Mass Death*. New Haven, CT: Yale University Press, 1985.
Žižek, Slavoj, *Tarrying with the Negative. Kant, Hegel and the Critique of Ideology*. Durham, NC: Duke University Press, 1993.
Žižek, Slavoj, *The Invisible Remainder: Essays on Schelling and Related Matters*. London: Verso, 1996.
Žižek, Slavoj, *The Plague of Fantasies*. London: Verso, 1997.
Zupančič, Alenka, *Ethics of the Real. Kant, Lacan*. London: Verso, 2000.

Current issues

Agamben, Giorgio, *Homo Sacer. Il potere sovrano et la nuda vida*. Turin: Einaudi, 1994.
Agamben, Giorgio, *Quel che resta di Auschwitz. L'archivio et il testimonio. Homo Sacer III*. Turin: Bollati Boringhieri, 1998.
Bernstein, Richard J., *Radical Evil. A Philosophical Interrogation*. Cambridge: Polity Press, 2002.
Cohen, Josh, *Interrupting Auschwitz*. New York and London: Continuum, 2003.
Copjec, Joan (ed.), *Radical Evil*. London: Verso, 1996.
Cugno, Alain, *L'Existence du mal*. Paris: Seuil, 2002.
Dews, Peter, *The Idea of Evil*. Oxford: Blackwell, 2009.
Donaggio, Enrico and Domenico Scalzo (eds), *Sul Male a partire da Hannah Arendt*. Rome: Meltemi, 2003.
Feinberg, Joseph F., *The Many Faces of Evil. Theological Systems and the Problem of Evil*. Wheston: Crossway Books, 2004.
Jullien, François, *L'Ombre au tableau. Du mal ou du négatif*. Paris: Seuil, 2004.
Lara, Pia Maria, *Re-thinking Evil. Contemporary Perspectives*. Berkeley, CA: University of California Press, 2001.
Lawrence, Joseph P., 'Schelling's metaphysics of evil' in *The New Schelling*, ed. Judith Norman and Alistair Welchman. London and New York: Continuum, 2004.
Lévy, Bernard Henri, *Réflexions sur la Guerre, sur le Mal et la fin de l'Histoire, précédé par Les Damnés de la guerre*. Paris: Grasset, 2001.
Maturstik, Martin Beck, *Radical Evil and the Scarcity of Hope. Postsecular Meditations*. Bloomington. IN: Indiana University Press, 2008.
Muchembled, Robert, *Une histoire du diable. XIIe–XXe siècle*. Paris: Seuil, 2000.
Neiman, Susan, *Evil in Modern Thought. An alternative History of Philosophy*. Princeton, NJ: Princeton University Press, 2002.

Oksenberg-Rorty, Amelie (ed.), *The Many Faces of Evil. Historical Perspectives.* London: Routledge, 2001.
Poché, Fred, *Penser avec Arendt et Lévinas. Du mal politique au respect de l'autre.* Lyon: Chronique sociale, 2003.
Portinaro, Pier Paolo (ed.), *I concetti del male.* Turin: Einaudi, 2002.
Todorov, Tzvetan, *Mémoire du mal, tentation du bien. Enquête sur le siècle.* Paris: Seuil, 2000.
Wirth, Jason (ed.), *Schelling Now. Contemporary Readings.* Bloomington, IN: Indiana University Press, 2005.

Index